Understanding Democratic Politics

Understanding Democratic Politics

An Introduction

Edited by

Roland Axtmann

SAGE Publications
London • Thousand Oaks • New Delhi

Contents

Contributors

David Arter is Professor of Nordic Politics and Director of the Nordic Policy Studies Centre at the University of Aberdeen, Scotland, UK.

Arthur Aughey is Senior Lecturer in Politics at the University of Ulster at Jordanstown, Northern Ireland, UK.

Roland Axtmann is Reader in Politics and International Relations and Co-Director of the Centre for the Study of Globalization at the University of Aberdeen, Scotland, UK.

John Barry is Reader in the School of Politics, Queen's University Belfast, Northern Ireland, UK.

David Beetham is Professor Emeritus of Politics, University of Leeds, UK.

Lynn Bennie is Lecturer in Politics and International Relations at the University of Aberdeen, Scotland, UK.

Vittorio Bufacchi is College Lecturer in Philosophy at University College Cork, Ireland.

Terrell Carver is Professor of Political Theory at the University of Bristol, UK.

Emma Clarence is a Research Assistant at the University of Aberdeen, Scotland, UK.

Patricia Clark is Lecturer in Philosophy at Cardiff University, Wales, UK.

Byron Criddle is Reader in Politics at the University of Aberdeen, Scotland, UK.

Alain Dieckhoff is Director of Research at the Centre d'Etudes et de Recherches Internationales, Paris, France.

Michael Dyer is Senior Lecturer in Politics at the University of Aberdeen, Scotland, UK.

Abdelwahab El-Affendi is Senior Research Fellow at the Centre for the Study of Democracy at the University of Westminster, UK.

Peter Ferdinand is Director of the Centre for Studies in Democratisation, University of Warwick, UK.

Sharif Gemie is Reader in History at the University of Glamorgan, Wales, UK.

Robert Grant was a Teaching Fellow in the Department of Politics and International Relations at the University of Aberdeen, Scotland, UK.

Wyn Grant is Professor of Politics at the University of Warwick, UK.

Thomas O. Hueglin is Professor of Political Science at Wilfrid Laurier University in Waterloo, Canada.

Kimberly Hutchings is Senior Lecturer in Politics at the University of Edinburgh, Scotland, UK.

Grant Jordan is Professor of Politics at the University of Aberdeen, Scotland, UK.

Michael Keating is Professor of Regional Studies at the European University Institute, Florence, Italy, and Professor of Scottish Politics at the University of Aberdeen, Scotland, UK.

Michael Lister is a PhD candidate in the Department of Political Science and International Studies at the University of Birmingham, UK.

William Maloney is Reader in Politics and International Relations at the University of Aberdeen, Scotland, UK.

George Moyser is Professor of Political Science at the University of Vermont, USA.

Noël O'Sullivan is Professor of Political Philosophy at the University of Hull, UK.

Antonino Palumbo is Post-doctoral Fellow in Political Philosophy at the Department G. Mosca, University of Palermo, Italy.

Nicholas Rengger is Professor in Political Theory and International Relations, University of St Andrews, Scotland, UK.

Michael Saward is Professor in Politics at the Open University, UK.

Judith Squires is Senior Lecturer in Political Theory at the University of Bristol, UK.

Linda Stevenson is a Research Fellow in the Department of Politics and International Relations, University of Aberdeen, Scotland, UK.

Neil Walker is Professor of European Law, European University Institute, Florence, Italy, and Professor of Legal and Constitutional Theory, University of Aberdeen, Scotland, UK.

Anders Widfeldt is Lecturer in Politics at the University of Aberdeen, Scotland, UK.

Daniel Wincott is Senior Lecturer in the Department of Political Science and International Studies at the University of Birmingham, UK.

Preface

With the end of the Cold War and the downfall of communism, the idea of democracy has become very widely accepted. The idea of 'rule of the people, by the people, and for the people' has been justified in a number of ways, and its institutionalization in political structures has taken a variety of forms. This textbook traces these different justifications and variations in institutional forms, and guides the student through the complexities of modern democratic politics.

The book is aimed at the student who comes fresh to the study of 'politics' as a student in Political Science. The book provides the reader with factual information about the forms and ways in which democratic politics is conducted and some of the ideological conflicts that inform political contestations, but it also introduces the reader to modes of analysis and vocabulary with which political scientists endeavour to understand democratic politics. The book covers much of what an undergraduate student should know about democratic politics, but it does not cover everything there is to know. Ideally, it is the first book to which students turn to gain an understanding of the themes and issues that political scientists pursue when they analyse democratic politics. And, ideally, it is the book students would wish to return to during their undergraduate years, while pursuing more in-depth studies, to remind themselves of the fundamentals they may already have forgotten.

The chapters in the book are quite short. There are no footnotes or endnotes, although many – but not all – chapters provide in-text references to other authors. Indeed, the editor suggested to the contributors that they should think of a one- or two-hour lecture they would deliver to students to give them an introductory over-view of their selected topic when writing their text. Each chapter therefore contains a 'bullet-point' summary, a section in which students are directed to further reading and a set of questions for tutorial discussion. This format will assist the first-year student to find a quick access to key issues in democratic politics. Yet, students will find that the chapters, although of an introductory nature, do need careful reading. The authors do not 'talk down' to the reader, nor do they engage in 'dumbing down' complex and controversial issues. The chapters deserve, and demand, the reader's engagement and sustained reflection. Indeed, such engagement and reflection is encouraged and assisted by the fact that individual chapters may not only be read profitably on their own, but can be grouped together. This does not just apply to the grouping of chapters as a result of dividing the volume into three parts: 'concepts'; 'institutions and political behaviour'; and 'ideologies and movements'. In addition, at the end of each chapter the readers will be advised of other chapters in the book that in certain respects complement the chapter they have just finished. But readers should not feel discouraged from starting, in a more conventional manner, with the first chapter and reading right through to the final chapter. It is hoped that, by the end, they will share the editor's view that the chapters have been brought into a sensible sequence.

A word of thanks is due to all the contributors. First of all, they agreed to write a piece on a topic of which they know so much, but had so little space to pursue the intricacies of the selected subject-matter. Furthermore, they all accepted that we were writing against a deadline, and I am pleased that, in the end, we all made it across the finishing line. But my most heartfelt thanks are owed to the contributors because they all responded with such good grace to my editorial suggestions on their draft chapters. I hope they will find that the end product does not betray the trust they have put in me and that our collaboration has resulted in a stimulating introduction to democratic politics.

My commissioning editor, Lucy Robinson, has offered sound advice from the start when I submitted the proposal for this book to the publishers and has given unstinting support for the project right through to the end. I hope that she, too, will be pleased with what we have achieved.

Roland Axtmann
Aberdeen

PART I

Concepts

1 Sovereignty

Roland Axtmann

In a liberal democracy, it is the people who have the right to determine the framework of rules, regulations and policies within a given territory and to govern accordingly (Held, 1996: chaps 3 and 10). Liberal democracy is premised on the acceptance of the notion of popular sovereignty and its institutionalization in citizenship rights. Sovereignty has been transferred from the (monarchical) ruler to the people, and the people have been defined as the sum of the legally equal citizens. Democratic rule is exercised in the sovereign, territorially consolidated nation-state. In a bounded territory, people's sovereignty is the basis upon which democratic decision-making takes place, and 'the people' are the addressees, or the constituents, of the political decisions. The territorially consolidated democratic polity, which is clearly demarcated from other political communities, is seen as rightly governing itself and determining its own future through the interplay of forces operating within its boundaries. Only in a sovereign state can the people's will command without being commanded by others.

STATE SOVEREIGNTY

'Sovereignty' has a spatial dimension in that it is premised on the occupation and possession of territory. This spatial dimension manifests itself most clearly in the drawing of territorial boundaries that separate the 'inside' from the 'outside'. This territorial exclusion is, in turn, the prerequisite for identifying the source of sovereignty within the bounded territory and for defining 'us' in contradistinction to 'them'. Historically, this idea of state sovereignty has come to dominate political thought since the Treaties of Westphalia in 1648 which ended the Thirty Years' War in Europe. Then, governments recognized each other's autonomy from external interference in the most important matter of the time, religious belief. No longer, so governments pledged, would they support foreign co-religionists in conflict with their states. This agreement changed the balance of power between territorial authority and confessional groups in favour of the state. It created the precondition for the build-up of an effective system of control and supervision by the state over the population. It was this 'sovereignty' of the state over its population that has been appropriated and transformed by the people into 'popular' sovereignty in the process of democratization since the late eighteenth century.

In 'pre-modern' Europe, political authority was shared between a wide variety of secular and religious institutions and individuals – between kings, princes and the nobility, bishops, abbots and the papacy, guilds and cities, agrarian landlords and 'bourgeois' merchants and artisans. The modern state project aimed at replacing these overlapping and often contentious jurisdictions with the institutions of a centralized state. This endeavour was legitimized by the theory of state sovereignty. This theory claimed the supremacy of the government of any state over the people, resources and, ultimately, over all other authorities within the territory it controlled. 'State sovereignty' meant that final authority within the political community lay with the state whose will legally, and rightfully, commanded without being commanded by others, and whose will was thus 'absolute' because it was not accountable to anyone but itself.

The 'idea' of sovereignty was premised on the notion of 'unity'. In Thomas Hobbes's classical formulation, without a common power man remains in a 'state of nature' in which his life is 'solitary, poore, nasty, brutish, and short' and men are nothing but a 'confusion of a disunited Multitude' (Hobbes, 1991/1651: 89, 122). 'Sovereignty' means the reduction of all individual wills 'unto one Will', thus establishing 'a reall Unitie of them all, in one and the same Person', and 'the Multitude so united in one Person, is called a Common-Wealth, in latine CIVITAS' (ibid.: 120). The sovereign, thus established, 'is the publique Soule, giving Life and Motion to the Common-Wealth' (ibid.: 230). The sovereign is the 'very able Architect' who designs 'one firme and lasting edifice' by abolishing diversity and irregularities or by explicitly sanctioning them (ibid.: 221).

'Governing' by the 'sovereign' thus aimed to take on the form of the artful combination of space, people and resources in territorialized containments, and the policing, monitoring and disciplining of the population within these spaces became the foundation, and the manifestation, of state sovereignty. As a result of historical developments that spanned several centuries, the modern territorial state came into existence as a differentiated ensemble of governmental institutions, offices and personnel that exercises the power of authoritative political rule-making within a continuous territory that has a clear, internationally recognized boundary. In the nineteenth century, the notion of the 'nation'-state came to stand for the idea that legitimate government could be based only upon the principle of national self-determination and that, at least ideally, state and nation ought to be identical to one another. The nation became the 'unitary' body in which sovereignty resided.

POPULAR SOVEREIGNTY

It is the key constitutional assumption in a liberal democracy that rule is exercised, or at least ultimately derived from, 'the sovereign people'. But what precisely does this notion of 'popular sovereignty' entail? Let us go back to the historical juncture at which the idea of 'popular sovereignty' gained wide currency, the late eighteenth century. It was during the struggle of the American colonies for independence from Britain and during the crisis and revolutionary overthrow of the French monarchy in the last third of the eighteenth century that a new principle for the political legitimization of political authority was established: the state is legitimate only insofar as it enacts the people's will and is thereby responsive and accountable to 'the public'. Not only had the people abolished, or overthrown, an established political order; they had also established a new political principle in that they replaced the idea of the state's authority to define public right and 'welfare' with their claim to a popular mandate to rule.

In the past, the claim of legitimacy of monarchical domination had been based on the notion that the rulers had received their authority 'by the grace of God' (*dei gratia*). Keeping the peace and providing justice under the rule of God as well as under the rule of law were the main responsibilities and justifications of royal authority well into the fifteenth century. The provision of peace and justice (*pax et justitia*) was to result in order (*tranquillitas*). But as developments in Europe showed during the sixteenth and seventeenth centuries, it was the attempt to enforce religious conformity after the Reformation that in effect undermined the establishment of *tranquillitas* in the course of the religious wars that swept across Europe in those centuries. As a result of these wars, political necessities and the concern with the maintenance of the political and geographical integrity of the territory increasingly came to inform the policies of the secular authorities. The notion of *raison d'état* (reason of state) reflected and legitimized this change: religious issues became subordinated to the secular concerns with the stability and order of the *political* commonwealth. The notion of *raison d'état* undermined the conceptualization of the political commonwealth as a *respublica christiana* in which the state-objective (and the duty of the ruler) was defined as the protection of the 'true' faith in order to provide for the best possible precondition for the subjects to attain eternal salvation. Instead of this religious foundation of the state-objective, the notion of *raison d'état* focused on the endogenous and autonomous determination of politics, and thus explicitly highlighted the tension between religious ethics and secular political prudence.

This shift in the meaning of monarchical authority found its most significant expression in the increase in the legislative activity of the ruler. The ruler now established himself as law-maker. But this very activity generated theoretical endeavours to assess more precisely the nature of that activity, the kind of power which it both presupposed and entailed. The notion of 'sovereignty' became central in the context of these reflections. It issued out of the basic assumption that

> there is somewhere in the community, whether in the people or in the prince, or in both the prince and the people united in one body, a *summa potestas*, a power which is the very essence of the State. The decisive contribution of the [rediscovered] Roman [law] doctrine was the new conception of law as an expression of this power, as an instrument which could be used and adapted in accordance with the changing needs of society, as a system of rules that were valid and effective as long as there existed behind them the control of a supreme will: a will which, in virtue of its supremacy, was *legibus solutus*,

> because it was not accountable to any but itself. (Passerin d'Entrèves, 1967: 93)

Henceforth it was one of the major concerns of political and juridical thinking to identify the 'will which legally commands and is not commanded by others' (Passerin d'Entrèves, 1967: 93). Jean Bodin in France and Thomas Hobbes in England conceptualized the king as the source of the law, and it was Hobbes who moved most decisively away from the notion of a sacred foundation of the ruler's legitimacy of rule derived from 'divine right' to a secular notion which saw the ruler invested with sovereignty by the people in the 'covenant'. For Hobbes, the state was constituted through the political contract. In this state, all men are subjects, except the man on whom all have agreed to confer power, and who thereby becomes sovereign over them. The rights of individuals and the sovereignty of the 'people' were dissolved in the *potestas* of the *Leviathan*, save the right of self-preservation; whatever the sovereign does is by virtue of the powers men have conferred on him.

Following on from this argument, since the mid-seventeenth century the purpose of the state was increasingly seen, both by the rulers themselves and the majority of political theorists, as going beyond the confines of preserving 'peace' and 'justice'; it comprised now the task of actively promoting the secular and material welfare of the state and its population. The promotion of this-worldly happiness of the population replaced the ruler's traditional duty to assist in its otherworldly salvation. Hence, to an ever greater extent, justification for monarchical rule was based on the claim that it would bring about and enhance the secular and material welfare of the state and its people. This 'state-objective' was particularly characteristic of the political regime of 'enlightened' absolutism that was embraced by many rulers across continental Europe in the eighteenth century. Looking back on the changes in the justification of monarchical domination, we notice that the magical and religious-sacral elements of the beliefs that legitimated domination as a 'divine right of kings' came to be replaced by the secular notions of safety, security and welfare which the rulers strove, and were expected, to provide for their subjects.

The idea of 'popular sovereignty', however, challenged this notion of the legitimacy of rule, grounded as that notion was in the rulers' performing their tasks and functions well. It stipulated that, henceforth, political authority was legitimate only if it was bestowed, and willed, by the people, and not because of the 'state-objectives', however defined, which it strove to achieve. The people, not the king, were now seen as the source of the law. Article 2 of the Virginia Bill of Rights of 1776 made this point succinctly: 'All power is vested in, and consequently derived from, the people. . . . [M]agistrates are their trustees and servants, and at all times amenable to them'. A related idea was the assertion in the French Declaration of the Rights and Duties of Man and Citizen of 1789 that: 'The source of all sovereignty is essentially in the nation; no body, no individual can exercise authority that does not proceed from it in plain terms.'

The radically new idea, which became prevalent in the late eighteenth century, was that 'the sovereignty of the people' was inalienable, that it could not be revoked by, or ceded to, some other body or person. The first and decisive act of exercising this sovereignty is for the people to give themselves a constitution under which they agree to live together. In designing a constitution, the people create a government and give it powers, but they also regulate and restrain the powers so given. In the revolutionary period, the idea was reinforced that the rule of law meant that the state and its rulers, as much as the citizens, had to submit to the laws of the land; that, in effect, not only had law to be independent of the state, constituting, as it were, an autonomous realm, but had also to be superior to it: then, and only then, could it be conceived of as binding, not only for the subjects or citizens, but for the state itself. This was the core idea behind revolutionary constitutional politics: political rule

was established through a constitution and, once established, also limited by it.

Once sovereignty of the people had been established as the principle of legitimate political authority, the question had to be confronted whether there could be any limits to their sovereignty. Could it be argued that certain areas of individual behaviour had to be delimited over which even 'the people' have no right to exercise control? One answer to this question typically referred to natural rights, rights of man, or, above all in the twentieth century, human rights. These rights have been seen as a barrier against the exertions of even the sovereign people. The Virginia Bill of Rights of 1776 (Article 1) claimed that

> all men are by nature equally free and independent, and have certain inherent rights, of which, when they enter into a state of society, they cannot by any compact deprive or divest their posterity; namely the enjoyment of life and liberty, with the means of acquiring and possessing property, and pursuing and obtaining happiness and safety.

And the American Declaration of Independence of 1776 expressed the same thoughts in the following famous words:

> We hold these truths to be self-evident, that all men are created equal, that they are endowed by their Creator with certain unalienable rights, that among these are life, liberty, and the pursuit of happiness. That to secure these rights, governments are instituted among men, deriving their just powers from the consent of the governed. That whenever any form of government becomes destructive of these ends, it is the right of the people to alter or to abolish it.

The Declaration thus put the defence of the rights and liberties of individuals against government at the very centre of the foundation of a new political commonwealth. The chapters in this volume by Neil Walker, Vittorio Bufacchi, Antonino Palumbo, Noël O'Sullivan and David Beetham provide important detailed arguments regarding the constitutional grounding of political rule and the debates on the limits of legitimate authority and political power – and ultimately of 'popular sovereignty' – as a result of the idea of the 'sovereign' individual.

In liberal democracies, the idea of popular sovereignty and popular control over political decision-makers is given empirical expression through a variety of institutions. Civil liberties, which, for example, guarantee freedom of movement, expression and association, enable citizens to organize independently of government and exert influence on government and governmental policies in their pursuit of shared interests and concerns. Mechanisms of representation are in place to allow the translation of social interests into political issues. There is the recognition of the necessity for public contestation for all political offices and political support. The most important institutional mechanism here is the electoral system which allows for frequent and fairly conducted elections of political decision-makers and serves thus also as one mechanism of elite recruitment and replacement. Electoral competition, and the system of representation more generally, are, in turn, premised on the existence of organized political groups, such as political parties or interest groups. Finally, popular control and its effectiveness are vastly dependent upon the institutional differentiation of the legislature, the executive and the judiciary, and upon the division and distribution of power among them. Many of these institutions are discussed in the various chapters of this volume.

RETHINKING SOVEREIGNTY

I have suggested that two suppositions underpin democratic politics. According to the first supposition, sovereign citizens exercise democratic rule in the sovereign, territorially consolidated state: only in the sovereign state can the people's will command without being commanded by others. 'State sovereignty' and 'popular sovereignty' are inextricably intertwined. According to the second supposition, the politically organized nation constitutes the 'self' whose own determination modern political liberalism aims to ensure. In the imagery of the 'nation', the plurality and antagonisms of 'society' are moulded into a political entity; the nation is the 'unitary' body in which sovereignty resides. A systemic linkage between democracy and 'nation'-state is therefore presupposed: citizens as co-nationals are seen as sharing both the same culture, or way of life, and the same fundamental rights and obligations in relation to the 'nation'-state.

In recent years, both suppositions have been subjected to sustained criticism. The increase in the number of transnational communities of migrants, asylees and refugees in the 'global age' have undermined the assumption of the cultural homogeneity of the 'nation'-state. The political backlash against members of these transnational communities, as well as the need for their political accommodation, have intensified the debate about uniformity and diversity. John Rex (1998) has distinguished between those migrant communities which embrace the goal of eventual return to their 'homeland' (and thus form 'diasporas') and other globally dispersed communities which intend to remain dispersed and take advantage from this dispersal. The term 'transnational migrant communities' includes both types. One characteristic of these 'transnational migrant communities' is that they all maintain various types of transnational linkage.

To sustain these transnational linkages, the migrant communities can avail themselves of the 'space-adjusting' innovations in communication and transport. Rex points out that 'ethnicity today often operates by E-mail', and we may easily add other elements of the global technological infrastructure that play an important part in community formation and network structures: reduction in travel costs and in travel time as well as safer travel to many parts of the world; a global mail service, instant telephone contacts and fax connections as well as satellite television.

This technological infrastructure allows for the build-up and maintenance of transnational linkages of migrant communities around the world in an intensity and density that would not have been possible even a decade ago. And given the widespread accessibility of multimedia systems, the government, associations and clubs in the 'homeland', as well as the migrant communities themselves, now find it easier to produce and publish newspapers, magazines, cassette tapes, videos, etc. for their dispersed members in which 'cultural belonging' may be represented and celebrated.

Since it has become easier to maintain transnational bonds, the incorporation and acculturation of immigrant minorities by the state in which they live have become more contested (Doomernik and Axtmann, 2001). As Robin Cohen has suggested, 'many immigrants are no longer individualized or obedient prospective citizens. Instead, they may retain dual citizenship, agitate for special trade deals with their homelands, demand aid in exchange for electoral support, influence foreign policy and seek to protect family immigration quotas' (Cohen, 1996: 519). In short, they may organize themselves into powerful collective political actors. The contested politics of 'multiculturalism' should be placed within this context. In the last few decades, ever more migrant communities have demanded the recognition and support for their cultural identity. At stake is the acceptance of the demand for group-differentiated rights, powers, status or immunities that go beyond the common rights of citizenship. These demands raise the question of the very nature, authority and permanence of the 'multicultural', or rather 'multicommunal', state of which these various cultural communities are part. Our prevailing assumptions of common citizenship, common identity and social and political cohesion come under scrutiny. The question has arisen how these communities can co-ordinate their actions in areas of common concern or common interest, for example, with regard to the environment, the economy

or military security. The much more fragmented, decentralized institutional pattern emerging from this diversity would have to allow for, first, democratic communal self-government; secondly, a public debate on the matters communities have in common; thirdly, protection of legitimate powers to uphold autonomy; and, fourthly, the political coordination of the communities that keeps them part of one larger community.

Questions of 'minority rights' have also moved to the forefront of democratic theory because the last few decades have witnessed the revival of ethnic nationalism in liberal democracies and secessionist threats by 'internal' nationalities as well as the related recognition of the 'multinational' character of most 'nation'-states. These issues have dominated the domestic politics in countries such as the United Kingdom (Scotland, Wales and Northern Ireland), Spain, Belgium, Canada (Quebec) and in southeast Europe. Furthermore, we are also witnessing the political struggle of indigenous peoples in white settler states (such as Canada, Australia and New Zealand, but also, to an extent, in the United States of America) for recognition as free, equal and self-governing peoples.

As 'nations within', 'stateless nations' (such as the Catalans, the Scots or the Quebecois) and indigenous peoples share the historical experience of an existence of complete and functioning societies on their historic homeland before being incorporated into a larger state. However, there are two major differences between the two 'national minorities' in democratic states. First, indigenous peoples in white settler societies were subjected to *de facto* 'genocidal' policies and generally threatened in their very physical survival to an extent quite incomparable to anything experienced by most 'stateless nations'. Secondly, most 'stateless nations' embrace a form of 'civic', or 'postethnic' nationalism (where group identities and membership are held to be fluid, hybridic and multiple), a form of nationalism they tend to share with the 'majority nation'. Indigenous peoples, on the other hand, are firmly (if not exclusively) mobilizing around a more static, descent-based and culturally exclusive conception of group identity and membership. To the extent that they do not (wish to) speak the political language of 'liberal nationalism', and make demands for official apologies for past humiliations and atrocities, indigenous peoples raise the stakes in the intercultural dialogue and challenge the assumption that political accommodation can be achieved within the institutional arrangements of liberal democracy.

The indigenous claim to 'sovereignty without secession' develops the idea of 'nested' sovereignty, which demands the right of self-determination over those jurisdictions of direct relevance to the indigenous people while at the same time acknowledging a shared jurisdiction over certain lands and resources on the basis of mutual consent. Indigenous demands raise, then, a number of questions. What does it mean to do justice to indigenous claims within the framework of a democratic and postcolonial state? More broadly, can liberal democracy become genuinely intercultural? Must we redefine democracy so that it should no longer be seen as an affair of a singular body of citizens who together constitute a singular people, but rather as an affair of citizens who constitute a plurality of diverse peoples, groups and associations (as Barry Hindess (2001) suggests)? The chapters by Judith Squires on 'Pluralism – Difference', by Michael Keating on 'The Territorial State', by Thomas Hueglin on 'Majoritarianism – Consociationalism' as well as Alain Dieckhoff's chapter on 'Nationalism' pursue some of these issues which have been put on to the political agenda by the 'nations within'.

Finally, the debate on 'globalization' has raised the issue of the decline in the policy capacity of the state and a transformation of state sovereignty as a result of 'sovereignty pooling' in multilateral arrangements. As a result of a high level of societal differentiation and the increasing transnationalization of a wide range of societal interactions, the effective political solution of ever more societal problems is being sought at a level above or outside the nation-state. Many political and academic observers claim that multilateral institutions such as the United Nations, the International Monetary Fund, the World Bank, and the World Trade Organization acquire ever more authority and thus curtail the 'sovereignty' of their nation-state members. And a similar argument is being advanced with regard to the European Union where ever more decisions are taken that affect the citizens in the member states. However, many transnational interactions, and the transnationalization of economic action in particular (often referred to as 'global capitalism'), have hurried ahead of the current possibilities for their political regulation. At the same time, the structures and mechanisms of international regulatory policy-making – such as International Governmental Organizations – are, in turn, more advanced than the institutions for their democratic control. This creates an extreme tension between the effectiveness of political problem-solving at the 'international' level, on the one hand, and democratic legitimacy which remains embedded in 'domestic' political institutional arrangements, on the other. This tension is aggravated by the repercussions of international policy-making on domestic societies. Democratic politics at the nation-state level is increasingly curtailed as a result of the binding force of international political agreements. While 'democracy beyond the nation-state' remains weak, 'democracy within the nation-state' is thus weakened as well – and the notion of 'popular sovereignty' becomes problematic.

While there is much debate and controversy in the social sciences about these developments, there is a consensus that the idea of 'sovereignty' – for a long time a 'taken-for-granted' idea – must urgently be reconsidered. Given the centrality of the concept of 'sovereignty' for our understanding of democracy, a re-evaluation of 'sovereignty' may also lead to a redefinition of democracy.

Summary

- In liberal democratic thought, sovereign citizens exercise democratic rule in the sovereign, territorially consolidated state.
- In liberal democratic thought, 'state sovereignty' and 'popular sovereignty' are inextricably intertwined.
- In liberal-nationalist democratic thought, the nation is the 'unitary' body in which sovereignty resides.
- Transnational migration, multinationalism and globalization make it imperative for us to rethink the assumptions of liberal democratic thought concerning sovereignty.

TUTORIAL QUESTIONS

1. **Critically discuss the following statement: 'Only in a sovereign state can the people's will command without being commanded by others.'**

2. **Why may a re-evaluation of 'sovereighty' also lead to a redefinition of democracy?**

3. **In which ways does the acknowledgement of the internal heterogeneity of democratic societies problematize the concept of sovereignty?**

FURTHER READING

Stephen D. Krasner (1999) *Sovereignty. Organized Hypocrisy* (Princeton, NJ: Princeton University Press) provides a wide-ranging account of the debates surrounding the idea of sovereignty as well as a challenging argument about the continued viability of the sovereign state.

David Held (1995) *Democracy and the Global Order. From the Modern State to Cosmopolitan Governance* (Cambridge: Polity Press) develops a sustained argument as to why our notion of democracy, and sovereignty, needs to be reconsidered in the age of globalization.

Alain-G. Gagnon and James Tully (eds) (2001) *Multinational Democracies* (Cambridge: Cambridge University Press) discuss from both a theoretical and empirical-comparative perspective multinational political associations.

Duncan Ivison, Paul Patton and Will Sanders (eds) (2000) *Political Theory and the Rights of Indigenous Peoples* (Cambridge: Cambridge University Press) problematize the Western notion of sovereignty by analysing the ongoing process of 'decolonization' of relations between indigenous and non-indigenous peoples.

The question of 'popular sovereignty' in heterogeneous political associations is – implicitly – addressed in Will Kymlicka (1995) *Multicultural Citizenship: a Liberal Theory of Minority Rights* (Oxford: Clarendon Press) as well as in Will Kymlicka and Wayne Norman (eds) (2000) *Citizenship in Diverse Societies* (Oxford: Oxford University Press).

REFERENCES

Cohen, Robin (1996) 'Diasporas and the Nation-State: From Victims to Challengers', *International Affairs*, **72**: 507–20.

Doomernik, Jeroen and Axtmann, Roland (2001) 'Transnational Migration, the Liberal State and Citizenship', in Roland Axtmann (ed.) *Balancing Democracy*. London/New York: Continuum, pp. 76–89.

Held, David (1996) *Models of Democracy* (second edition). Cambridge: Polity Press.

Hindess, Barry (2001) 'Democracy, Multiculturalism and the Politics of Difference', in Roland Axtmann (ed.), *Balancing Democracy*. London/New York: Continuum, pp. 90–106.

Hobbes, Thomas (1991/1651) *Leviathan*. Ed. Richard Tuck. Cambridge: Cambridge University Press.

Passerin d'Entrèves, Alexander (1967) *The Notion of the State. An Introduction to Political Theory*. Oxford: Clarendon Press.

Rex, John (1998) 'Transnational Migrant Communities and the Modern Nation-State', in: Roland Axtmann (ed.), *Globalization and Europe. Theoretical and Empirical Investigations*. London: Pinter, pp. 59–76.

See also chapters

2 Constitutionalism

Neil Walker

MEANING AND HISTORY

To make sense of the idea of *constitutionalism* we must first address what is meant by a 'constitution'. The standard view is that 'constitution' has two meanings. In a first and formal sense the *Constitution* refers to the written document of a state which outlines the powers of its main organs of government (in particular its parliament, executive and courts), and which also often specifies the main rights guaranteed to the citizenry by the state. In a second and material sense, the *constitution* refers to the wider collection of legal norms, customs and conventions which constitute and regulate the system of government. Most, but not all, states have a documentary Constitution, the best-known exception being the United Kingdom, but all states have a material constitution. The material constitution will include the documentary Constitution, if one exists, but also other less formal legal sources which complement, supplement, modify, marginalize or – where a documentary Constitution is lacking – substitute for the formal source.

The idea of *constitutionalism* finds its object of reference in the 'institutional fact' (MacCormick, 1974: 102) of the documentary or material constitution. Constitutionalism registers at two different but related levels. First, it registers at the cultural or sociological level, referring to the prevailing profile of attitudes – elite and popular – towards con-

stitutional government at any particular time or place. Secondly, constitutionalism registers at the normative level, concerning the specification of standards to which constitutional government should aspire, either universally or in a particular socio-political context. It is the second sense of constitutionalism with which this chapter is primarily concerned, although normative arguments about constitutionalism clearly provide the raw material from which constitutional discourse as a sociological phenomenon is formed, whether such discourse is affirmative or critical of prevailing constitutional arrangements.

Both as a sociological phenomenon and as a sphere of normative debate in and beyond the academy, constitutionalism reached maturity in the age of the modern state, although its origins pre-date the modern state and, arguably, it will survive the modern state. Historically, constitutionalism emerged from a number of different sources. One tradition, originating with Aristotle and the classical Greek city-state, developed a framework for thinking about government as a 'constitutional' mix or balance between different elements and institutions – monarchical, aristocratic and democratic. Another relevant tradition is Roman law, in which an absolutist trend vesting total authority in the emperor vied with other tendencies conducive to a more restrained sense of legal and constitutional order. Both in its classical phase and, more emphatically, when it was rediscovered at Bologna around 1100, Roman law is closely associated with a codifying and rationalizing process which certified a stable normative framework for dealing with a whole range of social and economic relations, although its main focus was the private relations of civil law (contract, property, etc.) rather than the public domain of government. Of perhaps more direct significance, Roman law also nurtured a conception of natural law – of the grounding of legal rules in 'natural' principles of reason concerning equality and justice rather than in the will of the law-maker – which was to provide a powerful resource for subsequent 'constitutional' claims to and justifications for 'good' government. A third and later source was the medieval conception of Germanic law and feudalism. The idea of *reciprocal* obligation between lord and vassal – between ruler and ruled – which is such a central theme of feudal institutions, helped to consolidate ideas of limited government and, through the gathering of various estates of the realm in a central body, to nurture institutions of representative government which were to become bedrocks of modern constitutionalism.

These ideas gradually came together from the sixteenth century onwards in the development of the modern state. It is important to recognize that constitutionalism is not simply an *external* account of the modern state but an *internal* set of ideas closely bound up with its very formation and character. Quentin Skinner (1984: 349–52) has identified the conditions of possibility of the modern state as (1) the development of a conception of politics or statecraft distinct from purely religious or ethical discourse, (2) the idea of a territorially bounded polity, and of an international society of autonomous sovereign states no longer subsumed within a wider imperial power or *universitas*, (3) the complementary idea of internal sovereignty – a single source and ordering of all forms of political authority within a territory, and (4) the idea that political organization is in service of secular ends – that its purpose and justification is to pursue the interests of the state and its populace, however narrowly or broadly defined. Con-

stitutional thought was crucial to the development of this idea of ordered, bounded and internally legitimated secular rule through its sponsorship of two sets of ideas associated with the delineating and delimitation of political authority. In the first place, the constitutional notion that the system of government should be internally differentiated and balanced provided a way of consolidating all political authority under the head of a single sovereign power yet ensuring that the *exercise* of that authority should not be the prerogative of any single person or institution. In the second place, the constitutional idea that there should be a 'public' domain of government and a 'private' domain of civil society, and that the private domain should be sustained and protected from arbitrary interference by a framework of civil rights (and later also political and economic rights), served the double function of consolidating the notion of a separate and self-contained state or political community (comprising distinct but mutually regarding 'public' and 'private' domains) and of asserting that the purpose and legitimation of government was conditioned by, or at least not independent of, the interests of an identifiable population or 'society'.

It is all too easy in the context of a broad overview to overestimate the coherence of constitutionalism as a body of ideas, to underestimate the difficulties and discontinuities involved as these ideas competed for acceptance within the ideologies and institutions of modern states, or, indeed, to pass over the continuing fragility, contingency and selectivity of their endorsement within the international society of states. It is an endlessly complex task to trace the connections between certain fundamentals of political theory and belief – liberal or republican, democratic or aristocratic, popular or elite – on the one hand, and certain constitutional forms of the modern state – written or unwritten, unitary or federal, parliamentary or presidential – on the other. Constitutional thought has always been and remains deeply controversial both as regards the basis of political authority upon which it is grounded and as regards the institutional implications to be derived from these foundations.

In the second section, a flavour of this atmosphere of contestation is provided through consideration of some of the most important and long-standing currents of debate within constitutional thought. Yet acknowledgement of controversy should not lead us to the opposite error of discounting the resilient influence of constitutionalism. Constitutionalism, both because its vocabulary of ideas is deeply sedimented within modern systems of practical reasoning about government and because 'actually existing' formal and material constitutions insistently condition the aspirations and strategies of those who would exercise or claim political authority, provides an important orienting framework for modern statecraft. Furthermore, as discussed in the third and final section, this deep framework continues to be of significance today even as it is challenged by developments which question the centrality of the very international society of states that cradled constitutionalism to the operation of a shifting global configuration of authority.

NORMATIVE QUESTIONS

Many of the controversies and disagreements within constitutionalism are underwritten and in some measure explained by a paradox at the centre of constitutional government. That paradox, which exercises constitution-builders and constitutional theorists today as much as it did the authors of the *Federalist* documents on the eve of the establishment of the United States Constitution of 1789, lies in the fact that constitutional law both *constitutes* and seeks to *constrain* the power of the state.

In constituting the state, constitutional law creates an institutional complex capable of wielding enormous power. The political project of the state incorporates, as the indispensable foundations and necessary incidents

of its claim to internal and external sovereignty, the maintenance of internal and external security. In turn, this requires a police force, a military defence capacity and, more generally, a system of courts and tribunals and an arsenal of enforceable sanctions through which the state's conception of normative order can be effectively institutionalized. In other words, constitutionalism is in one of its functions a means of drawing up a 'power map' (Duchacek, 1973) – a framework of 'coercive self-organisation' (MacCormick, 1993: 128) through which the state equips itself with the necessary authority to perform its basic functions *qua* state.

Yet constitutional law is also the means by which the power of the state is conditioned and limited. Through its doctrines of separation of powers, of checks and balances between the institutions of government, of division of powers between the centre and devolved or federated units, of government in accordance with general, transparent and accountable legal rules, of fundamental rights, of dispute resolution and grievance–remedy before disinterested tribunals, constitutional law seeks to contain the power of the state. In other words, having nurtured the beast, constitutional law also seeks to tame it.

Many of the problems typically associated with state power are linked to the paradoxical double function of constitutional law. Constitutional law creates institutions with significant authority over the society in whose interests they should act. Yet precisely because of the centrality of these institutions in the exercise of authority, constitutional law, even where it is entrenched against reform motivated by the short-term self-interest of any particular government regime, must in some measure also rely upon these institutions to restrain within acceptable limits the authority they are individually and collectively granted. The ensuing tensions affect each of the three major organs of government – legislature, executive and judiciary. Responsibility for the making and unmaking of laws which set limits on the capacity of the state rests with those whose role and loyalties within the system of government may encourage them instead to promulgate legislation that minimizes constraints upon public power. Those charged under the constitution with the execution of public power within legal limits may on occasion be able and willing to stretch, or even violate, these limits in the name of ideological commitment or bureaucratic convenience. A similar conundrum affects the judiciary, traditionally viewed as 'the least dangerous branch' (Bickel, 1986): the judges are entrusted with ensuring that the constitution means what it says, but their role as authoritative and final interpreters of fundamental law entails that the validity of their own pronouncements cannot be challenged, and so they may with impunity favour sectional interests or otherwise deny that law its 'best' interpretation.

Given the inherent dangers of the abuse of governmental power, it is unsurprising that the emphasis with constitutional theory and rhetoric has often been placed on the restraint rather than the constitution of government power. So much so, indeed, that constitutionalism is often *equated* with the doctrine of limited government. With the growth of universal adult suffrage in the nineteenth and twentieth centuries, this idea has taken on a particular meaning. For unlike the regimes of earlier ages, modern governments are typically constituted through *democratic* means, and so constitutionalism that is understood as an argument about the limitation of government power now becomes an argument about the restriction or moderation of democracy itself. The controversial implications of this are readily apparent. On the one hand, the idea of democratic self-government is a dominant, perhaps *the* dominant legitimating ethic of government in the modern age. On the other hand, constitutionalism, also a central theme in the legitimation of the state, appears to be predisposed to the restriction of this dominant ethic. The rich and varied arguments deployed to address this tension, considered in outline below, raise many questions but also suggest one modest conclusion: namely, that constitutionalism as a normative

thesis about the conditions of good government is the more compelling to the extent that it remains aware of its double function – where it does not simply present itself as a thesis about the limitation of governmental power but rather as a method of reconciling virtues associated with the constitution of government authority and reasonable fears concerning the abuse of that authority.

Scepticism about democracy in the name of constitutionalism takes a number of forms. One line of scepticism proceeds from the absence of direct democracy as a viable *general* option for decision-making given the scale and complexity of modern government (although more direct forms of democratic participation may well be possible in some areas and levels of government), and with the limits of representative democracy as the only realistic alternative to direct democracy. Representative democracy, echoing the general critique of overweening government power mentioned above, invites the danger of the representatives developing interests which are at odds with, and priorities which are not sanctioned by, the constituency that they represent. Another line of argument is based on the premise that in representative democracies typically only the interests of the majority are effectively represented. Majoritarian democracy thus courts the danger that the interests of unrepresented or underrepresented minorities are neglected or, worse still, sacrificed to the interests or passions of the majority. A third line of argument, which often embraces the above two but extends beyond them, is based upon a more general distinction between 'popular' and 'just' institutions and principles of government. In this view, the ethical underpinnings of just institutions, whether these take the form of a 'liberal' commitment to equal respect and concern for every citizen, or a 'republican' commitment to endow all citizens with the freedom and well-being necessary to participate adequately in the life of the 'republic', are not necessarily best identified or cultivated by simple resort to this or that conception of representative democracy.

Of course, there are democratic counter-arguments to this scepticism about democracy. To the extent, for example, that the constitutionalist solution may endow a Supreme Court with the power to overturn democratically endorsed legislation, it may be argued that the cure is worse than the illness: that the empowerment of judges offers as few or even fewer guarantees against the abuse of governmental authority than the balanced representation of all relevant interests and aspirations. Relatedly, it may be asked, on what authority other than that democratic will is it possible to offer a persuasive conception of just institutions? To those constitutionalists who offer the answer of an original contract of government founded upon the popular sovereignty of 'the people' and their strategy of pre-commitment to just institutions, one may respond that the original constitutional contract, even if promulgated in reasonable accord with popular sovereignty (a conclusion often not sustained by the historical record), should not override or constrain the wishes of the contemporary *demos*. To those constitutionalists who offer a theory of just institutions that rests on fundamental and supposedly objective moral principles, one may respond that there is simply no agreement in modern pluralist societies over the content of such moral principles and that democratic means remain necessary to reflect, channel and reconcile reasonable disagreement over these very principles. For example, if one particular conception of just institutions argues in favour of a fundamental charter of 'negative rights' – rights against governmental interference with liberty, religion, privacy, expression association, etc. – while another argues that the guarantee of rights should also extend to certain welfare rights concerned with material well-being (as, for example, in the *Sozialstaat* principle enshrined in the German Constitution), then democratic principles would argue for a constitutional settlement which is reasonably accommodating of the different conceptions rather than one which enshrines one conception over the others.

The arguments on either side are well balanced. Each position tends to be more persuasive in pointing to the shortcomings of other positions than in dealing with its own. This simply reflects the depth of the constitutional paradox, the unavoidability of having to take seriously in any adequate theory of constitutionalism the twin needs to constitute governmental power and to restrain it. That is why the more sophisticated theories of modern constitutionalism attempt to address the issues raised above within a framework which seeks to reconcile 'democracy' with 'constitutionally limited government' rather than treat these as opposing imperatives. It may be argued, for example, that certain individual rights are constitutive of and prerequisite to democracy rather than – or in addition to – imposing limitations on democracy. Relatedly, it may be argued that democracy itself is a contested concept, and that without additional justificatory arguments drawn from constitutional discourse, it cannot stipulate the ideal conditions of its own institutional realization. This sort of starting position tends to generate strongly proceduralist conceptions of constitutionalism, in which various institutional guarantees are required – whether in the form of procedural rights of voice and participation, in multi-level or federalized systems of government, or in new forms of representation, dispute resolution and conciliation (referendums, functional or expert fora and systems of representation, Ombudsmen, administrative agencies dedicated to specific tasks of 'good government' such as the regulation of private industries or the pursuit of equal opportunities, Truth and Reconciliation Commission, etc.), in order to optimize the conditions for democratic participation.

THE FUTURE OF CONSTITUTIONALISM

The currency of constitutionalism may never have been more in demand than today. Its core ideas are more energetically disputed than ever before, but this itself is tribute to their heightened profile and increasing pertinence. Over the last 15 years in particular, constitutional discourse has reinforced its influence over old territories and colonized new. In Central and Eastern Europe, the post-communist establishment of liberal democratic regimes was accompanied by the gradual emergence of new constitutional settlements. In Germany, reunification of its pre-war territory required significant adjustment to the existing constitutional machinery. In Britain, as the comfortable clothes of the unwritten constitution became increasingly threadbare, New Labour's project of institutional reform after 1997 marked an intensity of engagement with constitutional issues. In South Africa, the new Constitution of 1996 is generally regarded as crucial to the long-term viability and legitimacy of the post-Apartheid regime. Beyond the level of the state, too, we observe unprecedented constitutional stirrings. The development by the European Union of 'state-like' characteristics such as representative institutions of government, a common currency, influence over macro-economic and social welfare policy, a policing capacity and a concern with the security of its own external borders, has led to a new interest in its constitutional status and direction. To take one other example, the heightened profile of human rights institutions at the global (United Nations), regional (European Convention of Human Rights, Inter-American Charter, etc.) and domestic level (Canadian Charter of 1982, British Human Rights Act of 1998, etc.) has sparked a new concern with constitutional rights jurisprudence as a way of accommodating individual and group claims and aspirations within national, sub-national, transnational and supra-national political spaces on every continent.

Yet the development indicated by the last two cases of a 'post-state' element within constitutionalism not only testifies to its expansion, but also hints at a profound challenge. If the framework of political authority within which modern constitutionalism was nurtured is gradually altering and embracing

new regulatory domains, how appropriate does constitutionalism remain as a normative discourse for that changing framework? We will conclude our discussion by briefly considering the nature of this challenge under three related heads. The first challenge, most immediately suggested by 'post-state' constitutional expansionism, is the powerful *legacy of state-centredness* within constitutional thought. The second concerns a more general problem of 'constitutional over-reach'. The third concerns the problem of *systematic normative bias* within constitutionalism.

The legacy of state-centredness

It is now broadly accepted that the identity of territory, community and political capacity, which was the historical condition of the state of the Westphalian age, is coming to an end. Through the denationalization of capital investment, culture, travel and communications media we increasingly confront forms of power and social organization which escape the grasp of the state into local, private or transnational domains. Both responding to and reinforcing this dislocation we find new forms of legal rule and political community in and between sub-state, trans-state, supra-state and other non-state units and processes. One response to this is simply to deny that any of these developments have constitutional implications. Thus, for example, there are those who continue to view the European Union – surely the most developed form of post-state legal and political community – in terms of a traditional framework of international law. Traditionally, within the theory of the Westphalian society of states, international law has been to external sovereignty what constitutional law is to internal sovereignty. It concerns the external relations between (constitutional) states, and so requires an entity such as the European Union to be viewed as no more than a compact between states, with no claim to authority other than as a jurisdiction delegated by states. One need only consider that the European Union has its own parliamentary, executive and judicial institutions, its own extensive policy jurisdiction, its own budget, its own internal and external security capacity, its own (largely accepted) claim to the direct applicability of its laws to individuals (and not merely states) and to the supremacy of its laws over national laws, and even its own conception of European citizenship, to appreciate how impoverished such a view is.

But if it is in principle legitimate to think of post-state 'polities' or 'processes' in constitutional terms, the legacy of state-centred constitutionalism generates two sets of problems. To begin with, there are 'problems of translation' (Weiler, 1999: 270) of the core normative concepts of constitutionalism from the state domain – where they may not have originated but where they have certainly undergone centuries of development and refinement – to the non-state domain. Ideas such as democracy, separation of powers and citizenship make a particular kind of sense and suggest particular kinds of institutional and normative possibility in the context of the state as the predominant or exclusive site of political authority and community. They make a different kind of sense in the context of an entity such as the European Union, which involves a much 'thinner' form of political community and which must share (and so coordinate) power and normative authority with the state level.

A second, and perhaps even more profound set of problems, concerns the 'public institutional prejudice' of the statist constitutional legacy. On this view, the public institutional *form* of constitutional law and constitutionalism is every bit as disabling a legacy as its state-derivative *content*. Post-state legal authority is not just about the emergence of new but reasonably familiar institutional complexes in emerging political centres such as the European Union, or the Council of Europe or the World Trade Organization, but is also about the emergence of new forms of private or hybrid ordering – from transnational commercial law (*lex mercatoria*) to the self-regulation of powerful sports bodies such as FIFA and the IOC or of new

networked arrangements such as the Internet. Arguably, constitutional law, dominated by the image of public institutions holding the centre of political and economic life, is not sufficiently flexible to grasp and hold to account these new regulatory forms.

Constitutional over-reach

The development of post-state political forms and of constitutional responses to these new forms also tends to exacerbate the long-standing problem of constitutional over-reach. The problem of over-reach concerns the tendency of constitutionalists to overstate the explanatory and transformative potential of constitutional discourse. On this view, there is an inherent conceit in constitutional thinking, an overestimation of the extent to which individuals, institutions and political circumstances are moved by constitutional considerations. Constitutional law is only one ingredient in the recipe of legitimate government and sustainable political community, but often constitutionalists treat it as the main or only ingredient and tend to neglect factors such as traditions and symbols of community identity, shared political values and aspirations, common or intersecting economic interests, and the existence of dynamic institutions of civil society and communications media. This is not to say that constitutional norms cannot reinforce or facilitate the development of these other factors, but the relationship is a complex and variable one, and it cannot be assumed that constitutionalism is the decisive or even an independent variable. The tendency towards over-reach is accentuated in post-state domains as here the other ingredients of political community tend to be poorly developed and the burden on law as a tool of social engineering is consequently increased. This can be seen, for example, in the currently intense political and academic debate on the idea of a documentary European Union constitution as the catalyst for a mature sense of European political community and identity – an enterprise which unless linked to a more rounded understanding of the sources of solidarity risks a wide-ranging disappointment of expectations.

Systemic normative bias

Finally, there is the question of systematic normative bias. Particular constitutions are endlessly accused of any number of particular biases, as when their formulation or interpretation of this fundamental right or that limitation on the competence of any specific government organ works against a particular set of interests or aspirations. As regards more systematic bias, prior to 1989 socialist constitutions were typically accused (and readily plead guilty to) anti-capitalist bias, and, conversely, the defenders of socialist constitutions would accuse western constitutions, with their strong assertion of private property rights, of systematic bias against the socialist commitment to comprehensive public planning and control. As this particular wave of ideological conflict has ebbed, the main contemporary charge of systematic bias against constitutions has assumed a different form. This concerns the broad category of what is commonly known as identity politics or the politics of difference – once again a development which is closely linked with the drift away from the state as the centre of legal and political organization. The basis of the charge of normative bias in this domain is that the growing demand for recognition of distinctive group interests or rights, whether based on national or regional identity, aboriginal or ethnic minority status, gender or other cultural difference, cannot be adequately accommodated within available constitutional forms.

On what basis is this charge made? Particular constitutional arrangements provide many obvious critical targets for the proponents of identity politics, whether these be the imbalance of representation of diverse cultural identities within existing government institutions, the lack of veto or 'super-majoritarian' checks against the abuse of minority positions, or the absence of dedicated group institutions. The charge of systematic bias, however, must do more than cite a catalogue of constitutional disappointments. It must also look to underlying explanatory factors, two of which stand out. One has to do with the objective difficulty of resolving identity conflicts within any given constitutional framework. To apply a crude but suggestive taxonomy, *identity* conflicts tend to be more intractable than either *interest-based* conflicts, which can be resolved by marginal compromises in the light of awareness of mutual interdependence, or even *ideological* conflicts, in which opposing views may be strongly held but where there nevertheless often remains scope for mutual engagement and persuasion. In identity conflicts, by contrast, there is a tendency to deny or to ostracize the other, and less capacity, or often even willingness, to speak and negotiate beyond one's own reference group. As to the second explanatory factor, this concerns the typical blindness of the constitutional framework towards the significant objective difficulties involved in addressing the politics of difference. Constitutions in the final analysis provide unitary frameworks of political organization, and constitutionalism tends to track this unitary approach in suggesting the normative underpinnings of these frameworks. So the most authoritative discursive traditions within the constitutional canon, including liberalism, republicanism/communitarianism and nationalism, far from being sympathetic to deep diversity, rest upon a presumption of homogeneity, articulated respectively 'as a society of undifferentiated individuals, a community held together by the common good or a culturally defined nation' (Tully, 1995: 41).

CONCLUSION

The challenge posed by identity politics to constitutionalism should not be viewed as unanswerable. That constitutionalism has a tendency to assume a degree of uniformity within the political community which is in tension with a strong politics of recognition, does not mean that constitutionalism is fated to fail the challenge. As with the other pressing difficulties of the new age – the problem of state-centredness and the temptations of over-reach – the potential of constitutionalism to rise to the challenge depends upon the capacity of those involved in its theory and practice to reflect on its limitations and to adapt its formidable normative resources to rapidly changing circumstances.

Summary

- Constitutionalism involves the specification of standards to which constitutional government should aspire.
- Constitutions and constitutional discourse reached maturity with the advent of the modern state.
- Constitutionalism is required to address the permanent tension between maximizing the benefits of government and minimizing its abuses, a tension often expressed as an opposition between 'democracy' and 'fundamental rights'.
- As the international society of states is gradually transformed by new globalizing pressures and by the emergence of 'post-state' political forms, constitutionalism faces new challenges to its relevance and legitimacy as a normative framework for governance.

TUTORIAL QUESTIONS

1. **To what extent, if at all, should constitutionalism be viewed as in tension with democracy?**

2. **Identify and assess the major new challenges facing constitutionalism in the twenty-first century?**

FURTHER READING

Colin Munro (1999) *Studies in Constitutional Law* (London: Butterworths, second edition) provides an accessible and lively overview of the development and contemporary features of the British constitution.

Jan-Erik Lane (1996) *Constitutions and Political Theory* (Manchester: Manchester University Press, chapters 1–4) provides a concise and informative history of western constitutionalism.

Martin Loughlin (2000) *Sword and Scales: an Examination of the Relationship between Law and Politics* (Oxford: Hart) is another very good short history of constitutionalism, particularly in its assessment of the links between theory and politics.

Jeremy Waldron (1999) *Law and Disagreement* (Oxford: Oxford University Press) provides an excellent analysis of the debate between rights-based and democratic conceptions of constitutionalism.

The works by Weiler and Tully, cited below, provide original and readable accounts of the challenges faced by constitutionalism in the light of the development of the European Union and of the new politics of difference respectively.

REFERENCES

Bickel, Alexander (1986) *The Least Dangerous Branch: The Supreme Court at the Bar of Politics* (second edition). New Haven, CT: Yale University Press.

Duchacek, Isaac, D. (1973) *Power Maps: Comparative Politics of Constitutions*. Santa Barbara, CA and Oxford: Clio Press.

MacCormick, Neil (1974) 'Law as Institutional Fact', *Law Quarterly Review*, **90**: 102–32.

MacCormick, Neil (1993) 'Constitutionalism and Democracy', in Richard Bellamy (ed.), *Theories and Concepts of Politics*. Manchester: Manchester University Press, pp. 124–47.

Skinner, Quentin (1984) *The Foundations of Modern Political Thought. Vol. 1: The Renaissance*. Cambridge: Cambridge University Press.

Tully, James (1995) *Strange Multiplicity: Constitutionalism in an Age of Diversity*. Cambridge: Cambridge University Press.

Weiler, Joseph (1999) *The Constitution of Europe*. Cambridge: Cambridge University Press.

See also chapters

3 Human Rights and Democracy

David Beetham

The purpose of this chapter is to explore the relation between democracy and human rights, and to consider some of the problems of theory and institutional practice raised by their relationship. Since the agenda of human rights is a huge one, embracing economic, social and cultural rights as well as civil and political ones, it will be necessary to distinguish between them at least at an analytical level, although current human rights practitioners regard them as 'indivisible'. Most of this chapter will concentrate on issues in the area of civil and political rights, and will only at the end assess how far the same considerations apply to the remainder of the human rights agenda.

RIGHTS AS AN INTEGRAL PART OF DEMOCRACY

What, then, is the relation between democracy and civil and political rights, in which we can include the classic freedoms of movement, association, assembly, expression and information, as well as the rights to personal security, protection against arbitrary detention and access to a fair trial? Political scientists have tended to argue in the past that the relationship was a purely *empirical* one. That is to say, countries which we would recognize as democratic because their governments are freely and fairly elected on the basis of universal suffrage are also likely to have a good record in the protection of civil and political rights, in comparison with the record of non-democratic or less democratic political systems. This relationship can be demonstrated statistically, and is a *causal* one: governments that are accountable to their electorates have to be sensitive to their rights if they wish to be elected or re-elected to office. So the defence of basic rights has been seen as a consequence of having democracy in the first place.

However, this kind of argument begs the question of how we should define democracy to begin with. Increasingly, democracy is coming to be defined today in terms of the possession of civil and political rights as well as of a particular set of political institutions, and these rights are being seen as themselves intrinsically democratic rather than simply as a valuable addition to electoral democracy or a gratifying consequence of it. The reason is that electoral democracy itself cannot serve as an effective mechanism for citizen choice and accountable government unless citizens can express their opinions openly, freely associate with others, have access to impartial information about what the government of the day is doing, enjoy legal protection against arbitrary executive action or interference, and so on. Such freedoms are essential if the democratic principle of popular participation in, and control over, the collective decisions that affect people's lives is to be meaningful in practice. Democratic principle requires that these freedoms be available to all citizens equally under the law, and that they be guaranteed even in the face of a contingent electoral or parliamentary majority.

The idea that rights form an intrinsic component of democracy was expressed very clearly by the legal philosopher Ronald Dworkin when arguing the need for a British bill of rights:

> True democracy is not just *statistical* democracy, in which anything a majority or plurality wants is legitimate for that reason, but *communal* democracy, in which majority decision is legitimate only if it is a majority within a community of equals. That means not only that everyone must be allowed to participate in politics as an equal, through the vote and through freedom of speech and protest, but that political decisions must treat everyone with equal concern and respect, that each individual person must be guaranteed fundamental civil and political rights no combination of other citizens can take away, no matter how numerous they are or how much they despise his or her race or morals or way of life. That view of what democracy means is at the heart of all the charters of human rights. . . . It is now the settled concept of democracy in Europe. (Dworkin, 1990: 35–6)

However, if human rights lie as much at the heart of democracy as the mechanisms of electoral representation and accountable government, because there is an essential congruence between them, this congruence is not always evident at the level of institutional practice. There are considerable disagreements about how rights should be institutionally protected. What if the instruments for their protection should come into conflict with the will of a democratically elected government? Should the decisions of unelected judges be allowed to override those of an elected parliament? And can it possibly be democratic for a country's duly appointed governmental agencies to be overruled by a body which is external to the state itself and largely composed of foreigners? Does this not infringe a basic democratic principle of self-determination, that elected governments should be the final arbiters of a country's fortunes? These are the questions that the remainder of this chapter will address.

BILLS OF RIGHTS AND THEIR ADJUDICATION

First is the question of how the basic civil and political rights necessary to democracy should be protected. Most countries do this by means of a bill of rights which is constitutionally entrenched and can be amended only by special majorities of the legislature and/or a popular referendum. Until very recently the UK managed without such an explicit statement of 'fundamental rights and freedoms', and there was some opposition to the recent incorporation of the European Convention on Human Rights into UK law as our own domestic bill of rights. It is worth considering the arguments surrounding this issue, as they have a significance beyond the domestic politics of the UK.

Part of the argument concerned conflicting interpretations of British history, especially its recent history. 'Traditionalists' argued that fundamental freedoms had historically been protected by a combination of institutional factors: by a popularly elected parliament acting as watchdog of citizens' rights; by the common law interpreted by an independent judiciary and by common-sense judgments of the jury system; and by a broader 'culture of liberty' which underpinned the other two. They saw no need to tamper with these 'three pillars of liberty'.

On the other side, supporters of a bill of rights argued that this institutional framework was no longer adequate to defend essential freedoms in the UK, as the recent history of rights-restricting legislation demonstrated. Parliament, they contended, was now simply a creature of the executive through its tightly disciplined legislative majority, rather than an effective check upon it. The judgments of the judiciary showed that in practice they were executive-minded or executive-friendly, rather than fully independent. And public opinion could be readily stampeded behind oppressive legislation under the impact of some outrage or tabloid campaign in a manner that in calmer moments they might come to regret. Yet such legislation, once on the statute books, proved difficult to reverse. The extent to which the UK had fallen behind international standards of rights protection was demonstrated by the number of individual complaints of infringement against the government upheld by the European Court of Human Rights at Strasbourg. Even the Labour government in its White Paper on the Bill of Rights was forced to concede that existing legal protections were inadequate.

For all these reasons, so it was argued, the UK needed its own bill of rights, as had indeed been introduced in other long-established Westminster-type systems such as Australia, Canada and New Zealand. But how was such a bill of rights to be interpreted and adjudicated in practice? The most usual method is through a constitutional court or supreme court in which judges, often appointed for life or until retirement age, give decisions on cases brought before them. Such decisions then determine future interpretations of the relevant constitutional provisions. At this point opponents of the idea of a bill of rights made another objection: is it not profoundly undemocratic to hand over the interpretation of a country's basic rights from a popularly elected parliament and place them in the hands of an unelected judiciary which has no public accountability?

Let us be clear what exactly is being objected to here. It is not the existence of a professional and independent judiciary *per se*, since such a body is necessary for the protection of the 'rule of law'. This is the principle that breaches of the law should be impartially tried and appropriate punishment or restitution determined, without fear or favour, who-

ever the offender, including members of the government and its officials. Such a principle, and the separation of powers which underpins it, is necessary to a democratic polity, since without it the will of a popularly elected legislature cannot be enforced in practice. Rather, what is being objected to is the possibility that existing legislation approved by parliament, or executive actions and procedures endorsed by such legislation, or potential future legislation under consideration, might be struck down as unconstitutional because it infringes a given judicial interpretation of the bill of rights. Is this not to give the judiciary supremacy over the legislature, and over a democratically elected government?

Such arguments are given added weight by the fact that most bills of rights (the USA is an exception) explicitly allow for the rights to be overridden or derogated from in the event of pressing public need. So the freedom of assembly may be legitimately curtailed under the threat of public disorder; the freedom of speech may be limited by considerations of national security, or endemic ethnic or religious conflict; the right to privacy may be restricted to gain evidence of serious breaches of the law; the freedom of movement and even access to due legal process may be curtailed under the imminent threat of terrorism. Since no rights are absolute (except possibly the right not to be tortured), should it not be a matter for elected governments rather than judges to determine where the balance between individual freedoms and the requirements of public security (and hence the security of individuals) should be struck?

In reply, it could be argued that these are indeed matters for governments to determine, but that it makes all the difference if governments know that their actions can be open to public scrutiny in the courts, and challenged by those who believe that their basic rights have been infringed. All governments, even elected ones, tend to be too ready to restrict individual freedoms and then to deny the public the information necessary to assess whether the restrictions are justified.

A codified bill of rights gives the courts (and through them the public at large) the opportunity to test whether such restrictions are indeed required, and whether they are proportionate to the threat to public security that is being claimed. In other words, the courts can give extra weight in the balance to individual freedom when the scales are otherwise tipped substantially on the side of increasingly powerful executives. This is particularly important where there is a danger that a government may act in a partisan way against political opponents. In such contexts the fact that judges are trained to be impartial and above politics is a decided advantage, rather than the reverse. And while they may not be accountable in the sense that they can be dismissed for their judgments, they are accountable in a literal sense in that they have to give a public 'account' of the reasons for them.

HUMAN RIGHTS AND PARLIAMENTARY LEGISLATION

The issue, however, is not just whether it is democratic for the courts to have the final power of adjudication over instances of executive action. It is also whether they should have the power to strike down whole categories of legislation because they are contrary to a country's bill of rights. This concern is widely shared, even by those who are in favour of rights protection through a codified bill of rights. In view of this concern, a number of countries have developed mechanisms of parliamentary scrutiny so that it is not just left to the courts to determine. For example, some have entrusted the task of scrutinizing legislation, existing and proposed, for its compatibility with the bill of rights, to an impartial human rights committee comprising senior members of both chambers of the legislature. Or the task may be given to an independent Human Rights Commission, whose membership has to be approved by the legislature, to whom it is required to

make regular reports. The mechanism now in force in the UK under the recently passed Human Rights Act envisages that a court may make a 'declaration of incompatibility' between a legislative provision and the bill of rights, with the requirement that a minister of the relevant department should either bring forward proposals to amend the legislation or explain why this is not being done. In either case the ultimate authority over legislative matters rests with parliament.

However, it must be doubted whether in practice such procedures do more than maintain the fig leaf of parliamentary sovereignty, since it is unlikely that parliament would sustain the legislative provisions in question once a declaration of incompatibility has been made. In any case the traditional principle of all Westminster-type systems that no parliament can bind its successors has already been substantially eroded by the enactment of a bill establishing 'fundamental rights and freedoms' as the entitlement of all citizens without discrimination. The whole point of enacting such a measure is precisely to constrain the future competence of a popularly elected assembly by putting issues involving basic rights beyond the reach of any simple majority decision.

The question of whether such a limitation is democratic or not can be answered by appealing to two considerations, one substantive, the other procedural. The substantive one has already been discussed at the start of the chapter, namely that democracy cannot simply be equated with the majority decisions of a representative assembly, but also involves the guarantee to citizens of equality of the rights and freedoms necessary to engage in public activity.

The procedural consideration is that the content and procedures for a bill of rights should themselves have been democratically endorsed, preferably by a special majority of the legislature and confirmed in a popular referendum. In this way any limitation on the future discretion of an elected assembly can be seen as a process of democratic self-limitation rather than as an extraneously imposed limitation by an unelected judiciary. The fact that the UK Human Rights Act came into force without a referendum or even any substantial engagement by the government with the wider electorate indicates that the procedural legitimacy of its provisions is less secure than it could have been, however democracy-supportive their substantive content may be.

To argue in this way does not itself resolve difficult issues of practical judgement about what is democratic in particular circumstances. What it does is to question any simple conclusion that, where an unelected judiciary overrules the actions of an elected government, this must *ipso facto* be undemocratic or a defeat for democracy. Such conflicts should rather be characterized as a tension between one aspect of democracy and another, and it is a matter for legitimate debate which outcome is more democratic in a given situation, if indeed such a conclusion can be reached at all.

A CONTROVERSIAL EXAMPLE

To pursue this issue further, let us take the example of a situation where a constitutional court orders the disbandment of a political party because it might threaten the rights of citizens if its policies were implemented in the future. This has happened a number of times in Turkey. The Turkish Constitution contains quite specific limitations on the freedoms of association and expression, which are designed to protect the integrity of the state and the secular character of its political life. These limiting provisions have brought the country into conflict with the European Convention on Human Rights, to which it is a signatory, particularly in relation to Turkey's treatment of its Kurdish minority, which has also delayed Turkey's accession to the European Union. However, a number of decisions of Turkey's constitutional court outlawing particular political parties have been upheld by the European Court of Human Rights at

Strasbourg as being legitimate 'in a democratic society'.

The most recent case is also the most serious, since it involved the party (Refah Partisi or Welfare Party) which had obtained more votes than any other in a general election, and which also formed part of the governing coalition at the time. Some of its members, including its Chairman and one or two of its leading MPs, were on record as having advocated the introduction of sharia law for Turkey's Muslim majority, and different legal systems for other religious groups, though no such policies had been pursued by the party in government, nor had they ever been mentioned in the party's manifesto. On the strength of these statements Turkey's constitutional court ordered the dissolution of the party, the sequestration of its funds and the removal of the offending MPs from parliament (though the vast majority were allowed to retain their seats without a party label). The chief ground cited was that a secular state and legal system was a vital component of the country's democracy, and that the statements in question demonstrated a hidden party agenda to create an Islamic regime which would give the power of legislation and legal interpretation to extra-parliamentary and extra-judicial religious bodies. Subsequently, the dismissed MPs appealed to the European Court of Human Rights to have the decision overturned, on the ground that it violated their rights to free expression and association.

In July 2001 the European Court upheld the decision of Turkey's constitutional court by the narrow margin of four judges to three. The arguments for and against are worth summarizing briefly, since they illustrate in an acute form some of the dilemmas of defining what constitutes democracy in the light of human rights considerations. The majority of four argued that any party which advocates 'the infringement of the rights and freedoms afforded under democracy' cannot claim the protection of the European Convention. The introduction of sharia law would introduce discrimination into the legal system on grounds of both religion and gender, and would subordinate the guarantee of human rights and freedoms for all to the 'static rules imposed by the religion'. Political Islam, though tolerant of other religions, had never shown the same tolerance towards its own faithful. The fact that the party enjoyed such a measure of popular support, and even the prospect of winning a parliamentary majority in the future, made its disbandment even more urgent to pre-empt the threat to democratic rights. 'There can be no democracy,' they concluded, 'where the people of a state, even by a majority decision, waive their legislative and judicial powers in favour of an entity which is not responsible to the people it governs.' In effect what the judges were saying was that democracy had to be curtailed in the present in order to protect it in the future; more bluntly, that the people had to be protected from the consequences of their own electoral decisions.

In a dissenting judgment, the other three judges argued that the decision of Turkey's constitutional court did indeed constitute a violation of the MPs' rights to free expression and association. Democracy was meaningless, they argued, without the free expression of electoral opinion, and this was 'inconceivable without the participation of a plurality of political parties representing different shades of opinion'. The fact that a political programme was considered incompatible with the current principles and structures of a state did not make it incompatible with the rules of democracy, which required that diverse programmes should be proposed and debated, even if they called into question the way the state was organized. A principal characteristic of democracy was the possibility it offered of resolving a country's problems through dialogue, and there was simply no evidence from the party's actions in government that it sought to restrict public dialogue or the freedoms of expression and association more generally. (For the full text see Council of Europe, *Case of Refah Partisi and others v. Turkey*, Strasbourg, 31 July 2001.)

Part of the disagreement here involved a question of interpretation of the facts before the court, but it also serves to illustrate some much wider issues. First, it shows that judgments about what is democratic are far from straightforward in practice, since the different requirements of democracy may come into conflict with one another. Secondly, the different opinions show the judiciary engaged in a serious debate about the essence of democracy, of a kind that does not often take place even in legislatures. One reason is because the European Convention requires that any limitation on the rights it guarantees have to be such as are 'necessary in a democratic society', with the consequence that judges are compelled to debate what the requirements of a 'democratic society' amount to. This is not just an academic exercise, but one that may have far-reaching practical consequences. Thirdly, and perhaps most importantly, the case demonstrates that the final decision about the fate of a country's democracy lies in the hands of a judicial body outside the country, and one composed almost entirely of foreigners. Does this not conflict with the elementary principle of self-determination, that a people should be free to decide their own affairs, even if the consequences of their decision may prove unfortunate? This question brings us to a final issue to be considered, that of the internationalization of democratic and human rights standards.

DEMOCRACY AND THE INTERNATIONAL ADJUDICATION OF HUMAN RIGHTS STANDARDS

A significant feature of recent decades is that human rights standards, and with them the standards of democratic life, have been increasingly determined at the international level. Since human rights are, by definition, universal in scope, their adjudication has become the subject of international bodies. The International Covenant on Civil and Political Rights, to which the vast majority

of countries has subscribed, requires that signatory states provide quinquennial reports to
the UN Committee on Human Rights, showing how they have fulfilled the requirements
of the Covenant. On the basis of these
reports, together with submissions from non-
governmental organizations, the Committee
then issues a judgement on the country's
observance of the different items of the Covenant, with recommendations for action by
the government concerned. However, these
judgements have a persuasive force only,
backed up by the influence of public opinion,
and not the force of legally binding rulings.

Much more stringent are the procedures
governing the European Convention on
Human Rights, to which all members of the
Council of Europe (a wider body than the
European Union) are required to subscribe.
These procedures involve a fully-fledged
Court with an independent judiciary, to
which individuals from member states may
appeal once all domestic remedies for a
claimed human rights violation have been
exhausted. The decisions of the Court are
binding on member states, which are
required to bring domestic law or administrative practice into line with the European
standards if the judgment goes against them.
The ultimate sanction is suspension from
membership of the Council, which happened
to Greece under the rule of the colonels from
1967 to 1974. It is unlikely that any European
country today would allow the issue to be
pressed this far, especially as membership of
the Council is a precondition for membership
of the European Union. Indeed, annual
reports are required from candidate countries
for membership of the EU on their levels of
human rights observation and democratic
practice, none of which have had any part in
determining these standards in the first
place.

Admittedly there is provision in European
human rights adjudication for respect for
member countries' own political and cultural
traditions in the interpretation of the Convention. This is the doctrine termed the 'margin
of appreciation', whereby domestic courts

and governments are acknowledged to be
better placed than Strasbourg judges for
deciding some sensitive issues of proportionality in the limitation of their citizens' rights.
However, this 'margin' is itself limited by the
necessity of preserving the integrity of the
Convention, and its legal status is itself a
matter of dispute. Actual judgments by the
Court show that a number of practices which
could be claimed as 'traditional' in the UK
have been outlawed under the Convention.
These include some matters that are not
strictly to do with democratic rights, such as
the use of corporal punishment in schools.
The recent incorporation of the European
Convention into UK law as our own domestic
bill of rights has also put certain issues
beyond the scope of domestic legislation,
such as the right to privacy, and under a
recent protocol the abolition of capital punishment across Europe has been made
irreversible.

CONCLUSION

Should we be concerned about this internationalization of human rights standards from
a democratic point of view? Whatever we
may think about the desirability of these
standards, the effect they have is to remove
certain issues from the agenda of domestic
political debate. This effect would be even
more pronounced if economic and social
rights were to achieve the same justiciable
status as civil and political ones, as some
argue they should. Then a considerable area
of social and economic policy, which is currently contested between political parties,
would be removed from the political arena.
Indeed, this is already happening as the
European Union sets standards for consumer
protection, employment rights and so on,
which member states are required to enforce.

However, a similar argument can be made
for social and economic rights as for civil and
political ones, that they have a foundational
status for democratic citizenship. How can
civil and political rights themselves be

exercised without the personal and economic empowerment brought by access to health, education and economic security? Just as the civil rights of vulnerable minorities need protection, it can be argued, so too the economic rights of those on the margin of employment need protecting from the collusion of electoral majorities in their disempowerment. In other words, economic and social rights should no longer be seen as a desirable outcome of democratic politics, but a necessary *precondition* for them, and therefore rightly the subject of international standard setting and adjudication.

The conception of democracy we started with at the outset, which was eloquently expressed in the quotation from Ronald Dworkin, seems to have landed us in a paradox. The stronger and more extensive the constitutional guarantees of democratic rights, the less discretion is left for decision-making by the institutions of electoral democracy. As Michael Saward has put it: 'If a full range of demanding social and economic rights were to be constitutionalized, little would be left for "ordinary" democratic decision' (Saward, 1998: 102). Not only that. The rights to be constitutionalized would be, as they increasingly are, defined by international agencies beyond the state. And then we open up a new set of questions about the democratic accountability of these agencies and their processes of decision-making. In sum, resolving a *substantive* deficit in the rights dimension of democracy opens up a potentially worrying *procedural* deficit in the democratic mechanism of representation and accountability in the bodies involved in standard setting at the international level.

Summary

- There exists an integral connection between rights and democracy.
- The place of a 'bill of rights' in a democratic constitution is, however, highly controversial.
- A defence of 'human rights' must confront the following challenges:
  - Are the judgments of an unelected judiciary, which annuls parliamentary legislation on the basis of 'human rights' conventions, ultimately 'undemocratic'?
  - Given the internationalization of human rights issues, how can the democratic accountability of international human rights bodies be ensured?

TUTORIAL QUESTIONS

1 **'A bill of rights is inimical to democracy.' Discuss.**

2. **'The stronger and more extensive the constitutional guarantees of democratic rights, the less discretion is left for decision-making by the institutions of electoral democracy.' Can this paradox be resolved?**

FURTHER READING

A.H. Robertson and J.G. Merrills (1996) *Human Rights in the World* (Manchester: Manchester University Press, fourth edition) is a standard text explaining human rights. Chapters 4 and 5 deal with the institutions for the protection of human rights in Europe, and chapter 6 with the Americas.

I. Brownlie (ed.) (1992) *Basic Documents on Human Rights* (Oxford: Clarendon Press, third edition) is a useful reference work for the main human rights covenants and treaties.

Various aspects of the relation between human rights and democracy are dealt with in D. Beetham (1999) *Democracy and Human Rights* (Cambridge: Polity Press, chapter 5); M. Saward (1998) *The Terms of Democracy* (Cambridge: Polity Press, chapter 5); and A. Weale (1999) *Democracy* (Basingstoke: Macmillan, chapter 9).

R. Dworkin (1990) *A Bill of Rights for Britain* (London: Chatto & Windus) offers a classic justification for a bill of rights and its compatibility with democracy. An important contribution to the debate is Jeremy Waldon (1993) *Liberal Rights* (Cambridge: CUP), chapter 16.

REFERENCES

Dworkin, R. (1990) *A Bill of Rights for Britain*. London: Chatto & Windus.

Saward, M. (1998) *The Terms of Democracy*. Cambridge: Polity Press.

See also chapters

1 Sovereignty
2 Constitutionalism
4 Justice, Equality, Liberty
5 Power, Authority, Legitimacy

8 Pluralism – Difference
22 Democratic Citizenship in the Age of Globalization

4 Justice, Equality, Liberty

Vittorio Bufacchi

SOCIAL JUSTICE AND THE RESOLUTION OF CONFLICT

Social cooperation is the cement of political society. The structure and legitimacy of political power is determined by how the benefits of social cooperation are secured. The difference between a democracy and a non-democracy fundamentally comes down to whether social cooperation is voluntary or imposed by force: the more extensive the level of voluntary social cooperation, the stronger the democratic fibre of society.

Notwithstanding its benefits, people often fail to cooperate spontaneously for the common good. Many succumb to the tendency to benefit from the efforts of others without contributing anything of their own. The fundamental problem all democracies face is therefore how to find an acceptable equilibrium between allowing social cooperation to be voluntary, and avoiding missing out on the benefits of social cooperation because of widespread free-riding. This is where social justice enters the scene. We look to theories of social justice to help us solve two problems. First, given that in a democracy all citizens are free to act as they wish (as long as their actions do not harm others), inevitably there will be conflicts to be resolved. Such conflicts arise when too many individuals fight over the control of too few resources (widely defined to include both material goods and political rights). There is therefore a need

for principles that will establish just criteria for the distribution of the benefits of social cooperation across society. For example, to what extent should property by privately owned? Should public money be spent on improving our roads or public transportation? Should group rights protect minority cultures at the expense of the rights of single individuals within these communities?

Apart from resolving the conflicts that arise between individual citizens, a theory of social justice must also resolve conflicts between citizens and state authorities. In particular, principles of social justice should tell us when, where and how a state can legitimately use force to entice individual citizens to co-operate rather than free-ride. Should we be forced to pay taxes? Can the state force us to go to war?

Of all the conflicts of interests that a theory of justice is expected to resolve, one is so fundamental as to be enshrined in ideological trenches, namely, the conflict between liberty and equality. Should the distribution of social benefits and burdens aim to promote greater equality between individuals, even at the expense of certain individual liberties, or should it aim for the most extensive set of liberties in all areas, even if this will result in fundamental inequalities across society? This question is not as abstract as it may appear at first. Some people think that the Scandinavian model is the best effort yet to construct a just society, where for example the Swedish state will not shy away from heavily taxing wealthy citizens on their income in order to provide greater opportunities for everyone, especially the least advantaged members of society. Others think that a just society is embodied in the policies of President George W. Bush of the USA, whose first deed upon entering office in 2001 was to pass a $1.3 trillion tax cut, while trimming welfare provisions.

Another important policy issue that fully reflects the debate on social justice concerns the health care policy, such as the National Health Service in Britain. Is a just society one where everyone has a right to adequate health care provision, irrespective of their income potential, or should citizens be responsible for looking after their own health, and be made to pay for it? Here we have two different conceptions of social justice. Those who emphasize equality aim to bridge the gap between the haves and the have-nots, whereas those who emphasize liberty hold the belief that the state should not interfere with the lives of its citizens, other than for the sake of their protection and safety.

On all the major questions of social policy, it would appear that the principles of equality and liberty are pulling us in different directions. The challenge of a theory of social justice is to resolve this tension between equality and liberty. There are three ways of doing so: either by favouring equality over liberty, or liberty over equality, or by showing that equality and liberty are never truly at odds. But before this question can be settled, we need a deeper understanding of the concepts of equality and liberty.

WHAT IS EQUALITY?

Equality holds a central place in modern society, even though this is a very complex, multidimensional concept, open to many different interpretations. There are three questions regarding equality that demand closer inspection: *why* is equality important?; *what* is being equalized in an egalitarian society?;

and *who* should be the beneficiaries of an egalitarian society?

First, *why* equality – or, what are the values driving equality? Clearly it is not enough to say that we are all equal to the extent that we are all members of the same human species, or that we are all the same in the eyes of our creator, since these equalities are potentially compatible with gross social, economic and political inequalities. Equality is a moral value, not an empirical calculation. The fact that we are all different in our capabilities does not take away from the fact there is a fundamental respect which is owed to each person as a moral agent. From an ethical point of view, we want to say that all human beings are of equal worth.

To say that all human beings, notwithstanding race, gender or nationality, are of equal worth is to make a moral claim. What are the policy implications of this moral claim? Contrary to what may seem to be at first, being of equal worth does not translate automatically into a basic right to the same identical bundle of goods or opportunities as anyone else. Morally we may all be equal, but not socially or biologically. The fact that we are all uniquely different in our make-up should alert us to a simple reality of life, namely, that there are significant variations in our individual abilities to enjoy our lives, or, as Nobel prizewinner Amartya Sen puts it: 'The personal and social characteristics of different persons, which can differ greatly, can lead to substantial interpersonal variations in the conversion of resources and primary goods into achievements [and freedoms]' (Sen, 1992: 38). For example, it would be foolish to assume that your average ten-year-old child from Britain has the same needs as a ten-year-old child in Ethiopia; or that there are no basic differences between a pregnant woman and a man; or that physical and mental disabilities are irrelevant. It is a fact of life that some people need more resources than others to cope with life, which is why a better understanding of equal worth is in terms of having a right to equal concern and respect. Generally speaking, we show *concern* for others by acknowledging that they are capable of suffering and frustration, while we show *respect* for others by acknowledging that they are capable of forming and acting on their independently chosen life plans.

The second question is equality of *what*? How is equality to be measured, or what is being equalized (the *equalisandum*) in an egalitarian society? The answer to this question is not as straightforward as one might wish, since once again we are not confronted with an empirical question, but a qualitative one. There are two rival responses to the 'equality of what' question. We could be talking about equality of resources. Alternatively, we could be talking about equality of welfare. The difference between resources and welfare comes down to the following: do we aim to equalize starting points, or do we aim to equalize outcomes? We may want to equalize the opportunities people have, giving them access to resources but then letting them be responsible for any inequalities that may result from their actions, for example, by providing free education to each and every child. Alternatively, we may want to equalize the conditions in which they live, whereby our concern for their well-being is more important than any argument based on responsibility or merit; for example, we may want everyone in our society to enjoy a standard of living that bestows dignity and security, including those who may be responsible for any inadequacies in their lives. There are advantages and disadvantages with both positions, which explains why the debate has turned to middle-of-the-road solutions that aim to reconcile considerations of opportunities and responsibility (resources) with considerations of basic need-satisfaction (well-being).

The third question is *who* are the beneficiaries of an egalitarian society, or who is being targeted as the concerned party in an egalitarian society? Egalitarians are, yet again, divided on this question. On one side, *strict egalitarians* argue that it is bad if some people are worse off than others, therefore equality calls for greater uniformity across society. To defend their views, strict egalitarians argue

that apart from being an intrinsic value, being good in itself, equality is desirable because lack of parity may also have bad effects.

The possible bad effects of inequalities are innumerable. For example, inequalities may generate conflict, which in turn may lead to violence and misery. That crime rates are much higher in rich American cities than in Scandinavian countries can, perhaps, be explained by pointing to the inequalities that characterize life in America. Inequality may also damage the self-respect of those who are worst off. Considering that we construct the way we see ourselves by comparison to those around us, it is worth asking what it feels like to be among the worst-off groups in society. Perhaps those who are worst off, socially or economically, compared to others in the same community would blame themselves for their calamity. They might start to question their own abilities, feeling inadequate, incompetent or generally inferior compared to those who are better off. All this would contribute to undermining their self-respect. Finally, inequalities may lead to some members of society having power over others. Those who have more economic resources may be able to translate their advantages into other forms of power, both social and political. It is not simply a case of economic power translating into political power, as in the case of electoral politics just about anywhere in the world, from the Kennedy and the Bush dynasties in the USA, to Berlusconi in Italy. At a more personal level, for example, it can mean that employers may get away with sexually harassing workers who feel they cannot afford to lose their jobs, and therefore are forced to endure humiliations.

Notwithstanding these arguments, not all advocates of egalitarianism are convinced that the value of equality is best captured by the goal of equalizing welfare across members of society. After all, if parity is the goal, this may be secured by a policy of 'levelling down', that is, bringing down the level of welfare of those who have more to the level of those who have less. This may not be desirable. To have the entire population living in poverty cannot be better than having only a small minority living in poverty while the rest enjoys a healthy, satisfying standard of living. Those who are sceptical of the virtues of strict equality suggest a different way of capturing the spirit of egalitarianism, namely, increasing the well-being of the worst off in society.

This version of egalitarianism, known as the *priority view* or simply *prioritarianism*, suggests that it is more important to help those who are worst off, whether or not this leads to parity between the worst off and the better off. As Joseph Raz famously explains:

> What makes us care about various inequalities is not the inequality but the concern identified by the underlying principle. It is the hunger of the hungry, the need of the needy, the suffering of the ill, and so on. The fact that they are worse off in the relevant respect than their neighbours is relevant. But it is relevant not as an independent evil of inequality. Its relevance is in showing that their hunger is greater, their need more pressing, their suffering more hurtful, and therefore our concern for the hungry, the needy, the suffering, and not our concern for equality, makes us give them the priority. (Raz, 1986: 240)

Egalitarianism is a complex philosophy. There are many different ways of being an egalitarian, pulling us in opposite directions. As we have seen, there are disparate answers to the questions of how best to assess the value of equality, how to measure equality, and how to define the goals of equality, all of which are valid considerations which deserve to be taken seriously. To complicate matters even more, this multidimensionality is not unique to the idea of equality. The same applies for the idea of liberty, which is the other main contender for the sole, devoted attention of social justice.

WHAT IS LIBERTY?

The terms 'liberty' and 'freedom' (hereby used interchangeably) have a strong rhetorical force, although the exact meaning of these concepts remains a contested area. In an attempt to make sense of liberty, a useful and still immensely influential distinction is made between *negative* and *positive* freedom.

The terminology of 'negative' and 'positive' is potentially confusing, to the extent that our first reaction is to look favourably at what is labelled 'positive' and unfavourably at what is 'negative'. This is in fact the exact opposite of what Isaiah Berlin (1969), who coined the terms, was trying to convey. The reason for using these terms is the following. We say that one enjoys *negative* freedom when one is allowed to operate within an area of non-interference. Here negative simply refers to the lack of interference, obstacles or constraints; in short, freedom *from*. Alternatively, one enjoys *positive* freedom when one realizes a certain level of self-government, or in other words having the power or capacity to act according to one's wishes. Here positive refers to having the means required to pursue those goals which one has chosen for oneself; in short, freedom *to*.

The distinction between negative and positive freedom is very problematic, not being as clear-cut as the terminology may suggest. Contrary to what Isaiah Berlin argued, negative and positive freedom are not mutually exclusive. In fact, it is difficult to think of positive freedom as independent from negative freedom, as the following example suggests. In Britain women were not allowed to pursue a career in the legal profession until 1911. This means that before 1911, women were legally – and therefore physically – prevented from attending classes in higher education institutions imparting degrees in jurisprudence. In other words, before 1911 women did not have the negative freedom to do certain things. But after 1911, as these legal restrictions were lifted, women enjoyed both the negative freedom of not facing restrictions and the positive freedom to pursue a career in the legal profession, and in the process perhaps fulfil a life-long aspiration.

Intuitively, it would seem that freedom includes both a negative and a positive dimension. So why do philosophers still use this terminology of negative and positive freedom? What do we gain from the purely analytical distinction between a negative and a positive understanding of freedom? I believe the answer lies in the ethical underpinnings of these two ways of understanding what it is to be free. In other words, there may be even deeper, more fundamental moral values than freedom which become visible when we distinguish between negative and positive freedom, namely, self-ownership and autonomy.

Starting with negative freedom. Some extreme sympathizers of this conception of freedom, who call themselves *libertarians*, argue that we should think of freedom in physical terms, as physical non-interference or lack of physical obstructions. One is free as long as one is not physically constrained in one's actions. Critics of libertarianism are not persuaded by this, pointing to the fact that according to this physicalist approach a threat does not count as a violation of one's freedom. For example, if a bandit points a gun at you and demands 'your purse or your life', libertarians would not condemn this threat as a restriction of your liberty, since the victim is still physically free to move and to make a choice. Similarly, a violent husband who threatens his wife by raising his hand, but does not hit her, is technically not restricting her freedom. Of course this does not mean that libertarians condone the behaviour of bandits or violent husbands. Far from it. They simply want to make the point that while bandits and violent husbands are morally repulsive beings, what we find objectionable about their behaviour should not be confused with issues of lack of freedom.

Libertarians argue that there are many advantages to their physicalist approach to freedom. First of all, it means that freedom is not a subjective standard, but an objective reality that can be more easily measured. After all, if psychological harm is included in our list of impediments to freedom, then a university lecturer is infringing the freedom of a student every time he or she fails someone for not doing the assigned work, since he or she is causing the student great psychological harm. Secondly, by reducing freedom to a person's physical actions, we have a clear idea of what it is to be unfree. In the words of Hillel Steiner: 'A person is unfree to do an action if, and only if, his doing that action is rendered impossible by the action of another person' (1994: 8).

It is exactly because libertarians endorse a physicalist understanding of freedom that they are in a position to argue for a basic right that we all have over ourselves. This fundamental right is referred to in the literature as the right to self-ownership, or the claim of an individual to sovereignty over his or her person, typically taken to include not only his or her body, but also his or her energy, talent and labour (and perhaps even the fruits of his or her labour). The idea of self-ownership finds favour with opposing positions on the ideological spectrum, being championed by sympathizers of a free-market system to oppose most forms of state interference, but used by Marxists to expose the immorality of exploitation.

Those who are unhappy with the libertarian interpretation of freedom, such as *perfectionists*, inevitably want to defend a positive conception of freedom. In recent years there has been a tendency to equate the thesis of positive freedom with the notion of autonomy. But what does it mean to be autonomous? Literally meaning 'self-rule', 'self-law' or 'self-government', the idea of autonomy is open to many different interpretations.

It has been suggested, for example, that autonomy is a *condition*, defined as the psychological ability to be self-governing. This is promising, the only worry being that to define autonomy as a condition is to appraise it for its instrumental value, rather than for intrinsic reasons. Alternatively, autonomy can be seen as an *ideal*, whereby an autonomous person is one who identifies with one's desires, goals and values. To identify with one's own desires means that an agent reflects critically on a desire and, at a higher level, approves of having that desire. To act autonomously means not only being in a position to do what one wants, but also being able to want what one wants. To be free to act in accordance with mere desires or emotions is not to be autonomous. Instead, an autonomous person is someone who is in control of his or her desires, someone who has the power to reason over his or her appetites, longings and urges.

From a moral point of view, autonomy means endorsing moral principles as one's own. From a political point of view, autonomy can be contrasted with dogmatism or extreme forms of paternalism. To live an autonomous life is to formulate, revise and pursue one's conception of the good life, not to accept blindly and uncritically what others may suggest.

A JUST SOCIETY

Can justice reconcile the demands of equality and liberty? It is clearly not easy. As we have seen, there are many different ways of being an egalitarian, just as there are many different ways of interpreting the principle of liberty. Reconciling the two paradigms of equality and liberty is an onerous challenge, but one we cannot afford to dodge. We must resist the simplistic pessimism of equating social justice with an ideal beyond our reach. To argue that there are simply too many values involved for any reconciliation to occur is to make a dangerous mistake. It could even open the way to undemocratic forces.

Instead, we must try to think more creatively about how a just society can make equality and liberty work in harmony. This is exactly what the American philosopher John Rawls did in the second half of the twentieth century. Writing in the aftermath of the Second World War, Rawls formulated an ambitious, comprehensive and totally original theory of social justice that appears successfully to reconcile the demands of liberty and equality. Notwithstanding its length (587 pages) and complexity (25 years in the making), Rawls's book, *A Theory of Justice*, published in 1971, instantly became the most influential work in moral and political philosophy of the twentieth century. The importance of this book cannot be overemphasized. In three or four hundred years' time, when students of politics are taking courses in the history of political thought, after Hobbes and Locke in the seventeenth century, Rousseau and Kant in the eighteenth century, and Marx and J.S. Mill in the nineteenth century, they will be told about how Rawls's theory of justice in the twentieth century changed the course of political theory.

What is so special about Rawls's theory of justice? Rawls's stroke of genius is to bring back to life a philosophical approach that had been out of favour for at least two hundred years: the social contract. The basic idea behind a social contract is to establish the conditions for a hypothetical unanimous agreement, the assumption being that if we could all hypothetically agree to something, whatever it is we all agree to must have both validity and legitimacy. Historically, the device of the social contract had been conjured up to explain and justify the legitimacy of the state and the corresponding political obligation of citizens. What no one had ever attempted to do, until Rawls, was to employ the device of a social contract to determine principles of justice to which all free and equal citizens would consent.

Using the idea of a social contract, Rawls set out to find principles of justice that everyone would find acceptable. One would be tempted to label Rawls's exorbitant project as 'mission impossible', dismissing it as yet another utopian fantasy conjured up by a philosopher totally detached from the real world. But this would be a gross mistake. The way Rawls constructs a hypothetical unanimous agreement is both spectacular and overwhelmingly convincing, so much so that many over the years have been converted to the Rawlsian approach to social justice. Briefly, this is how it works. Rawls invites us to engage in a speculative thought experiment. Given that the agreement is supposed to be unanimous, meaning that it does not exclude anyone, it follows that you or I can partake in the experiment using our own heads (following our own desires, convictions, beliefs, etc.). All we need to do is answer a simple question: how would we want the most precious goods, both material (wealth) and non-material (human rights), to be divided across society, if we did not know our place in the world? For example, let us assume that we did not know our gender, our race or our sexual inclinations. Would we gamble on a world where non-whites are denied their fundamental rights, where women are powerless or where homosexuals are persecuted? Rawls argues that it would be irrational to run the risk of finding ourselves members of an oppressed group, which is why we would all agree to live in a world where everyone enjoys the same full set of rights and liberties.

Now, let us assume that we did not know our social class, nationality or our physical endowments. How would we want material resources to be divided? It is unlikely that we would choose the kind of world in which we live today, where a small percentage of individuals (mostly able-bodied, middle-class, westerners) controls a hugely disproportionate slice of the world's wealth, while millions of people worldwide face a daily struggle just to feed themselves. Not knowing our place in the world would make us very cautious about how we would want economic resources to be distributed. Which is why Rawls suggests that it would be irrational to want economic resources to be distributed so that the richest individuals in the richest nations take the lion's share of resources, as it is at the moment. Instead, just in case we happen to find ourselves among the less fortunate, for example born physically impaired or below the poverty line, or perhaps starving in Somalia, we would all agree that it would be

best for resources to be redistributed so that any inequality will be to the greatest benefit of those who are least advantaged.

It is important to emphasize that in Rawls's theory of social justice, the concepts of liberty and equality find their true nature in the idea of a social contract. The aspiration of a social contract is to seek a unanimous agreement, which must be grounded in the consent of each and every individual. It is this idea of consenting individuals that captures the value of liberty. Furthermore, apart from being free, all those who take part in this agreement are also equal. In Rawls's contractarian theory of justice, equality is not only defined in terms of the proviso that no one can be excluded from the agreement. There is more. Remember that in Rawls's thought experiment no one knows his or her place in the world. It is this basic ignorance that acts as a great leveller, since in seeking an agreement no one is in a position to take advantage of a potentially stronger bargaining position as a consequence of having undeserved privileges.

To recap: according to Rawls, a just society is a place where everyone enjoys the same set of rights and liberties, and where economic resources are distributed with the goal of promoting the greatest long-term benefit of the least advantaged groups or classes. In this model of a just society, liberty and equality appear to be fully reconciled. So, is this it? Has Rawls delivered the last word on social justice, equality and liberty? Of course not. Political theory, at least within democratic cultures, never reaches a final resting place. What makes democratic political theory vibrant is the fact that it is in constant movement, always changing and (one hopes) improving. Rawls is not an exception to this rule. Notwithstanding the universal acclaim and admiration Rawls's work has received, it has also been the target of many critical rebuttals. For example, those writing from an ideological perspective on the right reject Rawls's account of liberty, while those on the left reject his conception of equality. Others have taken issue with the universal aspirations of the social contract approach, suggesting instead that there may be many different ways of reconciling liberty and equality, and that each community should be allowed to define for itself what it understands by social justice.

While Rawls has come under considerable fire, there are many who share Rawls's vision, and have undertaken the task of defending him, while refining and improving upon his project. Paradoxically, those who want to defend Rawls's original project are sometimes forced to argue against Rawls's own attempt to develop his theory. In particular, Rawlsian-inspired philosophers have tried to defend, amend and ameliorate two pillars of Rawls's original theory of justice: universality and impartiality.

Many feel that holding on to the values of universality and impartiality is, arguably, the best way for a democracy to deal with conflicts. The reason we value justice, and the reason why it is worth fighting for a just society, is not to overcome conflict but to manage it. The point of a just society is not to avoid conflicts of value by aiming for eternal reconciliation, but simply to find ways for equality and freedom to co-exist within a just society. Justice demands the provision of an arena and a set of rules where questions of freedom and equality can be debated, on fair grounds, as each issue arises. In other words, a just society provides an impartial framework within which supporters of equality and liberty can fight their battles. Brian Barry captures this basic notion of justice with authority and clarity:

> Justice as impartiality is designed to provide a framework within which people can live, but does not purport to tell how to live. . . . Justice as impartiality does not have a substantive answer to every question. Rather, in very many cases it can set limits to what is just but has to leave the choice of an outcome within that range to a fair procedure. (Barry, 1995: 113)

The important lesson we learn from reading Barry is that a theory of justice is not the panacea for all our troubles. Just as it is an error to assume that in a conflict *every* conceivable outcome is equally valid, it is also an error to assume that there is *one* right answer to every conflict. The point of justice is to define fair procedures according to fair rules. While justice as impartiality has nothing to say about the outcome of specific conflicts, it does set limits on the range of acceptable outcomes by appealing to the fairness of the rules that define the decision procedure for adjudicating between conflicting interests.

By taking the impartiality approach to questions of justice we come to see conflict in a different light. A just society does not have a problem with the conflict of value between equality and liberty. It is not simply the case that conflicts cannot be avoided, but that some degree of conflict is desirable. A just society is one that provides the conditions for the peaceful co-existence of diverse and potentially conflicting conceptions of the good life. What makes a society just is the fact that diversity is not eradicated and conflict is not suppressed. In fact, it is heterogeneity that will make a just society and its citizens prosper. Diversity does not rule out compatibility, while conflict must be confined to legally recognized and acceptable channels of expression. Of course, where there are conflicts, there are winners and losers, but in a just society those who lose are not the victims of an injustice. As long as there are appropriate procedures to deal with such antagonisms, conflict is not a problem.

CONCLUSION

Throughout this chapter the discussion of justice and the conflict of equality and liberty has assumed issues arising within a single nation-state. As a concluding thought, it is important to remind ourselves that the demands of justice, equality and liberty cannot be confined within geographical boundaries. Our analysis of justice, equality and liberty applies equally to an international context, especially in the present era of growing globalization. The distribution of the world's natural resources, the obligation to assist the needy anywhere in the world, the responsibilities of international corporations and cooperation, the global environment, the legitimate use of violence across borders and the arguments for a world government, are as central to issues of justice, equality and liberty as issues of education, taxation and health care are within a single society.

Summary

- The aim of social justice is to resolve conflicts that arise within society. Such conflicts may arise between citizens, or between citizens and the state.
- The biggest challenge for a theory of social justice is to resolve the conflict between equality and liberty.
- There are many different ways of interpreting the concepts of equality and liberty.
- It is important to distinguish between equality of resources and equality of welfare and between strict equality and prioritarianism.
- It is important to distinguish between negative liberty and positive liberty and between self-ownership and autonomy.
- Justice can reconcile equality and liberty not by providing a single, universal principle that solves all potential conflicts, but by providing fair terms in the procedures to be followed when adjudicating between conflicting claims.
- The aim of justice is not to eliminate conflicts. There cannot be a just society without conflict and diversity.

TUTORIAL QUESTIONS

1. **Is equality intrinsic to our understanding of the concept of social justice?**

2. **What is the difference between freedom and autonomy?**

3. **Can equality and liberty co-exist within a just society?**

4. **Does Rawls's thought experiment work?**

FURTHER READING

John Rawls (1999) *A Theory of Justice* (Oxford: Oxford University Press, second edition) is the most influential and original work in political philosophy since J. S. Mill's *On Liberty* was published in 1859. A classic. A shorter, and more recent, text is John Rawls (2001) *Justice as Fairness. A Restatement* (Cambridge, MA: Harvard University Press).

Adam Swift (2001) *Political Philosophy: a Beginners' Guide for Students and Politicians* (Cambridge: Polity Press) is a very readable, jargon-free analysis of social justice, equality, liberty and the concept of community.

Anne Phillips (1999) *Which Equalities Matter?* (Cambridge: Polity Press) gives a very accurate but readable overview of the debate on equality, with many references to feminist issues.

Steven Luper-Foy (ed.) (1988) *Problems of International Justice* (Boulder, CO: Westview Press) is an excellent collection of essays dealing with issues of international justice.

REFERENCES

Barry, Brian (1995) *Justice as Impartiality*. Oxford: Oxford University Press.

Berlin, Isaiah (1969) *Four Essays on Liberty* (second edition). Oxford: Oxford University Press.

Raz, Joseph (1986) *The Morality of Freedom*. Oxford: Oxford University Press.

Sen, Amartya (1992) *Inequality Reexamined*. Cambridge, MA: Harvard University Press.

Steiner, Hillel (1994) *An Essay on Rights*. Oxford: Blackwell.

5 Power, Authority, Legitimacy

Noël O'Sullivan

POWER

Although power is a central feature of all politics, attempts to define its nature have reflected major differences of approach throughout western history. In the ancient and medieval worlds, for example, the dominant approach was normative because power was rarely treated as an independent feature of political existence but was instead submerged in a vision of an all-embracing ethical order – thought of as 'natural' or cosmological – in which both the individual and the community have a definite place assigned to them, and to which they must conform in all their actions.

In the modern world, by contrast, the idea of a natural or cosmological order of any kind has largely disappeared as the background for human life, and consequently for the analysis of power. The beginning of a new attitude to power following upon the loss of the old setting is already discernible at the end of the medieval period in the writings of Machiavelli, who was one of the first thinkers to focus attention on the power of the Prince in a way that extricated it – in some degree at least – from its previous subordination to ethical considerations. Machiavelli's tendency to adopt an empirical rather than an ethical approach to power was subsequently intensi-fied by the growth of the characteristically modern western desire to study all aspects of human life, including power, in a scientific, wholly neutral way. In recent decades, however, scepticism about the possibility of applying scientific method to the study of human society has become widespread, and the possibility of describing power in purely neutral, non-ethical terms has consequently been hotly contested. A good way of appreciating more fully the difficulties presented by the concept of power is to consider the debate between defenders and critics of the modern project of achieving a scientific analysis of power.

A century and a half after Machiavelli's pioneering endeavour to treat power in an empirical way, Hobbes applied the empirical approach even more rigorously. In its most general sense, Hobbes observed, 'The power of a man . . . is his present means to obtain some future end' (1651/1909: 66). This general definition of power, however, is unsuitable for purposes of social theory, where what is needed is a definition of power that concentrates attention more narrowly on relationships in which the exercise of power in some way constrains the behaviour of those over whom it is wielded. A common way of dealing with this is by distinguishing between 'power *over*' and 'power *to*'.

Hobbes himself, in fact, recognized the need to restrict the meaning of power in specifically political contexts to 'power over'. In doing so, he went a step further than Machiavelli when he attempted to define 'power over' scientifically – that is, by using the categories of cause and effect. 'Power over', Hobbes maintained, is the ability of one person to 'cause' another to produce the 'effect' at which he aims by carrying out his bidding. This way of describing 'power over', however, is too crude to provide a very satisfactory characterization of human relationships, mainly because it attempts to apply the mechanistic language of the natural sciences to the interpretation of human relationships, thereby confusing the language of inner reasons (that is, of motives and purposes) with the 'push–pull' language of physical causes and effects.

During the twentieth century, various thinkers have attempted to remove this confusion by redefining the scientific approach in a way that avoids Hobbes's mechanistic language. One of the most influential examples of this is the behavioural approach to the study of power represented in particular by Robert Dahl. Dahl defines 'power over' as follows: 'A has power over B to the extent that he can get B to do something that B would not otherwise do' (Dahl, 1961: 125). This definition, however, has been criticized for being too narrow because it ignores various kinds of hidden power. One of the most influential versions of this criticism is that developed by Steven Lukes.

In *Power: a Radical View* (1974), Lukes endeavours to expose hidden forms of power by taking account of the fact that A may exercise power over B not only by the visible, direct means studied by Dahl and others, but also by two indirect ones that do not involve A doing anything at all. One of these – the 'second dimension' of power – occurs when purely procedural conditions ensure that the policy agenda in a situation involving A and B is tabled in such a way that B's interests are not considered. The importance of this second dimension, Lukes notes, had previously been realized, albeit in a somewhat undeveloped way, by Peter Bachrach and Morton S. Baratz (1962: 947). He accordingly claims originality only for elaborating more fully the nature of a 'third dimension' of power which other thinkers have tended to neglect.

Lukes's third dimension, like the second, concerns a way in which A may exercise power over B without actually doing anything. It arises, Lukes maintains, when A is able to exercise power over B because B is unaware of his true interest, which is to enjoy '(relative) autonomy and choice' (1974: 34). The third dimension occurs, that is, because people may be socially determined in ways that prevent them from making choices that reflect their real interests.

Somewhat inconsistently with this analysis, which he claims is superior to other approaches to power, Lukes draws on the work of Gallie (1956) when he qualifies his position by asserting that, in the last resort, the meaning of the concept of power (like other key political concepts) is 'essentially contestable'. By this, he means that scholars can never reach ultimate agreement about the nature of power because ideological elements inevitably creep into their thought. This view has been rejected, however, by Terence Ball (1993: 548) who plausibly argues that the concept of essential contestability makes unintelligible the existence of politics itself, since it mistakenly implies that men are forever doomed to live in the equivalent of Hobbes's state of nature – a condition, that is, in which there are no shared meanings, but only those which each person gives to the concepts he himself uses.

A further difficulty presented by Lukes's three-dimensional concept of power concerns his concept of 'true interests'. Although Lukes acknowledges that different conceptions of what real interests actually *are* 'are associated with different moral and political positions' (1974: 34) and admits that it is well-nigh impossible to decide in a non-dogmatic way what someone would want in different circumstances, he nevertheless clings to the idea that the individual's own interpretation of his or her wants may in principle be overridden by an observer who claims to have a clearer view of his or her true or objective interest. Lukes attempts to protect his position against the danger of authoritarian interpretation which this view opens up 'by insisting on the empirical basis for identifying real interests', but the fact that the empirical element is either indiscernible in some cases, or may be variously interpreted in others, leaves the nature of the protection it affords questionable (1974: 33).

Perhaps the most unsatisfactory element in Lukes's three-dimensional concept of power, however, lies in a crucial, yet completely arbitrary, assumption upon which his whole analysis rests. This is that 'power over' is generally something negative – something to be equated with domination, in the sense of impeding the autonomy of those subject to it. What this overlooks, as Foucault (1980) has argued, is that power can perfectly well be benign. The main point at stake, however, is made by Terence Ball who argues that 'power *over* is not paradigmatic [as Lukes assumes] of power *per se*. . . . Political analysts are [in fact] more apt to speak about political actors' power to *do* things than their power *over* someone' (Ball, 1993: 551). As an example, Ball instances the power of the American president, which is pre-eminently the power to persuade rather than to exercise power *over* in the sense of domination.

As soon as it is acknowledged that power of this kind – namely power to persuade – is the paradigm of political power, rather than power *over*, the common link running through the work of such diverse thinkers as Arendt (1972), De Jouvenel (1993) and Habermas (1984) immediately becomes apparent. What they share is a view of power as the ability of free agents to create, through communicating in the political process, a public structure which permits them to act as a unified collectivity. At this point, it may be noticed, contact is restored with the concept of power found in ancient political theory. Thus Cicero, for example, describes power as *potestas*, which refers to the ability of the *pop-*

ulus Romanus to act in unity through mutual communication. Power in this sense, it should be emphasized, is diametrically opposed to concepts of violence and domination. Unlike them, as Anthony Giddens has remarked, it is not in principle an obstacle to freedom or emancipation, 'but is their very medium' (1984: 257).

What may now be briefly considered is a 'systemic' approach to power which overlaps with certain aspects of Lukes's third dimensional approach, although Lukes himself rejects the more extreme formulations of systems theory. Of these, one of the most striking is that of Louis Althusser, who identified the essence of the 'systemic' approach when he maintained that power is never exercised, properly speaking, by individuals or groups, but is always exercised impersonally, by social structures. The attraction of this approach lies in its claim not only to include what are considered to be the deepest sources of hidden power, but to be purely descriptive, or ideologically neutral. The systemic approach, however, creates at least three major problems. The first concerns the difficulty of determining what the 'structures' which are supposed to exercise power actually are. The second is that attributing the concept of power to impersonal systems or structures necessarily divorces it from the concepts of intention and purpose, thereby making it impossible to distinguish power from the kind of mere physical *force* that an elevator exercises when it moves passengers from the first to the fifth floor. The third is that a purely structuralist approach to power, such as that developed by Althusser and Balibar (1968), cannot avoid a crucial philosophical confusion. This consists, as Lukes notes, in illegitimately moving from the idea that *all action is in some sense socially conditioned* to the mistaken conclusion that no action involving the exercise of power is a matter of personal responsibility.

A variety of approaches to the nature of power have now been considered, ranging from empirical and systemic ones which treat it as a given or pre-political phenomenon, to ones which treat it as essentially a creation of the political process itself. For this latter approach, power is not a given but a difficult and always provisional achievement, attained by free agents cooperating through speech – that is, by non-coercive means. There is, however, one further way of approaching power which must now be noticed. This is the analytical approach practised by political theorists such as R. Flathman (1973) and R. Friedman (1973) in the USA, and R.S. Peters (1967) and M. Oakeshott (1975) in Britain. What these thinkers offer, despite their manifest differences, is a concept of power sufficiently precise for the purpose of political theory, yet sufficiently modest for it to be free from the charge of ideological orientation. Oakeshott's analysis, in particular, is especially illuminating in this respect.

Oakeshott's starting point is the general characterization of power as a relationship in which one party 'has the ability to procure with certainty a wished-for response in the conduct of another' (Oakeshott, 1975: 333). Here, 'ability to' is coupled with 'power over', and no reference is made to whether or not B, over whom A exercises power, wishes to act otherwise than A requires: the simple fact of B's compliance is a sufficient condition for power. This, however, leaves the precise character of the power relationship in need of further specification. Oakeshott offers two illuminating comments which tighten up his characterization of it.

On the one hand, Oakeshott notes, relationships *purely* based on power are a rarity. For such a relationship to exist, there must be absolutely no shared understanding between the parties involved about the worth or propriety of the response sought by the one making the demand, and the responding party must be concerned solely with the consequences for himself of compliance or non-compliance with that demand. The reason why such a relationship of pure power is rare, Oakeshott remarks, is because relationships are usually moralized in some degree at least: the power element in a relationship is

normally present, that is, only as a subordinate consideration in subscribing to what is acknowledged to be an obligation.

On the other hand, in the case of power as it relates specifically to the state, Oakeshott notes that the unique feature of the state consists 'in having the authorized monopoly of certain sources of power, the chief of which are military force and the power to execute the judgements of a court of law' (Oakeshott, 1975: 334). He recognizes, however, that the vocabulary of power is unable to do full justice to the nature of the state because it does not permit any distinction to be made between power and authority. At this point, then, it is necessary to turn to the subject of authority.

AUTHORITY

The main feature of authority, as it occurs in legal and political contexts, is that it connotes a *right* to issue directives which *obligate* (Connolly, 1993: 108). In this respect authority is very different from power, which merely coerces. The reason why authority obligates is that, in modern state structures, it is conferred by an office whose occupant is regarded by those obligated as in some sense their representative. It is this that entitles the office holder to make declarations that are morally binding. Authority, in other words, is never possessed by individuals or groups in their personal or private capacity but is always conferred solely by their special status. What is remarkable about this concept of authority, which is in many respects a modern invention, is that those who possess it are entitled to require the performance of their claims without either the approval of them by those subject to their authority, or any acknowledgement of the rational or persuasive nature of their declarations.

It is with this novel characteristic of the modern concept of authority in mind that Richard Flathman has defined it as follows:

Words are taken to be authoritative by a

listener when he recognizes that the claim they make to be heeded is not conditional on his own personal examination and assessment of the reasons or arguments on which they rest, but rather on the consideration that they come from a particular speaker who, because of some identifying characteristic that sets him apart from others, is acknowledged to be entitled to receive this special response. (Flathman, 1987: 29)

In state contexts, the 'identifying characteristic' referred to in this definition concerns, as was just noted, the office held by the person who claims authority. The precise nature of the relationship between authority, office and obligation, however, must now be more fully explored.

The first modern thinker to deal with this relationship systematically was (as in the case of power) Hobbes. For Hobbes, what creates civil unity is the acknowledgement by fellow citizens of what he terms an 'artificial person', by which he means what we now describe as an office holder. The office holder (or artificial person) can obligate those in his (or her) jurisdiction because each citizen acknowledges him as the sole rightful representative of the state and agrees to (as Hobbes puts it) 'own' – that is, *authorize* – his acts in that capacity.

Hobbes's way of describing political authority relies on a fundamental contrast between 'being in' and 'being an' authority. Experts – in philosophy or building or music – can all lay claim to 'being an' authority, without them 'being in' authority. In practice, however, the two concepts of authority do not exclude each other. An office holder such as the prime minister, for example, may not only be *in* authority, but may also be *an* authority, perhaps on economics. But if the two kinds of authority are not exclusive, they nevertheless always remain distinct. A tutor at a university, for example, is usually knowledgeable about his (or her) subject. He does not, however, acquire his right to require his students to write essays from the fact that his knowledge of the subject is generally superior to theirs; he acquires it, rather, from his

formal appointment to a lectureship by the university. Tutors who hoped to run tutorials by relying on the terms of their appointment rather than by commanding the respect of their students through their knowledge of their subject, however, would soon find that their authority simply faded away. Many political theorists would argue that the same thing holds of those who possess political authority.

An important qualification remains to be made about the concept of 'being in' authority. It is that authority in this sense is found only in constitutional states: in other kinds of state, in which a formal constitutional commitment is replaced by a substantive commitment to a particular vision of the good society, possession of authority is detached from the concept of office and connected instead to the ideology of the rulers. This was obviously the case with totalitarian systems of government of the kind found, for example, in the USSR and Nazi Germany. In both cases, the authority claimed by the government had nothing to do with constitutional procedures but derived instead from the government's assertion of a monopoly of ideological orthodoxy – its insistence, that is, that it alone embodied the historical destiny of the people (whether defined as the proletarian masses or as the racially pure *Volk*), and was alone capable of leading them into the utopia of the communist society or the Third Reich. The result of connecting authority with ideological orthodoxy is to make government intolerant of dissentients: only the constitutional states, with their formal concept of authority, can adopt a more or less inclusive approach to social pluralism.

A final point to be made about the impersonal nature of authority concerns the confusion sometimes caused by what Max Weber termed 'charismatic' authority, which owes nothing to possession of an office but derives directly from the personal qualities of the individual to whom it is ascribed. Charisma, however, can never create the *right* to obligate which is essential to legal and political authority, even if people do in fact comply with the declarations of those who possess it. As Oakeshott remarks, the term 'charismatic authority' is in fact a contradiction in terms, except 'where the mystique alleged is that of an office and not that of the personal magnetism of the agent or the transparent wisdom of his utterance' (1975: 321).

Political authority, then, consists in the right of a state office holder to issue rules and directives which obligate those within his or her sphere of competence. As it features in liberal democratic societies, the most striking characteristic of such authority is that one who holds it can demand compliance even when the laws or policies in question are not regarded as rational, persuasive or substantively acceptable by those who acknowledge their validity. This is because the authority, being formal, does not demand substantive consensus. It was remarked earlier that this characteristic of authority in constitutional states provides a means of political coordination in social conditions in which a high degree of moral and political diversity exists.

LEGITIMACY

What has provoked inevitable resistance to the modern concept of authority outlined above is the fact that it appears incompatible with the ideal of individual autonomy that stands at the centre of modern western morality. Since this concept of autonomy acknowledges the moral validity only of self-chosen limits on human conduct, it presents authority as something external and alien. It is this opposition, first theorized by Rousseau, that gives rise to the problem of legitimacy.

How then is the potential gap between rulers and ruled created by concern for individual autonomy to be bridged? It can only be through the construction of a public realm that transcends the gap, while simultaneously protecting the diversity of modern western societies. Three different ways of doing this have been proposed. A review of

all three suggests that none is entirely satisfactory.

The liberal theory of legitimacy

The first proposal locates the key to constructing a public realm in a consensus based upon a universally acceptable ideal of rationality. The work of Joseph Raz provides a good illustration of this version of the liberal enterprise. For Raz, 'The basis of legitimacy is relative to success in getting people to conform to right reason' (1990: 13). Right reason refers here to an objectively valid, 'non-relativized' (in Raz's phrase) standpoint implicit in, but independent of, the 'relativized' ones of those subject to authority in specific social and cultural contexts. What is problematic, however, is the precise nature of the 'non-relativized' concept of rationality upon which Raz relies. In particular, three aspects of Raz's philosophy are especially difficult to reconcile with his quest for an overarching, universally valid concept of rationality.

One aspect is Raz's belief in value pluralism, understood as the existence of an irreducible diversity of worthwhile ways of life, each of which is reasonable, and each of which possesses, in addition, virtues and excellences that inevitably conflict with those of alternative ways of life. A second is his belief in multiculturalism, in the sense of a recognition of 'the equal standing of all the stable and viable cultural communities existing in [a] society' (1994: 67). A third is his commitment to the ideal of individual autonomy as the aim which every truly liberal state must pursue. It is Raz's handling of the last of these three aspects which is perhaps the most puzzling, mainly because he assumes that autonomy is a culturally neutral value that can be deemed rationally acceptable to all members of society. In reality, autonomy is a fundamentally western ideal, intimately tied to a long tradition of individualism which attaches only a subordinate significance to group identity.

It would seem, then, that far from resting upon a 'non-relativized' concept of rationality, Raz's theory of legitimacy is tenable only within the confines of a very definite cultural tradition (Lukes, 1990). Despite his deep awareness of the difficulty of tying legitimacy to a universal rational consensus in an age marked by profound moral, cultural, religious, ethnic and sexual diversity, Raz seems reluctant to abandon the liberal quest for an objective concept of rationality that critics regard as relying upon an unattainable 'view from nowhere'. A possible way out of the difficulties this creates is suggested by proponents of the discourse theory of legitimacy.

The discourse theory of legitimacy

Discourse theory abandons the liberal attempt to ground legitimacy in a universally valid concept of rationality arrived at independently of the political process and endeavours instead to ground it in what Seyla Benhabib has described as 'the free and unconstrained public deliberation of all matters of common concern' (1994: 26). The most intellectually ambitious defender of this ideal is Jürgen Habermas.

Habermas's starting point is the contention that classical liberal theory fails to recognize that legitimacy involves something far more fundamental than protecting rights and interests. What is at stake, to be precise, is our sense of identity as free and equal agents. This sense of identity, however, can only be awakened by abandoning the self-centred 'monological' view of reason associated with the individualist tradition and recognizing instead the inherently 'dialogical' character of reason itself. In practice, Habermas stresses, this recognition can be achieved only through actually experiencing the communicative dimension of political life, in the course of which a deeper sense of mutual dependence is generated – provided, Habermas insists, that free and equal participation in the political process is open to all citizens. When this latter condition is met, the principal condition for legitimacy set by discourse theory is satisfied.

The main difficulty with this theory is that it appears to leave little place for the existence of deep-seated social conflict which cannot be removed by communicative rationality. Unfortunately, Habermas offers no reason to suppose that there is any connection between the achievement of rational communication and the creation of political consensus. Indeed, his attempt to connect legitimacy to communicative rationality has left him exposed to the charge of ultimately evading the problem of legitimacy by retreating from politics into philosophy in order to 'protect the idea of democracy by placing it beyond the reach of practical imperatives' (Connolly, 1983: 326). In other words, Habermas replaces politics with a 'metatheoretical question' about the nature of valid moral knowledge (Connolly, 1983: 325).

Like the liberal theory of legitimacy, then, discourse theory fails in the end to respond adequately to the diversity of modern western society. This has provoked the creation of a third theory of legitimacy which is in some respects sympathetic to discourse theory while also claiming to confront the fact of diversity more directly. This is termed the agonal theory of legitimacy.

The agonal theory of legitimacy

The starting point for the agonal theory of legitimacy is brought out very well by Chantal Mouffe, for whom agonalism entails, above all, a willingness to abandon the quest for an unattainable ideal of rational consensus. The supreme folly of that quest, Mouffe (2000: 113) maintains, is that it is grounded in abstract principles which fail to acknowledge the inescapably political character of social experience, by which she means the ineradicably conflictual character of all human relations. In particular, what that quest entails is the imposition of an illiberal ideal of total inclusion on the radically plural character of contemporary western democracies. By warning against the illusion that a final, fully inclusive form of democracy can ever be achieved, Mouffe observes, agonalism 'forces us to nurture democratic contestation, to accept responsibility for our actions, and to foster the institutions in which political action, with all its limitations, can be pursued. Only under these conditions is a pluralist democracy possible' (Mouffe, 2000: 113). Two main problems are presented by this theory. One is that it fails to allow for the political apathy of modern western populations. The other is that it appears unduly optimistic about the possibility of finding peaceful means of accommodating the vast range of social differences it seeks to empower.

An alternative version of agonal theory has been developed in the United States by William Connolly, whose aim is to construct what he terms a theory of 'critical legitimism', the nature of which is fully developed in *Identity/Difference* (1991). In that work, politics is characterized as an unending struggle with the problem of evil, defined by Connolly in secular terms as the universal experience of cruelty (especially in the form of the systematic exclusion of others) as an inescapable part of the social process in which our identities are forged. As Connolly himself puts it, 'every form of social completion and enablement also contains subjugations and cruelties within it. Politics . . . is the medium through which these ambiguities can be engaged and confronted, shifted and stretched' (1991: 94).

On this view, legitimacy is possible only when we try to ensure that our actions do not result in needless cruelty, especially in the form of demonizing and excluding otherness. The difficulty with this version of the legitimation enterprise is that it is inspired by a quasi-religious vision of society as entailing universal moral guilt, as a result of the inescapable cruelty inherent in all existence. Legitimacy therefore becomes entangled in a liberal form of guilt complex which can be assuaged only by transforming politics into the quest for a morally vindicated life. This quest, however, not only threatens political paralysis through moral sensitivity but also fails to provide safeguards against the conversion of politics into a means by which a self-righteous minority might seek to impose its views of how 'the other' should be treated upon a majority that it despises for its lack of civic sentiment.

Although the agonal model attempts to achieve legitimacy by embracing maximum social diversity, then, it fails to provide a coherent account of how this can be achieved.

CONCLUSION

For at least two centuries western political thinkers have generally insisted that the defence of limited government requires three distinct vocabularies, namely those dealing with power, authority and legitimacy respectively. At the present time, however, concern with two of those three concepts, namely authority and legitimacy, appears to be declining, mainly because western populations have become increasingly willing to discuss politics primarily in terms of the various social and economic benefits governments can offer. If what governments offer is considered sufficiently attractive, then constitutional issues, which are the focal point of the concepts of authority and legitimacy, tend to get ignored, leaving only a 'politics of power'.

Contemporary indifference to constitutional issues is intensified by the advent of the European Union which, it has been suggested, is likely to mean a chronic and continuous crisis of legitimacy at both the national and the European Union levels (Beetham and Lord, 1998: 124). The danger, in brief, is that the European Union has already eroded the legitimacy of national institutions, without bringing any corresponding growth in acceptance of the legitimacy of its own supra-national ones. Whether the European world will succeed before too long in creating a new, supra-national public realm, in which the problem of a 'democratic deficit' is gradually resolved, remains to be seen: for the immediate future, opinion will inevitably continue to be deeply divided on the issue.

It would be wrong to conclude, however, that the prospect of a single vocabulary for western politics – a vocabulary, that is, of power – would necessarily mean the reduction of politics to an unpleasant system of coercion. On the contrary, a politics of power may well be both comfortable and popular, if power is used for benign purposes. If a decline of the traditional concern for authority and legitimacy does materialize, however, and modern liberal democracies are left with only a politics of power, then ideals such as the rule of law, an independent judiciary and respect for individual rights would be reduced to indulgences granted by the executive on a discretionary basis. As de Tocqueville remarked long ago, the fact that this kind of government may well prove to be both comfortable and popular should not conceal the fact that it is no longer the government of a free social order, whether at national or supra-national level.

Summary

- Attempts to adopt a purely empirical approach to power assume that the concept can be adequately defined by a detached spectator. This ignores the fact that, in politics, power is a creation of the political process and, as such, can be defined only in relation to the 'internal' standpoint of those who are participants in the political process itself.
- Authority, unlike power, involves the concepts of obligation and of office.
- The nature of legitimacy in liberal democracies remains controversial.
  - For classical liberal theory it derives from the contribution government makes to the protection of individual rights.
  - For discourse theory, it derives from the creation of a public world in which equal participation permits the formation of a shared popular will.
  - For agonal theory, legitimacy depends upon the willingness to abandon the quest for consensus, affirm diversity, and embrace positively political conflict.
  - These three different concepts ultimately involve different, and conflicting, views of the human good.

TUTORIAL QUESTIONS

1. **'Every political realist knows that the state is power, and nothing but power.' Do you agree with the realist?**

2. **What is 'hidden' power? Can it be analysed objectively?**

3. **What is the relationship between authority and legality?**

4. **Which theory of legitimacy best reconciles citizens to state authority?**

FURTHER READING

William E. Connolly (1983) *The Terms of Political Discourse* (Oxford: Blackwell) is a valuable introduction to all three concepts of power, authority and legitimacy.

William E. Connolly (ed.) (1984) *Legitimacy and the State* (Oxford: Blackwell) offers a more extended and varied analysis of the subject of legitimacy.

John Gray's chapter on 'Political Power, Social Theory, and Essential Contestability', in David Miller and Larry Siedentop (eds) (1983) *The Nature of Political Theory* (Oxford: Clarendon Press, pp. 75–102) provides a lively analysis of some of the most important recent approaches to the subject of power.

P. Morris (1987) *Power: a Philosophical Analysis* (New York: St Martin's Press) is a comprehensive treatment of the subject.

Michel Foucault's afterword on 'The Subject of Power' in Hubert L. Dreyfus and Paul Rabinow (eds) (1983) *Michel Foucault: Beyond Structuralism and Hermeneutics* (Chicago, IL: University of Chicago Press) is a useful introduction to the thought of this influential but somewhat elusive thinker.

Richard B. Flathman's article 'Authority' in *Blackwell Encyclopedia of Political Thought*, ed. D. Miller et al. (Oxford: Blackwell, 1987) is a clear and concise introduction to this topic.

REFERENCES

Althusser, L. and Balibar, E. (1968) *Lire le Capital*. Paris: Maspero.

Arendt, H. (1972) 'On Violence', in *Crises of the Republic*. New York: Harcourt Brace Jovanovich.

Bachrach, Peter and Baratz, Morton S. (1962) 'The Two Faces of Power', *American Political Science Review*, **56**: 947–52.

Ball, T. (1993) 'Power', in Robert E. Goodin and Philip Pettit (eds), *A Companion to Contemporary Political Philosophy*. Oxford: Blackwell, pp. 548–57.

Beetham, D. and Lord, Christopher (1998) *Legitimacy and the European Union*. London: Longman.

Benhabib, S. (1994) 'Deliberative Rationality and Models of Democratic Legitimacy', *Constellations*, **1**: 26–52.

Connolly, William E. (1983) 'The Dilemma of Democracy', in John S. Nelson (ed.), *What Should Political Theory Be Now?* Albany, NY: State University of New York Press.

Connolly, William E. (1991) *Identity/Difference: Democratic Negotiations of Political Paradox*. Ithaca, NY: Cornell University Press.

Connolly, William E. (1993) *The Terms of Political Discourse*. Oxford: Blackwell.

Dahl, R. (1961) 'The Concept of Power', in Sydney Ulmer (ed.), *Introductory Readings in Political Behavior*. Chicago, IL: Rand McNally.

De Jouvenel, B. (1993) *On Power*. Indianapolis, IN: Liberty Fund.

Flathman, Richard B. (ed.) (1973) *Concepts in*

Social and Political Philosophy. New York: Macmillan.

Flathman Richard B. (1987) 'Authority', in *Blackwell Encyclopaedia of Political Thought*. Oxford: Blackwell, pp. 28–31.

Foucault, M. (1980) *Power/Knowledge*. ed. C. Gordon. Brighton: Harvester.

Friedman, Richard (1973) 'On the Concept of Authority in Political Philosophy', in Richard E. Flathman (ed.), *Concepts in Social and Political Philosophy*. New York: Macmillan, pp. 121–46.

Gallie, W. (1956) 'Essentially Contested Concepts', *Proceedings of the Aristotelian Society*, **56**: 167–98.

Giddens, A. (1984) *The Constitution of Society*. Berkeley and Los Angeles, CA: University of California Press.

Habermas, J. (1984) *The Theory of Communicative Action* (2 vols). Boston, MA: Beacon Press.

Hobbes, Thomas (1651/1909) *Leviathan*. Oxford: Clarendon Press.

Lukes, S. (1974) *Power: a Radical View*. London: Macmillan.

Lukes, S. (1990) 'Perspectives on Authority', in J. Raz (ed.), *Authority*. Oxford: Blackwell, pp. 203–17.

Mouffe, Chantal (2000) 'For an Agonistic Model of Democracy', in Noël O'Sullivan (ed.), *Political Theory in Transition*. London: Routledge, pp. 113–30.

Oakeshott, M. (1975) 'The Vocabulary of a Modern European State', *Political Studies*, **23**: 319–41.

Peters, R.S. (1967) 'Authority', in A. Quinton (ed.), *Political Philosophy*. Oxford: Oxford Univeristy Press, pp. 81–96.

Raz, J. (ed.) (1990) *Authority*. Oxford: Blackwell.

Raz. J. (1994) 'Multiculturalism: a Liberal Perspective', *Dissent*, Winter: 67–79.

See also chapters

6 Representative and Direct Democracy

Michael Saward

The concepts of 'representation', 'representative democracy' and 'direct democracy' are critical to our understanding of democracy – its past, present and possible futures. But the first thing to notice about each of these concepts is that there is no one 'proper' meaning for any of them. They are *concepts*, to be sure, but serious political and philosophical debates begin when we look at competing *conceptions* of each of them. The relationships between these concepts have proven to be no less contentious; for example, there have been many historical debates about whether direct or representative democracy is the 'true' democracy. My aim in this chapter will be to illustrate some of these key debates and disputes. Along the way, I hope to provide a snapshot of the meanings, histories and possibilities of each of them, both separately and as they intertwine in theory and in practice.

A RANGE OF CONCEPTIONS

Is representative democracy true democracy?

'Representation' is most prominent today in a political context that is so familiar to us that we often do not think about it: the fact that what we call 'democracies' today are *representative democracies*. Representative democracy comes in many varieties, but whatever precise form it takes in a given country, it primarily means that 'the people' do not rule directly; rather, they do so indirectly through elected representatives. This is normally taken to be an uncontroversial thing to say, but note how much there is to dispute or contest even in that simple sentence – for example, the idea that the people 'rule' in any tangible sense when in fact they take no formal part in governing. In the textbooks, representative democracy is almost always (a) separated out from other types of democracy, such as direct democracy, and (b) marked down as *the* modern form of democracy, the form which operates and is more or less entrenched and accepted in all countries that are regarded as 'democratic'. There is widespread acceptance of the idea that representative democracy *is* democracy, and that it is thoroughly 'democratic' (though, as we shall see, putting representation and democracy together so easily is unusual in historical terms).

Representative democracy is defined primarily by its embodying certain institutions and practices, above all the uses of more or less free and fair elections in which citizens of a country are entitled to vote to choose those who will govern them, with their consent, for a limited period: their representatives. Of course, events like those surrounding the contest in Florida in the US presidential election of 2000 between George W. Bush and Al Gore raise many questions about what might count as 'free and fair' elections, but I leave such issues to one side here. Representative democracy is also defined by the roles played within it by legislatures, executives, accountable bureaucracies and political parties, among other institutions. The merits and demerits of various models of representative democracy, such as the 'consensus' and 'majoritarian' models, are debated in detail by political scientists.

WHAT SHOULD REPRESENTATIVES DO?

Delegates or trustees?

There is also continuing debate in political science and political theory regarding the proper *role* of elected representatives. What, for example, should a good member of the UK House of Commons or the US House of Representatives *do*? On one view, members should do what their constituents want them to do. According to this perspective, elected representatives should not try to exercise independence of thought. They are *delegates*, sent to the legislature to argue and to vote for outcomes which embody the actual or expressed wishes of their constituents; in this respect, they are sometimes said to be *mandated* to act in a certain way. On the other hand, representatives can be seen as not being bound – or not tightly bound – by what their constituents happen to think or want on an issue. According to this perspective, the proper role of the representative is to exercise his or her own judgement, to act in the larger interests of his or her constituents, and not to follow slavishly the latters' whims and passing wishes. In this way, according to the classic language used in these debates, representatives can be regarded not as delegates but as *trustees*. Their role is to look after the interests of their constituents but in a context where those interests are not the same thing

as their momentary opinions or preferences. A good trustee-representative may legitimately vote in a legislature against the wishes of a majority of his or her constituents on the grounds that to do so is to serve the larger or longer-term interests of those same constituents.

Beyond these debates, 'representation' in the daily politics of 'representative democracies' is often enough about political parties and their leaderships and policies. Debates and arguments continue about the responsiveness of elected leaders, especially presidents and prime ministers and members of the government of the day. Are they being 'representative'? Or are they exposed to claims that they are distant from voters' concerns, failing to respond to voters' or constituents' or the parties' or the nations' interests? Are they acting in the interests of groups other than 'the people' in some sense – in the interests of the unions, the farmers, of big business, of another country? And if they are (or seem to be), are they therefore 'unrepresentative'? Scandals and corruption and personal character and ability matter in everyday political discourse too – what do we (whoever 'we' are in a given context) expect, demand, require of our representatives, in order that we may think them properly 'representative'?

Does it matter who representatives are?

What representatives should *do* is one thing; who the representatives *are* matters in many contexts too. In recent years there has been much discussion, for example, about whether it matters that minority religious or ethnic communities in representative democracies should be guaranteed representation in national legislatures (and perhaps other institutions too). Some countries use quotas, such as Belgium where new laws require parties to have a certain proportion of women candidates for elections; or guarantee a certain number of seats in the national legislature, such as for members of the indigenous Maori minority in New Zealand. Certainly, many representative systems build in an element of cultural 'proportionality' as a way to include or to incorporate a wide range of religious, ethnic, regional, gender and other interests in their representative decision-making institutions (perhaps the most extreme example has been in post-war Lebanon, where each of the various Christian and Muslim faith communities has been guaranteed certain key governmental and legislative positions broadly in proportion to its numbers in the general population).

Elections and beyond: making 'representative claims'

'Representation' in daily politics is a messy matter of rhetoric, communication, presentation (of self and others). It is not a question of whether a representative is really a 'delegate' or a 'trustee' – or not primarily, at any rate. The central point may be that he or she can play both of these roles at different (or even the same) time: depending on personal and party skills a representative may be able to shift between 'roles' and forge new ones as circumstances permit and make it desirable to do so. Another way of making this point is to say that the concept of representation finds its meanings and roles played out in the myriad spaces of political practice more than in the abstract simplifications of books of political theory, though the latter can in turn help to orient us through the political world's complexities.

So far, I have concentrated upon political representation as it is linked to elected offices, above all national legislatures. This has been the context for considering briefly issues such as 'how do you get to be a representative?', and 'what makes your actions representative when you are in office'? But the role of ideas of 'representation' in politics goes beyond institutional and elective boundaries. Many different kinds of group and leader, elected and non-elected, make claims to 'represent' certain ideals, interests, people. One could go so far as to say that the making of 'representative claims' is the primary reflex in poli-

tics, and should perhaps be the primary focus in our efforts to understand politics in particular contexts. In the so-called 'war on terrorism' which was launched in 2001, for example, George W. Bush and Tony Blair *claimed* to represent democracy, freedom, decency, international order, and so on. Opponents of the 'war' or its conduct *claim* (variously) to represent justice, victims of colonialism, the downtrodden and the neglected. Winning the 'propaganda war' is a vital part of winning the real war, in the contemporary era – indeed, the propaganda war is inseparable from the real war.

Another provocative example of a representative claim is that of anti-globalization protesters claiming to represent the real interests and concerns of economically vulnerable communities in many different countries. Nobody *elected* them to be such representatives in formal terms, but if by their actions or words they manage to establish a credible claim with enough people to be somehow representative of certain interests, then their efforts can become an important part of the dynamics of 'political representation' more generally.

DIRECT DEMOCRACY

But what of direct democracy? Political scientists tend to define this term in two quite different ways. First, it refers to face-to-face decision-making in an assembly (or forum, more broadly) of citizens, without the election or use of representatives. Thus, it has an important element of proximity (citizens or members of a community actually gathered together) and, of course of directness (the people make decisions for their community together, directly, without formal mediation). At various points in history, types of what is sometimes called '*assembly democracy*' have been practised, beginning most notably in the ancient Athenian city-state in Greece more than 2,500 years ago. This type of direct democracy – anything that approximates the Athenian experience reasonably closely –

is quite rare today. The most prominent contemporary example may be the *Landesgemeinde* or face-to-face assemblies by which the affairs of certain Swiss cantons are governed (and in some cases have been for centuries). In New England in the USA, a long tradition of face-to-face town meetings continues to today.

The second major sense in which political scientists refer to direct democracy is in the form of the *referendum*, sometimes called 'referendum democracy'. A referendum is a vote on an issue in which the outcome or decision is reached directly by the people's vote. The decision is not taken by representatives or anyone else other than by the body of voting citizens themselves. Referendums have, for example, become more common in the making of major constitutional decisions in recent years in the UK and in the European Union. The ratification of European Union treaties, such as those of Maastricht and Nice which advanced the deepening and extension of the EU, were ratified by referendum in many member states; Danish referendums in particular have become passionate, close-fought affairs on the European issue.

Referendum politics

But the undoubted historical and contemporary spiritual home of the referendum is Switzerland. Something like two-thirds of recorded referendums historically have been held in Switzerland; direct democracy in both of its basic forms is a deeply entrenched part of Swiss political culture. Swiss citizens can find themselves voting a number of time each year on a wide range of issues, deciding the outcomes directly. Although there has never been a *national* referendum on any issue in the United States, about half of the 50 states in the US federal system of government have some provision for the use of referendums. Referendums were widely advocated by the Progressive movement around the turn of the twentieth century in the USA, partly as a way of using more direct forms of democracy in order to tackle widespread political corruption. Considerable debate accompanies the pros and cons of referendum democracy in the USA. Opponents argue that referendum campaigns play on voter fear and ignorance, allow an avenue into politics for special interests with their own (hidden?) agendas, and often act as a stage for the playing out of existing political inequalities in the sense that big money interests can more readily sponsor referendum votes on issues that matter to them, and likewise to campaign for their preferred outcomes. Defenders counter that there is little evidence that people make irrational decisions in referendum votes, and further that referendums should not be tarred with the brush of separate problems within the political system – such as lack of limits on campaign spending by single people or interests.

Among other countries, Australia, New Zealand and Italy have in recent decades made regular use of the referendum to decide contentious and constitutional issues (such as voting rights for Aboriginal peoples in Australia, and fundamental changes to the electoral systems in New Zealand and Italy). Even a country with a constitutional tradition of parliamentary sovereignty, and therefore little constitutional space for the use of the referendum, such as Britain, has seen referendums used more often (and prominently) in recent years. This is because Britain has undergone considerable constitutional change. Accordingly, referendums have been conducted to decide upon the creation of national parliaments or assemblies for Scotland and Wales, and a new elected mayor for London. In the early 2000s a key referendum on Britain adopting the euro as its national currency is due to be held. So even in hostile contexts, referendums are becoming almost common, and a key too in legitimating major constitutional changes.

The referendum is not an instrument with a single dimension. Direct democracy in the form of the referendum comes in a range of types. If the referendum is desirable in principle, then some basic choices must be made about how it might be deployed. First of all, should it be:

- conducted nationally, regionally or locally, depending on the issue?
- controlled by government, or the product of citizen initiatives (petitions) or some form of independent commission?
- confined to use on constitutional questions (basic rules of the system, such as who has voting rights), or extended to cover some legislative questions (everyday laws) as well?
- binding on governments, so that they must enact the outcome, or merely consultative, so that they can ignore the outcome if they wish?
- one-vote-decides-the-issue, or serial or renewable so as to reflect changing citizen attitudes?

In addition, other specific questions about the context in which referendums are held will invariably arise, such as: how should the question be framed?; how can more or less equal publicity for all sides be achieved?; and what is the appropriate timing?

Direct politics beyond votes

The idea of 'directness' in democratic politics – or the potential for people to act politically in a direct manner, not having their actions or views mediated by officially sanctioned or other representatives – resonates beyond issues of Athenian-style assemblies or referendums. Consider, for example, an argument that 'democracy' is not simply about the formal or institutional features of a governmental system – elections, how governments are formed, how many houses of parliament there are, and so on – but also about self-organization and protest and action at all sorts of different levels and layers of national and international political life.

There is well-documented and widespread disillusion among the populations of the older representative democracies about the capacity of their elected political leaderships

effectively to respond to their needs and concerns. Certainly, voting rates are declining nationally and locally in many representative democracies. The more serious politicians and observers regularly worry about this lack of participation and apparent political apathy.

At the same time, it is evident that new and innovative forms of 'direct politics' have come to the fore in recent years, and have provided new types and avenues of political participation for many young people in particular. I think especially of anti-globalization and anti-capitalist demonstrations and actions from Seattle to Genoa and beyond; boycotts of products, countries and corporations; direct action movements such as Reclaim the Streets in the UK and in radical environmental groups more generally. New interactive and communications technologies have enhanced opportunities and avenues for direct political action by citizens; information about governments and private institutions is more widely available than ever before, and so the potential for focused and effective action by even quite small groups of individuals is heightened.

Without going into further detail here, I suggest that the phrase 'direct democracy' ought not perhaps to be *reserved* any longer for its traditional signifying role in political science – direct assemblies of citizens and the referendum, respectively. If 'democracy' includes importantly political participation, action and initiative by ordinary citizens, then self-initiated, creative and informal 'direct' action by citizens constitutes a form (or set of forms) of 'direct democracy' in action. Up to a point, concepts gain their meanings from the contexts in which they operate – or indeed contexts in which they are deployed as political weapons. And accordingly, their meanings shift and reshape constantly, and students and others need to be sensitive to these shifts and the larger forces that lie behind them.

WHICH IS THE MOST DEMOCRACTIC – REPRESENTATIVE OR DIRECT?

But finally, what of 'democracy' *in itself*, without these prefixes? Is it a concept which just takes the flavour of its prefixes – social, liberal, deliberative, radical, representative, direct, and so on – having no real character or meaning on its own? If it is not, then we are entitled to ask further difficult questions, notably: (a) how democratic is representation as a concept and a practice?; (b) how democratic is direct democracy?; and even (c) which of the two is more democratic?

Representation and democracy

Representation had a complex political life long before modern democracy was invented in the American and French Revolutions in the late 1700s. The word and the idea expressed a range of claims and facts about Roman emperors, and kings and feudal lords in the Middle Ages. For most of its historical life, the idea of political representation had little or nothing to do with elections, or other tangible means of choice. 'Democracy', until about two hundred years ago, meant something very different from 'representation'. Until American and French adaptations, 'democracy' *meant* face-to-face assembly decision-making as practised in ancient Athens (one reason why to be a 'democrat' was to be derided as a foolish idealist or worse). Many imagine, for example, that the American 'founding fathers' were self-consciously creating a new type of democracy at the birth of the USA. However, the US Constitution's chief architect, James Madison, was perfectly clear that he was *not* establishing a 'democracy'. What made the new republic different from ancient democracies – and therefore not at all a 'democracy' – was 'the total exclusion of the people, in their collective capacity, from any share' in the government. It was not a democracy, but a republic – for Madison, a government 'in which the scheme of representation takes place' (Wood, 1992: 97). In a few years, calling this 'republic' a 'representative democracy', or later simply 'democracy', became common (Wood, 1992: 98). By such a process, the opposite of democracy *became* democracy.

Today we tend to see 'representative democracy' as normal and natural in politics, certainly not a contradiction in terms. But the difficulties we have today in seeing how it *may* be internally contradictory is the product of major historical shifts in meaning and practice. Acknowledging this fact can be the first step towards questioning the democratic character of systems built around representation. Certainly, the main arguments in democratic theory over the past 50 or 60 years have been between advocates of purely representative democracy and their critics, the advocates of 'participatory democracy'. The latter, despite the great value they place on direct participation by ordinary people in the making of decisions which affect their lives (in the workplace, in local communities, within political parties, and so on), have acknowledged the necessity of representative government to the possibility of *any* kind of democracy in the governing of a large, modern nation-state. However, they have gone on to argue that this is not nearly enough, and that we must move beyond minimal models of democratic possibility. They argue that highly direct and participatory forms of democracy can operate and thrive within broader representative structures, lending dynamism and legitimacy to those larger structures in the process.

The implications of this 'participative' critique of representative democracy are compelling, above all the view that representation itself is not anti-democratic, but that it does offer a rather thin, minimal vision of democracy's potential on its own. If democracy is a good thing, then presumably we want more of it if we can; we may want to promote democracy beyond representative institutions, a theme I return to in a moment.

How democratic is direct democracy?

As mentioned above, the most common type of direct democratic institution in operation today is the referendum. Many countries have used it to ratify or to legitimize constitutional changes (or, in other words, changes to the basic rules of the game of a political system, such as how elections are conducted). For these purposes its use is on the increase, in the countries of the European Union as the EU's constitutional structure continues to evolve, for example. One can be an opponent of 'direct democracy' and still favour the use of the referendum for these purposes. Used in this way, the referendum is a device deployed sparingly for special changes to a polity. It does not disrupt or undermine the representative character of modern democratic politics, but rather supports it by enabling occasional, strategic doses of direct democratic legitimacy.

Opponents of direct democracy take aim at varied targets. First, they often decry ancient Athenian democracy as not being remotely 'democratic' at all, by modern standards. One can see what they mean. In Athens, women, foreigners and slaves made up the bulk of the population of the city-state, but they were not 'citizens', and hence had no right or expectation of political participation – at least formally, in the sense of attending the assembly. Athenian direct democracy was direct democracy for the few, the minority. Critics of Athens (and of models derived from it) also point to the ways in which demagogic leaders can exploit irrational or vengeful impulses of the 'mob', leading direct democracy away from restraint, appropriateness or 'balance' in its policies. In short, 'Athens' has been something of a whipping boy down the ages for opponents of democracy (since democracy meant Athenian-style direct democracy until 200 years ago) who fear mob rule, rule by the ignorant, or the overturning of all balance, order and sometimes gentility in politics and government.

Opponents of direct democracy today take aim at the use of the initiative and the referendum in particular to decide policies. (Using referendums to legitimize or to ratify major constitutional changes has a broader acceptance.) The Netherlands in 1999 came very close to adopting a new policy-making arrangement nationally whereby a range of policies passed by the parliament would have to be endorsed also in a popular referendum before moving on to become law. In a number of US states, a wide range of policies and proposals – on the environment, education, health, taxes and so on – have been and are subject to referendum votes. There are many other examples (again, Switzerland provides most of them). What the opponents worry about here is low voter turnout leading to inconsistent and unrepresentative decisions, skewed campaign funding granting too much influence to powerful special interests, and voters being ill-informed about the consequences, and even the nature, of the proposals upon which they vote. Proponents reply that if democracy means 'rule by the people' in some tangible sense, then surely one has to trust the people and abide by votes they produce directly, not simply cut ordinary people out of any formal political role beyond the occasional choice of representatives.

CONCLUSION: ONLY CONNECT?

Direct and representative forms of democracy have tended to be seen in black-and-white terms, historically and today. Increasingly, however, observers are coming to the view that representation and direct decision-making can make perfectly good bedfellows in the right circumstances; favouring one need not exclude extensive use of the other in political decision-making. One needs to adopt a pragmatic viewpoint. 'Representation' is a device or a mechanism; so too is the referendum, or the direct assembly even.

Making political or collective decisions means having a decision procedure which uses different devices or mechanisms (elections, debates, consultation, etc.). Why not combine different devices in order to achieve distinctive democratic outcomes? Recently there has been prominent advocacy of combining representative democracy as we know it with extensive use of the referendum to ratify policies passed by legislatures (see especially Budge, 1996).

So, why not citizens' initiatives to set the agenda, subsequent parliamentary and public deliberations, followed by parliamentary decision to be endorsed by popular referendum, as a vision of a *single* democratic procedure? Such a procedure should provide political elites in particular with incentives to explain key proposals and to defend them in public. Including a referendum requirement for major new laws would create an incentive for policy advocates to present their proposals in clear accessible language. Picked up from different streams in democratic theory debates, these devices taken together enact specific versions of democratic principles of equality, public interest, inclusion and participation.

In sum, we do not have to choose between representative and direct forms of democracy. Instead, we can think creatively about deploying both together as part of efforts to meet the political challenges faced by democracy today.

Summary

- This chapter has discussed two types of 'democracy': 'representative' and 'direct' democracy.
- In a 'representative' democracy, the people do not rule directly, but indirectly through elected representatives. There has been considerable debate as to whether representatives should be seen as delegates, mandated by the people to act as instructed by them, or as trustees, acting more independently of their constituents.
- 'Direct' democracy may refer to face-to-face decision-making in an assembly of citizens, without the election of representatives. It may also refer to a political system that makes frequent use of referendums in decision-making ('referendum democracy').
- It has been suggested in this chapter that the term 'direct democracy' should be used more broadly to include the self-initiated, creative and informal 'direct' actions by citizens.
- A convincing argument can be made that representation itself is not anti-democratic, but that it does offer a rather thin, minimal vision of democracy's potential, and that it should be complemented by elements of 'direct democracy'. The common stark distinction between representation on the one hand and direct democracy on the other is not tenable.

TUTORIAL QUESTIONS

1. **Can ordinary people be trusted with the making of political decisions?**

2. **Should we have more direct democracy, on the grounds that democracy is a good thing and direct forms are more democratic than other forms?**

3. **Can anyone really represent your interests? Can you rightly claim to represent others' interests, and if so in what circumstances?**

FURTHER READING

Advocacy of combining referendums with representative institutions can be found in Ian Budge (1996) *The New Challenge of Direct Democracy* (Cambridge: Polity Press).

Maija Setala (1999) *Referendums and Democratic Government* (Basingstoke and London: Macmillan) provides an up-to-date account of the theory and practice of direct democracy.

Arend Lijphart's account of the varieties of representative democracy has most recently been set out in A. Lijphart (1999) *Patterns of Democracy* (New Haven, CT: Yale University Press).

Bernard Manin (1997) *The Principles of Representative Government* (Cambridge: Cambridge University Press) provides a compelling history (and criticism) of representative government.

The modern classic on political representation remains Hannah Fenichel Pitkin (1972) *The Concept of Representation* (Berkeley, CA: University of California Press).

REFERENCES

Budge, Ian (1996) *The New Challenge of Direct Democracy*. Cambridge: Polity Press.

Wood, Gordon S. (1992) 'Democracy and the American Revolution', in John Dunn (ed.), *Democracy. The Unfinished Journey, 508 BC to AD 1993*. Oxford: Oxford University Press, pp. 91–105.

See also chapters

2 **Constitutionalism**	13 **Parliaments**
7 **Majoritarianism – Consociationalism**	14 **Parties and Party Systems**
8 **Pluralism – Difference**	15 **Elections and Electoral Systems**
9 **Civil Society – National and Global**	18 **Political Participation**

7 Majoritarianism – Consociationalism

Thomas O. Hueglin

HISTORICAL INTRODUCTION

The discovery of consociational democracy in small countries

At the end of the Second World War, the United States and the United Kingdom emerged as the two dominant models of democracy. It became the prevalent view that stable democracy was best served by a political culture of individual liberalism, and by the political institutions of parliamentary majority rule based on party competition. Almost universally, it seemed, the main focus of comparative political science was on mass democracy in large countries.

Then something unexpected happened at the 1967 World Congress of the International Political Science Association in Brussels. Two scholars, Gerhard Lehmbruch (1974) and Arend Lijphart (1974), presented papers that significantly changed the course of political science history. Both papers drew attention to some of the smaller democratic countries such as Switzerland, the Netherlands and Belgium, and they both questioned the assumption that majority rule was the only legitimate and successful form of democracy.

The political culture in these countries was characterized less by individual liberalism and based more on cultural segmentation among a small number of different linguistic and/or religious groups. Majority rule of one group over another was not acceptable. Consequently, political stability depended on negotiated compromise among these groups and their political parties. Instead of party competition and majority rule, governance in these countries typically relied on grand coalitions of all major parties, and on strict proportionality in the distribution of executive and administrative powers. This form of governance was called consociational democracy.

Two models of democratic governance

Ever since these papers were first presented, the interest in non-majoritarian forms of democracy has increased. Moreover, comparative political science gradually discovered that majoritarianism in its pure form is limited to political and institutional practice in a few countries only, and that most democracies are in fact governed by a mix of majoritarianism and consociationalism. Arend Lijphart, who has remained the leading political scientist investigating both forms from a comparative perspective, now distinguishes two basic models of democratic governance, the majoritarian *Westminster Model of Democracy*, and the consociational or *Consensus Model of Democracy*.

Comparative significance in a complex world

This distinction is important for the comparative study of politics in several ways. First, it continues to help us understand how democratic politics works in those countries where majority rule is not acceptable due to the segmented nature of their societies. Secondly, it draws attention to consociational practices in other countries normally associated with majority rule. And thirdly, it allows us to think about the prospects of democratic governance in a globalizing world characterized by integration as well as segmentation. Indeed, as the European Union demonstrates already, the consensus model may become the dominant form of governance in such a world.

TYPOLOGICAL DISTINCTIONS

Assumptions

Majoritarianism and consociationalism are not only typologically distinct institutional forms of government. As all *-isms*, they are embedded in a number of distinct ideological assumptions about the nature of society and the political process.

Majoritarianism evolved from the Glorious Revolution of 1688 in England when absolute power was wrestled from the king and gradually bestowed upon parliament. Its main ideological foundation was individual liberalism as celebrated in the works of Thomas Hobbes and John Locke. According to these social philosophers, all men (and women only much later) are equally free and autonomous in the pursuit of their selfish interests. Because of this equality and the resulting homogeneity of society, majority rule came to be seen as the most practical way of making decisions. The minority would accept such decisions because its interests were not fundamentally different from those of the majority. Transferring the absolute powers of the king to a parliamentary majority did not

violate the principle of liberalism because the minority in opposition would have a fair chance of winning the next election.

The majoritarian British Westminster model, named after the palace where the British parliament met, came to be the principal yardstick of legitimate parliamentary government worldwide.

Consociationalism is embedded in a different set of assumptions. It also represents an older tradition of political thought and practice. During the Middle Ages, continental European society had been organized into a plurality of organic groups and territorial communities, and each of these was governed by distinct sets of overlapping rights and privileges. If conflict was to be avoided, differences had to be settled by mutual agreement. As in England, the relative stability of this system broke down during the religious wars in the aftermath of the Reformation. At the beginning of the seventeenth century, the first modern theorist of consociationalism and federalism, Johannes Althusius, designed a political system in which the self-governing autonomy of subcultural groups and communities would be preserved. Universal governance would be based on an elaborate scheme of multilevel power-sharing. Althusius's theory was sustained by his underlying faith in the cooperative – or as he called it for the first time, consociational – rather than selfish nature of human beings. But he was also convinced that this consociational predisposition of society required adequate organization in a plurality of smaller and larger communities.

The Peace Treaties of Westphalia in 1648 eventually ended both the old plural order and Althusius's visions of a consociational world. A territorial state system was brought on its way with sovereign powers over all internal groups and communities. In the same treaty, however, the new territorial rulers were admonished to settle religious differences among themselves by 'amicable agreement' rather than majority rule. This is the spirit of consociationalism that lived on in some of the smaller territories such as Switzerland, the Netherlands and Belgium.

Preconditions

Assumptions about human nature are not enough to explain why some societies chose consociationalism over majoritarianism. Yet they point to important differences in political culture. In England, individual liberalism was able to forge a homogeneous political culture of nationalism early on, and English hegemony could neglect the interests of national minorities. This is how majoritarianism was established. Consociationalism, on the other hand, typically developed when no cultural group was able to dominate the others and some form of compromise became inevitable. External threat and country size played a role as well. In Switzerland, consociationalism evolved as a necessary response to foreign domination, and power-sharing was facilitated by the physical proximity of ruling elites. By comparison, the geographic expanse of the United States of America required the development of strong executive governance unencumbered by power-sharing in grand coalitions. Today, in the age of instant electronic communication, consociationalism no longer appears tied to the proximity of space in principle.

Institutional majoritarianism in a nutshell

The logical starting point is a majoritarian electoral system. Each electoral district is represented in parliament by the one candidate who has won the most votes. This favours large parties with broad popular appeal and typically results in a two-party system although a few third parties may be successful as well if they enjoy regionally concentrated support.

Government is then formed by the majority party. If no party wins an absolute majority of seats, it will have to form a minority government, or join forces with one or several of the smaller parties in order to bring about a bare-majority coalition.

There is a fusion of executive and legislative powers because the prime minister and her or his cabinet are elected members of parliament. The political process is characterized by the competitive interplay between government and opposition. As long as there is majority support, usually enforced by strict rules of party discipline, the government is nearly unassailable and can impose its will upon the minority. If the government loses a parliamentary vote, on the other hand, it has to step down and call for an election.

Parliamentary majoritarianism is usually associated with a unitary form of government. In a number of British settler colonies, however, notably Canada, Australia and India, a hybrid form of parliamentary federalism has been established. In these cases, the paramountcy of majority rule in the parliamentary chamber limits the political legitimacy of regional representation in second chambers. The same holds true for second legislative chambers in unitary states. Majoritarianism therefore generally makes for a case of weak bicameralism.

Institutional consociationalism in a nutshell

The logical starting point here is a proportional electoral system whereby each party wins parliamentary seats roughly proportional to the percentage of the national vote it has won. This favours multi-party systems representing the more segmented interests in plural societies.

Political accommodation requires the formation of grand coalition governments, including all major parties. Governing in consociational democracies consequently relies on executive power-sharing among these parties. The positions in cabinet and ministerial bureaucracy are distributed according to principles of strict proportionality. The political process is characterized by negotiated consensus and compromise.

In order to make such negotiations possible, executive and party elites need room to manoeuvre. Typically, therefore, consociational governance is patterned by a legislative–executive balance of power. The executive does not dominate the parliamentary process but cooperates with it. The government also does not have to step down if it loses a decision in parliament. Since it is based on a broad coalition of all major parties, a new election would only reproduce the same situation.

An essential characteristic of consociationalism is segmental autonomy. Subcultural groups will have a large degree of autonomy to govern their own affairs. If these groups are territorially concentrated, federalism is the most obvious technical solution. Dividing powers between two levels of government provides regionally based cultural groups with autonomy over matters of language and education, for instance, while allocating powers over trade and commerce at the federal level. Another option is decentralization which does not require a formal division of powers. A satisfactory degree of segmental autonomy can be achieved by formulating general national standards (policy-making) but leaving programme design and administration to subcultural groups (policy implementation).

A typical institutional feature of consociationalism in federal systems is strong bicameralism. In order to safeguard the regional and/or subcultural interests they represent, second chambers are vested with powers equal to those of the parliamentary chamber.

Related concepts and practices

Consociationalism is not the only concept and institutional practice that differs from majoritarianism. Related concepts that seek to temper the blunt force of majority rule include federalism, corporatism and communitarianism.

Federalism has already been mentioned as an institutional component safeguarding segmental autonomy in some consociational democracies. It is also an important non-majoritarian form of government in its own right, recognizing territorial group rights alongside of individual citizenship rights (see Chapter 11 by Michael Keating).

Corporatism is an informal practice of negotiating specific tripartite agreements between business associations, labour unions and the state as mediator. As in consociational regimes, this is likely when neither side can easily overrule the interests of the other. To be successful, corporatism has to rely on highly organized business and labour organizations. Their privileged recognition by the state narrows the wide range of interest group pluralism typical for majoritarian regimes. Corporatism generally requires the presence of strong social democratic parties that can back up the interests of unions in parliament and/or government. The main focus of corporatist intermediation is on incomes policy and price stability. Its practice is limited to time and circumstance. Insofar as it is carried by a genuine political culture of social partnership, however, it is an important modification of the adversarial style of policy-making in majoritarian democracies.

Communitarianism challenges individualist assumptions about human nature by arguing that people's lives are embedded in social, cultural and historical communities that cannot be chosen freely. Individual rights therefore do not make much sense unless they can be exercised within the context of such communities. Again, this obviously means that such communities need protection from majority rule. Both consociationalism and federalism are institutional means providing such protection. However, communitarianism challenges majoritarianism more radically from an anthropological perspective of human behaviour according to which most people seek to live in stable communities held together by some special sense of mutual belonging.

CRITICAL EVALUATION

Democratic governance is expected to be representative of all citizens. All elected officials must be held accountable for their decisions and actions, and the process of governing must result in an efficient output of policies and regulations. These are the main criteria by which majoritarianism and consociationalism can be evaluated as to their general democratic qualities.

Representation

Majoritarianism typically produces mass parties driven by vote maximizing strategies. Such parties represent general interests. Especially since the end of the Cold War and the decline of democratic socialism in its wake, party competition has been characterized by appeals to bland populism rather than clear choices. Minority interests and issues are rarely at the forefront of political debate. When bare-majority governments require the inclusion of a small third party, however, such parties, and the interests they represent, can gain disproportionate influence upon the government agenda.

In Germany in 2002, for instance, the government coalition of Social Democrats and Greens resulted in a greater emphasis on environmental issues than would have been the case if the Social Democrats had been able to govern with an outright majority. However, the political success of the Greens is owed to the fact that Germany has a mixed system of representation. While the governing style is majoritarian, the electoral system is proportional. In systems of pure majoritarianism, such as the United Kingdom, the inclusion of third party interests in government is unlikely.

The emphasis on proportionality and power-sharing makes consociationalism appear more inclusive as a system of representation. A larger number of parties and the proportionality of seat distribution constitute a more accurate representation of voters' preferences. More importantly, power-sharing in grand coalition cabinets requires a more balanced course of policy-making, taking into consideration the interests of all major societal segments. A major problem of consociationalism, however, is

exactly this emphasis on political accommodation among the major segments of society. Some minority interests may be left out permanently.

In Switzerland, for instance, the same grand coalition of four parties has governed for more than half a century. More than half a dozen of the other parties therefore have been relegated to a permanent and ineffective opposition status. The representative system is split between governmental and non-governmental parties. Since the governmental parties routinely receive about two-thirds of the national vote, one-third goes without any chance of contributing towards the formation of a government.

Accountability

The competitive dynamic of government and opposition among two major parties as in the British Westminster model allows for the clear allocation of responsibility. Governing majority cabinets cannot conceal responsibility for their actions or inactions by pointing the finger to the compromise requirements typical for grand coalitions or, in federal systems, by blaming the other level of government. Accountability is further enhanced by the fact that the prime minister and cabinet are themselves members of parliament and are therefore directly exposed to the questions and inquiries levelled against them by a vigilant opposition. However, the role of parliament as a vigilant provider of accountability is diminished when the policy platforms of the major parties do not significantly differ from one another. Parliamentary debates then tend to degenerate into exercises of political grandstanding, and citizens lose interest in electoral participation.

Grand coalition governments typically operate at arm's length from parliamentary scrutiny, and they can continue governing in unperturbed fashion even if they lose important decisions in parliament. In Switzerland again, the members of the federal government are individually elected for fixed four-year terms by parliament, and parliament cannot upstage them during that period of time by a vote of no confidence. However, the reliance of consociationalism upon negotiated compromise at the same time requires a more balanced relationship between executive and legislature similar to a system of checks and balances. As in the American system, for instance, the governing executive needs to negotiate the passage of bills with party leaders and committee chairs.

Because negotiations work best behind closed doors, this reliance upon negotiated compromise among executive and party elites, and with the segmental interests they represent, often leads to secrecy. Similar to the Council meetings of the European Union, consociational policy-making takes on the character of diplomatic relations. Parliaments are perhaps less dominated by the executive as is the case in majoritarian systems, but their role is more one of providing complicity than accountability. Again, one of the side-effects of this, and of the lack a credible alternative, is political complacency and a low voter turnout.

Efficiency

The general assumption is that majoritarianism is a more efficient mode of policy-making than consociationalism. Negotiating consensus among a plurality of political actors is time-consuming. Moreover, the suspicion prevails that the perpetual need for compromise will lead to the mediocrity of watered-down or second-best solutions. Some do even speak of a decision trap resulting in policy blockages. The comparative record somewhat belies these views and concerns. Indeed, there is considerable evidence that consociationalism scores higher than majoritarianism on both traditional issues of class-based politics and new issue politics, and that it can also handle constitutional conflict more flexibly.

Industrial relations have been far more stable and efficient in Germany than in Britain, for example. Germany is not a classical consociational democracy, of course, but the federal system, with its possibility of different party majorities in the two chambers of the federal legislature, requires negotiated compromise on most policy issues. Politically backed by the two major parties, Conservatives and Social Democrats, business and labour organizations have been generally cooperative in finding negotiated settlements on incomes policy. By comparison, the adversarial style of British politics has been an impediment to efficient policy-making. Alternating majority governments have resulted in discontinuous policy approaches, and productivity has been slowed down by a high rate of industrial conflict.

In the field of issue politics, environmentalism commands centre stage. And again it seems that the more consensus-oriented political systems can cope with the demands of environmental policy-making very well. In the European Union, for instance, Germany and the Netherlands are among the leaders pushing for efficient regulation. France and Britain, on the other hand, together with the poorer Mediterranean countries, are among the laggards. The assumption that consensus politics at best leads to lowest common denominator agreements cannot be sustained. Environmental protection standards in the European Union are now higher than in most member states.

Finally, there is the question of how societies cope with fundamental political conflict requiring constitutional adjustment and change. Two countries that have experienced such conflict are Belgium and Canada. Because of bicultural tensions, both have been at the brink of a break-up in recent years. In Belgium, the conflict between Flemings and Walloons has found a – however precarious – solution in the federal constitution of 1993. In line with Belgium's consociational tradition, this constitution emphasizes proportionality, power-sharing and arbitration. In Canada, the adversarial style of competing majoritarianism at the federal and provincial level of government has thus far precluded a similar resolution of the historical conflict between English and French Canadians.

More generally, consociationalism and majoritarianism both have their strengths and weaknesses. The strength of majoritarianism lies in its capacity of unencumbered policy formation. Decisions can be made quickly and without ambiguity. Policy implementation, on the other hand, can be fraught with inefficiency when majority decisions fail to gain universal acceptance. Exactly the opposite is the case with consociationalism. Based on negotiated agreements and compromise, policy formulation is often slow and cumbersome, but once an agreement has been reached, policy implementation may be more efficient because it is received with broad acceptance in politics and society.

Democratic qualities

According to Arend Lijphart (1999), consensus democracies generally score high on a kinder and gentler social policy agenda because a more consultative and participatory style of policy-making fosters inclusiveness and social consciousness, a more feminine approach than the masculine type of power politics prevalent in majority democracies.

Maybe the comparative record is somewhat misleading, here. In Switzerland, often cited as the model case of consociational democracy, women were given the right to vote in federal elections only in 1971, and it took another decade before legal, social and economic equality was formally introduced. For a long time, at least, political accommodation in Switzerland has been very much in the masculine hands of closed fraternities of interest and influence. While this is still so at the commanding heights of private business and public administration, the share of women in politics, both at the legislative and executive level, has increased dramatically in recent years.

Overall, Lijphart's data clearly show that majoritarian democracies spend less on welfare and foreign aid, are less environmentally

responsible, and incarcerate more people. One explanation is that majoritarianism, with its emphasis on competitive power politics and individual liberalism, leaves society less organized in the pursuit of collective public interests and therefore more vulnerable to the dictates of the market and powerful business interests. Consociationalism, on the other hand, with its reliance upon political accommodation among different segments of society, can provide for a more balanced mix of policy priorities.

THE GROWING RELEVANCE OF CONSOCIATIONALISM IN A GLOBALIZING WORLD

In the end, why should we be interested in the deviant political practice of a number of mostly small countries? It ought to be clear by now that consociationalism does not automatically make for a better form of democratic governance. Just as majoritarian party governance is vulnerable to the pressures of dominant interests with superior means of organization and influence, so can consociationalism degenerate into a closed shop of elite accommodation among the usual suspects.

Comparative relevance

Obviously, consociational systems and practices should not be neglected as part of the real world of politics. Apart from a cynical perspective of power politics, there is no systematic reason why knowledge about France or the United Kingdom is more important than knowledge about Switzerland or Belgium. Moreover, the comparative record shows quite clearly that elements of consensus democracy are present in many, if not most, political systems, and their importance is often neglected. This is so especially in federal systems where the formal existence of two levels of government requires cooperation and compromise. But there, as elsewhere, consociational practice depends on a societal predisposition to understand politics as a form of amicable agreement among different interests and preferences rather than as a competitive struggle between them. Thus consensus democracy is a central feature in federal Germany as well as in the unitary Scandinavian welfare democracies, whereas it is overshadowed by strong British parliamentary traditions in federal systems such as Canada and Australia.

American exceptionalism

A peculiar case is that of the United States of America. In the Congress, pragmatic bipartisan compromise prevails but it is commonly driven by a competitive spirit of 'you win some and you lose some' rather than by negotiated agreements over different visions of politics and society. The relationship between federal government and the states, on the other hand, is clearly dominated by Congressional supremacy and differences of opinion usually end up in the courts. The checks and balances between president and the Congress, on the other hand, typically require some level of negotiated accommodation because the president cannot automatically count on support even from his own party. Rooted in its strong tradition of individual liberalism, American society is a litigation society that is ultimately opposed to the idea of consociationalism.

Kinder and gentler

The overall comparative record cannot be ignored. In terms of social inequality, the United States of America and the United Kingdom are at the bottom of the scale among industrialized democracies. Consensus democracies generally have a better record which is largely owed to the Scandinavian welfare democracies. While countries like Sweden or Denmark are not typical cases of consociationalism, their political cultures are cooperative and problem-oriented rather than competitive and adversarial. This consociational predisposition is evidenced by the fact that minority governments are tolerated almost as a matter of fact, and that multipartisan parliamentary committees play a central role in policy formulation.

Again, however, the virtues of institutionalized consociationalism should not be overestimated. Switzerland, once again, a classical case of consociational federalism with a permanent coalition government including a social democratic party, has the worst record of net income disparity in Western Europe. Canada, by comparison, and despite its far more adversarial system of federalism, finds itself roughly in the same league with the consociational Netherlands. The lesson to be drawn is that institutional differences ultimately make a significant difference only if they are put to the right kind of use by societal forces so predisposed.

Complex societies

Majoritarianism evolved with the nationalist assumption that all individuals are essentially alike within territorial nation-state boundaries. This assumption was always a tenuous one because it neglected the presence of cultural, regional or social minorities and their interests. In an age of increased transnational mobility and migration, it may become even more problematic. Despite or, rather, precisely because of the forces of transnational integration and globalization, national societies are becoming less homogeneous, not more. Multiculturalism and identity politics are on the rise everywhere, joining the forces of older regional and cultural movements that have existed all along.

Ethnicity

Particularly salient issues are religion and ethnicity which appear to have replaced the Cold War as the world's most serious source of violent conflict. At least some central elements of the consociational model are widely seen as prerequisites for stable solutions. There is widespread agreement that group autonomy and power-sharing are inevitable institutional means to overcome such conflicts. There is not a single voice, for instance, that would not insist that a peaceful and stable solution for Afghanistan must become based on shared governance by all ethnic and religious factions in that country, including the Taliban.

Some critics of consocationalism, however, argue that group autonomy can deepen uncompromising attitudes which in turn will make power-sharing arrangements unstable and short-lived. Yet the exact reverse argument can be made as well. Once in place, institutions also shape the attitudes of those participating in them. Take Northern Ireland, for example: the fact that Sinn Fein leader Gerry Adams finally and successfully urged the IRA to begin the process of disarmament may well be owed to his previous experience with power-sharing arrangements under the Good Friday Agreement.

Globalization and regional integration

Despite transnational market integration, nation-states still provide the prime focus of civic identity. Majoritarianism on a world scale is as unthinkable as it is undesirable. International regulatory institutions such as the World Bank or the World Trade Organization lack accountability and legitimacy. As the civic protests since Seattle have shown, there is a need of enhanced inclusiveness. Again, a world federal system of states would not be able to accommodate sufficiently the concerns and interests of civic

groups and social movements that are now transnational in nature and organization as well. Consociationalism, with its emphasis on proportional access to the process of governing by all major segments of society, can at least infuse the debate about global democracy with some new ideas.

The subsidiarity principle as enshrined in the Maastricht Treaty of the European Union can be interpreted as such an idea. Its stipulation that decisions are to be taken at the lowest possible level of governance requires ongoing political negotiations about who *should* do what in the name of accountability and efficiency. It therefore provides decision-making in the Union with a discursive quality akin to consociational practice. This is different from the constitutional separation of powers in conventional federal systems which leaves room only for judicial interpretation.

Likewise, the consultative voice given to regions and interest groups in the Committee of the Regions and the Economic and Social Committee at least recognizes the need for inclusion and dialogue. Strengthening the powers of the European Parliament would mean pushing Europe in a more majoritarian direction. Giving formal powers of co-decision to these committees would strengthen consociationalism. These are choices that sooner or later will become inevitable both for the European Union and the global community.

Summary

- Majoritarianism and consociationalism are two alternative traditions in political thought and practice. While consociationalism as a dominant form of governance prevails in some of the smaller European countries, elements of consociational practice can be found in most political systems.
- Majoritarianism is grounded in a social philosophy of individual liberalism. Its main institutional elements are:

- a majoritarian electoral system
- a two-party system
- bare-majority governments
- fusion of executive and legislative powers
- competition between government and opposition
- weak bicameralism.

- Consociationalism is grounded in a social philosophy of group identity and autonomy. Its main institutional elements are in turn:
  - a proportional electoral system
  - a multi-party system
  - grand coalition governments
  - executive–legislative power balance and proportionality
  - negotiated compromise among all major participants
  - strong bicameralism.
- Related concepts and practices are federalism, corporatism and communitarianism.
- Consociationalism can lead to a more inclusive mode of representation but may leave out some minorities permanently. Secretive elite bargaining can also lower the level of public accountability.
- The main strength of majoritarianism is efficient policy formulation. The advantage of consociationalism in turn is policy implementation based in previous agreement across all segments of society.
- Consociational democracies overall show a more generous social policy record.
- The growing relevance of consociationalism lies in the fact that complex multicultural societies and international communities defy the logic of majority rule and require new forms of governance based on agreement.

TUTORIAL QUESTIONS

1. **Review the main institutional differences between consociationalism and majoritarianism.**

2. **Is consociationalism more democratic than majoritarianism?**

3. **Discuss globalization from a majoritarian and from a consociational perspective.**

FURTHER READING

The theoretical foundations of consociationalism in the history of political thought have been reconstructed in Thomas O. Hueglin (1999)

Early Modern Concepts for a Late Modern World: Althusius on Community and Federalism (Waterloo: Wilfrid Laurier University Press).

The original debate on consociational democracy can be found in Kenneth D. McRae (ed.) (1974) *Consociational Democracy: Political Accommodation in Segmented Societies* (Toronto: McClelland and Stewart).

On consensus and majority democracies from a comparative perspective the state of the art is now Arend Lijphart (1999) *Patterns of Democracy: Government Forms and Performance in Thirty-Six Countries* (New Haven, CT: Yale University Press).

An excellent introductory textbook of comparative European politics sensitive to the consociational dimension in politics is Jürg Steiner (1998) *European Democracies* (New York: Longman).

REFERENCES

Lehmbruch, Gerhard (1974) 'A Non-Competitive Pattern of Conflict Management in Liberal Democracies: the Case of Switzerland, Austria and Lebanon', in Kenneth D. McRae (ed.), *Consociational Democracy: Political Accommodation in Segmented Societies*. Toronto: McClelland & Stewart, pp. 90–7.

Lijphart, Arend (1974) 'Consociational Democracy', in Kenneth D. McRae (ed.), *Consociational Democracy: Political Accommodation in Segmented Societies*. Toronto: McClelland & Stewart, pp. 70–89.

Lijphart, Arend (1999) *Patterns of Democracy: Government Forms and Performance in Thirty-Six Countries*. New Haven, CT: Yale University Press, pp. 275–300.

See also chapters

8 Pluralism – Difference

Judith Squires

Pluralism: 'A belief in diversity or choice, or the theory that political power is or should be widely and evenly distributed.'

(Heywood, 1998: 336)

Pluralism is currently a key concept in the social sciences. Originally a description of a particular, ideologically conservative, school of thought in American political science, it has now become an increasingly important concept for a wide variety of social and political theory. The fact of pluralism appears to epitomize the very nature of the contemporary life, while the normative desirability of pluralism exudes from an ever-growing range of theoretical literatures.

METHODOLOGICAL, SOCIOCULTURAL AND POLITICAL PLURALISM

Within the social sciences the term 'pluralism' is applied in diverse ways: methodological, sociocultural and political (McLennan, 1995). Methodological pluralism entails various perspectives, ranging from the endorsement of a multiplicity of research methods, and a multiplicity of interpretative paradigms, through to the belief in the existence of many truths and – in more postmodern articulations – many 'worlds' (McLennan, 1995: 57–76). Sociocultural pluralism similarly entails a range of perspectives, including the claims that there are many types of important social relations, many subcultures, multiple identities and multiple selves. Political pluralism, which will be the focus here, entails a commitment to diversity, with this ranging from the recognition of sociocultural difference, to the determination to facilitate these differences, to the demand that difference be represented in democratic structures (McLennan, 1995: 77–97). It is these various forms of political pluralism that are of particular interest in relation to democratic theory.

CLASSICAL PLURALISM

Until the 1970s 'pluralism' was most often used as a description of a school of empirical democratic theory, which emerged in the United States in the 1950s. One of the key exponents of this school of American pluralist theory was Robert Dahl (1956, 1971). Dahl's study of who had power over what in New Haven politics led him to the conclusion that America was a 'pluralist democracy'. What defined it as pluralist was the fact that religion, race, ethnic group, class and regional identities were all deemed to be significant divisions in society, generating many competing interests (Dahl, 1971: 106–7). In making this claim classical pluralists rejected a Marxist account of the state, and invoked Max Weber's view that there are many determinants of the distribution of power other than class. They suggested that power was distributed competitively, with all interest groups able to make some impact on the process of political decision-making. Dahl called this polyarchy, or rule by 'minorities government' (Dahl, 1956: 133). This expression of factional interests, while clearly falling short of the democratic ideal of popular self-government, was deemed to be a positive articulation of democratic practice in that it maintains equilibrium in complex modern societies. Accordingly, pluralists of this classical school argued that democracy should be defined as the rule by multiple minority oppositions.

CRITICS OF CLASSICAL PLURALISM

This classical pluralist position has been widely criticized as offering a naïve celebration of American society, failing to pay attention to the systematic imbalances in the distribution of power in society. By assuming the existence of diverse interests and the propensity of one group to offset the power of another, with the state acting as a neutral arbitrator, classical pluralist theory implied that pluralism was an accurate empirical account of existing democracies (Held, 1989: 57–64). This was increasingly felt to be an inadequate position by those who were concerned about the unequal distribution of power among groups. Classical pluralism was, as McLennan notes, 'taken by many radicals as representing little more than an apology for corporate capitalism, a western Cold War ideology parading as mature social science' (McLennan, 1995: 1). As a result, classical pluralism has largely been dropped, though a series of more refined pluralist perspectives did develop from this tradition.

Neo-pluralists, such as Charles Lindblom, for instance accepted that the state was systematically constrained by the needs of private enterprise (Lindblom, 1977: 122–3). However, contemporary social and political theory is still marked by a manifest concern with the 'fact of pluralism' (Rawls, 1993).

LIBERAL PLURALISM

Where classical pluralism offered a putatively descriptive account of the distribution of political power in democratic polities, contemporary liberal theory offers a more overtly normative endorsement of the desirability of the multiplicity of ethical values. Accordingly, while the former focused attention on the claim that interest group competition secures democracy, the latter emphasizes the extent to which moral pluralism safeguards individual liberty. As Bellamy suggests: 'Recent liberal philosophers share the belief that the prime virtue of pluralism lies in its being neutral between rival conceptions of the good' (Bellamy, 1999a: 42). These philosophers share a commitment to a pluralist framework that provides scope for people to live according to these diverse conceptions of the good. In *Political Liberalism* for instance, Rawls (1993) articulates a conception of liberalism that is 'political not metaphysical' in that it is a response to the 'fact of pluralism' in modern societies. Here people disagree over fundamental values, they disagree over how to rank values, and even about how to reason and debate about values, and such disagreements are intractable.

In response to this 'fact of pluralism' liberal theory has developed various strategies for managing pluralism. Richard Bellamy offers a useful schema of the central liberal pluralist strategies, which he labels trading, trimming and segregation. Trading, as advocated by Hayek, focuses on the possibilities for mutually advantageous bargains. This libertarian strategy treats values as personal opinions and suggests that they be treated as synonymous with consumer preferences. It assumes that ideals and identities can be treated in the same way as interests (Bellamy, 1999b: 17–41). Trimming, as advocated by Rawls, simply attempts to avoid conflict. Rawls takes the incommensurability of value differences much more seriously than traders: so seriously indeed that value differences are thought to make politics impossible and so need to be confined to a private sphere rather than aired in public. This limits political debate to the clash of interests only (Bellamy, 1999b: 42–66). Segregation, as advocated by Walzer, assumes interests and ideals to be determined by cultural identity, homogeneous within identity groups and incommensurable across them. This communitarian liberal strategy recommends that different groups avoid one another (Bellamy, 1999b: 67–89).

CRITICS OF LIBERAL PLURALISM

Contemporary liberal pluralists, like the earlier classical pluralists of empirical democratic theory, are frequently criticized for being politically and sociologically naïve. In starting from the premise of the autonomous individual agent, both traders and trimmers 'ignore the forces shaping our choices and the limits of our ability rationally to control or harmonize them' (Bellamy, 1999b: 46). Pluralism, in other words, cannot be understood in terms of a plurality of interests alone: it must also engage with the plurality of ideas and identities.

The traders and trimmers not only overlook the tensions caused by social deprivation and economic inequality, they also fail to comprehend the appeal of fundamentalist religions. As such they are accused of being unable to deal with the reality of contemporary pluralism. Rawls works with an understanding of people as citizens who regard their private aims and attachments as contingent and open to revision. But as private individuals we may have religious and moral convictions that are definitive of our identity. The problem, Miller suggests, 'is to

see why people whose identities are encumbered in this way should give priority to an unencumbered citizen identity' (Miller, 2000: 47). Certain moral convictions will be incompatible with the language of liberal pluralism, as with those who hold that their religious moral standards should be inscribed in law. Neither, its challengers claim, offers a viable response to the fact of pluralism. Liberals, it is argued with increasing frequency, 'underestimate the difficulty of "liberalizing" nonliberal identities' and so fail to offer an adequate response to pluralism (Miller, 2000: 49).

What then of the segregationists' strategy? This approach has become highly influential with the emergence of identity politics. Many feminist and multicultural theorists have come to argue that differences of identity, as opposed to those of interests and ideals, require an assertion of difference that is not amenable to erasure and therefore pose a distinctive challenge to liberalism, which has always claimed to tolerate differences of ideas (Phillips, 1995). Multicultural critics commonly argue that if this tolerance is based on a commitment to autonomy, the pluralism that it endorses will be one limited to a liberal horizon. As Bhikhu Parekh (2000: 1) argues, their demand for recognition 'goes far beyond the familiar plea for toleration'. Multicultural theorists, such as Parekh, tend to emphasize the distinctiveness of identity-based claims: 'Unlike differences that spring from individual choices, culturally derived differences carry a measure of authority and are patterned and structured by virtue of being embedded in a shared and historically inherited system of meaning and significance' (Parekh, 2000: 3).

GROUP REPRESENTATION

Political pluralism entails a commitment to diversity then. This commitment may take the form of a simple recognition of sociocultural difference, but is increasingly taken to entail the demand that difference be represented in democratic structures. The endorsement of political pluralism, in other words, has come to include a commitment to group representation, where the groups are not conceived primarily as interest groups but rather as 'identity groups'. Rainer Baubock, for example, suggests that a 'pluralistic conception of liberal democracy with institutionalized group rights offers the best hope for resolving . . . conflict by political means rather than by force' (Baubock, 1999: 152).

This makes the issue of identity central to current debates about political pluralism. As Jeremy Waldron notes: 'The idea of identity plays an increasing role in modern politics. It affects the way people perform their duty of civic participation; and it affects their conceptions of what it is to perform that duty responsibly' (Waldron, 2000: 156).

Among those theorists who argue for some form of group representation there are three quite distinct understandings of the nature and significance of identity. These can be labelled the autonomy, authenticity and contingency perspectives on identity. One can argue for group representation from each of these perspectives, but there are significant differences between them.

The autonomy argument for group representationfocuses on the centrality of 'rational revisability': the ability of individuals rationally to assess and revise their current ends. What distinguishes this perspective from more universalist forms of liberalism is the claim that a theory of culture is needed in order adequately to consider the context of choice. People's capacity to make meaningful choices depends on access to cultural structures which require 'institutional cement' if they are to survive (Kymlicka, 1995). Group-differentiated rights provide such cement and are a requirement of citizenship. Will Kymlicka, the key advocate of this perspective, argues that all individuals have the same right to choose how to lead their lives. Culture provides the context within which individuals make meaningful choices. So, given this, people need the security of their own culture in order to enjoy the same individual

rights as others. Such security may require policies of group representation.

The authenticity argument for group representation focuses on the capacity of individuals to be in touch with their moral feelings. Our moral salvation, Charles Taylor – the key advocate of this perspective – argues, comes from recovering authentic moral contact with ourselves (Taylor, 1992: 29). Such an identity politics is concerned with authenticity as distinct from dignity, self-realization as opposed to rational revisability. Where autonomy requires cultural structures, authenticity requires dialogical interaction. The discovery of one's true identity is not, on Taylor's account, a monological process; it cannot take place in isolation, but rather needs to be negotiated with others and therefore depends upon one's dialogical relation with others. Recognizing the unique identity of everyone requires not an identical set of rights for all, but public acknowledgement of the particular worth of each.

In contrast to each of the above, the contingency argument for group representation focuses on the centrality of transgression. Rather than seeking to discover true identities, this approach aims to explode such expressions of 'identity', viewing all claims to coherence and unity as produced rather than uncovered, 'as artefacts of analysis rather than its finds' (Ferguson, 1993: 12). Identity is not only socially constructed, it is here understood to be constituted through a disparate and shifting network of interrelated discourses, with no single causal or determining factor. As William Connolly notes: 'Identity is thus a slippery, insecure experience, dependent on its ability to define difference and vulnerable to the tendency of entities it would so define to counter, resist, overturn, or subvert definitions applied to them. Identity stands in a complex, political relation to the difference it seeks to fix' (Connolly, 1991: 64).

Notwithstanding the clear theoretical differences between these three accounts of identity, each has been used to justify an endorsement of group representation. Liberal critics of this endorsement tend to assume, however, that the practice of granting group rights will inevitably strengthen the authenticity model of identity, to the detriment of individual autonomy. They express concern at the essentialism implicit in these arguments, suggesting that all advocates of group rights necessarily rely on the idea that members of groups have some sort of primordial attachment to certain cultural practices or social perspectives which need to be sustained. Brian Barry, for instance, points to Taylor's view that the interests of 'those who value remaining true to the culture of our ancestors' should be given priority over the interests of 'those who might want to cut loose in the name of some individual goal of self-development' (Taylor, 1992: 58). Barry argues that this is an essentialist stance, which stands in opposition to the liberal commitment to autonomy.

Of course many advocates of group representation do not accept the charge of essentialism. Indeed, those within the autonomy and contingency camps have good theoretical grounds for claiming that their understanding of subjectivity precludes the possibility of essentialism. So, for instance, James Tully and Iris Marion Young, both self-identified contingency theorists, claim to reject a notion of groups as clearly bounded, mutually exclusive and maintaining specific determinate interests (Tully, 1995: 11; Young, 1990: 186). However, liberal critics, such as Barry, argue that their political proposals 'do not make sense in the absence of essentialist assumptions' (Barry, 2001: 2). In other words, liberal critics of group representation reject this form of a 'politics of difference' because they suspect that it can only really be defended from an authenticity perspective, which they cannot accept.

THE POLITICS OF DIFFERENCE

Iris Marion Young, in her book *Justice and the Politics of Difference* (1990), articulated a significant critique of liberal strategies of pluralism. She suggests that attachment to specific traditions, practices, language and other culturally specific forms is a crucial aspect of social existence. Groups that have suffered oppression need guaranteed representation in order that their distinct voice can be heard. A just polity requires the participation and inclusion of all groups, which is secured only by differential treatment for oppressed groups.

This rejection of the assimilationist ideal is based on a belief that attachment to specific traditions, practices, language and other culturally specific forms is a crucial aspect of social existence. A democratic public should therefore provide mechanisms for 'the effective recognition and representation of the distinct voices and perspectives of those of its constituent groups that are oppressed or disadvantaged' (Young, 1990: 184). These mechanisms will involve three distinct features. First, the provision of public resources, which will be used to support the self-organization of group members, 'so that they achieve collective empowerment and a reflective understanding of their collective experiences and interests in the context of the society' (Young, 1990: 184). Secondly, the provision of public resources to enable the group to analyse and generate policy proposals in institutionalized contexts, and the formal requirement that decision-makers show that they have taken these perspectives into account. Thirdly, group veto power regarding specific policies that affect a group directly, '. . . such as reproductive rights for women' (Young, 1990: 184).

Rather than transcending particularity, Young proposes that '. . . attention to social group differentiation is an important resource for democratic communication' (Young, 1997: 385). But social groups are not, Young stresses, to be confused with either interest groups or identity groups. Social groups are neither 'any aggregate or association of persons who seek a particular goal, or desire the same policy . . .' nor 'a collective of persons with shared political beliefs' (Young, 1990: 186). Rather, '. . . the social positioning of group differentiation gives to individuals some shared perspectives on social life'

(Young, 1997: 385). Young is keen to point out that these groups should be understood in relational, not essentialist, terms.

The social groups argued by Young to require special representation are, on the other hand, defined with reference to a specific vision of justice which generates criteria for assessing social oppression, and hence criteria for establishing which groups require such representative guarantees. This vision of justice offers guidance regarding which groups require special representation rights, and how they should act in the political realm. A distinction is made between demands stemming from self-interest and those stemming from justice: 'the test of whether a claim upon the public is just or merely an expression of self-interest is best made when those making it must confront the opinion of others who have explicitly different, though not necessarily conflicting, experiences, priorities and needs' (Young, 1990: 186). In other words, to engage in deliberation with other social groups marks a just political dialogue as opposed to a simple expression of instrumental interest.

How much does the new politics of difference literature differ from the earlier classical pluralism literature? As McLennan notes: 'some of the older pluralist observations and goals have been rediscovered by radicals as if they were entirely new' (McLennan, 1995: 95). Interestingly, McLennan directly compares Dahl's *Democracy and its Critics* (1989) and Young's *Justice and the Politics of Difference* (1990). He suggests that the phraseology of Dahl and Young is extraordinarily similar: both focus on the harm caused by the notion of the 'common good', both articulate a notion of groups that are 'multiple, cross-cutting, fluid and shifting' and both stress the dangers of an essentialist identity-based pluralism (McLennan, 1995: 96–7). The most notable difference is that while Marxist critics accused Dahl's pluralist stance of being politically conservative, Young's politics of difference is widely perceived to be politically radical today.

DEMOCRATIC LIBERALISM

Young depicts her 'politics of difference' as a rejection of the assimilationist liberal and republican traditions. However the widespread concern with cultural diversity has also led to the articulation of new forms of pluralism located within these two traditions. For instance, in contrast to the earlier liberal strategies of pluralism, Bellamy proposes a fourth: that of democratic liberalism, which is characterized by a focus on politically negotiated compromises. This strategy, like Young's, is a democratic and contextualist one. It relies on political deliberation to negotiate reciprocal solutions.

Bellamy suggests that this politics of compromise is superior to the other forms of pluralism articulated to date in that it alone can encompass three distinct forms of political conflict: conflicts of interests (for limited resources), ideals (involving rival-rights claims) and identities (each seeking recognition) (Bellamy, 1999b: 103). The more differences turn on a clash of ideals or identities rather than interests, the less satisfactory trading or trimming become. Yet, the segregationists, who do focus on identities, argue that no compromise is possible. What is needed is a strategy that can generate compromise in relation to interests, ideals and identities.

As Young attempts to defend a conception of social groups as distinct from both interest groups and identity groups, so Bellamy attempts to defend a model of pluralism that engages with more than just interests or identities. He acknowledges that the models of pluralism offered by the traders and segregationists have twin dangers inherent within them: the establishment of a mere '*modus vivendi*' or the creation of 'Balkanization'. Given these dangers, both classical interest-group pluralism and essentialist identity politics are rejected. In their place Bellamy proposes that a liberal politics must be about negotiation. Negotiators 'practice reciprocal accommodation as part of a search for conditions of mutual acceptability that reach towards a compromise that constructs a shareable good' (Bellamy, 1999b: 101).

Such negotiation, it is argued, cannot be confined within an unquestioned constitutional framework. The constitutional framework itself must be a product of negotiation. Bellamy's (1999b: 116) model replaces the legal constitutionalism favoured by liberal democrats with a 'republican style of political constitutionalism'. On this conception of constitutionalism liberty is viewed as civic achievement rather than natural attribute. Its aim is not to ensure the absence of interference, but rather to prevent arbitrary domination. Here the constitution is not a precondition for politics; rather, political debate is the medium through which a polity constitutes itself.

This argument echoes in certain respects the important contribution made by Tully, who questions whether a modern constitution can recognize and accommodate cultural diversity. His strategy is to show that if constitutionalism is approached from the perspective of marginalized minority groups, the limitations of existing constitutions are revealed (Tully, 1995: 4). By exploring the historical formation of particular constitutions, one perceives the extent to which the sovereignty of the people is in some way denied and suppressed rather than affirmed and expressed. Tully argues that 'culture is an irreducible and constitutive aspect of politics' (Tully, 1995: 5) and that the cultural ways of citizens must be recognized as a first step in shaping constitutional arrangements. It is not sufficient, in other words, to demand group recognition within the existing constitutional framework (as both Kymlicka and Taylor have done). What is needed is a constitutional dialogue of mutual recognition. Like Bellamy, Tully argues that 'constitutions are not fixed and unchangeable agreements reached at some foundational moment, but chains of continual intercultural negotiations and agreements . . .' (Tully, 1995: 183–4). So, while Bellamy identifies his model as democratic liberalism and Tully identifies his as post-imperial, they share a common commitment to a negotiated constitutionalism that recognizes the diversity of cultural identities.

In proposing this model of democratic liberalism Bellamy is, in effect, drawing on the insights of difference theorists to develop a strategy of liberal pluralism that has the resources to engage with the diversity of not only interests and ideals, but also identities, that increasingly characterize modern societies. As Andrea Baumeister (2000: 200) notes: 'the central challenge for liberals today is not to find grounds for universal rational agreement, but to develop a set of institutions which can effectively manage the conflict and antagonism that inevitably accompanies diversity.

Summary

- The term pluralism is used in various distinct debates: methodological, sociocultural and political.
- In the 1950s and 1960s 'pluralism' described a school of empirical democratic theory, now referred to a 'classical pluralism'.
- Critics of classical pluralism argue that, while claiming to offer an accurate empirical account of existing democracies, the theory actually served normatively to endorse the *status quo* in America.

- Recent liberal philosophers share a commitment to pluralism because it is believed to allow people to live according to diverse conceptions of the good.
- Liberal theorists offer distinct pluralist strategies. Each of the liberal strategies of pluralism has been accused of being unable to deal with the reality of contemporary pluralism.
- An adequate account of contemporary political pluralism is increasingly felt to demand a focus on identities as well as interests.
- Arguments for group representation tend to rest on one of three distinct accounts of identity: autonomy, authenticity or contingency.
- Critics of group representation tend to argue that the policy entails essentialism and/or creates 'ghettoization'.
- In her defence of a model of group representation that is based on social groups, Young stresses the importance of deliberation.
- The 'politics of difference' developed by Young shares many similarities with the earlier classical pluralism of Dahl.
- Recent attempts to articulate a compelling account of political pluralism entail a synthesis of some of the insights of a politics of difference (notably its focus on the recognition of identities) with the more traditional liberal concern with conflicts of interests and ideals.

TUTORIAL QUESTIONS

1. **Which theoretical perspective offers the most compelling response to cultural diversity?**

2. **Can liberalism accommodate the demands voiced by advocates of a politics of difference?**

3. **Are group rights a threat to individual self-determination?**

FURTHER READING

Andrea Baumeister (2000) *Liberalism and the Politics of Difference* (Edinburgh: Edinburgh University Press) offers a useful account of the 'politics of difference' as it operates within feminism and multiculturalism, the challenges this politics poses to liberal theorists, and the manner in which liberalism has responded.

Richard Bellamy (1999) *Liberalism and Pluralism: Towards a Politics of Compromise* (London: Routledge) offers a very readable account of various existing liberal strategies of pluralism, along with their short-comings, and offers a persuasive alternative vision.

Gregor McLennan (1995) *Pluralism* (Buckingham: Open University Press) provides an excellent, lucid overview of the concept of pluralism as it is used within the social sciences generally.

Bhikhu Parekh (2000) *Rethinking Multiculturalism: Cultural Diversity and Political Theory* (Basingstoke: Macmillan) provides fascinating reflections on the forms of monism and pluralism that have operated within the history of political thought, and also offers a new multi-cultural perspective on cultural diversity.

Iris Marion Young (1990) *Justice and the Politics of Difference* (Princeton, NJ: Princeton University Press) provides one of the most influential statements of a politics of difference, to which liberal accounts of pluralism have been concerned to respond.

REFERENCES

Barry, Barry (2001) 'Essentialism and Multi-culturalism', *Ethnicities*, 1: 255–81.

Baubock, Rainer (1999) 'Liberal Justifications for Ethnic Groups Rights', in Christian Joppke and Steven Lukes (eds), *Multicultural Questions*. Oxford: Oxford University Press, pp. 133–57.

Baumeister, Andrea (2000) *Liberalism and the 'Politics of Difference'*. Edinburgh: Edinburgh University Press.

Bellamy, Richard (1999a) 'Liberalism', in Roger Eatwell and Anthony Wright (eds), *Contemporary Political Ideologies* (second edition). London and New York: Continuum, pp. 23–49.

Bellamy, Richard (1999b) *Liberalism and Pluralism: Towards a Politics of Compromise*. London: Routledge.

Connolly, William (1991) *Identity/Difference: Democratic Negotiations of Political Paradox*. Ithaca, NY: Cornell University Press.

Dahl, Robert (1956) *A Preface to Democratic Theory*. Chicago, IL: University of Chicago Press.

Dahl, Robert (1971) *Polyarchy: Participation and Opposition*. New Haven, CT: Yale University Press.

Dahl, Robert (1989) *Democracy and its Critics*. New Haven, CT: Yale University Press.

Ferguson, Kathy (1993) *The Man Question: Visions of Subjectivity in Feminist Theory*. Berkeley, CA: University of California Press.

Held, David (1989) *Political Theory and the Modern State*. Cambridge: Polity Press.

Heywood, Andrew (1998) *Political Ideologies*. Basingstoke and London: Macmillan.

Kymlicka, Will (1995) *Multicultural Citizenship*. Oxford: Oxford University Press.

Lindblom, Charles (1977) *Politics and Markets*. New York: Basic Books.

McLennan, Gregor (1995) *Pluralism*. Buckingham: Open University Press.

Miller, David (2000) *Citizenship and National Identity*. Cambridge: Polity Press.

Parekh, Bhikhu (2000) *Rethinking Multiculturalism: Cultural Diversity and Political Theory*. Basingstoke: Macmillan.

Phillips, Anne (1995) *The Politics of Presence*. Oxford: Clarendon Press.

Rawls, John (1993) *Political Liberalism*. New York: Columbia University Press.

Taylor, Charles (1992) 'The Politics of Recognition', in Amy Gutmann (ed.), *Multiculturalism and the Politics of Recognition*. Princeton, NJ: Princeton University Press, pp. 25–74.

Tully, James (1995) *Strange Multiplicity*. Cambridge: Cambridge University Press.

Waldron, Jeremy (2000) 'Cultural Identity and Civic Responsibility', in Will Kymlicka and Wayne Norman (eds), *Citizenship in Diverse*

Societies. Oxford: Oxford University Press, pp. 155–74.

Young, Iris Marion (1990) *Justice and the Politics of Difference*. Princeton, NJ: Princeton University Press.

Young, Iris Marion (1997) 'Difference as a Resource for Democratic Communication', in J. Bohman and W. Rehg (eds), *Deliberative Democracy: Essays on Reason and Politics*. Cambridge, MA: MIT Press, pp. 383–406.

See also chapters

9 Civil Society – National and Global

Roland Axtmann

THE RENAISSANCE OF 'CIVIL SOCIETY' IN ITS POLITICAL CONTEXT

The concept of 'civil society' has been employed in political thinking for many centuries, but mainstream political science has by and large neglected the term. It was only in the last two decades or so that, as a result of political developments mainly in Eastern and Western Europe, 'civil society' has become a popular term in both political debate and academic analysis.

First, the dissident movements in the state-socialist societies in Eastern and Central Europe in the 1970s and 1980s developed the idea (and ideal) of civil society in their political and cultural struggles against a totalitarianpolitical regime that denied any difference between political and social power and prevented the formation of independent centres of power outside the state. 'Civil society' was conceptualized as juxtaposed to a despotic state; indeed, as the main weapon against it. What had to be defended was the ideal of an independent life of society against the despotic encroachments by the state upon its terrain:

> What is this independent life of society? . . . It includes everything from self-education and thinking about the world, through free creative activity and its communication to others, to the most varied free, civic ini-

tiatives, including instances of independent self-organization. In short, it is an area in which living within the truth becomes articulate and materializes in a visible way. (Havel, 1978/1991: 177)

Within civil society, every person must have the right of free speech and of free association, and through the exercise of these rights discover what they have in common, recognize each other as peers and begin to regain their liberty. 'Civil society' was the expression of a new ethical vision of social order, signalling a clash of different moralities between the state and society. At issue was the restoration of the dignity of autonomous citizens' initiatives and the creation of a space for the independent formation and activity of grassroots movements. For the Hungarian writer György Konrad, civil society and the activities in it were, approvingly, analysed as amounting to a depoliticization of life; they were seen as 'antipolitical', geared towards limiting the state's interference with the individual's private affairs:

> Antipolitics is the emergence of independent forums that can be appealed to against political power; it is a counterpower that cannot take power and does not wish to. Power it has already, here and now, by reason of its moral and cultural weight . . . Antipolitics neither supports nor opposes government; it is something different. Its people are fine

right where they are; they form a network that keeps watch on political power, exerting pressure on the basis of their cultural and moral stature alone, not through electoral legitimacy. That is their right and obligation, but above all it is their self-defense. (Konrad, 1984: 230–1)

Politics, he argued, had flooded nearly every nook and cranny of people's lives; these lives ought now to be depoliticized, ought to be freed from politics 'as from some contagious infection'.

In the setting of the authoritarian state-socialist societies we find here a 'liberal' conceptualization of 'civil society' that perceives state power as the nemesis of the liberty of the individual. Liberty resides in 'civil society', which is understood as the totality of relationships voluntarily entered into by self-determining individuals in the pursuit of their self-chosen goals and the network of voluntary associations outside the state which are essentially contractual in nature.

Secondly, the breakdown of the post-war welfare state consensus among the main political parties in the 1970s and 1980s led to an embrace of the idea of civil society in Western Europe. In the twentieth century, the West European state had become ever more proactively involved in the planning and management of the economy and in structuring society by meeting social needs and providing utilities and services. As a result, '[b]y the 1960s, both right- and left-leaning political parties had endorsed statism, and accepted the idea that public agencies should manage the economy, regulate commercial and industrial activities, subsidize incomes, provide a wide range of services, manage sizeable social security funds and even own and operate large industrial enterprises' (Midgley, 1991: 9). In 1985, on social expenditure alone the OECD countries spent on average almost 25 per cent of their Gross Domestic Product. By that time, however, the welfare state consensus had already come under severe attack, particularly from intellectual forces in Britain and the United States.

The state was no longer seen as the solution to society's problems, but as their cause. The critique of the welfare state was comprehensive. It was argued that the welfare state eroded individual responsibility and initiative; created a large, inefficient bureaucratic welfare apparatus that intruded and violated the privacy of the citizen, diminishing choice and individual preferences; and harmed economic productivity and growth by 'confiscating' private resources in the form of taxation for welfare expenditure, thus depriving the private sector of money needed for capitalization. Instead of the proactive interventionist welfare state, there was now much support for the liberal idea of a free market and limited government. The privatization of state functions should lead to a 'minimal state', and the strengthening of the private sector as a result of widespread marketization was perceived as releasing 'civil society' from the clutches of 'big government'. In this 'neo-liberal' conceptualization of civil society, state power was to be curtailed through the activities of 'civil society'.

Thirdly, this neo-liberal attack on the welfare state was in some ways taken up by the 'new social movements' that had been forming since the mid-1960s. In many ways, the women's movement, the environmental movement, the gay and lesbian movement as well as (increasingly) the anti-racist movement, were developing strategies to by-pass the state in their struggles. They perceived the state as a bureaucratic and centralized apparatus that interfered with every individual's life, moulded individual life chances and, instead of combating economic, gender, sexual and racial discrimination, reinforced capitalism, patriarchy, racism and sexual stereotyping through its policies. These movements grew increasingly sensitive to 'the alienating, decapacitating, and depersonalizing effects that the welfare state and its legal-bureaucratic or professional modes of distribution, treatment, and surveillance can have upon communities and individual "lifeworlds"' (Offe, 1987: 506). For the neoliberals, the state's interventions had to be limited by returning the allocation of welfare to markets. For the 'new social movements', on the other hand, the state's interventions had to be limited because they inhibited cultural diversity and individual 'permissiveness'. And it was not the market that should take over the state's task of providing for certain forms of welfare; rather, welfare should be returned to 'more localized, non-hierarchical and non-bureaucratized forms of communal self-administration' (Pierson, 1991: 217). Whereas the neo-liberals proposed, in effect, the depoliticization of welfare issues through the privatization of welfare concerns in the form of private insurance schemes, the 'new social movements', in effect, opted for the re-politicization of welfare issues by making them a central concern for the institutions and organizations of a self-governing civil society. Communalization, not marketization, should follow the state's extrication from (some) welfare provisions.

While these developments, reaching back to the 1970s, helped reintroduce the concept and idea of 'civil society' into political and academic debate, there are also three further, and more recent, developments that entrenched 'civil society' as a key notion of democratic politics.

First, since the 1990s left-of-centre governments in Western Europe (as well as the Clinton presidency in the United States) have endeavoured to formulate a 'third way' of progressive politics beyond the radical neo-liberalism of the 1980s and the old statist-corporatism of social democracy after the Second World War that had led to the interventionist welfare state. While the 'third way' is not a coherent political ideology, it is fair to say that it envisages a revised role for the state – 'as a facilitator, as an enabler: still involved in the funding and regulation of services but not necessarily in their provision' (Latham, 2001: 27). While handing over certain state functions to the private sector through marketization remains a possibility (and an actual policy), civic groups in civil society – the voluntary sector – are charged

with generating creative and energetic strategies to cope with social problems and with taking over the delivery of public services (Giddens, 2001). The goal is thus the formation of a strong society which 'can only come from strengthening the bonds of trust and mutuality between each of its citizens. In a solid society, with its dense networks of respect and cooperation, people are likely to value altruism as much as self-interest. This is why the third way seeks to strengthen civil society through its policies of devolution' (Latham, 2001: 27). This political debate is taken up in academic analyses of 'social capital' (see Chapter 19 by Maloney and Stevenson in this volume).

Secondly, to the extent that 'third way' ideology emphasizes the need to match individual rights with civic responsibilities of the individual and to foster a culture of duty within 'strong communities', there is some ideological overlap with the debate on communitarianism (Driver and Martell, 2001). As Benjamin Barber has argued:

> communitarians do not believe that the private domain is simply one of solitary, rights-bearing individuals. . . . Rather, since they assume that people are embedded in communities and tied to one another by bonds that precede and condition their individuality, they envisage civil society as a complex welter of ineluctably social relations that tie people together, first of all into families and kinship associations like clans, and then into clubs, neighborhoods, communities, congregations, and more extended social hierarchies. (Barber, 1998: 22–3)

Civil society has thus been conceptualized as the arena where people interact and are embedded in identity-bestowing communities and where they experience solidarity and social bonding. The main difference between a more 'conservative' communitarianism and a 'third way' communitarianism would appear to be that, whereas the 'conservative' variety tends towards emphasizing the need for one community for all citizens (a 'national' community), 'left' communitarianism is more likely to endorse the idea of a 'community of communities', of a 'plural' civil society.

The third of the more recent developments deserves a somewhat more detailed presentation.

GLOBAL CIVIL SOCIETY

The idea of a 'global' civil society has in recent years become a key feature in debates on globalization. During the last few decades, the threats to the survival of the human race posed by nuclear, biological and chemical warfare and by dangers of an eco-catastrophe as well as a concern with political and social injustice worldwide, be it with political prisoners, discrimination on the basis of race or gender or 'Third World' poverty, have led to the formation of movements that do not limit their activities to any one particular territory. For activists in the environmental and peace movements, in Amnesty International or the more recent 'anti-globalization movements', for example, the 'one world' has become the point of reference for their concerns. This also holds true for the women's movement or the transnational movement of 'indigenous peoples'. Such a global orientation is also becoming prominent within religious organizations. The participants in these movements act on the basis of a global consciousness:

> [Their] ethos implies a reorientation of citizenship in order to go beyond loyalty and diligent participation in the collective life of a territorially delimited society that qualifies as a sovereign state. The citizen sensitive to the claims of this emergent ethos needs to extend his or her notions of participation in dimensions of both space (beyond the territory of any particular state) and time (beyond the present, reclaiming past wisdom and safeguarding future generations). (Falk, 1992: 153–4)

'Think globally, act locally' as much as 'Think locally, act globally' is the core of this ethos that is 'necessarily deferential to the local and the diverse' (Falk, 1992: 153). It is now often argued in political and academic debate that these 'citizen-pilgrims' are participating in the creation of a 'global' civil society.

Alejandro Colás (2002) has highlighted two aspects of the debate on 'global civil society'. First, the growing economic, technological and cultural integration of a globalizing world is believed to be impelling a deeper and more extensive cooperation among socio-political activists across the globe. That extension of social movement activity beyond state boundaries is considered to be opening up previously closed arenas of world politics, thereby gradually replacing the sovereign nation-state as the major locus of political power. Secondly, concomitantly with this wave of transnational movement activity, we witness the formation of a global governance structure. The international governmental organizations (IGOs) that have been the building blocks of the multilateral arrangements entered into by sovereign states, are being drawn into a system of 'complex multilateralism' where international non-governmental organizations (INGOs), citizens' movements and multinational corporations share in the task of governance.

One prominent understanding of 'global governance' is provided by James Rosenau in his analysis of the 'turbulent world' of the late twentieth century. For Rosenau, global governance is the (mainly) unintended consequence of the conscious pursuit of goals by distinctive collective actors through the exercise of control mechanisms that have transnational repercussions:

> To assess global governance . . . is to trace the various ways in which the processes of governance are aggregated. The cumulation encompasses individuals, their skills and orientations, no less than private and public collectivities at the local, provincial, national, transnational, international, and global levels. . . . Global governance is not so much a label for a high degree of integration and order as it is a summary term for highly complex and widely disparate activities that culminate in a modicum of worldwide coherence. (Rosenau, 1997: 10–11)

In this world, governance is no longer the exclusive domain of national governments and the state. Rather, the sites out of which authority can be exercised and compliance can be generated have been dispersed and authority has been relocated 'outwards to transnational and supranational organizations, sidewards to social movements and NGOs, and inwards to subnational groups' (Rosenau, 1997: 43–4). Rosenau pays scant attention to the question as to what makes for a *democratic* 'global governance'. He organizes his thoughts on democracy around the idea of 'checks and balances':

> The decentralization of rule systems in disparate and localized sites has greatly inhibited the coalescence of hierarchical and autocratic centers of power . . . authority is so widely dispersed that neither tyrannical majorities nor autocratic leaders are likely to gain much of a foothold in this emergent domain and, if they do, the constraints against their tyranny are likely to be too numerous and resistant for them to expand the scope of their power. (Rosenau, 1997: 40–1)

This rather mechanistic model with its emphasis on the dispersal of power among a multiplicity of groups and collective actors is reminiscent of American pluralist political theory of the 1950s and 1960s. As Colás (2002: 152) rightly suggests, such a conceptualization of 'global governance', and of 'global civil society' as a key element of its material infrastructure, is the rule rather than the exception in contemporary discussion. 'Transnational', or 'global', civil society is seen as a fairly homogeneous, non-hierarchical and disinterested counterpoint to the power-driven system of states, representing an otherwise marginalized or disenfranchised 'global citizenry'.

Against such an understanding of 'global civil society', Colás raises a series of pertinent questions. Empirically, he points to the fact that 'global civil society is what states make of it' (2002: 153). Many NGOs are organized by governments (GONGOs), are quasi-non-governmental organizations (QUANGOs) or are even government-run or initiated (GRINGOs). Their participation in conferences organized by international governmental organizations such as the United Nations is premised on their state-approved accreditation. This observation raises the question about the adequacy of a 'liberal' conceptualization of ('global') civil society as pitted against the 'state' (and the states in the inter-state system) and points us to a hypothesis that posits the state as a significant component of international social movement activity (Colás, 2002: 75–83). On the one hand, it is therefore necessary to pay due attention to the interaction of transnational civil society and inter-state relations. On the other hand, we must not forget that the 'transnational' social movements and movement organizations are formed mostly within national civil societies and, to a great extent, depend for their success, and even their survival, on other institutions such as political parties, trade unions, churches and the media. A global civil society that is built around the global linkages of these nationally 'embedded' movements is thus inherently fragile and premised upon a 'national' environment congenial to movement politics.

Furthermore, a considerable number of NGOs have been boosters, and often willing executioners, of neo-liberal policies, more concerned with spreading, and entrenching, a particular form of capitalism rather than promoting democracy. More generally, NGOs as 'functional' organizations represent the interests of their members rather than a nascent global 'demos'. That there are, in the various 'anti-globalization movements', forces that struggle against the logic of global capitalist accumulation and its political and cultural ramifications, cannot be doubted, although fighting against capitalism in itself does not make a social movement democratic.

A BRIEF NOTE ON THE HISTORY OF THE CONCEPT OF 'CIVIL SOCIETY'

There is one commonality between the various notions of 'civil society' that I have sketched above: 'civil society' is contrasted to 'the state'. In the history of the concept of 'civil society', which stretches back to ancient Greece, this conceptualization is quite recent, eventually becoming dominant in the late eighteenth century. Before then, 'civil society' was used predominantly as a synonym for 'political society': *civitas sive societas civilis sive res publica*, 'the city-state or civil society or common wealth'. For Aristotle the *societas civilis sive politica*, that is, the *polis*, was a community of citizens who are united in order to live a 'good', 'virtuous' life. In this self-governed community, citizens engage with each other as free and equal persons and rule themselves through law, not through force, coercion and subjection. This political community is contrasted with the *societas domestica*, the sphere of (economic) production and (social) reproduction, the realm of the *oikos*, that serves the satisfaction of the needs and necessities of life.

Aristotle's equation of civil society with political society, remained a main feature of the conceptual history of civil society over the centuries. One of the major deviations from this tradition occurred in the contractual theories of political authority in the seventeenth and eighteenth century. For the English philosophers Thomas Hobbes and John Locke in the second half of the seventeenth century, for example, civil society was no longer defined by setting it apart from domestic society, but from the 'state of nature'. For Hobbes (1651/1991), the 'state of nature' is a state in which individuals are not bound by the force of any agreed human laws. To escape from this violent, dangerous and unsociable 'state of nature', men constitute a civil society through mutual agreement. By covenanting to become subjects of a commonwealth, the individuals put themselves under the authority of the civil laws. By providing for the 'Leviathan', the strong state as that agency that enforces the social contract and secures the *status civilis* against any internal or external threats, the member of the commonwealth is now no longer seen as a peer among peers, sharing in governing

and being governed – as in Aristotle's thinking – but as a subject of a 'sovereign' political power.

Locke, too, argues that civil society occurs 'wherever any number of Men, in a state of Nature, enter into Society to make one People one Body Politic under one Supreme Government' (Locke, 1689/1989: § 89). Locke thus conceptualizes civil society as synonymous with legal authority and the executive apparatus of the law. Although Locke does not describe the state of nature in Hobbesian terms as anomic, but populated by rational, property-owning individuals with fundamental rights, civil society is given its relief by comparing it to a (hypothetical) *status naturalis*. For both Hobbes and Locke, civil society is pacified society; a society in which the use of force by private individuals is banned. By designating (collective) actors who are empowered to deploy legitimate force in (civil) society, either of these theoretical positions creates a space for conceptualizing the actors and agencies involved in the enforcement of order as an analytically distinct sphere of society, as 'the state'.

Arguably, however, the contemporary dominant 'liberal' conceptualization of 'civil society' that emphasizes (the need for) the separation of 'state' and 'civil society' has taken its cue from Alexis de Tocqueville. Writing in the first half of the nineteenth century, de Tocqueville conceived of modern society as a democratic society in the sense that it has led to an increasing equalization of social conditions. The collapse of the 'old regime' (as a result of the political transformations triggered by the French Revolution) set individuals free by cutting them loose from the affective and social ties to families, groups and corporations, membership in which had given them their identity and a sense of belonging. Furthermore, the structure of modern society is such that it also reinforces this process of individualization by privileging self-centred competitive actions by 'possessive individualists'. As a result, 'democratic' citizens 'do not scruple to show that they care for nobody but themselves' (Tocqueville, 1945, vol. II: 100).

Democracy as that society that, in the name of the sovereignty of the people, the equal treatment of individuals and the uniform provision of public goods, aims for the abolition of inequalities of power and wealth, inexorably leads to the gradual concentration of power in the hands of a centralized state: the political demand for the equality of conditions means in reality the institutionalization of public regulation in the form of the social-welfare state in which the state becomes regulator, inspector, adviser, educator and punisher of social life. Centralization thus creates a framework for the peaceful pursuit of private interests and can therefore be interpreted as aiding the development of self-centred individualism. Yet, this incessant increase of the prerogative of centralized government will also lead insensibly to the surrender of individual independence as the people perpetually fall under the control of the public administration: 'The eye and finger of government are constantly intruding into the minutest detail of human actions' (Tocqueville, 1945, vol. II: 325, 313). Atomization and individualization are intrinsic features of 'democratic' society; and so is the danger of state despotism that feeds on the 'democratic' demand for equality of conditions and thrives on the individualization in modern society (Tocqueville, 1945, vol. II: 318). Tocqueville argued that only a vibrant civil society that was structured through a plurality of associations could secure liberty. On the one hand, these associations would contain the processes of atomization, giving individuals a sense of solidarity and interdependence. On the other hand, they would provide a barrier against the encroachments by the state on the life of individuals.

It would go beyond the bounds of this chapter to trace more references to past conceptual discussions in the contemporary usage of 'civil society'. It would be possible, for example, to identify in ('conservative' and 'left') communitarianism traces of an understanding of 'civil society' as 'civilized' society

in the sense of 'polite' and 'sociable' society grounded in a shared notion of 'civility'. This is an understanding that can be found in the texts of the Scottish Enlightenment of the eighteenth century. It could also be argued that, whereas the neo-liberals read Adam Smith, one of the most prominent philosophers of the Scottish Enlightenment, as a political economist who spoke about the market, utility and the rational self-interest of the individual, the ideologues of the 'third way' re-discovered him as a moral philosopher. He, together with other theorists, argued that a 'commercial society' was not simply held together by human interaction and relationships that are governed by material needs that are best satisfied by market exchanges and an intricate division of labour. Rather, 'commercial society' produced and sustained a 'realm of private friendship and free interpersonal connections, of morals, affections, and sentiments . . . commercial societies at once circumscribed the realm of need, consigning it to the market, and simultaneously created a sphere of non-instrumental human relations, governed by "natural sympathy", the moral affections' (Khilnani, 2001: 20; cf. Latham, 2001: 29).

When we turn to the debate on 'global civil society', we may discern the 'classical' reference to the idea of civil society as the companionship of strangers; the imagining of a systematic set of (global) relationships between human beings which gradually is being institutionalized into a 'global' society, an imagining that underpins the contemporary development of an enforceable system of human rights. There is also a clearly discernible reference to the 'liberal' understanding of 'civil society' as a universe of voluntary organizations, set apart from the state and as the arena where enlightened opinion-formation is possible. Yet, what is not sufficiently well analysed is civil society – in its 'global' as much as in its 'domestic' form – as a contested space and the power relations that structure it.

The issues at stake crystallize when we raise the question of capitalism as a problem for conceptualizing 'civil society'. In the mid-nineteenth century, Karl Marx conceptualized civil society as comprising exclusively material and economic relations; and the complex of economic relations was seen as coterminous with society itself. As a member of civil society, man is of necessity 'egoistic man': 'an individual separated from the community, withdrawn into himself, wholly preoccupied with his private interest and acting in accordance with his private caprice. . . . The only bond between men is natural necessity, need and private interest, the preservation of their property and their egoistic persons'; he 'treats other men as means, degrades himself to the role of a mere means, and becomes the plaything of alien powers' (Marx, in Tucker, 1978: 43 and 34). In his description of civil society as capitalist society, Marx transformed the picture of the (hypothetical) Hobbesian 'state of nature' into the (historical) reality of bourgeois society.

It is not necessary for us to accept Marx's understanding of 'civil society' as nothing more than the sum total of the material conditions of life in order, nevertheless, to accept the need to locate capitalism in its relation to 'civil society'. It would appear reasonable to make at least two assumptions. First, if we include the economy in civil society, then we have to pay systematic attention to the oppressive forces operating within it. A theory of civil society that does not do so is seriously deficient. Secondly, a conceptualization that keeps 'the economy' outside the conceptual reach of 'civil society' is also unsatisfactory if it neglects to analyse the ways in which 'the economy' can be as much a despotic force prone to coerce civil society as can the state. This ambiguity towards capitalism betrays the essentially 'liberal' tradition of the dominant thinking about 'civil society'.

CONCLUSION

I have suggested that the dominant understanding of 'civil society' relates, and juxtaposes, the concept to 'the state'. In this essentially 'liberal' understanding, 'civil society' has been conceived as the realm of consensus and unforced communication and cooperation – the realm of liberty. The state, on the other hand, has been analysed as the monopolist of (legitimate) violence, needed, though, to enforce order, yet, because of its control of the means of coercion, also a threat to individual liberty. This positioning of 'civil society' allows for three distinctive argumentative moves. First, 'civil society' can be defined as a kind of 'pre-political' sphere in which individuals enter into relationships with each other in pursuit of their idiosyncratic interests, unimpeded by the state. It is the sphere of individual freedom as long as the right to be left alone (by the state) is upheld. Secondly, the network of associations and organizations that make up 'civil society' are the bulwark against a potentially despotic state. Thirdly, 'civil society' is the space where citizens acquire and deploy the resources they need to exercise the right of political participation. 'Civil society' constitutes the social and cultural dimension of democracy in that it allows for the formation of those identities, values and institutions without which a democratic public life could not exist. It is here that some of the current debates on political legitimacy may be located. In a move 'from voting to talking', an increasing number of political theorists see the debates in civil society that precede the act of voting as the important mechanism that lends legitimacy to policy outcomes.

I have pointed out that power relations that obtain in 'civil society' are in need of much more focused analysis. I have made this point with regard to capitalism, but a similar case could be made with regard to the unequal distribution of other social and cultural resources – some of these maldistributions have been discussed, for example, with regard to gender inequality or in the context of multiculturalism. Without a theory of social power civil society theorists will not be in a position to analyse the conflicts and tensions within civil society.

Summary

- The concept of 'civil society' has a long history, stretching back to ancient Greece.
- Since the mid-seventeenth century, 'civil society' gradually acquired its dominant modern meaning as the sphere of social interaction juxtaposed to the 'state'.
- The concept of 'civil society' has lost its marginal position within modern political science since the 1970s. The dissident movements in state-socialist Eastern Europe; the 'new social movements' in Western Europe; and the neo-liberal 'New Right' reintroduced the concept into political debate – although, in each case, giving the concept a different meaning.
- In recent years, the concept of 'civil society' has been taken up by the ideologues of the 'third way' as well as 'communitarian' political thinkers.
- The notion of a 'global' civil society' has become a central aspect of the debates on globalization.
- Insufficient attention is paid in analysis of 'civil society' to the power relationships that constitute this sphere of social interaction.

TUTORIAL QUESTIONS

1. **What is 'civil' in 'civil society?**

2. **To what extent does 'civil society' express a moral vision?**

3. **What is the relationship between 'civil society' and 'the state'?**

FURTHER READING

Baogang He's chapter on 'Civil Society and Democracy', in April Carter and Geoffrey Stokes (eds) (2001) *Democratic Theory Today*

(Cambridge: Polity Press, pp. 203–27) is a good introductory text that complements the chapter in this book.

John Keane's 'Introduction' and 'Despotism and Democracy', in John Keane (ed.) (1988) *Civil Society and the State* (London: Verso, pp. 1–31 and 35–71) are still extremely valuable overviews of the history of the concept of 'civil society'. The other chapters in the volume provide an excellent introduction to the debates in the 1970s and 1980s.

Sudipta Kaviraj and Sunil Khilnani (eds) (2001) *Civil Society. History and Possibilities* (Cambridge: Cambridge University Press) is a collection of pieces that reflect current debates on 'civil society', including chapters on the debate in developing countries.

Krishan Kumar (1993) 'Civil Society: an Inquiry into the Usefulness of an Historical Term', *British Journal of Sociology,* **44**: 375–95 discusses 'civil society' from a sociological perspective.

Keith Tester (1992) *Civil Society* (London: Routledge) places the conceptual history of 'civil society' in the context of the formation of modernity.

Alejandro Colás (2002) *International Civil Society* (Cambridge: Polity Press) provides an excellent account of the varied conceptualizations of 'civil society' and places the concept in the context of developments in International Relations as an academic discipline.

Benjamin Barber (1998) *A Place for US* (New York: Hill and Wang) discusses for the American situation, as the subtitle states, 'how to make society civil and democracy strong'.

REFERENCES

Barber, Benjamin (1998) *A Place for US: How to Make Society Civil and Democracy Strong.* New York: Hill and Wang.

Colás, Alejandro (2002) *International Civil Society.* Cambridge: Polity Press.

Driver, Stephen and Martell, Luke (2001) 'Left, Right and the Third Way', in Anthony Giddens (ed.), *The Global Third Way Debate.* Cambridge: Polity Press, pp. 36–49.

Falk, Richard (1992) *Explorations at the Edges of Time. The Prospects for World Order.* Philadelphia, PA: Temple University Press.

Giddens, Anthony (ed.) (2001) *The Global Third Way Debate.* Cambridge: Polity Press.

Havel, Vaclav (1978/1991) 'The Power of the Powerless', in Vaclav Havel, *Open Letters.* London: Faber & Faber, pp. 125–214.

Hobbes, Thomas (1651/1991) *Leviathan.* Ed. Richard Tuck. Cambridge: Cambridge University Press.

Khilnani, Sunil (2001) 'The Development of Civil Society', in Sudipta Kaviraj and Sunil Khilnani (eds), *Civil Society. History and Possibilities.* Cambridge: Cambridge University Press, pp. 11–32.

Konrad, George (1984) *Antipolitics.* San Diego, CA and New York: Harcourt Brace Jovanovich.

Latham, Mark (2001) 'The Third Way: an Outline', in Anthony Giddens (ed.), *The Global Third Way Debate.* Cambridge: Polity Press, pp. 25–35.

Locke, John (1689/1989) *Two Treatises of Government*. Ed. Peter Laslett. Cambridge: Cambridge University Press.

Midgley, James (1991) 'The Radical Right, Politics and Society', in Howard Glennester and James Midgley (eds), *The Radical Right and the Welfare State. An International Assessment*. Hemel Hempstead: Harvester Wheatsheaf, pp. 3–23.

Offe, Claus (1987) 'Democracy Against the Welfare State? Structural Foundations of Neoconservative Political Opportunities', *Political Theory*, **15**: 501–37.

Pierson, Christopher (1991) *Beyond the Welfare State? The New Political Economy of Welfare*. Cambridge: Polity Press.

Rosenau, James (1997) *Along the Domestic–Foreign Frontier: Exploring Governance in a Turbulent World*. Cambridge: Cambridge University Press.

Tocqueville, Alexis de [1835/1840] (1945) *Democracy in America* (2 vols). New York: Alfred Knopf.

Tucker, Robert C. (ed.) (1978) *The Marx–Engels Reader* (second edition). New York and London: Norton.

See also chapters

10 Class – Elites

Roland Axtmann and Robert Grant

As Noël O'Sullivan demonstrates in his chapter of this book, 'power' is a philosophically and analytically difficult concept. In this chapter, we shall deal with the nature of power as it relates to two distinct categories of collective actors who have been identified in political analyses as the chief bearers of social and political power, social classes and elites.

CLASS

In this section, we shall concentrate mainly on the views espoused by Karl Marx, the nineteenth-century revolutionary political activist and theorist of capitalism and modern society. For Karl Marx and his friend and collaborator, Frederick Engels, classes are the collective actors that make history. They famously stated in the *Communist Manifesto* in 1848 that

> the history of all hitherto existing society is the history of class struggles. Freeman and slave, patrician and plebian, lord and serf, guild-master and journeyman, in a word, oppressor and oppressed, stood in constant opposition to one another, carried on an un-interrupted, now hidden, now open fight, a fight that each time ended either in a revolutionary reconstruction of society at large, or in the common ruin of the contending classes. (Marx/Engels, in Tucker, 1978: 473–4)

In capitalist society, the capitalists as the owners of the means of production are in an antagonistic conflict with the wage workers who are separated from the means of production and have nothing to sell to gain a livelihood and ensure their very survival but their own labour power, that is, their capacity to work. On the basis of the private ownership of the means of production it is possible for the capitalists to exploit the workers by paying them less in wages for what they collectively produce than the price that product achieves on the market: to make a profit, the capitalists must exploit their workers.

Marx and Engels, therefore, posited a polarized class structure – under capitalism, the two dominant classes are the capitalists and the proletariat. Their relationship involves a mutual conflict of interest, engaging the two classes in an incessant struggle with each other. However, as capitalism develops, so class struggle matures: ultimately, capitalism is its own gravedigger. The main reason for this development is, according to Marx and Engels, that the working class increases in number and becomes spatially concentrated in greater masses in factories, factory towns and working-class districts. The various interests within the working class are more and more equalized, in proportion as machinery obliterates all distinctions of labour, and there is a trend towards nearly everywhere reducing wages to the same low level. These developments allow for the formation of a working-class consciousness: the proletariat becomes aware that its members share the same class position and class interests because they are all equally subjected to exploitation. This realization is the foundation for the creation of working-class organizations. The political organization of the working class follows, if not 'automatically' from economic conditions, then at least 'logically' from shared class position and the joint experience of exploitation.

Since, for Marx, modern society was class society, 'all struggles within the State, the struggle between democracy, aristocracy, and monarchy, the struggle for the franchise, etc., etc., are merely the illusory forms in which the real struggles of the different classes are fought out among one another' (Marx, in Tucker, 1978: 160–1). In this sense, then, as Marx and Engels remarked in the *Communist Manifesto*, '[p]olitical power, properly so called, is merely the organized power of one class for oppressing another'. Economic power, therefore, translates into political power: the ownership and control of society's productive resources is the power-base upon which the capitalist class erects its political domination – and its ideological predominance as well – as Marx argued in *The German Ideology*:

> The ideas of the ruling class are, in every epoch, the ruling ideas: i.e., the class which is the ruling *material* force in society is at the same time its ruling *intellectual* force. The class which has the means of material production at its disposal, has control at the same time over the means of mental production. . . . The ruling ideas are nothing more than the ideal expression of the dominant material relationships . . . grasped as ideas; hence of the relationships which make one class the ruling one, therefore, the ideas of its dominance. (Marx, in Tucker, 1978: 172, original emphasis)

This view on class-based power led Marx and Engels to argue in the *Communist Manifesto* that 'the executive of the modern state is but a committee for managing the common affairs of the whole bourgeoisie' (Marx, in Tucker, 1978: 475). The state is thus seen as (nothing but) the political instrument wielded by the economically dominant class to sustain its class rule. Though the state may well act on behalf of the ruling class, this does not necessarily mean that it works at its behest. Marx went beyond this position in his study on the *Eighteenth Brumaire* where he analysed the 'exceptional' historical situation in mid-nineteenth-century France where the class struggle was 'frozen' by an inability of any one class to exhibit its power over the state. In this situation of a precarious power equilibrium of the antagonistic classes, the state (bureaucracy) may gain autonomy from class control. But since the Bonapartist state did not change the capitalist relations of production, 'in the last instance', it remained dependent on the bourgeoisie for capital accumulation to secure tax revenues for its own consumption and military expansion.

More recent Marxist theories of the capitalist state took their cue from Marx's analysis of the Bonapartist state. Their central tenet has been that the state is compelled to fulfil certain 'functions' in capitalist societies that objectively serve the common, long-term interests of the capitalist class. It has been argued that the nature of the state and its activities can be deduced from the changing systemic requirements of capitalism as a mode of production rather than from the composition of state and government personnel and the attempts by capitalists to influence its operation and policies. The containment of class struggle as well as the creation of legal and monetary frameworks for market capitalism, investment in infrastructure and welfare, or provision for the reproduction of the labour force have been analysed as functional contributions of the state to the reproduction of the capitalist mode of production in the long term. In order to fulfil these functions the state had to be 'relatively' autonomous. But functionalist Marxists remain aware of the fact that the capitalist state depends on the investment decisions of the large capitalist interests because it is excluded from the organization of capitalist production and the allocation of private capital. Both for the achievement of its policy goals and the maintenance of its revenues the state has to depend on economic growth generated within the capitalist economy. The state thus has to operate in such a way that the long-term needs of capital are met.

Contemporary Marxist theorists have also had to take a critical look at the idea of a polarized class structure, taking account of the continued existence of the 'middle class(es)'. How best to define these 'inter-mediate classes' has been a major problem in both Marxist class analyses and non-Marxist analyses of the social stratification of modern society. One often used typology distinguishes between the 'old', the 'new', and the 'lower' middle class. The 'old' middle class is composed of the self-employed who run and own small businesses – from the plumber and the hairdresser to the newsagent and decorator. To characterize this group, Marx spoke – disparagingly – of the 'petty bourgeoisie'. The 'new' and the 'lower' middle classes used to be seen as being composed of the property-less, non-manual or 'white-collar' workers. The 'new' middle class developed with the expansion of professional, managerial and administrative occupations. It is composed of highly educated professionals with formal qualifications, working mainly in the service sector – and, increasingly, in the culture industry. Their main internal differentiation is between those professionals who work in the public sector, for example, in the health and education sector, or in social welfare, and those working in the private sector as, for example, lawyers, accountants or doctors. The increase in recent years in the number of self-employed professionals, for example, in the areas of information technology or the media, and the restructuring of the welfare state and hence the limiting of the number of occupational positions in the public sector has reinforced this internal dividing line. But arguably, in terms of education, status and life-style, the self-employed professionals have less in common with members of the 'old' middle class

than with public sector professionals. And both groups within the 'new' middle class can clearly be distinguished from the 'lower' middle class, composed of routine, non-manual employees in clerical, secretarial and similar occupations, a sector that has become increasingly feminized over the last few decades.

The middle class of white-collar workers and professionals, but also the 'lower middle class' made up, for example, of those who work as office staff or ancillary staff, created problems for class analysis because they did not adequately encapsulate what had historically been understood by the term 'class'. Rather than being an homogeneous entity with its own peculiar set of norms, values and aspirations, they were perceived to lack the cohesion that – allegedly – had held the working class together; indeed, the 'middle class' was considered hardly to constitute a class at all. It was identified more by its heterogeneity than by its homogeneity. Orthodox Marxists had argued that there was no middle class as such and that any social strata lying in between the bourgeoisie and the proletariat would ultimately drop into the ranks of the proletariat. In time the tendency of capitalism to create ever deepening class division would lead this 'class' to realize where their interests lay, firmly with the rest of the working class. However, with the rise of the new middle class in the 1950s and 1960s there appeared to be something of a culture shift throughout society as a whole. It was apparent that the new middle class was not destined to disappear. Indeed, the aspirations of this class appeared to define an era marked by consumerism, a set of aspirations to be shared by a whole generation of people across North America and Western Europe. The new middle class, it was claimed, had aspirations and values that were altogether quite different from those of both the old industrial working class and the 'old' middle class.

In addition, it was also obvious to many in the labour movements of North America and Western Europe that the appeal of Marxism was beginning to lose its grip on the mass of the population. Its appeal had in any case always been somewhat marginal in all except Southern European countries. It was no longer the case, if it had ever been, that a politics committed to the overthrow of capitalism, would fall on receptive ears. Far from having nothing to lose but their chains, the workers now had cars, televisions, holidays and job security. The workers were not just 'workers' but were now consumers and as consumers their interests were tied closely to the success of capitalism. They had a degree of economic prosperity that allowed them more leisure time, greater job security and more access to consumer goods than ever before. On the part of the social democratic parties across Western democracies, these developments were deemed to require a shift in emphasis away from the ideologically more pure days of the inter-war period to an emphasis on a welfarist pragmatism.

With the decline and fall of state socialism since the 1970s there has been a marked decrease in the level of discussion concerning class. For many, 'class' has had its heyday and we have entered a period where the divisions that gave rise to the class conflicts that had marked the past are now gone. The reality, however, is somewhat different. Societies remain divided on a number of different levels whether they are class, race, religion or gender. Class may not be the central dividing line between social groups, but it is one of many and will continue to be so in societies where social inequalities exist that are grounded in the position of individuals within the economic structure. Those people who control, if not outrightly own, the means of production and hence determine the structure and the development of the economy, will always attempt to defend their position, and one way to do so is to mobilize political power. The control over economic resources will remain politically significant. But as the development of the new middle class amply demonstrates, control of knowledge (rather than the ownership of economic resources) may also translate into political power.

ELITISM

Elite theorists argue that in every type of society there is a continuous struggle for power between elites and the domination of the ruling elite(s) over the mass of society. The population is divided into those who rule and those who are ruled. A creative, self-conscious leadership group, variously described as the 'establishment', the 'political class', the 'ruling class', 'oligarchy' or, in short, the elite, rules, of necessity, over the unstructured, unorganized multitude, which is ultimately passive and incompetent, immature, irrational and easily manipulated. Any attempt to establish rule by the mass of the population is doomed to failure.

Against Marxists, elite theorists argue that those who claim to represent the working class themselves develop a self-interest, which often manifests itself in a sharing of characteristics and mannerisms of the very class they seek to overthrow. A working-class elite that became differentiated – economically, politically, culturally – from the rest of the working class was an elite that ceased to pursue the same aspirations as those they were supposed to represent. Consequently, the democratic ideal of representation is marred by the reality that those who 'represent' in fact *mis*-represent those in whose name they fight. Elitists also argue that rather than overthrowing class domination, Marxism sets up new and potentially more pernicious forms of domination, the rule of the 'avant-garde' party and its organizational elite. Since in a socialist society both economic and political power would be concentrated in the hands of this group, this elite's domination would be firmly entrenched.

Elitists are also critical of liberal democracy. Whereas liberal democracy is built around such notions as the rule of law, one person one vote and political equality, elitists argue that such ideas simply do not reflect the reality which consists of fundamental inequalities in power between the rulers and the ruled. The very existence of the state and its various tools for repression indicated that power was exercised unequally. Some writers have further argued that the existence of a ruling elite *ensured* democracy by preventing the rise of the masses to power. If the masses were too easily mobilized, then there would be the danger of mob rule and the rise of 'mass society'. The consequence would be an atomization of society and a breakdown of the institutional and social supports that give rise to a democratic culture among the populace at large. The existence of an elite, far from undermining democracy, would in fact act as a stabilizing force on democracy, allowing for the circulation of elites within set rules. This argument is drawn from the aristocratic rejection of democracy that has its roots in the work of Plato and Aristotle. The masses are seen as a potentially dangerous, irrational 'mob' that is easily aroused and prone to promoting the rise of demagogic power. Democracy is here best conceived as an arrangement in which the power of the mass or the mob is checked by the concentration of power in the hands of the elite.

Typologies

The elite theorists can be usefully divided into three types: classical, radical and democratic.

Classical elitism. Classical elitists emerged at around the turn of the twentieth century and were concentrated in Italy and Germany. In Germany, the expansion in support for the socialist Social Democratic Party had inaugurated a period of unprecedented electoral success for a working-class political party. Furthermore, as a result of (state-led) industrialization and national unification, bureaucratic structures came increasingly to dominate the state administration and political parties as well as the economy.

Among the classical elite theorists, the Italians Vilfredo Pareto and Gaetano Mosca and the German Robert Michels were the most prominent. Pareto famously stated that 'history was the graveyard of aristocracies'

rather than, as Marx had claimed, the battleground where antagonistic classes fight it out with each other until the oppressed class has overpowered the initially dominant, ruling class. He developed a 'psychological' elite theory, according to which elite power stems from particular psychological qualities that fit their carriers for leadership roles. Skilful, manipulative, cunning and inventive 'foxes', on the one hand, struggle against 'lions' which show strength of purpose, a willingness to use force, but who are also incorruptible. History shows a constant circulation between these two types of elite. Acquiring political power through manipulating the political machine to obtain the consent of the population, the 'foxes' would ultimately be overpowered through sheer force by the 'lions', employing coercion and violence to achieve their ends. Rule, however, cannot be routinized on the basis of force alone, and moves towards gaining consent would allow the 'foxes' to regain power – and so a new circle would begin.

Mosca and Michels, on the other hand, argued that elite power stems from superior organization and the possession of skills by certain members of society that are key to the functioning of society. Mosca famously stated that the organized few, acting in concert, will forever triumph over the unorganized masses. For Roberto Michels, taking his cue from the German sociologist Max Weber, elite power was based on bureaucratic power. Modern complex organizations are bureaucracies, and bureaucracies are inherently oligarchic and exclusive: rule by the elites of bureaucratic organizations was inevitable because only they can manage the organizational needs of modern, industrial-capitalist society. He showed that the 'iron law of oligarchy' also applied in the case of the German Social Democratic Party. He claimed that the move away from revolutionary socialism towards a reformist position, and thus, ultimately, an accommodation with capitalism and bourgeois society, can be explained by the self-interest of the oligarchic party elite which was at odds with the class interests of the movement as a whole.

Radical elitism. With the rise in bureaucracy that characterized 1950s North America there emerged the notion that all societies were beginning to take on a largely similar appearance. While some authors, such as Robert Dahl, argued in the 1950s and 1960s that America was a pluralistic society where numerous different interests throughout society were being represented in a competitive, democratic encounter, some had other ideas. C. Wright Mills argued in *The Power Elite* (1956/1959) that a trio of elites largely determined the fate of the United States: top corporation executives ('corporate chieftains'), military leaders ('warlords') and the political executives of the Washington administration. These elite groups share a similar set of social and cultural values as well as psychological affinities. As a 'power elite', they exercise power over the direction of society that is democratically not legitimated.

Crucial to the ascendance of economic, political and military power was the centralization and concentration of power into fewer hands. The American economy had become dominated by 200 or 300 giant corporations, administratively and politically interrelated, which together gained decisive influence over economic decisions. The political order had become a centralized, executive establishment which concentrated previously scattered powers and had permeated every sphere of social life. Finally, the military order had grown into one of the largest organizational clusters of government, drawing heavily on its financial resources and becoming increasingly bureaucratized. The leaders of each of these domains, so it was argued by Mills, tended to come together to form the 'power elite' of America. However, Mills ultimately grounded his analysis of the power elite in a theoretically even more intricate analysis of the United States' socio-political and socio-economic structure:

In so far as the structural clue to the power elite today [1956!] lies in the economic order, that clue is the fact that the economy is at once a permanent-war economy and a private-corporation economy. American capitalism is now in considerable part a military capitalism, and the most important relation of big corporation to the state rests on the coincidence of interests between military and corporate needs, as defined by warlords and corporate rich. Within the elite as a whole, this coincidence of interest between the high military and the corporate chieftains strengthens both of them and further subordinates the role of the merely political men. (Mills, 1956/1959: 275–6)

Arguably, at the beginning of the twenty-first century and with the rapid further militarization of US foreign policy in the context of 'the war on global terrorism', this analysis remains highly suggestive. Yet, lest Mills's theoretical position should be misconceived, it needs emphasizing that he developed the notion of 'power elite' as an alternative to the Marxist notion of 'ruling class'. For him, 'ruling class' was a phrase that combined the economic concept of class with the political concept of rule and thus contained the theory that economic class ruled politically. Because, so Mills claimed, this term 'does not allow enough autonomy to the political order and its agents, and it says nothing about the military as such' (Mills 1956/1959: 277, fn), Mills rejected it and substituted the concept of 'power elite'.

Democratic elitism. Mills's conception of a concerted power elite that could be neither controlled nor held accountable by the public is quite at odds with the position of 'democratic elitism' whose lineage can be traced back to the 1940s and an interpretation of elite behaviour that was most notably developed by the Austrian economist and sociologist Joseph Schumpeter. In the tradition of Gaetano Mosca, Max Weber and Roberto Michels, Schumpeter argued that the twentieth century had witnessed a growth in the complexity of modern industrial societies, and, consequently, the inexorable rule of organized and organizational elites. For Schumpeter, democracy was not 'government by the people', but 'government approved by the people'; democracy was the rule of the politician:

> [T]he role of the people is to produce a government, or else an intermediate body which in turn will produce a national executive or government. And we define: the democratic method is that institutional arrangement for arriving at political decisions in which individuals acquire the power to decide by means of a competitive struggle for the people's vote. (Schumpeter, 1976/1942: 269)

Democracy is thus an arrangement for the establishment of political leadership. The citizens' role in a democracy is limited to the act of voting. Furthermore, once politicians have been elected, the voters should withdraw from politics. Hence, this position set itself clearly apart from 'classical' democratic thinking. In the 'classical' democratic tradition, the direct participation of citizens in all aspects of public affairs was considered to be imperative for the person to achieve the full development of his (!) individual capacities. Whereas such direct involvement of an active citizenry in public life was seen to enhance freedom, for democratic elitists such direct popular democracy is impossible and undesirable: democracy needs competent leadership, not the irrationality of the masses; in complex societies democracy presupposes organization, and organization implies oligarchy – democracy and oligarchy are not starkly contrasting types of political rule (as Aristotle had suggested), but two sides of the same coin.

It is within this tradition that contemporary democratic elitism considers elite competition for electoral support as a key element of a democratic system. In elections, the passive and disorganized mass of voters becomes the arbiter of the political conflict. Elections enable the masses to remove from power an elite group which is unresponsive to their wishes. Furthermore, the multiplicity of sectional elites, their relative autonomy from each other on the basis of their respective control of resources, and the relative autonomy of societal elites from the elites of the state and government restrict elite power.

CONCLUSION

On first sight it might appear as if the theories of class rule and elite rule respectively have little in common. However, as John Scott's analytically innovative discussion of the question, *Who Rules Britain?* (1991), has brilliantly demonstrated, this is not necessarily the case. Scott develops an analytically intricate conceptual framework, as can be seen from the following key passage:

> A ruling class exists when there is both political domination and political rule by a capitalist class. This requires that there be a power bloc dominated by a capitalist class, a power elite recruited from this bloc, and in which the capitalist class is disproportionately represented, and that there are mechanisms which ensure that the state operates in the interests of the capitalist class and the reproduction of capital. In this sense . . . Britain does still have a ruling class. (Scott, 1991: 124)

Scott thus introduces a number of distinctions. First, he defines the 'power bloc' as an alignment of social groups, generally under the dominance of one of them. This alignment is able to monopolize the levers of political power in a society over a sustained period. While such an alignment brings together groups with divergent and partially conflicting interests, it is united through a common focus on the exercise of state power. In democracies, this power bloc is supported and sustained in electoral competition by an electoral bloc that comprises a wider alignment of social groups. It 'gives continued long-term support to the political party or parties of the power bloc in parliamentary or local elections, though its members are themselves outside the power bloc' (Scott, 1991: 122). One task in political analysis is thus to understand the linkage between power bloc and electoral bloc. Secondly, an analysis of state power has to focus on the institutional hierarchies of the state. As such, it is concerned with the 'state elite' which operates in and through the state apparatus, and thus comprises the key formal positions of authority within the state. Those who fill these positions at a particular time constitute a 'political elite'. Thirdly, political elites can take different forms: 'Where the political elite is strongly rooted in a power bloc, the political elite takes the form of a power elite. While all state societies will have a state elite, not all will have a power elite. The occupants of positions within the state elite comprise a power elite if [and only if, R.A./R.G.] they are recruited from a particular power bloc' (Scott, 1991: 37). Hence, another task in polit-ical analysis consists of determining whether the 'state elite' must be understood as a 'power elite'. On the basis of these conceptual distinctions, which draw on both class theory and elite theory, Scott arrives at his hypo-thesis that he then sets out to prove through an empirical analysis of the particular case of Britain: 'A capitalist class may be regarded as forming a ruling class when its economic dominance is sustained by the operations of the state and when, alone or through a wider power bloc, it is disproportionately represen-ted in the power elite which rules the state apparatus' (Scott, 1991: 38).

Scott's book shows impressively that it is possible to bring together different theoretical traditions and, through theoretically informed concept-building, to develop an analytical framework for empirical analysis.

Summary

- In this chapter, we have looked at social classes and elites as bearers of social and political power.
- For Marx, classes are defined by the position of their members within the economic system and, in particular, with regard to the ownership of the means of production.
- For Marx, economic power translates into political and ideological power.
- For Marx, political power is merely the organized power of one class for oppressing another.
- For elite theorists, politics is not conducted as a series of class struggles, but is a continuous struggle for power between elites and the domination of the ruling elite(s) over the mass of society.
- While there are elite theorists who are manifestly anti-democratic, such a stance is not immanent in elite theory. Mills's 'radical elitism' critically analyses the forces that impede democracy, and 'democratic elitism' sees democracy embedded in elite competition.

TUTORIAL QUESTIONS

1. **What are the key characteristics of a class?**

2. **How do elite theorists differ from Marxist theorists?**

3. **Can elitism be considered in any way 'democratic'?**

FURTHER READING

Robert C. Tucker (ed.) (1978) *The Marx-Engels-Reader* (New York and London: Norton, second edition) contains a good selection of texts by Marx and Engels on class, politics, ideology and the development of capitalism. The 'Communist Manifesto' of 1848 is the starting point for an engagement with Marx's concept of 'class'.

Peter Calvert (1982) *The Concept of Class: an Historical Introduction* (London: Hutchinson) remains a concise guide to the historical development of the concept of 'class', placing Marx's conceptualizations in a wider context in social and political theory.

Anthony Giddens (1981) *The Class Structure of the Advanced Societies* (London: Hutchinson) complements Calvert's text, but is theoretically more ambitious and has, since its publication, acquired the status of a 'classic' text itself.

Peter Saunders (1990) *Social Class and Stratification* (London: Routledge) covers theories of social class as well as evidence on class inequalities mainly in contemporary Britain in a brief introductory text.

C. Wright Mills (1956) *The Power Elite* (Oxford: Oxford University Press) is a splendid polemic and a modern 'classic'.

John Scott (1991) *Who Rules Britain?* (Cambridge: Polity Press) provides an excellent analysis of power in British society, combining aspects of class analysis and elite theory.

Eva Etzioni-Halevy (1993) *The Elite Connection: Problems and Potential of Western Democracy* (Cambridge: Polity Press) is a good introductory text to elite theory and develops 'democratic elitism' in interesting ways.

REFERENCES

Mills, C. Wright (1956/1959) *The Power Elite*. New York: Galaxy Books (imprint of Oxford University Press).

Schumpeter, Joseph (1976/1942) *Capitalism, Socialism and Democracy*. London: Allen & Unwin.

Scott, John (1991) *Who Rules Britain?* Cambridge: Polity Press.

Tucker, Robert C. (ed.) (1978) *The Marx-Engels-Reader* (second edition). New York and London: Norton.

See also chapters

PART II

Institutions and Political Behaviour

11 The Territorial State

Michael Keating

TERRITORY AND DEMOCRACY

In one sense we might say that all politics is territorial, since it takes place within a territorially defined political system, usually the sovereign nation-state. It is when we open up the nation-state box and look at the territorial divisions within it, however, that the close connection between territorial structures and power relationships becomes most apparent. Systems of representation, institutions and processes of policy-making can advantage particular actors and groups and favour particular outcomes depending on how they are organized.

There is no agreed view on the relationship of territorial government to democracy. On the contrary, there are radically opposed views, one of which has insisted on the need for a centralized state to give effect to the will of the people, while the other has associated democracy with decentralization and divided power. Nor is there a clear association between centralization and the political right and left. Most of the main political ideologies contain both centralist and decentralist traditions, although there is a strong tendency in the modern world to favour decentralization in principle, if not always in practice. Each country in the world has its own system of territorial government and its own political traditions but, for the sake of clarification, we can group them under three headings: the unitary state, the federal state and the de-volved or regionalized state. After discussing these constitutional models, we will consider the particular case of the plurinational state.

THE UNITARY STATE

The archetype of the unitary state is the Napoleonic system established in France after the Revolution of 1789, which swept away the traditional order inherited from the Middle Ages. The Revolution had established the principle of the sovereignty of the people and declared that the relevant people was the French nation. There could therefore be no room for rival centres of power in the provinces and localities, since this would undermine the principle of popular sovereignty itself. Equality of citizens meant, further, that rights and duties should be the same throughout the national territory, with no room for traditional privileges or differences. As elaborated in the course of the nineteenth century, this philosophy, known as Jacobinism, insisted that democracy and progress could be ensured only by rigorous uniformity. Napoleon's own contribution to this following the Revolution was to complete the work of the monarchs by establishing a centralized bureaucracy and a uniform system of law and administration. In due course this Napoleonic model was adopted by other countries, especially in Southern Europe and including Italy, Spain and Greece.

The key features of the Napoleonic system are, first, uniformity of policy. A story is told of a French Minister of Education in the nineteenth century who boasted to visitors that he could tell them the precise page of the exact book that every school pupil of a particular year was reading across France. Uniformity of policy is ensured by entrusting the administration of services to central civil servants operating on the ground, the 'field services'. So schoolteachers, police officers or road engineers would be employees of central government. Central officials known as prefects were appointed for each administrative division to represent the central government and coordinate its services. Elected local governments do exist in Napoleonic systems but they do not have extensive powers or resources and are under the tight control of the prefect.

In practice, matters are more complicated and the effort at centralization is often self-defeating. In order actually to get things done, prefects and the field services have to bend the rules to local circumstances. Local political figures, unable to act on their own, seek to penetrate the central state and exercise influence in national politics. In France this takes the form of the accumulation of mandates, by which it is common for a local mayor also to be the member of parliament or even a government minister. Indeed, the prime minister and the minister of the interior (in charge of local government) have often themselves been serving mayors. In this way, centralization merely generates new forms of local power and the central government, far from being all-powerful, becomes captured by local interests. At the same time, local government in Napoleonic systems tends to be rather important politically, even when it has little power. Turnouts in local elections tend to be high and the mayor is an important figure in the community. This further forces central government to take local interests seriously. So central–local relations become less a matter of top-down imposition than of elaborate bargaining.

A different model of unitary state is represented by the tradition of local self-government. Here democracy is associated with decentralization and pluralism rather than uniformity, but within an overall framework of unity. In this model, found not only in the United Kingdom but also in other English-speaking countries and within the federal units of federal states, there is a relatively small central administration. Most services are run by elected local governments, which have a substantial degree of autonomy in deciding how to provide them. In this way provision of services can be tailored to local needs and preferences. The locality is respected as a forum for self-government and democracy, as well as being a school for citizenship and responsibility. Yet while local government possesses a degree of independence, central government can have the last word and is free to change the shape and powers of local government when it judges it necessary. Such a system requires a delicate balance between central and local power, a mutual respect and a willingness for each level to play the game by the conventional rules. When the two levels are controlled by parties with very different ideologies, there may be conflict and a breakdown of relations.

These varieties of unitary state are ideal types and, as we have seen in the cases cited, cannot be taken as precise descriptions of reality. The territorial structure of the state is something that is always subject to political argument and contestation. So Napoleonic countries have always contained admirers of the British model of local self-government. In France they are known as Girondins, after the Jacobins' main opponents in the post-revolutionary politics. Conversely, Britain has seen its 'Jacobins', who sought centralization in order to secure equality and unity. Hence each unitary state in practice contains a balance of centralist and decentralist elements reflecting its own history and politics.

With the advance of the welfare state in the twentieth century, there has been a tendency for local government to lose power as national standards are imposed in the name of equity. So local democracy and equal treatment came increasingly into conflict. In the United Kingdom itself, local self-government has suffered from the constant reorganizations over the last 30 years and the centralist tendencies of governments of both parties, but especially the Conservative governments of 1979–97.

By contrast, Napoleonic systems have seen a tendency to decentralization. In the 1980s in France itself, the powers of local government were enhanced and those of the prefects reduced in a massive process of change. Democratization in Spain following the death of the dictator Franco in the 1970s was accompanied by decentralization to the regions or 'autonomous communities'. Italy in the 1990s has seen a shift of power away from the centre to the cities and regions and a similar process has begun in Greece. The motives for decentralization are varied. States have gradually realized that centralization may be counter-productive, since it overburdens the centre without increasing its ability to get its way. Paradoxically, it may be easier for central governments in more decentralized states to get their way than in centralized ones. This is because local interests in a decentralized state are external to the government, while in France the local mayors are sitting in the national parliament and even the cabinet. Transferring powers and responsibilities to local government may thus be a way for the centre to free itself politically and administratively and gain a degree of autonomy for itself. Decentralization is also seen as a way of increasing the accountability of local politicians, who will have to answer for their own decisions rather than blaming the centre when things go wrong or when there is not enough money for new projects. In this way, it is hoped that local democracy can be invigorated and local citizens can be encouraged to participate more fully in civic affairs. Where local government has been weakened, on the other hand, as in Britain or in the provinces of Canada, local interest declines, election turnouts fall and citizens become disenchanted.

Local government systems since the Second World War have undergone radical reforms, under the twin imperatives of democratization and efficiency. Often the two principles seem to be in conflict. Democracy points to small units permitting face-to-face deliberation and a sense of community. Efficiency has often pointed to larger units, especially as the expansion of public services has required the mobilization of large resources, the hiring of specialist staff and heavy investment in infrastructure. Most countries have consolidated their local governments into larger units, notably the United Kingdom, which has emphasized managerial considerations above all and has reorganized repeatedly over the last 120 years. At the other extreme is France, which still has over 36,000 communes, more than the rest of the European Union put together and has preferred to establish mechanisms for inter-communal cooperation rather than forcible mergers. The reason is the powerful position of local politicians within the French centralized state, giving them the ability to block reforms which might undermine their own power bases.

THE FEDERAL STATE

The main competitor to the unitary state is the federal state, in which power is formally divided between the federation (at the centre) and the federated units (which are called states in the USA, provinces in Canada and *Länder* in Germany). The political principle here is that democracy and liberty are best served by a division or sharing of power rather than by vesting it all in one institution. This represents the exact opposite to the Jacobin principle that democracy requires unity and uniformity. For the federalist, democracy is best conducted in smaller communities, reflecting people's local experience and identities, rather than in large, anonymous units. Federalists, unlike Jacobins, also harbour a certain suspicion of government, even democratic government, and believe that it should be balanced by countervailing powers and divided authority. In a federation, unlike a unitary state, the distribution of powers between the levels is guaranteed by the Constitution, and neither level can alter it without a formal constitutional change, normally requiring the consent of both the federal level and all or most of the federated units. Disputes over the relative powers of the two levels are settled by a constitutional court, which sometimes doubles as the supreme court of the federation. In principle, federations should have a second chamber in the federal parliament representing the constituent units, while the first chamber represents the citizens as individuals. In this way, unity is enhanced as the federated units are drawn into the national policy process. This principle is applied in Germany where the *Bundesrat* represents the *Länder* governments. In the United States, each state has two senators but as these are directly elected they do not really represent the states as institutions. In Canada, senators are nominated by the federal prime minister and merely deemed to be from the various provinces although neither the provincial governments nor their electors have any say in the matter.

Within the family of federal states, two varieties can be recognized. One is the separation-of-powers federalism found in the United States and Canada. Here the competences of each level are spelled out fully, with anything not mentioned falling to the states (in the USA) or the federation (in Canada). Each state is a self-contained political system and should be able to pursue its policies on its own. In practice, there is a great deal of overlap and interdependence between the responsibilities of the two levels so that 'layer cake' federalism, with each level sharply distinguished, has given way to 'picket fence' federalism, with lines of responsibility running both horizontally and vertically, or even to 'marble cake' federalism, where responsibilities are completely mixed up. Observers have also noticed a certain tendency for the emergence of vertical policy communities to emerge, of people who are involved in a given policy field and operate across the levels of government.

The other model is 'cooperative federalism', which accepts at the outset that the responsibilities of the two tiers are interdependent and that they must work closely together. This is the German tradition, kept alive in the Constitution and practice of modern Germany. While the *Länder* do keep some exclusive responsibilites in a few fields, most tasks are shared on the basis that the federal level passes broad, framework legislation, and the *Länder* are responsible for filling in the details and for implementation. The *Bundesrat*'s approval is required for all laws affecting *Land* responsibilities, which means in practice about two-thirds of all laws, as well as for taxation matters. Most taxes are set nationally, with *Bundesrat* approval, and the proceeds are distributed according to a formula. This contrasts with the United States and Canada, where states and provinces determine their own taxation levels. So while in US-style federalism, powers and responsibilities are divided, in the German model they are shared. As government has assumed new responsibilities, these have often been handled as 'joint tasks', a form of partnership between the two levels provided for in the Constitution. German cooperative federalism puts a heavy premium on national unity, consensus and willingness to compromise. The principle of 'federal loyalty' enjoins both sides to respect the rules and spirit of the game and not to press its advantage too far. These are cultural and political traits that cannot be reproduced at will; hence, while the German model has attracted a lot of interest and admiration, it has proved difficult to export it to other countries. Even within Germany, it has come in for criticism as the need for consensus can prevent needed adaptation to change. The wealthier *Länder* have also been increasingly critical of the financial distribution system which, they complain, makes them share too much of their wealth with their poorer compatriots. Inclusion of the poor eastern *Länder* into the system following unification in 1990 has further strained the system.

There are some common trends across federal systems although their impact is rather different according to the case. All have experienced a growing interdependence of the two levels as the tasks of modern government escape the old functional categories on which the division of powers was based. A second one, which goes rather in the opposite direction, is a growth in competition as federated units seek to position themselves within the international economy, seeking investment, technology and markets. Transnational integration and the panoply of effects captured by the term globalization impel them to look beyond national borders, seeking resources and allies elsewhere, and the wealthier ones often complain that the need to contribute to the support of their poorer neighbours damages their competitive potential. As the problems faced by government become more complex, governments are encouraged to seek more innovative solutions and this has revived the role of federated units as laboratories for policy experimentation, long recognized as one of the advantages of federalism. Yet as government becomes more complicated and policy-making retreats into complicated networks dominated by executives at both levels, the role of legislatures is diminished and there are increasing complaints about the democratic deficit, a familiar term in the debates about the European Union.

DEVOLUTION AND THE REGIONAL STATE

Since the 1960s a third model of territorial government has emerged in European unitary states, the devolved or regional state, sometimes described as the 'meso' level between centre and locality. This development has been fuelled by functional trends as well as democratizing impulses. The main functional impulse has been the need for planning and economic development machinery at the regional level, now recognized as a key level for the understanding and management of economic change. States which in the past managed their spatial economies by centralized regional policies, distributing public investment and steering private firms, find themselves less able to do this in conditions of European and global competition. Emphasis has thus shifted to more bottom-up policies, with regions taking more responsibility for their own development. Less stress is put on financial incentives or the steering power of big government, and more on the conditions for locally induced growth, including entrepreneurship, training and technology transfer, all of which are better delivered at the regional level. A second motivation lies in the old desire for central governments to reduce the political and administrative burden on themselves and to engage local and regional actors more fully. Then there is the democratic impulse as in many parts of Europe regions have become the focus of popular demands for self-government and participation. This is most clearly the case in historic nations like Scotland or Catalonia or in regions with a strong identity and culture like Flanders or Brittany.

Devolution is a formula whereby the state transfers powers down to the region or historic nation but without giving the regions the recognition as constitutional equals or limiting its own powers as would happen in a federal system. Devolution can take stronger or weaker forms. In France and Italy regional governments are rather weak and confined to specific tasks. Many of the regions are rather artificial and do not rest upon a strong sense of popular identity, although others have historic roots. Both countries hesitated long before setting up regions, fearing their power to disturb the workings of the centralized state. In France, the gestation of regions lasted from the 1950s, through a period of indirectly elected councils, until 1986 when they were finally elected. Although regions featured in the Italian post-war Constitution of 1946 they were not actually set up until 1970 and received their powers only in 1976. In both France and Italy, regions must co-exist with local governments and a third level, known in France as the department and in Italy as the province. Spain has a stronger system of regional governments, known as autonomous communities, recognized in the Constitution of 1978. Although the Spanish political parties had hoped to confine devolution to the historic territories of Catalonia, the Basque Country and Navarre, they included a provision allowing any region to claim it, and in the event all of them did. Spanish autonomous communities are protected by the Constitution and have rather broad competences, to the point that some people argue that Spain is becoming a federation in practice if not in name. In a similar way, Belgium evolved during the 1980s and 1990s from a devolved state, with regions and language communities, to a fully-fledged federation, recognized in the constitutional changes of 1993.

Since 1999, the United Kingdom has been a partially devolved state, with very different settlements for Scotland, Wales and Northern Ireland, reflecting the distinct conditions in each territory. Scotland has a legislative parliament with wide powers and a government responsible to it. Northern Ireland has a legislative assembly with an executive formed on a power-sharing basis by all the main parties. Wales has an assembly with only administrative and secondary legislative powers. There is a longstanding debate about establishing regional government within England but so far there are only indirectly elected assemblies responsible for guidance on planning and economic development. The United Kingdom settlement is thus highly asymmetrical. There are elements that look rather federal, such as the broad powers of the Scottish Parliament and Northern Ireland Assembly, but central government and the main parties have set their faces against a full federal system and have insisted that devolution is merely an act of the central parliament, which thus retains ultimate power and authority.

THE PLURINATIONAL STATE

Democracy, as understood in the western state tradition, presupposes the existence of a *demos*, or people. In most cases this is taken to be the nation and the nation is in turn defined by the boundaries of the state. It is not that the nation is somehow a natural unit or precedes the state. Much of the history of France is about moulding a diverse set of peoples and cultures into a national unity. This in turn allowed France to develop its Jacobin conceptions of democracy, in which a unitary people expresses a unitary will. In Germany, the nation largely preceded the state, based on common language, culture and historic experience. So the German federal system with its division and sharing of power is held together by a common national identity. In other cases, however, state and nation do not coincide so easily. Despite the efforts of its monarchs over the centuries, Spain remains a complex state in which a Spanish identity co-exists with rival national identities in the three historic nationalities of Catalonia, the Basque Country and Galicia. Most Spanish people in the central regions feel only Spanish, but in the three historic nationalities most people have a dual identity while some have only a single loyalty, to their local nation, and do not feel Spanish at all. The United Kingdom contains three historic nations, England, Scotland and Wales and part of a fourth, Ireland. As in Spain, identities are complex, with many English people conflating the categories of British and English, while most Scots and Welsh have a dual national identity, or identify only with their local nation. Similarly, in Canada, the people of Quebec have a complex identity, with Canadian and Quebecois elements mixed in different proportions in individual citizens.

In these cases, democratic principles would

seem to require a recognition of the complexity and plurality of the *demos* or people. For some of the peoples of the minority nations, this can be achieved only by secession and setting up a separate state. Mostly, however, it points to a degree of self-government for the nations within an overall state framework shared with the others, thus allowing people to express their dual sense of belonging. The problem is that these national identities and demands tend to be highly asymmetrical. There has been a strong demand in Scotland for a local national parliament, but almost none whatever in England. Quebeckers are almost united in their desire for special recognition as a nation and most of them would like to see this nation remaining within Canada. Citizens elsewhere in Canada, however, insist that there can be only one nation and the Quebeckers should get no special recognition. Even in France there are nationalist movements in historic territories like Brittany and Corsica, despite centuries of assimilationist policies, but the French political class, steeped in Jacobin assumptions, finds it almost impossible to recognize them. In Belgium, demands for recognition and further autonomy are greater in Flanders than in Wallonia.

The United Kingdom has grappled with this problem for nearly 200 years and its politicians historically resisted giving autonomy to its constituent nations, fearing that they would become the main focus of citizen loyalty and legitimacy. A rival tradition, associated since the nineteenth century with Liberal Prime Minister Gladstone, favoured giving 'home rule' to the component nations in order to reconcile them to the union with England. Finally, in 1999 the Gladstonian tradition triumphed in the form of a highly asymmetrical form of devolution to three of the four constituent nations. There are pressures in Spain to follow a similar route, allowing greater powers to the historic nationalities and even the French have talked about making some special provision for Corsica. Critics point out that asymmetrical devolution, while giving more self-rule to the minority nations, creates problems at the centre which has to function both as a general government for the whole country and as a particular government for the non-devolved parts. The main one concerns equal democratic rights when representatives from the home rule nationalities continue to vote in the national parliament on matters that affect only the majority nation, being devolved elsewhere. In the United Kingdom this is known as the West Lothian Question after a Scottish MP who asked why, after devolution, he could vote on domestic matters in a range of English towns but not in his own Scottish constituency. Similar questions have been posed in other countries.

There is in fact no answer to the West Lothian Question. It is an inevitable result of the existence of overlapping and multiple national identities and the need to give them recognition in democratic institutions. Further complications arise in territories where identity is contested or a historic culture or nation straddles two states, as in Northern Ireland or the Basque Country. Here too recent British experience is instructive. In the Good Friday Agreement of 1998 there is a highly complicated set of mechanisms allowing citizens to express identities as British, as Irish or as Northern Irish, and an elaborate form of power-sharing and divided authority involving the United Kingdom, the Republic of Ireland and a Northern Ireland Assembly itself designed on power-sharing principles. Another complex arrangement exists in Belgium, where there are three regions – Flanders, Wallonia and Brussels – and three language communities – the Flemish, the French and the German. These largely coincide in Flanders to the point that the Flemish region and language community have merged their institutions, but do not coincide on the French side since the French-speaking population of Brussels do not consider themselves to be Walloons.

CONCLUSION

There is therefore no one answer to the question of territory and democracy. Rather, the debate about territorial government reflects the age-old debate about representation itself, and the extent to which it should be based on individuals as in the Jacobin conception or on communities. It also reflects the argument between those who would centralize authority in the name of efficiency and democratic unity and those who would divide it in the name of pluralism and liberty.

Summary

- We can divide systems into unitary and federal ones.
- Unitary systems may be more or less centralized, varying from the Napoleonic state to the traditional system of local self-government.
- Centralized states have tended to decentralize, while more decentralized states have tended to centralize, leading to some convergence between the two.
- Federal states can be divided into the separation-of-powers model and the cooperative model.
- There has been a tendency to interdependence and cooperative federalism over the years.
- At the same time there is a trend to competitive federalism.
- In recent years, unitary states have seen the growth of a regional or 'meso' level, creating an intermediate category between unitary and federal states.
- Plurinational states, containing more than one national community, raise specific issues of accommodation, often met by asymmetrical devolution.

TUTORIAL QUESTIONS

1. 'Apoplexy at the centre, paralysis at the extremes.' Why might this description be applied to Napoleonic systems of centralization?

2. What are the key differences between separation-of-powers federalism and cooperative federalism?

3. Have centralized systems tended to decentralize and decentralized systems to centralize? If so, why?

FURTHER READING

John Loughlin (2001) *Subnational Democracy in the European Union* (Oxford: Oxford University Press) offers a review of local and regional government in the 15 states of the European Union.

Michael Keating (1998) *The New Regionalism in Western Europe. Territorial Restructuring and Political Change* (Aldershot: Edward Elgar) is an analysis of territorial politics in Western Europe and the rise of regions as economic, political and institutional systems of action.

Ronald L. Watts (1999) *Comparing Federal Systems* (Montreal: McGill–Queen's University Press) provides a comparative analysis of federations across the world.

Michael Burgess (1995) *The British Tradition of Federalism* (London: Leicester University Press) traces the influence of federal ideas in British politics.

Daniel J. Elazar (1987) *Exploring Federalism* (Tuscaloosa, AL: University of Alabama Press) is an overview of federal theory and federal systems and of modern trends in federalism.

Daniel J. Elazar (ed.) (1991) *Federal Systems of the World* (London: Longman) provides a comprehensive description of all the world's federal systems.

See also chapters

1   Sovereignty
7   Majoritarianism – Consociationalism
12 Government, Civil Service and Public Policies
22 Democratic Citizenship in the Age of Globalization
25 Socialism – Marxism
26 Anarchism and Democracy

12 Government, Civil Service and Public Policies

Grant Jordan and Emma Clarence

A simplistic image of public policy envisages governments deciding what a policy should be and civil servants implementing that policy – or at least that is how the policy-making process may appear judged by political and parliamentary conventions. However, the reality of public policy is far more complex than this image allows. The relationships between governments, the civil service and the public policy-making process need to be examined in order to make sense of how policy is made and implemented. Following on from this, it is possible to explore the important changes that have occurred in how governments govern and how those changes have impacted upon citizens. Specifically, accountability – or the ability to hold someone to account for the actions done in his or her name – has been altered by the changes in the relationship between governments and the civil service. This has profound implications for the ways in which individuals can interact with governments. While this chapter draws widely on British examples, its key themes are ones that have a resonance for many other western countries.

PUBLIC POLICY-MAKING

Broadly, public policy is the term given to the decisions and direction of a government as well as the ideas which lead to actions to achieve certain aims and objectives. How that policy is made is important to consider. Governments alone do not make policy. Practically, policy-making is a complex process in which a multiplicity of actors can have a role. The government, the civil service, interest groups, 'think tanks', the media and 'popular opinion' among others can all influence policy-making.

Briefly, the policy process can be divided into four stages: policy initiation, formulation, implementation and evaluation. The policy initiation stage is where issues are identified as needing to be addressed by government. Such issues can emerge from within government or, alternatively, the government may be forced to react to issues that have developed away from the government, possibly through public concern or from events or a 'crisis'. It is at this stage that the problem to be addressed will be defined and its importance will be established. 'Agenda-setting' is a crucial stage for all those involved in the policy process as they seek to ensure that their interpretation of the problem and how important it is dominates. Two approaches can be identified in policy initiation: 'top-down' and 'bottom-up'. A top-down approach is one in which governments and civil servants identify the issue and seek to control its definition. A bottom-up approach is one where pressure is exerted to have an issue recognized and defined from 'below' – such pressure may come from interest groups, public opinion and the media. Policy initiation can be seen as a process of discussion, negotiation and contestation since how a problem is interpreted has far-reaching consequences for how public policy will be formulated.

The next stage is policy formulation, during which decisions are taken on how a problem will be addressed. This incorporates the development of different options and assessments of what resources (financial, time, staffing) are available, who will implement the policy and how it will be implemented. The problem will be examined and analysed, various options set out before government and possibly others involved in the process, and an option selected for implementation. Different models for policy formulation exist and it is important to recognize that the policy formulation process can vary between different countries and over time.

Implementation is the process by which the issue first highlighted in the policy initiation stage is practically addressed. At this stage it is possible again to use the ideas of 'top-down' and 'bottom-up' to explain policy implementation. A top-down approach to policy implementation will focus on those at the top having greater control over how a policy is implemented than those who are actually implementing the policy. Alternatively, a bottom-up approach will allow for greater flexibility in policy implementation and will enable those implementing the policy to respond to different circumstances and needs that may arise. There are benefits and problems associated with both approaches which must be considered during the processes of formulating and implementing policy.

It is not surprising that there are often significant differences between a policy as it was formulated, a policy as it was implemented and the results of a policy against the stated aims. Such changes may occur as a result of implementing a policy responsive to the needs of users and/or other events. Alternatively, it may be because a policy was not adequately or appropriately developed. There are many factors that impact on the implementation of a policy. Problems are not static, they shift and alter over time and are subject to other issues and events affecting them. Other factors include the level and appropriateness of resources, the time span available for the policy to be implemented, the flexibility of a policy to take account of changes in circumstances and a clear chain of command and responsibility. The evaluation stage is important in providing evidence of not only what policies worked best in given situations but also what did not work and what could be improved upon. It can be seen as both the end and the beginning of the policy process, with new policies often emerging from the evaluation of previous policies.

While the policy process can be neatly divided up on paper, the reality is significantly more complex and interlinked. Crucially, distinguishing between policy and operational (or implementation) matters, both in terms of activities and staffing, is not easy. The way in which an issue is defined, the policy chosen to be implemented, the resources given to implement a policy and other policies that may impact on the implementation of a policy are effectively outside the remit of those whose sole purpose is to implement a policy if such a distinction is made. It is important to remember this distinction, and the problems associated with it, when considering accountability.

Understanding the policy process is important in order to explore the changes that have occurred in the way governments govern. Even in the basic rendering of the policy process outlined above it is possible to see that governments alone do not initiate and decide policy, and the civil service alone are not responsible for producing the options set before governments and implementing and evaluating. Practically, it is even clearer. Government ministers have neither the time nor necessarily the expertise to be solely responsible for policy-making; they are reliant on advice and guidance. Such advice and guidance can come from civil servants, political advisers and outside organizations. Furthermore, the nature of the policy process means that governments are not solely responsible for devising policies. Pressure from below, events and crises, make policy-making a messy and complex business.

ACCOUNTABILITY

The conventions surrounding who is accountable for government decisions are based on a version of the policy process which assumes the dominance of politicians. While the academic debates on accountability have long since recognized the inadequacy of this model, it is one that continues to be upheld by the overwhelming majority of politicians and civil servants. Constitutionally, governments are responsible to parliament for their decisions and actions. The centrality of this point to the British constitution should not be underestimated. Within government, traditional accountability conventions, specifically on collective responsibility and individual ministerial responsibility (IMR), continue. Collective responsibility is where government ministers must accept and advocate a decision that has been taken collectively in cabinet – even if privately they disagree with it. This is not always maintained although the political consequences of apparent government disunity are often sufficient to limit the public visibility of such disagreements.

A more problematic convention is that of IMR. The convention demands that ministers accept responsibility for matters within and actions taken by their departments. In effect this means that ministers are responsible for the actions, and errors, of civil servants within their department. It is the vicarious nature of IMR that has been important – the apparent willingness of ministers to sacrifice themselves for the errors of others. It is also the vicarious nature of IMR that has made it

honoured more in the breach than in the practice. Ministers have proved themselves unwilling to accept responsibility for the errors of others, preferring instead (at best) to account for what has gone wrong and seek to improve, if not rectify, the problem. This has important consequences when considered with the changes that have occurred in the structures of government that will be explored further below.

Unlike governments and ministers, conventions do not permit civil servants to be held directly accountable to parliament; for civil servants, accountability runs upwards to their minister. The accountability of civil servants is further illustrated by what is known as the 'Osmotherly Memorandum' (Pyper, 1996: 67). The memorandum offered civil servants guidance on appearing before parliamentary select committees and made clear that they appear only to further the accountability of their ministers and are subject to the instructions given by ministers. While in theory such a model may appear to provide a clear articulation of who is responsible for what and to whom, the changes that have taken place in government in the past decades have served only to highlight the inadequacy of the model (Barberis, 1998). Civil servants are more than policy implementers; they formulate policy and advise on the formulation of policy. By accepting that civil servants are policy-makers, it becomes necessary to incorporate civil service actions into models of accountability.

NEW PUBLIC MANAGEMENT

New Public Management (NPM) was the term given by Christopher Hood (1991) to a set of ideas that appeared to underpin the changes that had been taking place in public policy. These 'mega-trends', as Hood (1991: 3) called them, included attempts to check the growth of government, both in size and in spending, the privatization or quasi-privatization of services, automation (specifically information technology) and the internationalization of the public policy agenda. Despite the looseness of the label it is possible to identify important characteristics of NPM. Briefly, these are:

- A shift away from issues of policy towards the management of service provision. Named individuals become responsible for government service delivery through agencies (and other government bodies or through the private sector) rather than the traditional anonymous, hierarchical structure of civil servants with a minister at the top.
- An emphasis on being able to measure (quantifiably) the performance and efficiency of agencies and other service providers.
- A greater focus on results rather than procedures. The idea of 'what works' is more important than how the work is done.
- The break-up of large units/departments into smaller ones; the smaller units being granted greater autonomy. Such units would interact, potentially providing each other with goods and services, but this would be done on a 'user-pays' basis, with units paying for the real cost of the goods and services they use.
- A move towards greater competition within the public sector. Rivalry between these smaller units becomes central to driving down costs and improving the standard of goods and services delivered.
- An emphasis on 'proven' private sector management techniques. This incorporates performance-related benefits and greater employment flexibility.
- Attempting to 'do more with less' by limiting resources and demanding greater financial discipline. (Hood, 1991: 4–5)

These ideas resonate with developments in the last two decades, but their novelty can be oversold. It is important to remember that Hood saw NPM as a trend rather than a destination in itself, and that accordingly not all the characteristics of NPM are evident in all of the reforms made to government.

The 'rolling back of the state' thesis is one that has been associated with many of the reforms and changes that have taken place in government. The social democratic consensus that had emerged after the Second World War, which saw a planning and interventionist role for governments in economic issues, was challenged by the emergence of a neo-liberal consensus, which argued for governments to withdraw from such areas and allow the market (and market mechanisms) to take its course, with governments only taking a regulatory role. Government would decrease both in size and expenditure, it would retreat from some areas altogether and limit its role in others – the state would effectively be 'rolled back'. However, while it is clear that the language used by government has shifted, there is conflicting evidence in support of a practical shift. Government expenditure (as a proportion of Gross Domestic Product) has not fallen significantly in the period following the decline of the social democratic consensus. Furthermore, the processes of centralization, whereby central government has extended its power over areas that previously had greater autonomy, contradict the rolling back of the state thesis. Regulatory powers have also been used by central government to influence and interfere in economic issues. Thus, the claim that the state has been 'rolled back' with the shift towards a neo-liberal consensus is less well founded than the rhetoric appears to indicate.

IMPLEMENTING NEW PUBLIC MANAGEMENT: NEXT STEPS AND BEYOND

A series of changes to the structure of the civil service has altered both the traditional lines of service delivery as well as accountability. The first big, if strangely invisible, development in organization in the NPM era was the invention of departmental agencies announced in 1988 in the 'Next Steps initiative' (Efficiency Unit, 1988). The civil service was to be radically changed by distinguishing between a core of civil servants who would make policy and numerous executive or Next Steps agencies that would focus on the delivery of services. Ultimately, civil servants involved in executive agencies would develop an expertise in delivering services while the expertise of the smaller core would lie in policy-making.

Executive agencies were to be developed out of existing government departments by 'hiving off' particular functions. Functions that were to be transferred to agencies were those where ministers were not required to have 'day-to-day' management and there was the potential for managerial innovation. Agencies remained part of government in that ministers appointed chief executives and agency staff were civil servants. However, Next Steps agencies were given a significant degree of autonomy and freedom over how they spent their budgets and structured their operations. Furthermore, senior managers within agencies could be appointed on fixed-term contracts and with performance-related pay. Crucially, however, accountability to parliament for the operation of an agency was to remain with the minister.

Next Steps agencies were based on the premise that it was both possible and desirable to draw a distinction between policy formulation and policy implementation. They were also founded on the idea that ministers would seek to maintain that distinction and therefore refrain from intervening (or interfering) in agencies. The reality of these assumptions were to be tested repeatedly as ministers sought to distinguish between what was a policy matter (and therefore their responsibility) and what was an operational matter (and, despite commitments that ministers would remain accountable for agencies, a matter for agency managers). Nor were ministers necessarily able to restrain themselves from involving themselves in matters that were meant to be the province of agency managers. The basic premises on which agen-

cies were founded were compromised by the realities of government.

The design and structure of agencies clearly contributed to the tensions that arose between agencies and ministers. If ministers were to be accountable for the actions of an agency it was unlikely that they would be willing not to intervene in the running of an agency, particularly in politically sensitive areas such as, for example, prisons. The unsustainable policy/operation split further compounded the difficulties. If ministers had sought to maintain this division and the ideas and conventions surrounding parliamentary accountability, it is clear that agencies would have had to be made accountable to parliament. Instead, accountability structures remained unchanged, regardless of the challenge Next Steps agencies posed to parliamentary accountability.

Executive agencies are seen to be part of the NPM agenda as it was developed in Britain. However, agencies are not full-blown examples of NPM in that they do not operate by competitive bidding and enforceable contracts. Central to bringing about change through executive agencies was the use of stated efficiency and performance targets. Departments were meant to set challenging targets for agencies, the attainment of which would drive down costs. This route to efficiency differs from the market competition that is central to NPM.

In other areas of government service provision, markets have been introduced to the delivery of public services in ways that appear to provide more direct NPM elements. The introduction of Compulsory Competitive Tendering (CCT) to various local services throughout the 1980s and 1990s is a clear example. CCT required local authorities to put out to tender various services, with service delivery contracts being awarded to the lowest bidders. This was one of the bluntest examples of the introduction of the market to public service delivery and while it may have been successful in lowering costs, it did not necessarily lead to improvements in the services provided. In central government 'market testing' was used in the belief that subjecting aspects of the civil service (such as legal and accountancy services) to a tendering process would increase efficiency either by improving the quality and cost of 'in-house providers' or by allowing external organizations to provide the services at a lower cost.

There has been significant disagreement regarding the desirability of market perspectives in public services. Such disagreements were initially seen as being along ideological lines, with the Conservative Party being associated with the drive to introduce the market into public services, and the Labour Party opposing such changes. However, the election of the Labour government in 1997, far from reversing the role of the private sector, has actually sought to increase it. Following the 2001 general election the Prime Minister, Tony Blair, made a speech outlining increased private sector involvement in government service delivery. In particular, the private sector was to be closely involved in the planned wave of new specialist schools, the programme of hospital building and social services (*The Times*, 17 July 2001).

The idea of 'what works' has been crucial to the Labour government. Opposition to the role of both the market and the private sector in service delivery has been dropped. Many of the previous reforms have continued. However, problems associated with previous initiatives have not gone unrecognized. In particular, the failure of government departments and agencies to work together, across organizational boundaries, has prompted a drive for a 'joined-up' approach to policy-making and implementation. This approach recognizes that there are difficult, 'cross-cutting' issues that fall within the remit of various departments and agencies that can be addressed only by coordinating the government's response. Furthermore, there have been attempts to lessen the negative aspects of the introduction of the market into government services by shifting the focus away from the cheapest supplier to taking a broader approach which looks for the 'best

supplier'. Thus, the quality of the goods and services, overall efficiency and value for money is examined along with the total cost. The dilemma is of course that competitive tendering was introduced to avoid the unacceptable face of partnership – collusion, inflated prices and feather bedding.

The private sector and the voluntary and community sectors are integral to the delivery of government goods and services. A number of initiatives have emanated from the Labour government which have sought to draw the private sector even further into the provision of government goods and services, and the trend towards NPM characteristics already evident has continued. Coordination of government activities has been accompanied by a move towards greater partnership working with organizations outside government. Public Private Partnerships (PPP) and the Private Finance Initiative (PFI) are indicative of the ways in which government has sought to access private sector resources. PFI has been used to fund projects which government has argued could not be funded directly by government due to resource limitations. Thus, private money has been used to build and operate projects, with the private sector recouping the cost (and profits) by charging users (including individuals and government). The PFI is a very formal and large-scale example of PPP and there are numerous examples of smaller PPPs.

RESPONSIBILITY AND DEMOCRACY

The conventions of accountability outlined previously have clearly been challenged by the changes that have occurred to the way in which governments govern. The (false) split between policy-making and operations has allowed government ministers to distance themselves from policy failures, claiming instead that the failure was a result of poor implementation rather than any fault with the policy itself. Civil servants, even within Next Step agencies, find themselves unable to account for their actions, governed as they are by the Osmotherley Rules. Ministers are able to evade parliamentary accountability by asserting that ministers are responsible only for policy matters, not operational matters. The increased use of the private sector further complicates who is accountable for government service provision.

However, does it, or should it, matter who delivers services or is it enough to focus on 'what works'? For a citizen there are important implications for responsibility and accountability with regard to who delivers services. For a consumer the provision of the most efficient and effective services may be the central concern. Individuals within society are both citizens and consumers of government services and there is an apparent tension between the two roles. The relationship between government and individuals as citizens – with duties and responsibilities accompanied by rights and access to goods and services provided by government – has been affected by the changes that have taken place. Increasingly, individuals are seen as consumers – individuals who use services provided by governments. Thus, the 'what works' mantra has dominated government policy-making, arguably to the detriment of procedures and structures which at least nominally sought to ensure adequate levels of accountability.

To view individuals as consumers significantly alters the relationship between people and government. In a marketplace consumers can select their supplier; if one supplier is unsatisfactory, there will be another company that will be able to provide satisfactory goods or services. However, in many areas of government (such as health care and education), most of the public have no realistic consumer rights and no capacity to take their business elsewhere. In such circumstances accountability for individuals comes through parliament, with individuals exercising their rights as citizens to demand changes to government policies, rather than as consumers, with the

consumers' ability to find an alternative supplier.

The use of PPPs and PFI are important to consider in this context. The incorporation of the private sector into the provision of public services, and the government's role as a contractual overseer, removes service provision from an overtly political forum to one where the politicized nature of the environment is less clear. In this instance, the reduction of citizenship to consumer choice is not as important as the impact of the 'government as manager' construct on democratic accountability.

Given the reluctance of ministers to accept responsibility for the errors of civil servants and the work of agencies, as the convention dictates, it is not surprising that ministers have proven themselves to be even more unwilling to accept responsibility for the failures of the private sector in service provision. The shift towards market-driven government has led to a move away from IMR towards what can be termed 'managerial accountability'. Managerial accountability focuses on attempts to ensure that those to whom the responsibility of carrying out tasks has been devolved – managers – have actually to meet agreed criteria. Thus, contracts signed between governments and organizations chosen to deliver services or goods will clearly specify what is to be delivered and at what cost. Implicit in this shift is the assumption that politicians will be accountable for the policy direction of governments while managers will be accountable for the implementation of those policies. There should be both political and managerial accountability.

However, political accountability through parliament, as discussed previously, has been seriously weakened. Therefore, what remains is managerial accountability. From the citizen's perspective there is little ability to call managers to account. Contracts and agreed performance criteria are between governments and outside service providers, not citizens and service providers. Managerial accountability is a tool used by governments, but one which citizens can access only through political accountability. If governments construct citizens as little more than consumers of government goods, it is not-surprising that people do not necessarily view citizenship as about rights and responsibilities. If it is unclear who is accountable and individuals feel that governments cannot be held to account because issues are identified as being about managerial not political accountability, then citizens may feel distanced from government. In return, the importance of the responsibilities of citizenship become diluted, if not lost.

The choice that has been presented by successive governments – between improved public services if provided through market mechanisms and decaying public services if provided directly by governments – is false. To construct the choice in such a way creates a perception that until the shift towards market-based mechanisms occurred governments were unconcerned about efficiency. All governments are concerned about efficiency; it is how that efficiency is achieved and at what cost, or benefit, that is crucial to political debate. In political practice we have strayed from a picture-book image of democracy, of parties competing with ideologically informed manifestos and the public selecting a broad programme to be implemented by selecting one or another set of politicians. Instead, what has appeared are competing politicians and rhetoric but with only a very narrow set of policy differences. Governments have settled on politically prioritizing efficiency because they think that electoral success is the reward for maximizing public services and restricting taxation.

CONCLUSION

The changes to government structures and the introduction of procedures and ways of working characterized as NPM have had far-reaching effects upon the civil service. More than three-quarters of civil servants worked in agencies only a decade after they were first introduced. These changes provide powerful evidence of the shift away from ideological discussions about what policies should be implemented to a pragmatic approach of 'what works'. They also indicate the declining importance of meaningful and practical concepts of accountability. Policy implementers are not accountable to parliament except through ministers who absolve themselves of responsibility because it was an operational matter, rather than a policy matter.

Governments envisage individuals as consumers of government services, concerned only with the quality of services provided. Accountability through parliament is replaced with accountability through contract, a process from which citizens, who are limited by the system of representative democracy that underpins parliamentary accountability, are excluded. The rights of citizens to hold, through parliament, governments to account has been lost in favour of the promise to deliver more efficient and effective government services. Governments, by slowly whittling away parliamentary accountability have, by their actions, tried to persuade citizens that there was a choice to be made between intangible notions of accountability and tangible service delivery. However, no such choice was ever necessary; it is possible to balance democratic accountability for service delivery with the effective provision of services if governments and ministers have the political will to do so.

Summary

- The process of making public policy is far more complex and messy than parliamentary and government conventions on responsibility and accountability allow for.
- Changes to the structure of government, with the introduction of agencies, have led to attempts to draw a distinction between policy-making and policy implementation. Such a distinction cannot be drawn convincingly.
- The changes to government and the increased role of the private sector in service delivery have challenged conventions on accountability.
- Ideas about 'what works' have come to dominate policy debates.
- The relationship between individuals and governments is based on the assumption that individuals consume government goods and services and that accountability is irrelevant.

TUTORIAL QUESTIONS

1. **Examine the policy process. Is it possible to draw meaningful distinctions between the various stages of the process?**

2. **To what extent is 'what works' more important than issues of accountability? Should individuals be concerned about accountability?**

FURTHER READING

P. Barberis (1998) 'The New Public Management and a New Accountability', *Public Administration*, **76**: 451–70 outlines the problems which NPM has exacerbated in accountability. It is illustrated with British examples.

P. Barberis (ed.) (1996) *The Whitehall Reader: the UK's Administrative Machine in Action* (Buckingham: Open University Press) provides a valuable collection of material covering all aspects of British administration.

Efficiency Unit (1988) *Improving Management in Government: the Next Steps* (London: HMSO) was the document which set out the Next Steps initiatives.

P. Greer (1994) *Transforming Central Government: the Next Steps Initiative* (Buckingham: Open University Press) outlines the shift to agency government and its impact.

H. Heclo and A Wildavsky (1974) *The Private Government of Public Money* (London: Macmillan) is a classic text on how decisions are taken on spending government money.

P. Hennessy (1989) *Whitehall* (London: Secker and Warburg) provides an important historical overview of the British bureaucracy.

C. Hood (1991) 'A Public Management for All Seasons?', *Public Administration*, **69**: 3–19 establishes the concept of New Public Management.

W. Kickert and R. Stillman (eds) (1999) *The Modern State and its Study: New Administrative Sciences in a Changing Europe and United States* (Cheltenham: Edward Elgar) offers an international perspective on public policy.

R. Pyper (ed.) (1996) *Aspects of Accountability in the British System of Government* (London: Tudor Business Publishing) examines ideas of accountability as well as providing practical illustrations of accountability in the United Kingdom.

REFERENCES

Barberis, P. (1998) 'The New Public Management and a New Accountability', *Public Administration*, **76**: 451–70.

Efficiency Unit (1988) *Improving Management in Government: the Next Steps*. London: HMSO.

Hood, C. (1991) 'A Public Management for All Seasons?', *Public Administration*, **69**: 3–19.

Pyper, R. (ed.) (1996) *Aspects of Accountability in the British System of Government*. London: Tudor Business Publishing.

See also chapters

10   Class – Elites   16   Interest Groups

13 Parliaments

David Arter

Parliaments are a virtually ubiquitous phenomenon. The number of countries that have never had one (mainly in the Middle East) can be counted on the fingers of two hands. The Pitcairn Island, with fewer than 100 inhabitants, has one (Norton, 1990: 1). Parliaments exist at the national, transnational and regional levels. Even the Samis or Lapps of northern Norway, Sweden and Finland have their own assemblies. The age of parliaments varies enormously. Some are extremely old. The Icelandic *Althing* dates back to 930, when its creation marked the unification of the various Norse settlements within a single nation. Some, like the legislatures of post-communist Central and Eastern Europe, are in their adolescence (Norton and Olsen, 1996: 231–43). Others, such as the devolved Scottish and Welsh assemblies, are in their infancy.

The structure of parliaments has also varied. In the century or so before the achievement of mass democracy, legislatures represented the social estates (*états/Stände*) – typically the nobility, clergy, burghers and peasants, and this type of quadricameral Diet of Estates survived in Prussia until the First World War. In communist Yugoslavia there was a quinticameral assembly with one chamber elected using the corporate rather than territorial principle of representation. There has also been a measure of corporatist representation in the Irish Senate (upper chamber). In Scandinavia since the Second World War, constitutional change has witnessed a shift in Denmark (1953), Sweden (1970) and Iceland (1991) from bicameral to unicameral systems. New Zealand in 1951 also abolished its second chamber. While in much of Western Europe, two-chamber assemblies are the norm, only four of the post-communist legislatures – Poland, the Czech Republic, Croatia and Romania – are bicameral. Bicameralism is, of course, a functional prerequisite of federal systems, although not all the upper (regional) assemblies are as powerful as the German *Bundesrat*. The Austrian Federal Council is notably lightweight.

Parliaments form the spine of liberal democratic states, comprising elected representatives of the people from whom an executive (government) is constituted. The central principle of parliamentarism is that governments are elected from, and in turn are responsible to, parliament. While parliaments are the centrepiece of democratic systems, each develops a distinct legislative culture and no two parliaments are exactly the same. Jean-Jacques Servan-Schreiber's characterization of proceedings in the French National Assembly as 'litany, liturgy and lethargy' stands in sharp contrast to the rumbustious and confrontational exchanges on the floor of the British House of Commons. Yet in Westminster, as in most western parliaments, plenary debates are often badly attended. There is not a little truth in the adage that: 'If you have a secret, tell it in the *Folketing* [Danish parliament] because there will be nobody there to hear it!'. Members can, of course, follow plenary debates on the television monitors dotted around the assembly or on the radio in their own rooms. The legislative culture of a parliament will be moulded by the formal rules, structures and procedures, the attitude of MPs to their work, especially committee work, and the dynamics of the parliamentary party system. The literature has distinguished between 'chamber-oriented legislatures' and 'committee-oriented legislatures'.

Yet irrespective of their age, structure and contrasting cultures, parliaments throughout the world share a core defining function. 'They give assent, on behalf of a political community that extends beyond the executive authority, to binding measures of public policy' (Norton, 1990: 1). That assent may be given unanimously or by a majority vote. Some parliaments require qualified majorities to enact certain types of legislation – constitutional amendments, for example.

FUNCTIONS OF PARLIAMENTS

Parliaments may be said to perform five main functions. First, there is the *representative function*. Parliaments are constituted to represent the interests or will of the people. MPs may in practice give primacy to constituency interests, especially in plurality electoral systems; party interests, as was notably the case in communist legislatures; or particular sectional interests, where election involved an element of vocational representation. In most West European assemblies, however, parliamentarians are charged with representing the nation as a whole. This latter view, classically propounded by Edmund Burke, that an MP's freedom is not limited by particular interests – which stands in contrast to the 'imperative mandate' associated with the political left – is enshrined in the French and German constitutions, among others.

Next, there is the *elective function*. Elected by the people, parliaments in turn elect, or at least sanction, a political executive. This is done either by an affirmative vote, which confirms the new government in office or, passively, by not expressing no confidence. In some countries, like Sweden, an incoming cabinet must receive a vote of approval on the floor of the assembly. In others, such as Italy, *non sfiducia* or 'not no confidence' will suffice. The re-election in November 2001 of David Trimble as First Minister required a majority of both nationalist and unionist MPs in Stormont, the Northern Ireland assembly. When two defections in the ranks of Trimble's Ulster Unionist Party narrowly denied him the required support, three members of the cross-denominational Alliance Party redesignated themselves 'unionists' for the day. Trimble was re-elected though not without tempers fraying in Ian Paisley's hardline loyalist Democratic Unionist Party.

Thirdly, there is the *recruitment function*. Parliaments are said to perform a significant role in the recruitment and socialization of political leaders. They provide a pathway to cabinet office and serve as a recruitment base from which a governing hierarchy emerges. In the case of single-party cabinets (majority or minority) the choice of ministers is largely in the hands of the prime minister. In the process of coalition formation, however, parliamentary parties often have a decisive say in the nomination of their allocation of ministerial portfolios and that, it is argued, facilitates a measure of assembly control. The situation in presidential systems is, of course, different, with the head of state naming a cabinet, which is often neither recruited from nor responsible to parliament. In some countries (France, Holland and Sweden, for example), there is an incompatibility rule which prevents members of the government being at the same time members of parliament. However, this does not prevent the vast majority of ministers taking office with a substantial body of parliamentary experience behind them. Accordingly, it is argued, parliaments facilitate the socialization of ministers who have internalized the rules and norms of parliament and broadly respect them after obtaining ministerial office.

Fourthly, there is the *communication function*. Parliaments, it is claimed, provide a trunk road through the political process, linking voters, parties, organized interests and the government. Voters can observe the plenary proceedings of parliament from the public gallery or via the Internet and may communicate with an individual MP by letter or e-mail. Parties and ministers are in contact at the meetings of the parliamentary party group and organized interests and ministers are quizzed by the parliamentary committees. To pursue the transport imagery, parliaments serve as an arterial route between state and society.

Finally, there are the *legislative and scrutiny functions*. Parliaments are charged with enacting legislation (which may originate in the government or assembly) and with scrutinizing the executive (that is, holding it to account). The latter function is performed *inter alia* by means of parliamentary committees of inquiry; plenary debates on government bills; committee scrutiny of legislation; committee inquiries and hearings; questions to ministers; and votes of censure or no confidence. For example, between 1980 and 2002, the Belgian parliament set up 13 committees of inquiry.

To an extent, a perception of the main functions of parliament will vary between countries and over time. *The Commission on Strengthening Parliament* (in the UK), which reported in July 2000, identified a rather different set of functions, which were said to operate in Westminster systems of government. They were: (1) to create and sustain a government; (2) to ensure the business of government is carried out; (3) to facilitate a credible opposition; (4) to ensure that the measures and actions of government are subject to scrutiny on behalf of citizens and that the government answers to parliament for its actions; and (5) to ensure that the voices of citizens, individually and collectively, are heard and that, when necessary, a redress of grievance is achieved (Norton, 2000: 2).

Parliaments are not, of course, monolithic entities: they comprise chambers, committees, parliamentary parties, MPs and a variety of agenda-setting bodies, bringing together the Speaker, Deputy Speaker(s) and party business managers. Much of the recent literature has focused on committees and parliamentary party groups. Strong committees are likely to be small, permanent and specialist, and combine the legislative and scrutiny functions. They may also – as in Austria, Estonia, Iceland and Sweden – be empowered to initiate legislation. Crucially, the ability to launch inquiries, cross-examine ministers and acquire a range of relevant evidence may be regarded as a prerequisite of strong committees. As Kaare Strøm has asserted: 'Parliaments can play distinctive and deliberative roles only if [the committees] have the capability to obtain information and expertise independent of the government' (Strøm, 1998: 53). The methods of obtaining information vary. Several parliaments, including Belgium (1985), Sweden (1988), Finland and France (1991) and Norway (2001) have recently established public hearings. In contrast, the standing committees of the House of Commons can consider only the text of the bill before them. They do not have the right to take written or oral evidence from witnesses.

Longley and Davidson have argued boldly that: 'Parliaments have, in the past three decades, become more influential bodies globally, and this has been due particularly to their newly created or revived committee systems' (Longley and Davidson, 1998: 5). Yet in the debate about the relative influence of committees and parliamentary groups, Lars Bille, writing on Denmark, is unequivocal: 'It is beyond any reasonable doubt that the work in government and in particular the permanent committees of the parliament is strongly influenced by the parliamentary party groups' (PPGs) (Bille, 2000: 142). The authors of the country chapters in Heidar and Koole's (2000) collection of essays on the PPGs in European democracies confirm this impression.

It may be stretching the point too far to think of the acronym MP as *member of party,* but in all West European parliaments party discipline requires MPs in practice to put the interests of the party first, that is, to place party loyalty before committee loyalty and, especially in floor debates, to vote according to the party whip. Not all whips are menacing figures like the British variety, although several countries number whips among the parliamentary party managers. In Norway the *innpisker* is a direction translation of the term 'whip'. While back-bench dissidence is relative rare in Western Europe, it does occur and, though not often threatening the very existence of a government, it can be influential. The Labour back-bench revolt early in 2002 against the (low) proportion of elected members (20 per cent) in the government's proposal for a reformed House of Lords is a case in point. Especially in the radical rightist (populist) parties that have emerged in Western Europe since the early 1970s, an authoritarian leadership style and/or strict party discipline have contributed to factionalization and fragmentation. Exceptionally, moreover, more than one in five MPs in the Italian Chamber of Deputies changed parties at least once between 1996 and 2000.

LEGISLATIVE CHANGE

Parliaments do not exist in a vacuum. Rather, they operate in dynamic socio-political environments. Parliaments, in short, both reflect and respond to changes in society as a whole. Indeed, there has been increasing academic interest in the subject of *legislative change*. Several broad trends may be observed in the West European context. First, there is the *professionalization of parliaments*. There has been a concern to enhance the *legislative capacity* of parliaments by reference to the five 'S's' described by Alan Rosenthal in his study of US state legislatures. These are *space* (offices for MPs, party group facilities, hearing rooms for standing committees, etc.); *sessions* (the removal of limitations on the length of regular sessions); *structural changes* (cameral reform or reform of the standing committee systems); *staff* (those attached to individual parliamentarians and standing committees); and *salaries* (Rosenthal, 1998). The professionalization of western parliaments has been in large part the corollary of the increasing complexity of modern society, the attendant growth in the scale and scope of government and the related increase in the parliamentary workload. Parliaments can no longer be part-time bodies.

Secondly, there has also been a *professionalization of the role of parliamentarian*, which is now viewed as a full-time job. The preponderance of career legislators, often lacking experience of the wider world of work, has not been universally welcomed. In the view of a veteran Swedish Conservative Party parliamentarian, the professionalization of *Riksdag* members has represented a deleterious development. In his words: 'Gone are the likes of Bertil Ohlin, who combined a professorship with his duties as an MP; no longer is the chairman of the blue-collar federation LO automatically an MP; and the representation of the private sector has dropped dramatically' (Arter, 2000b: 106).

Thirdly, their changing composition has reflected an *increasing feminization of parliaments*. Of the 1998–2002 *Riksdag*, 43 per cent are women. Helle Degn, a Danish Social Democrat, who in autumn 1998 became the first woman in the *Folketing* to celebrate a quarter of a century in parliament noted: 'There have been huge alterations in the climate during my twenty-five years in Christiansborg. Women are more visible and that is important. There is a different tone, style and prioritization' (*The Copenhagen Post*, 29 October–3 November 1998). This raises central issues related to the *politics of presence* and especially 'threshold presence' in Will Kymlicka's phrase – that is, the numbers required in a legislature to ensure a group's concerns are adequately addressed (Kymlicka, 1995). What, in short, is the threshold presence of women (and indeed other social groups) in legislatures for effective agenda-setting?

Fourthly, there has been a wholesale *internationalization of parliamentary activity*. From study trips to video conferencing, legislators are brought in contact with their counterparts in other countries. 'Best practice' is compared, the potential for institutional diffusion increased and an understanding of other parliamentary systems and cultures developed. There are more polyglots in parliament and a more outward orientation than ever before.

Finally, although parliaments have their own websites, *the media revolution may be said to have contributed to a marginalization of parliament as an agenda-setting institution*. Parliaments need the oxygen of publicity and yet the media have tended to focus on government rather than parliament and ministers have generally proved more adept than MPs at exploiting the media.

Philip Norton was clearly right in pronouncing that 'there is more to legislatures than their relationship to the executive in the policy cycle' (Norton, 1990: 5). There is the constituency role of MPs, which will differ from one electoral system to the next. There is the overall standing of the assembly in the eyes of the population at large. Survey data make a *prima facie* case for a crisis of popular legitimacy, even in countries with the newest legislatures. The devolved Scottish Parliament is one of the most open and accessible in the world, yet a male member of one of the MORI focus groups declared only two years after its inception: 'We don't know what's going on in Parliament. I don't think anyone in this room knows what's going on in Parliament. The taxpayer is paying for that. We have a right to know what is going on' (Scottish Parliament Procedures Committee 2001).

TYPES OF PARLIAMENTARISM

Aside from a delineation of their functions, much of the focus of the legislative studies literature has been on legislative–executive relations and, by extension, the power of parliaments. In the 1960s and 1970s the 'decline of parliaments' thesis held sway. In essence, the case for a 'decline of parliament' was predicated on the increased influence of both civil servants and organized interests at the crucial policy formulation stage and the control of parliament by cohesive political parties at the deliberative (assembly) stage of public policy-making. Neo-corporatist analysis relegated parliaments to becoming an appendage of the policy machine and Stein Rokkan's axiomatic formula that 'votes count but resources decide' became the orthodoxy of the day. Symptomatically, Richardson and Jordan's study of pressure groups in Britain in 1979 was sub-titled 'The policy process in a post-parliamentary democracy' (Richardson and Jordan, 1979). Thereafter, work in the Nordic context (Arter, 1984; Damgaard, 1992) detected a modest revival in the role of the parliaments in the region. The swing of the pendulum was complete when in 1998 Longley and Davidson declared, as noted, that parliaments had become more influential bodies globally and that this was due in no small measure to the modernization of their committee systems.

Anders Sannerstedt has produced an ambitious attempt to classify the western democracies by reference to the character of their parliamentarism. He employs three variables: (1) the numerical strength of the political executive in relation to the legislature; (2) the extent of party cohesion in the assembly; and (3) the institutional structure and focus of parliament.

Britain exemplifies type 1, in which majority single-party governments and strict party discipline have been accompanied by an orientation towards plenary debate. The relationship between the legislature and executive is essentially an adversarial one and inter-party negotiations 'across the floor of the House' are rare. Moreover, since the *bill committees* of the House of Commons are non-specialist and *ad hoc*, and all the chairs are appointed by and from the ruling party, the government controls the standing committee system and the position of parliament is weak. Indeed, after the June 2001 general election, at which the Labour Party emerged with an overall majority of 167 seats, a former Labour chief whip, Graham Allen, described the Commons as a 'six stone weakling helpless before a muscle-bound executive' (*The Guardian*, 23 June 2001). The government has also controlled the specialist select committees that were set up in 1979 to oversee the work of government departments.

The United States illustrates type 2. The Constitution vests the legislative function in Congress, cohesive and disciplined parties have not emerged at the federal level and Congress is a 'working parliament' with a powerful committee system. Accordingly, there is extensive negotiation in parliament on legislative measures, but this proceeds on the basis of logrolling and issue groupings rather than political parties. Sannerstedt may well paint a rather dated picture of modern American legislative practice. It is true that the Congressional committee system remains at the very heart of the law-making business on Capitol Hill. As Campbell and Davidson have noted: 'the influence of committees in Congress varies inversely with the strength and influence of political parties' (Campbell and Davidson, 1998: 124). The less cohesive the party caucuses – and they were almost non-existent for two decades after the Second World War – the more powerful the role of committees. However, they also demonstrate the way the hegemony of the committees has been increasingly challenged and weakened by stronger party leaders and the growth of cross-cutting issues that are often resolved by extra-committee bodies. Still, in Congress the centrality of the committee system has survived and stands in sharp contrast to the weak standing committees in Westminster.

Several West European countries, including Belgium and Holland, exemplify type 3. Majority coalitions are the norm, parliamentary parties are cohesive and disciplined and the assemblies incline to the 'working' variety. Accordingly, inter-party negotiations are largely confined to government formation and, thereafter, it is the political executive (the coalition government) and not parliament that is the principal negotiating site.

Again this represents something of a simplification since, as Ken Gladdish has observed about the Netherlands, 'under conditions of multi-party cabinets there is a relentless need to maintain accords at both governmental *and parliamentary levels*' (Gladdish, 1990: 111, my italics). This, it is implied, has resulted in a process of multilateral negotiation and makes it possible to identify three distinct patterns of legislative–executive relations. Gladdish speaks of 'a continuous imperative towards collaboration between ministers and their own parliamentary parties [the intra-party mode], between ministers and their cabinet colleagues [the intra-governmental mode] and between *fracties* [parliamentary party groups] in parliament which are expected to sustain the coalition [the inter-party mode]' (Gladdish, 1990: 112, my additions in parentheses). Nevertheless, while negotiations in situations of majority coalition, such as in Holland, appear to be much less unilinear than Sannerstedt suggests, his point that inter-party negotiation between government and opposition is exceptional seems fair.

Denmark, Norway and Sweden alone possess the features of type 4. Minority governments have become the norm, parties are disciplined and cohesive and their parliaments are very much of the 'working variety' with specialist standing committees. This combination has seen the government provide opportunities for the opposition to participate in the preparation and deliberation of political decisions. In Sannerstedt's words, 'negotiations between the political parties in parliament are more common in the "Nordic model" than in other types of democratic systems' (Sannerstedt, 1996: 54). In his analysis of 'Parliament and Government' in the Nordic countries, Erik Damgaard, too, concludes that inter-party bargaining is crucial across the region, but legislative–executive relations exhibit cross-national variations. In Iceland and Finland, where in recent times there have been majority governments, inter-party bargaining does take place – and at the parliamentary as well as ministerial level – but negotiations are concentrated on the coalition parties. In Denmark, Norway and Sweden, where minority cabinets have become the norm, they are obliged to include the opposition parties too. In short, Damgaard insists there is a Scandinavian model of inter-party relations (Damgaard, 2000: 279).

In contrast to the West European assemblies, where parties are the dominant actors, the post-communist legislatures of Central and Eastern Europe boast much less stable party systems. Factionalization and fragmentation are high and personality politics still takes precedence over coherent party programmes. The weaker position of parties has led Georgi Karasimeonov to suggest that: 'The short experience of post-communist legislatures leads to the conclusion that for a certain time to come they will be much more active in setting the policy agenda and initiating new bills than legislatures in established democracies' (Karasimeonov, 1998: 52).

Finally, there is the supranational European Parliament, which was described in the 1970s by a British Labour Party opponent of the (then) European Economic Community (EEC) as 'neither European nor a parliament'. Since then, it has acquired significant legislative powers, while comprising 626 representatives (MEPs) from 15 nation-states elected by a variety of electoral systems (closed list, ordered list, open list and single transferable vote), all working within the same parliamentary institution. The European Parliament today has co-decision-making powers with the European Council in selected policy areas (giving it an effective power of veto) and, as a consequence, MEPs are confronted with an ever-growing workload. Compared with most national assemblies, there is a relatively low level of party group cohesion and the defection of national party delegations from the party group line has become commonplace. Low turnout at European Parliament elections, moreover, suggests that for a majority of the 375 million EU citizens its work is little understood and its legitimacy open to question.

CONCLUSION: CLASSIFYING PARLIAMENTS

Political scientists have not resisted the temptation to classify legislatures. Particularly influential has been Mezey's (1979) distinction between active, reactive, marginal and minimal legislatures. An *active assembly* plays a major role in law-making and/or in making and breaking governments. A *reactive assembly* is more executive-dominated, but still commands considerable scope to influence and scrutinize government. *Marginal assemblies* are controlled by the executive and have only a marginal influence on policy, while a *minimal assembly* is there simply to provide a regime with the tinsel of legitimacy. In contrast to the focus on the functions of parliaments, attempts to classify them have been concerned in the main with their relative involvement in the formulation, deliberation and implementation of public policy. For example, building on Mezey, Philip Norton has referred to policy-making, policy-influencing and policy-legitimizing assemblies.

The US Congress is viewed as an example of a *policy-making assembly*. The mix is weak parties, strong committees and powerful regional interests, combining in such a way that major policy emanates from the floor of Congress. This may well be, as noted earlier, a somewhat dated picture of modern American legislative practice, but Congress probably approximates the policy-making assembly more closely than any other existing parliament. There are no policy-making assemblies in Western Europe, although the Icelandic *Althing* is distinctive in terms of the success rate of private member's bills. The point, however, is that these do not involve major public policies.

The West European parliaments fall into the category of *policy-influencing assemblies*, although the extent of influence and the point at which it is exerted vary. Sweden may be regarded as a strong policy-influencing assembly in that, uniquely in Western Europe, members of the *Riksdag* have been extensively involved on the commissions of inquiry (*utredningar*) that form the core component of the pre-legislative (formulation) stage of policy-making. Certainly in their prime in the 1970s, commissions represented, according to the *Riksdag* Speaker Birgitta Dahl, 'the first stage in Sweden's negotiating democracy' (Arter, 2000a). For most parliaments, however, policy influence is exerted at the deliberative stage via their committee systems, which scrutinize and amend government bills and hold the executive to account through hearings, both open and closed. Clearly, the policy influence of parliaments in the formulation and deliberation of public policy will be integrally tied to the mathematics of the legislative–executive balance. Independent of the latter, perhaps the greatest parliamentary influence will be brought to bear on regional questions since they are not infrequently the object of cross-party collaboration (or 'logrolling' in American parlance). Parliamentary influence over the implementation of policy – how laws are actually working – has operated largely through the appointment of a special commissioner (Ombudsman) whose remit has been to investigate complaints and report back (often in the form of an annual report). Recently, there has been growing concern to vest parliamentary committees with the task of post-legislative scrutiny.

The demise of communism has meant there are fewer *policy-legitimizing assemblies* left – that is, assemblies convened for only a very short session annually (perhaps a month) simply to rubber-stamp measures in purely ritualistic fashion. In the former Soviet bloc, parliaments have played an integral role in the democratization process and, not yet dominated by cohesive political parties, their legislative impact has been far from exiguous. Yet in both Eastern and Western Europe, the primary challenge appears to be making the work of parliament more visible to ordinary citizens and, by extension, increasing the popular legitimacy of the institution. This is as true for the 'mother of parliaments' in Westminster as, for example, the Polish *Sejm*. Parliaments often work far more effectively than is generally thought, but the rather negative general perception is a reality and needs changing.

Summary

- Parliaments are a virtually universal phenomenon and, in connecting people and politicians, form the spine of liberal democratic polities.
- Each parliament will have a legislative culture of its own, moulded by the formal rules, structures and procedures in the assembly, the dynamics of the parliamentary party system and, above all, the attitude of MPs to their work.
- All parliaments share a core defining function: they approve binding measures of public policy on behalf of a political community that extends beyond the executive authority.
- The 'decline of parliaments' orthodoxy has given way to research which shows that parliaments have, in the past three decades, become more influential globally.
- In considering the case for a 'revival of parliaments', the relative influence of legislative committees and the parliamentary party groups needs careful examination.

- The post-communist legislatures appear to have been much more active in setting the policy agenda and initiating new bills than the parliaments in Western Europe.
- Parliaments often work far more effectively than is generally thought, although the rather negative perception is a reality and needs changing.

TUTORIAL QUESTIONS

1. **How relevant are the traditional functions of parliament to the way they function in the early twenty-first century?**

2. **How would you go about assessing 'strength' and 'weakness' in parliaments?**

3. **What were the main threads in the 'decline of parliaments' thesis? Is there evidence of a revitalization of legislatures in the world today?**

FURTHER READING

Philip Norton (ed.) (1990) *Parliaments in Europe* (London: Frank Cass) is not getting any younger, but is a good introduction and contains solid descriptive and analytical country chapters.

Lawrence D. Longley and Roger H. Davidson (eds) (1998) *The New Roles of Parliamentary Committees* (London: Frank Cass) is written in a generally straightforward style and includes chapters on the US Congress and the post-communist legislatures of Central and Eastern Europe, as well as the UK, Norway, etc. Strøm's chapter, in particular, covers a good deal of ground.

K. Heidar and R. Koole (2000) *Parliamentary Party Groups in European Democracies* (London and New York: Routledge). The current orthodoxy views the PPGs as both parliamentary actors and the most important arenas for legislative deliberation. This volume contains a multitude of case studies, although the conventional wisdom should not be accepted lying down.

REFERENCES

Arter, David (1984) *The Nordic Parliaments. A Comparative Analysis*. London: Hurst.

Arter, David (2000a) 'Change in the Swedish Riksdag: From a "Part-time Parliament" to a "Professionalised Assembly"?', *Journal of Legislative Studies*, **6**: 92–116.

Arter, David (2000b) 'From a "Peasant Parliament" to a "Professional Parliament"? Change in the Icelandic Althingi', *Journal of Legislative Studies*, **6**: 45–66.

Bille, Lars (2000) 'A Power Centre in Danish Politics', in K. Heidar and R. Koole (eds), *Parliamentary Party Groups in European Democracies*. London and New York: Routledge, pp. 130–44.

Campbell, Colton and Davidson, Roger H. (1998) 'US Congressional Committees: Changing Legislative Workshops', in L.D. Longley and R.H. Davidson (eds), *The New Roles of Parliamentary Committees*. London: Frank Cass, pp. 124–42.

Damgaard, Erik (ed.) (1992) *Parliamentary Change in the Nordic Countries*. Oslo: Scandinavian University Press.

Damgaard, Erik (2000) 'Parliament and Government', in P. Esaiasson and K. Heidar (eds), *Beyond Westminster and Congress. The Nordic Experience*. Columbus, OH: Ohio State University Press, pp. 265–80.

Gladdish, Ken (1990) 'Parliamentary Activism and Legitimacy in the Netherlands', in P. Norton (ed.), *Parliaments in Europe*. London: Frank Cass, pp. 103–19.

Heidar, K. and Koole, R. (eds) (2000) *Parliamentary Party Groups in European Democracies*. London and New York: Routledge.

Karasimeonov, Georgi (1998) 'The Legislature in Post-Communist Bulgaria', in L.D. Longley and R.H. Davidson (eds), *The New Roles of Parliamentary Committees*. London: Frank Cass.

Kymlicka, W. (1995) *Multicultural Citizenship: a Liberal Theory of Minority Rights*. Oxford: Oxford University Press.

Longley, Lawrence D. and Davidson, Roger H. (eds) (1998) *The New Roles of Parliamentary Committees*. London: Frank Cass, pp. 1–9.

Mezey, M. (1979) *Comparative Legislatures*. Durham, NC: Duke University Press.

Norton, Philip (1990) 'Parliaments: a Framework for Analysis', in Philip Norton (ed.), *Parliaments in Europe*. London: Frank Cass, pp. 1–9.

Norton, Philip (2000) 'Reforming Parliament in the UK: the Report of the Commission to Strengthen Parliament', *Journal of Legislative Studies*, **6**: 1–15.

Norton, Philip and Olsen, David M. (1996) 'Parliaments in Adolescence', *Journal of Legislative Studies*, **2**: 231–43.

Richardson, J.J. and Jordan, A.G. (1979) *Governing under Pressure*. Oxford: Martin Robertson.

Rosenthal, Alan (1998) *The Decline of Representative Democracy Process: Participation and Power in State Legislatures*. Washington, DC: Congressional Quarterly Press.

Sannerstedt, Anders (1996) 'Negotiations in the Riksdag', in Lars-Göran Stenelo and Magnus Jerneck (eds), *The Bargaining Democracy*. Lund: Lund University Press, pp. 17–58.

Scottish Parliament Procedures Committee (2001) *Official Report*, Meeting 9, 2001, 23 October.

Strøm, Kaare (1998) 'Parliamentary Committees in European Democracies', in L.D. Longley and R.H. Davidson (eds), *The New Roles of Parliamentary Committees*. London: Frank Cass.

See also chapters

5   Power, Authority, Legitimacy
6   Representative and Direct Democracy
14 Parties and Party Systems
15 Elections and Electoral Systems
16 Interest Groups
17 Social Movements
18 Political Participation
21 Cyber-democracy

14 Parties and Party Systems

Byron Criddle

Political parties and their interaction within party systems are the central feature of the political process in all democratic states. With the arrival of universal suffrage voters came to exercise their choice by opting between policy-specific parties instead of independent politicians, parliaments came to comprise organized parties not disparate groups of personnel, and governments formed out of a party or parties with distinctive policy objectives. It follows from this that parties provide the principal means by which voters express political preferences, are the primary means by which policy options are aggregated, and the sole means whereby ambitious politicians acquire access to government office. Rare is the politician without a party identity, and even in those states where political crises prompt the intrusion of soldiers or business-people into political leadership, such leaders inevitably create political parties to legit-imize and sustain their intervention, as in de Gaulle's case in 1950s France and Berlusconi's in 1990s Italy. The fact that the organizations so created might eschew the title 'party' in no way alters the fact that a party has been created in pursuit of political power.

All parties formally seek power through electoral competition and even if some never achieve power in the form of government office, they will still exercise influence on those parties which do merely by putting on the agenda their specific policy preferences. Thus, although sub-state nationalist parties may never govern the states from which they seek to secede, they oblige governing parties to address the issue of regional assertion. Parties do not have to govern to count.

PARTY FUNCTION

As described, the central function of parties is to govern, and thus to staff the political elite; hence the governing function and the elite-recruitment function. Additional functions are aggregation, mobilization and integration. Parties aggregate and mobilize interests and opinions. While most parties are coalitions of opinions, some are virtually single-issue parties, but all parties are inevitably drawn by their competitive environment to seek to mobilize a variety of interests and opinions. By so doing they structure voting behaviour around a series of options, which is both reflective of voter opinion and yet moulding of that opinion. The voter is thus integrated into a political system which to a degree constrains voter-choice, if allowing the voter the option of removing support from parties whose policy options he or she dislikes.

POLITICAL BRANDS

The kinds of policy preference represented by parties in European liberal democratic states are relatively few in number and persistent over time. From the origin of universal suffrage, achieved in most states by the first quarter and certainly the first half of the twentieth century, eight discernibly distinct brands have emerged, some more recently than others. They are liberalism, conservatism, Christian democracy, socialism or social democracy, communism, regionalism, environmentalism and nationalism. These brands or 'spiritual families', as they have been termed, are not entirely distinct, nor are they equal in electoral strength. For example, liberalism and conservatism overlap in their policy preferences, while regional, environmental and nationalist (in the sense of xenophobic or racist) parties all tend to have relatively low levels of electoral support. Few parties are unclassifiable under one or other of these headings (the small Scandinavian agrarian parties come to mind), and there are few countries in which most of these brands are not present in one form or another.

Parties based on liberalism, whether called Liberal or Radical, originated in the late nineteenth century, endorsed the free market and free trade and were hostile to state intervention in economic activity, though their liberalism was political as well as economic in advocacy of legal and political rights for all citizens. Such parties tended also to represent a secular alternative to religion in predominantly Catholic countries or, in post-Reformation countries such as Britain, non-conformist Protestants as distinct from Anglicans. Contemporary Liberal parties tend to favour, if in variable degrees, the market over the state, and to be permissive in matters of social policy.

Conservative parties originally developed as opponents of nineteenth-century Liberal parties, defending social elites and opposing franchise extension. They tended to greater pragmatism than Liberals on the role of the state but were less permissive on social rights. Franchise extension to lower strata required such parties to adapt in order to survive, and this they did by wrapping themselves in the national flag to mobilize beyond their higher strata support, whether by Disraelian jingoism in the 1880s or by Gaullism in the 1960s. However, contemporary Conservative parties have tended to become less distinguishable from Liberal ones by their support for the free market and advocacy of low taxation.

Christian Democratic parties developed after the Second World War as a consequence both of more liberal social theory emanating from the Vatican, and of a need for new, uncompromised parties to fill a vacuum created by the contamination of Conservative parties by collaboration with fascist regimes in Occupied Europe during the War. Such parties, predominantly Catholic in inspiration, anxious to mitigate class conflict, adopted a fairly statist position in economics and welfare provision, and a more conservative stance on social questions, but with post-war secularization threatening the appeal of such parties, they came to accept many of the free market nostrums of the Liberal and Conservative parties, so blurring the distinction between all three such party brands in the latter decades of the twentieth century.

Social Democratic (originally often 'Socialist') parties developed with franchise extension to the manual working class at the beginning of the twentieth century. Originally firmly statist, by the 1920s shorn of their Marxist wings which left to create Communist parties after 1917, Social Democratic parties entered government in many countries and in the process came to 'manage' capitalism, so diluting their hostility to the market, first by accepting a mixed economy in exchange for a welfare state, and then, with their own late twentieth-century voters' resistance to taxation, adapting further to free market values.

Communist parties, the product of the Russian Revolution and Moscow-directed in all cases at least until the 1950s, were Marxist-

Leninist anti-system parties, rigidly statist in economic policy and broadly permissive in social policy. Their electoral strength, inflated in some countries by their identification with wartime anti-fascist resistance, abated in the 1970s and declined further with the end of the Soviet Union.

Regional, or sub-state nationalist parties, representing distinct territorial or cultural entities, appeared in the 1960s as evidence of a re-emerged distinction between the interests of the often cosmopolitan centre and those of the particularist periphery, and usually mobilize ethnically distinct electorates whether Scots, Basques or Catalans.

Environmental parties developed in the 1970s with support drawn from young, educated, middle-class voters anxious over ecological degradation, and tend to statist preferences in economics and permissive stances on social policy.

Nationalist parties, identifying with the existing nation as a whole and not merely with a part of the territory seeking to secede, and largely a development of the last two decades of the twentieth century, developed as the voice of populist protest against multiculturalism as represented by immigration and by European integration, and with a predominantly racist or xenophobic perspective. They tend to the free market in economics, anti-permissiveness in social policy and a populist criticism of all existing political elites.

These eight party types may be further differentiated, first into those that usually govern and those that do not, and secondly into two camps of left and right. The first four brands – Liberals, Conservatives, Christian Democrats and Social Democrats – habitually govern; the latter four – Communists, Regionalists, Environmentalists and Nationalists – habitually oppose. The 'governing' parties moreover tend to much larger vote shares than the non-governing ones. More significantly, most of the eight brands may be assigned to either of two camps of left or right, depending on their positions on the state versus the market in economics, and

permissiveness versus conservatism in social matters. Thus on the state–market distinction, Liberal, Conservative and Nationalist parties cluster to the rightward end of the left–right spectrum, Christian Democrat parties cluster to the centre-right, Social Democrats and Environmentalists to the centre-left, and Communists to the left. On social policy issues, Conservative, Christian Democrat and Nationalist parties cluster to the right, Social Democrat, Environmentalist and Communist parties to the left, with Liberal parties more broadly dispersed across the centre and the left. On both measures, therefore, there is policy coherence across the various parties within each brand on the left–right continuum. The exception to this pattern are the Regionalist, or sub-state nationalist parties which, on both measures – economic and social – are well distributed across the spectrum, some to the left, others to the right, so lacking definition in terms of a dominant conceptual framework to which all other types of party conform. With this exception, salience of the left–right spectrum is clear, and is one of the most important factors ensuring party systems are characterized more by continuity than change.

PARTY SYSTEMS

The term 'party system' refers to the competitive interaction of parties. Originally it was suggested that party systems were of two sorts, two-party and multi-party, but such a distinction failed to acknowledge the very small number of countries in the two-party category and the absence of a single model of party competition in the multi-party category. Accordingly, a classification was devised that distinguished between three types of system: two-party systems where one of two parties usually wins over half the parliamentary seats and forms a one-party government; multi-party systems with upwards of five parties where at least one party may be large or dominant enough to govern alone, but where the government is normally provided by alternating *coalitions*; and multi-party systems with more than five parties where fragmentation precludes alternating coalitions. This schema, adduced by Giovanni Sartori (1976), took account of the number of parties significantly present in the parliament, their relative strengths and their ideological patterning (the assumption being that the greater the number of parties, the greater the likelihood of ideologically distinct brands).

The three types of system are distinct in ethos and in operational characteristics. Two-party systems involve competition between large consensus-based parties alternating regularly in power; opinion is bipolarized, but the parties are not 'poles apart'. The Anglo-American party systems are of this type. Multi-party systems with limited (3–5) party proliferation are operationally similar to the two-party type because competition, though involving more parties, is still bipolarized. The Scandinavian model of a large Social Democratic party facing a coalition of 'bourgeois' parties is of this type, with the still limited ideological differentiation permitting bipolarized competition on the Anglo-American model. Operationally similar, with competition still bipolarized between left and right blocs of parties, is post-1980s France, where a 'plural left' of Socialists, Communists and Greens compete against a coalition of centre-right parties, and Germany, where a Socialist–Green combination competes with centre-right opponents; the defining characteristic is consensus-based bipolarization. But multi-party systems with a larger range of parties, reflecting greater ideological diversity and with a greater scattering of the vote across the spectrum, often involving significant 'anti-system' extreme right and extreme left parties, are operationally distinct from the foregoing types; here competition is more likely to be tripolar, with a centre-placed group of parties governing in opposition to both hard left and hard right parties. Admittedly, systems of this type appear somewhat historical, as in immediately post-war France, and pre-Nazi Germany, though Italy, for much of the period from 1945, showed such characteristics, with, arguably, the end of the Cold War removing the bases for such highly polarized systems.

DETERMINANTS OF PARTY SYSTEMS

Party systems reflect social and institutional phenomena. Seymour Lipset and Stein Rokkan (1967) identified four cleavages around which parties have formed: centre versus periphery, church versus state, rural versus urban, and employer versus worker. The centre–periphery cleavage came first, as states were formed, with culturally or regionally distinct 'peripheries' being incorporated by a dominant 'centre', or resisting such assimilation. The church–state cleavage saw conflict between secular state and religion, usually in the form of the Catholic Church resisting the encroachment of secular power, and was thus a feature of Latin European party systems. The rural–urban cleavage pitted pre-industrial landowning interests against urban industrial interests in the nineteenth century, as in the Conservative versus Liberal politics of Victorian Britain, or more recently as a base for Agrarian parties in Scandinavia. The employer–worker cleavage, historically the most recent in origin, with the enfranchisement of the manual working class at the beginning of the twentieth century, is the basis for 'class' politics and has shaped contemporary party systems more than the other three cleavages.

These cleavages involved differences in occupation, religion and ethnicity, but varied in force in different countries. Where electorates have been largely urbanized, where the power of the Catholic Church was removed by the Reformation, and where cultural or ethnically distinct peripheries were incorporated, occupation – class – served as the salient cleavage in party formation. An example would be the British party system in its mid- to late-twentieth-century heyday, once the Irish periphery rebelled and seceded. Where other cleavage lines rivalled class, as in Latin Europe, the way the cleavages cross-cut, as in the case of the secular–religious cleavage and the class cleavage in France, would influence the shape of the party system, with secular workers voting Socialist and Catholic workers voting Christian Democrat. In mid-1950s France, the highly industrialized Moselle department had one of the lowest votes for the Socialist Party, but was an MRP (Christian Democrat) fortress.

Of the eight major party brands, most may be ascribed to Lipset and Rokkan's four cleavages: Socialist, Communist, Liberal and Conservative parties to class; Christian Democratic parties to religion; and regional sub-state nationalist parties to a persistence or resurgence of the centre–periphery cleavage. Only the Environmental and xenophobic parties derive less obviously from the identified cleavages.

If party systems reflect cleavages, so also are they shaped by institutions. Electoral systems, for example, are either permissive of parties or, as in the Anglo-American case, discouraging to small parties. Some voting systems, for example the French presidential election decisive ballot, impose two-party confrontation. Federal systems of government permit different party systems in different parts of the federation, as in Canada. Given that rules and structures rarely change, however, institutional constraints on party competition are fairly constant over time.

PARTY SYSTEM STABILITY

Party systems are characterized more by stability than by change. If electoral support for each of the eight party brands is measured over 50 years from the 1950s to the 1990s in 16 West European democracies, the picture is one not of substantive change but of trendless fluctuations. Thus the Social Democrat parties averaged 34 per cent in the 1950s and 30 per cent in the 1990s; Christian Democrats 21 per cent and 15 per cent; Conservatives 18 per cent and 18 per cent; and Liberals

9 per cent and 10 per cent. Other brands have shown a downward trend, if from a low base, such as the Communist parties, reduced from 8 per cent to 4 per cent. Nationalist and sub-state nationalist parties (taken together) went from 1 per cent to 6 per cent, and Environmental parties – a more recent development – went from a 1980s average of 2 per cent to 4 per cent in the 1990s. What these figures reveal is that the major governing parties broadly retained their level of support, some parties (such as the Communists) have declined, and some small parties have increased their vote share but are still small parties.

A further measure of stability is obtained by grouping the parties into left and right blocs. Thus, parties of the left have seen their aggregate support change from 42 per cent in the 1950s to 40 per cent in the 1990s, and parties of the right have seen theirs change from 55 per cent to 56 per cent, confirming remarkable stability, with such change as there has been confined to transfers between parties within the left and right blocs and not between the blocs themselves. Intra-bloc transfers do not of course preclude change in the sense of supporting new parties within each bloc but, as already noted, new parties such as Greens on the left and nationalists on the right remain small parties.

Explanation of party system stability relies first on the freezing hypothesis, according to which contemporary party systems still reflect the cleavage structures prevalent at the onset of universal suffrage. Alignments formed at that time have endured because parties have preserved them by organizational devices to retain voter loyalty. Electoral systems are seen primarily to have a conservative effect, either making new party intrusion difficult, as in the Anglo-American system, or by being permissive as under systems of proportional representation and so enabling existing parties, even if based on declining cleavages, to persist. Major governing parties, moreover, such as Social Democrats, Conservatives, Liberals and Christian Democrats, have in-built advantages over the non-governing brands. Their leaders are familiar as ministers; the parties have records in office by which they may be judged. Parties in government have the means of setting agendas favourable to themselves and damaging to their non-governing opponents; they have the option of adopting policies to stop support drifting to their opponents, especially to small new parties; they can 'structurally engineer' to reduce sources of support for opponents. Thus the British Conservatives in office in the 1980s managed the agenda to reduce support for Labour through the Falklands War, council house sales, trade union curbs and lower taxation, while Labour in office after 1997 headed off Conservative revival by adopting policies on crime and taxation favoured by Conservative voters, and on devolution favoured by voters who would otherwise vote for secessionist nationalist parties. Party system stability owes much to the incumbency factor.

Such change as there has been in relative party strengths remains to be explained. First, incumbency is a two-edged sword. Incumbent parties may disaffect as well as attract voters, and where governing parties of left and right lose appeal simultaneously, or in rapid succession, there is scope for protest voting for habitually non-governing parties. Such was always the basis for Communist voting, but the 1980s saw the emergence of new protest parties of left and right, whether Green parties or nationalist and sub-state nationalist parties. Secondly, the predominant class cleavage has weakened, opening the way to a re-emergence of the centre–periphery cleavage, and to xenophobia and environmentalism. Changing social structure has eroded the size of the manual working class; many workers – white or blue collar – are now self-employed; consumer affluence has reduced distinction between life-styles; social boundaries have melted; class consciousness diminished. Taken with the weakening bonds of religious affiliation in a secularized society, this removes two of the traditional sources of political mobilization. If politics is not to be structured around class or

religion, it is as likely to be structured by race in some form or another, whether that of sub-state nationalism, as in the case of Scottish Nationalism, or the integral nationalism of the French National Front seeking immigration controls and a recovery of sovereignty lost to the European Union. Racial politics of this kind seems to account for more of the 'new' voting since the 1980s than environmentalism, which reflects a rather different protest of the young, graduate class.

All emergent new brands, however, still suffer from the capacity of established parties to incorporate some of their demands in order to stifle their growth. New brand parties are also damaged when they are drawn into coalition governments, notably Green parties which then lose either their pacifist or anti-nuclear credentials. Party system stability is thus frayed at the edges, but the core remains intact. Crucial to this is the enduring conceptualizing of politics as a competition between left and right. The major governing parties are all centre-left or centre-right parties, so positioned that if they are unable to govern alone they are well placed to head centre-left or centre-right coalitions. Parties either side of the governing parties are drawn ineluctably by the left–right ordering of politics into alliances with them from time to time, so eroding their appeal as parties of protest. Even sub-state nationalist parties, uneasy with the distinction between left and right, are nevertheless obliged to choose, and in so doing risk absorption. Until such time as a distinction between left and right in the sense of high tax or lower tax, the state or the market, and permissive or restrictive social attitudes ceases to reflect voter concerns, contemporary party systems are unlikely to change significantly.

PARTY 'DECLINE'

Notwithstanding the evidence of party system stability, there is nevertheless the view, popular from the 1980s, that parties as such are in 'decline'. It is certainly the case that parties have lost members and activists. Nor do parties any longer reflect deeply embedded subcultures – whether religious, as in the case of Catholic-inspired parties, or class-based, as in the case of the French Communist Party which was rooted in the class-consciousness of a ghettoized working class. Mass communication and consumerism have eroded such cultural particularisms. Voters have also become more volatile, so that whereas the vote share of major party brands has remained stable, support for parties has become broader and shallower. Voter loyalties have become more conditional, partly as a consequence of the incumbency factor, in that parties of both left and right have, in the memories of most voters, sequentially failed in office. Thus in 1981 the French Socialists came to power after 23 years of Conservative governments, and proceeded to disillusion their voters with high unemployment, spending cuts and corruption scandals. Failed incumbency feeds voter dealignment; fewer voters identify with parties, more voters back 'protest' parties, and fewer voters actually vote at all. A more extreme version of this critique is to suggest that all major governing parties, whether of centre-left or centre-right, have, with the decline of the social democratic agenda of 'tax and spend', come to converge on a defence of business interests, prompting protest voting and

abstention. More radical still is the suggestion that political power is now monopolized by a professional elite of party leaders, political advisers, lobbyists and pollsters, who seek to manipulate the electorate, by-passing all 'unrepresentative' intermediaries.

That being said, the case for parties remains strong. Some of the above-mentioned examples of 'decline' are discountable. The fall in membership – indeed the end of mass membership – does not concern party leaders who seek a broad electoral appeal to weakly aligned voters with as few membership- or activist-inspired programmatic constraints as possible. Nor need unpopular incumbent parties fear repeated rejection if 'protest' party rivals are themselves obliged to govern and so to disappoint. The very fact of voter disengagement may well herald a fundamental change in the form of 'the end of politics', in the sense of the attainment of universal affluence for most of the two-thirds of the western democratic electorates who habitually vote. Meanwhile, however, parties, regardless of lower membership levels and increasingly conditional voters, continue to structure the vote, control the nomination of election candidates, recruit governing personnel, staff government and set the policy agenda.

Summary

- Political parties are the essential characteristic of pluralistic liberal democracy, as instruments of winning and administering power, and of determining policy outcomes.
- Parties seek to monopolize mediation between government and governed, and unlike non-electorally competitive agents of representation such as interest groups or social movements, their relative strengths are precisely measurable.
- Notwithstanding claims about the 'decline' of parties, they and their interaction within party systems are characterized by stability, not change,

since the achievement of universal suffrage; changes in party electoral strengths have reflected trendless fluctuations rather than new alignments or replacement of old parties by new ones.

- Such stability derives from the enduring conceptualization of political competition in terms of a left–right dimension, enabling absorption by old parties of new demands, and the exclusion of new parties unable to locate on the left–right continuum.

TUTORIAL QUESTIONS

1. **'Party systems are characterized more by stability than change.' Discuss.**

2. **'Party systems are shaped by social and institutional forces.' Discuss.**

3. **Are parties in decline?**

FURTHER READING

Alan Ware (1994) *Political Parties and Party Systems* (Oxford: Oxford University Press) provides the most comprehensive coverage of contemporary parties and party systems.

Peter Mair (1996) *Party System Change* (Oxford: Oxford University Press) authoritatively examines party system change and concludes that party systems are characterized less by change than by stability.

Michael Gallagher et al. (2001) *Representative Government in Western Europe* (London: McGraw Hill) contains an account of different political brands and their measurement from the 1950s to the 1990s.

Klaus von Beyme (1985) *Political Parties in Western Democracies* (London: Gower) examines the various party brands or 'spiritual families'.

Giovanni Sartori (1976) *Parties and Party Systems* (Cambridge: Cambridge University Press) is the classic text on its subject.

Michael Laver et al. (1992) *Policy and Party Competition* (London: Routledge) measures the ideological location of different political brands on the left–right continuum.

REFERENCES

Lipset, Seymour M. and Rokkan, Stein (1967) 'Cleavage structures, party systems and voter alignments: an introduction', in Seymour M. Lipset and Stein Rokkan (eds), *Party Systems and Voter Alignments: Cross-National Perspectives*. New York: Free Press, pp. 1–64.

Sartori, G. (1976) *Parties and Party Systems*. Cambridge: Cambridge University Press.

See also chapters

15 Elections and Electoral Systems

Michael Dyer

Electoral systems are employed by a wide variety of bodies, but in this chapter they relate to the means whereby politicians are elected to public office. The processes of such systems are regulated both by the state through legislation and judicial rulings, and private associations, notably political parties. Like other public institutions, electoral systems are not politically neutral, reflecting the diverse values and purposes of those who construct and sustain them, though time and chance have frequently led to unintended consequences. Electoral systems, therefore, act as variables in the distribution of political power, though the measurement of that influence has proved difficult and controversial.

THE FRANCHISE AND REGISTRATION

The biases of electoral systems have been most obviously evident in the composition of the franchise. In the United Kingdom, for example, the preamble to the 1832 Reform Act(s) expressly states it was designed to enfranchise 'men of property and intelligence', and the differences between the borough and county franchises, 1832–1884, underpinned the Whig–Liberal constitutional settlement: the transference of power to the middle class in urban areas but the maintenance of landlord domination elsewhere. The more liberal yet still discriminatory franchise of 1884 was expressly intended by Gladstone to extend the vote to 'capable citizens', only around 60 per cent of adult males, while the 1928 Equal Franchise Act established the principle of universal adult suffrage independent of property, intelligence, capacity and sex. Changes to the franchise had a major impact on the content of legislative programmes and the evolution of the party system. The biases of the franchise also reflect dimensions other than class. In the Dominion and Republic of South Africa, the exclusion of blacks and coloureds (post-1948) from the voters' roll was crucial to the evolution of its white settler and apartheid regimes, and the democratization of the franchise in the last decade marked and sustains a fundamental shift in the character of its political system.

A further consideration is the territorial extent of the franchise. The generous registration of British Guyanese emigrants to the United Kingdom, for example, is thought to have been crucial in determining the outcome of closely fought Guyanan elections. Similarly, in the United Kingdom, the last Conservative government hoped to gain advantage through the greater enfranchisement of Britons living abroad, though it proved a damp squib. The complexities which such arrangements raise concerning the territorial nature of the state and democratic citizenship are further reflected in the right of 'foreign' European nationals to vote in local and European but not national elections in the United Kingdom.

Closely associated with the franchise is the registration of electors, because the process can vitiate the generosity of basic qualifications. Indeed, the most important role of political associations and parties before democratization was to ensure that supporters were registered and to challenge the credentials of electors mobilized by opponents. In the United States, the employment of literacy tests, grandfather clauses, and the poll tax were extensively used in the South to bar blacks from the register. Southern politicians also sought to limit the electoral rolls by requiring potential electors to register long before the primaries at a small number of offices which were closed outside normal working hours and at weekends. Consequently, not only was the Old South undemocratic until at least the late 1960s, but its disproportional political influence through Congressional seniority and filibuster compromised the integrity of American democracy as a whole. Elsewhere in the western world the technicalities of voter registration have not attracted great interest among political scientists, suggesting that they pose no serious barriers to universal adult enfranchisement. In many parts of the third world, however, voter registration faces considerable practical difficulties, though lack of research makes it impossible to indicate what are the consequences for the realization of fully democratic registers.

Seemingly, across all societies the franchise has been by far the element in the electoral system that has most engaged public attention. Since the late eighteenth century, people have petitioned, marched, suffered imprisonment, fought and died from Peterloo to Tattenham Corner, Cape Town and Selma, for the opportunity to participate as electors. Concerns about other aspects have been largely restricted to politicians, political parties, and a few political scientists.

CONSTITUENCIES/DISTRICTS

If the franchise is the most important influence on an electoral system, the constituency system follows a close second because it determines whether a vote is of similar value from one electoral district to another. Equality of voter-size is particularly important in a system based on single-member constituencies. In nineteenth-century Britain, for example, the redistribution of parliamentary constituencies was slow to recognize the claims of the growing cities and industrializing counties, whose electors remained significantly under-represented even after the equalization of the franchise between county and borough in 1884; and although there was robust equality established in 1918, no mechanism for periodic constituency redistribution was established until after 1945. Even so, the influence of nationalism vitiated the democratic principle with the guarantee of a minimum number of seats for Scotland and Wales. The 72 seats allocated to Scotland were 15 above its democratic entitlement by 2001. Although the United States is the home of the gerrymander (the corralling of opposition voters in a small number of constituencies), a precise mathematical reallocation of Congressional districts between the states follows each decennial census. While each state remains responsible for the distribution of its own allocation, providing opportunities for partisan manipulation, the Supreme Court in recent years has declared unconstitutional variations of more than 1 per cent in population size between one district and another (Grofman and Lijphart, 1986: chapter 17). In democratic electoral systems based on proportional representation, the number of electors per constituency can vary, though that should be reflected by variation in the allocation of seats between electoral districts. More problematical for the satisfaction of democratic values, however, are legislatures whose constituencies rest on principles other than population. The United States Senate, based on two senators for each state regardless of size, is the major case in point.

What neither the US Supreme Court nor the politically independent United Kingdom Boundary Commissions can resolve is the problem that the fewer the number of candidates to be elected per constituency the greater the difficulty in constructing politically neutral districts. In First-Past-the-Post systems it is virtually impossible. Thus, in 1983, while the Labour Party won 32.2 per cent of the seats with 27.6 per cent of the votes the Liberal/Social Democrat Alliance carried only 3.5 per cent of the seats with 25.4 per cent of the votes. As between Labour and the Conservatives, it appears over most post-war elections that for any given distribution of support between them Labour performs better, as the comparison between Labour in 1983 and the Conservatives in 1997 and 2001 illustrates.

In some cases constituencies are reserved for specific ethnic groups, or constructed in such a way as to promote their representation. New Zealand, for example, has set aside three seats in the North Island and one in the South Island for Maoris, and Cyprus had separate multi-member districts for Greeks and Turks. In Lebanon, complicated nomination rules determine the ethnic mix of seats within multi-member constituencies, ensuring the return of a fixed proportion of Maronites, Druze, Shia and Sunni Moslems (Grofman and Lijphart, 1986: chapter 6). And in Mauritius, a system of 'best-losers' is designed to guarantee the election of Muslims and ethnic Chinese. A recent development in the USA has been the growth of majority-minority Congressional districts, whereby black and Hispanic seats of curious shapes have been manufactured to promote ethnic balance in the House of Representatives. Although the ethnic arrangements illustrated here have been designed to promote national integration, they have historically been related to colonial and neo-colonial systems designed to divide and rule (India in the 1930s) (Mackenzie, 1954) and preserve the privileges of ethnic elites (Rhodesia-Zimbabwe). A fundamental problem for liberal democrats is that of deciding how ethnic groups are to be defined, which are to be recognized as meriting mandatory representation, and why one particular social cleavage should be institutionalized at the expense of others. South Africa's adoption of List-PR with generous district magnitudes seems to have reconciled the question of ethnic representation with liberal democratic sensibilities because it facilitates minority representation along social cleavages, ethnic or otherwise, determined by the parties and electors rather than the state, as recommended by Lijphart (1987).

An important variable is *district magnitude* (the number of seats allocated to each constituency) because it has a critical bearing on the proportion of votes required to ensure election and the degree of party proportionality across the polity as a whole (Taagepera and Shugart, 1989: 112–41). In single-member constituencies, such as in the United Kingdom and the USA, for example, a candidate may need to win more than half the votes to secure election. In the Netherlands, however, where the whole country is a single constituency of 150 seats, a candidate/party can be returned/represented with less than 1 per cent of the poll. A classic example of the importance of district magnitude is its manipulation preceding the French elections of 1951, when the centre parties, fearful of Communist and RPF (Gaullist) strength in the Paris region, created only eight constituencies to return the 75 deputies from the capital. Outside Paris, however, where the democratic parties were stronger, they established much smaller constituencies, thereby making it more difficult for their anti-system opponents. Thus, while in Paris the outcome was highly party-proportional, thus minimizing any bonuses accruing to the Communists and RPR, it was less proportional in the provinces to the advantage of the centre (Cole and Campbell, 1989: 78–85). It should also be noted that the method of seat allocation was different between Paris and the provinces to further disadvantage the Communists and

RPF. There were, in fact, two electoral systems: one for Paris, another for elsewhere.

CANDIDATE SELECTION

The competence of formal and informal institutions in candidate selection varies from one country to another. As we have seen, ethnic considerations can be an important statutory requirement, and state law largely determines the selection of Democrat and Republican candidates in the United States. In most countries, however, and particularly in the United Kingdom where there has been a strong bias towards treating political parties as self-regulating private institutions, party organs dominate the nomination process.

Formally, democratic states place few restrictions on candidate eligibility other than those applicable to franchise qualification, and have not, therefore, attracted much attention from either academics or political activists. Excluded groups tend to be the youngest voters, for example, 18–20 year olds, those suffering from mental incapacity, criminals, and perpetrators of electoral fraud. In practice, of course, the menu of candidates presented to the electors, reflecting the preferences of party selectors, tends to be socially unrepresentative of the electorate as a whole. Franchise extension, nevertheless, broadened the bases of class representation, liberal parties advancing the professional classes and the industrial bourgeoisie, while social democratic parties catapulted manual workers into the political establishment. By contrast, females have been much slower to exploit their domination of most electorates. In multi-member constituencies the parties may take steps to maximize the appeal of the ticket. Thus, in rural Ireland, for example, geographical factors play an important part in candidate selection (Gallagher, 1980), and in Mauritius the Indian-based parties ensure that the different castes are represented.

Control of the nomination process is an important variable in the distribution of political power, having implications for the territorial aspects of representation. In this matter district magnitude is significant because it influences the degree of centralization in the parties. Single-member districts aid the influence of local notables and politicians, regional lists strengthen the hand of *Länder* politicians in Germany, and national leaderships are advantaged in the Netherlands and Israel because the countrywide lists have to be determined centrally. Of course, other factors play a role. Economic and social change in the United Kingdom, for example, have undermined the power and influence of local elites, for example landowners and coalminers, which have enabled national leaderships in both the Conservative and Labour parties to assume increasing control over candidate lists from which the constituencies nominate, replacing negative with positive vetting. It was through the dictation of the centre that the UK Labour Party was able to promote female representation at Westminster with the introduction of all-women short-lists before the 1997 general election. Similarly, even more draconian fiats, dividing the constituencies between the sexes, ensured Labour gender balance in the Welsh Assembly and Scottish Parliament.

The most radical departure from the dominant pattern of party nomination is the employment of *direct primaries* in the United States for the selection of Democrat and Republican candidates for most offices, apart from the presidency. By permitting the registered electorate to choose the main party nominees the parties have very little influence over the process. It also follows that power within the parties is fragmented, local constituency interests heavily influence legislators, there is a weak focus on national policy, and party discipline is minimal. The costs and conduct of primary contests make candidates heavily dependent on the financial and human resources of pressure groups, and party organization has become candidate-specific even for formal inter-party contests. Thus, while the system has made politicians more independent of party than elsewhere, they are more beholden to the interests, as the Enron collapse has recently illustrated.

THE BALLOT

The structure of the ballot itself is important, because the choices and manner of their presentation to the elector have implications for party identification and voter empowerment. Differences between types of electoral system are clearly critical variables in this matter, but even within broad types the variations are not to be ignored.

A major distinction is to be made between *categoric* and *ordinal* ballots. In categoric ballots the voter indicates a specific preference(s) for 'that (those) particular candidate(s)', or 'that party', whereas ordinal ballots require the voter to rank the candidates in order of preference. A second distinction is made in *closed* and *open* lists. Closed lists are where the party decides the order in which its candidates in (mostly) multi-member constituencies are to be returned, whereas the open list allows the electors to decide the ranking. (Farrell's *Comparing Electoral Systems* (1997) is particularly well illustrated with facsimiles of ballot forms).

Political parties tend to prefer the single categoric vote, for by denying the opportunity or need for ticket-splitting it sustains a focused partisanship. Parties also prefer closed to open lists because they help maintain the patronage and power of leaders and activists. Thus, in a Westminster election the voter can express only a single categoric choice for a list of one, and in South Africa an elector can cast only a single vote for a closed party list, the names of the candidates not even appearing on the ballot. Most List-PR systems are effectively of this type, the candidates being listed for information only.

Ordinal ballots effectively require the elector to vote for candidates of parties other than his or her own, thereby weakening his or her sense of party identification. In the case of the Alternative Vote, where the successful candidate is required to get more than half the votes cast in a single-member constituency, the weaker candidates are progressively eliminated (if necessary) and their votes are redistributed according to their lower order preferences until the winner achieves the mark. Similar conditions apply to the Supplementary Vote, which also operates in a single-member constituency, though the preferences are restricted to first and second choices. Under the Single Transferable Vote (STV), ordinal voting in multi-member constituencies, the temptation to indicate a preference for a candidate or candidates of 'another' party or parties before all of one's 'own' party candidates have all been ranked is clearly high. The system also ensures that the voters rather than the party rank the order in which a party's candidates are to be returned. Indeed, the unstated objections to STV by political parties is its high degree of voter empowerment and the tensions it creates between candidates of the same party for precedence.

It is not, however, always the case that ordinal ballots give greater effective power to the elector than categorical ballots. For example, there are contrasts between the STV ballot in Ireland, where the candidates are listed alphabetically, irrespective of party, and Malta, where they are listed alphabetically but in party groupings, and Australia, where they are ranked by the parties in party groupings. In Australia, the 'donkey' ballot encourages the elector to rank the parties rather than the candidates, thereby accepting the party rankings and rendering the system hardly different from List-PR (Farrell et al., 1996). Similarly, while most List-PR systems are either closed or effectively closed, that is the elector cannot determine the party rankings, the quasi-list systems used in Finland and Chile (prior to 1973) require the voter to select a party by selecting a candidate. The candidates are then ranked according to those preferences for the purposes of intra-party seat allocation. In Switzerland and Luxembourg, where the minimization of partisanship is a general feature of the political institutions and process, there is a system of panachage and accumulation. Each elector has as many votes as there are seats to be filled, can vote for candidates across party lists, and two votes can be placed on a specific candidate(s). Thus, as with STV, an elector can support different parties at the same time.

The number of votes cast by each elector in relation to the number of seats to be allocated can also be a highly significant variable. Traditionally in the United Kingdom there were a number of constituencies returning more than one member through the exercise of a Block Vote, where the elector was invited to cast as many categoric votes as there were vacancies. Respecting Westminster, the system lasted until the general election of 1950 and, while partisanship mostly ensured that candidates of the same party were returned, the system nevertheless permitted ticket-splitting, with locally important consequences for electoral outcomes and the party system (Craig, 1974, 1977). A variation of the Block Vote is the Cumulative Vote, where again the elector has as many votes as there are candidates to be returned, but can concentrate those votes on a certain candidate or candidates. This system was used for the election of school boards in order to assist the representation of minorities, for example, Roman Catholics.

In some systems the number of votes in categoric non-proportional systems might be less than the number to be returned. Between 1868 and 1885 in the United Kingdom each elector had only two votes in borough constituencies returning three members. Similarly, in Japan until recently, the Single Non-Transferable Vote in multi-member constituencies was designed to assist party proportionality. Such systems, including the Cumulative Vote, create considerable problems because the parties are uncertain as to how many candidates they should present and how to direct their supporters between their respective candidates. Under-nomination, over-nomination and maldistribution between candidates introduce a level of uncertainty that makes it particularly difficult for both parties and voters to make

rational choices (Lijphart, Pintor and Sone, in Grofman and Lijphart, 1986). That is probably a major reason why such ballots have fallen out of favour.

A novel ballot, but as yet untried in public elections, is the Approval Vote, designed to promote the return of a single candidate on the basis of as wide a consensus as possible, for example, a president. The voter is requested to cast as many categoric votes for all candidates he or she regards as fit to assume the post. While such a ballot would return a candidate commanding widespread support, his or her mandate would be particularly uncertain.

THE ELECTORAL FORMULA

The translation of votes into seats is broadly divided between plurality/majority and proportional systems, and it is around the respective merits of these types that most current debate over electoral reform takes place.

Under the plurality system the candidate(s) in any constituency with the most votes is returned whatever the number or proportion of votes he or she has received. This system applies to First-Past-the-Post (though there is no post, and would be more appropriately described as furthest down the course when the voting stops), the Block Vote, the Cumulative Vote, the Single Non-Transferable Vote, the Limited Vote, and Approval Voting. Majority systems, such as the Alternative Vote and the Supplementary Vote, require the winning candidate in any single-member constituency to receive more than half the votes, usually necessitating the progressive elimination of the weakest aspirants and the redistribution of their votes. A variant is the Two Ballot system, popular in France, which requires a second round of voting when none of the candidates receives more than half the votes first time round. The second ballot, however, requires only a simple plurality, though rules may allow only the top two on the first round to go through, and electoral pacts may produce voluntary withdrawals.

The basic objection to plurality and majority systems is that they fail to reflect the national distribution of party support because far too few votes fall on successful candidates, and they capriciously favour parties whose voters are fortuitously concentrated. The Nationalist/Afrikaner Alliance came to power in South Africa in 1948, for example, when it carried 79 of the 150 seats with only 42 per cent of the vote, as against the 71 seats won by the United Party/Labour Party with 52 per cent of the ballot (Butler and Bogdanor, 1983: 51–3). Unsurprisingly, critics regard plurality and majority systems as unfair and undemocratic. Supporters, however, claim that such deficiencies are offset by their capacity to produce clear-cut electoral outcomes, thereby establishing a powerful link of democratic accountability between executives and their electorates.

Proportional systems are of two types, candidate proportional, namely STV, and party proportional, List-PR. In the case of STV, each candidate has to achieve a specific number of votes determined by the application of the Droop quota (the number of votes cast divided by the number of seats to be allocated plus one), and a system of progressive elimination and the redistribution of surplus votes takes place until the requisite places have been filled. Respecting List-PR, within each multi-member constituency various formulae are applied for deciding how the seats are to be distributed between the various parties. It is important to emphasize that although proportional systems allocate seats proportionately, they vary in the extent to which they reflect either constituency or national distributions of party support. It is erroneous to assume, however, they are mostly designed principally to hold a mirror up to nature. According to Carstairs: 'The central problem which has influenced to the greatest extent the devising of the various electoral systems had been whether PR is intended to achieve the most accurate degree of proportionality or whether, in the real or supposed interest of stable government, a bias is introduced to favour of the larger or largest parties' (Carstairs, 1980: 218).

As discussed earlier, district magnitude is a critical variable, to which may be added the influence of any additional regional or national seats designed to mitigate the consequences of surplus constituency votes. Additionally, electoral law may require a certain level of support before a party qualifies for an allocation of seats. In Germany and Greece, for example, there are 5 per cent and 17 per cent thresholds, respectively. Proportional systems are also capable of producing what may be considered perverse results. In Malta, for example, a constitutional crisis arose when the Labour Party with fewer first preferences than the Nationalists won the election of 1981. Only a change in the electoral law guaranteeing victory for the party with most first preferences resolved the matter (Zanella, 1990).

In recent times there has been a growing attraction for Additional or Mixed Member systems, where the voter casts one ballot for a constituency member and a second for a party list. In Germany, the additional members, essentially equal to the number of First-Past-the-Post members, are allocated at the national level in such a manner as to ensure perfect PR based on second votes, once the 5 per cent threshold has been satisfied. By contrast, in Russia the distribution of additional members is not linked to the initial allocation. In Scotland and Wales the distribution of additional members, taking into account First-Past-the-Post results, is regionally rather than nationally based, and as there are significantly more constituency than additional members their systems are less proportional than Germany. The Jenkins Report (1998) recommends that four-fifths of Westminster MPs be returned by the Alternative Vote, and one-fifth by Top-Ups designed to mitigate the excesses of the constituency results, though not to produce a proportional outcome. The Russian system apart, the credibility of these systems rests heavily on the aggregate support for the parties being the same respecting first and second votes, that is, as much on voting behaviour as the electoral rules. The German system is more or less secure in this regard, but the Welsh and Scottish and Jenkins's variants are highly vulnerable to ticket-splitting and partisan manipulation (Dyer, 1998, 1999).

The democratic merits of proportional systems are that they more faithfully reflect the strength of political parties nationwide than plurality and majority systems applied to single-member constituencies. Such greater 'fairness', however, should not be confused with a proportionate distribution of political power. In former West Germany, the Liberals (FDP), with barely more than 5 per cent of the votes, enjoyed the fruits of office almost continuously as an essential coalition partner in both Christian and Social Democrat administrations, and because of their strategic position small religious parties have exercised inordinate power in the Israeli Knesset. At the same time in both those states the second largest parties have been excluded from office for varying periods. The problem is resolved in Northern Ireland, where not only is the legislature elected by proportional representation but so also is the administration. Setting aside the peculiar circumstances of Northern Ireland, the danger of such an arrangement is that by removing strong opposition it weakens executive accountability and elides the main avenue for the legitimate expression of popular discontent, an important element in the processes and maintenance of liberal democracy.

CONCLUSION: DO ELECTORAL SYSTEMS MATTER?

Perhaps the strongest assertion of the centrality of electoral systems is Hermens's classic *Democracy or Anarchy* (1972), where the author asserted that 'P.R. was an essential factor in the breakdown of German democracy' (Hermens, 1972: 293), and 'P.R. is entirely to blame for the end of Austrian democracy, [and] also had a share in the loss of Austrian independence' (Hermens, 1972: 299). By contrast, he applauded the 'integrating effects' (Hermens, 1972: 120) of the election system in the United Kingdom, because it forced parties to reject divisive sectional appeals. While few would have the temerity to make such widespread claims for the general significance of any electoral system, many have seen connections between them and other aspects of political life. Finer (1975), for example, has been among those arguing that Britain's economic failures have been a function of the adversarial politics promoted by the plurality method of returning MPs; Duverger (1964) has seen causal connections between electoral systems and party systems; and Katz (1980) has theorized on the consequences of electoral systems for electoral competition.

Inevitably, the impact of electoral systems on other aspects of the political process is more demonstrable and measurable at the micro rather than macro level, so that linkages become more convincing the more discrete and less important they become. Electoral systems may determine who become legislators, but their influence on system maintenance and policy outputs is much more difficult to establish. Furthermore, as comparative examples demonstrate, there are few necessary consequences arising from the application of any given electoral system because the social context, the evolution of the political culture and short-term events are powerful determinants of the way a system operates.

Finally, in assessing the power and influence of an electoral system in the distribution of political power one has to take into account other institutional features: whether a system is parliamentary or presidential, whether the state is federal or unitary, whether the system has a bias towards representative or direct democracy, not to mention such features as consociationalism and the power of unelected bodies such as central banks and constitutional courts. The efficacy of an electoral system in the promotion of democracy is heavily dependent on the degree to which other institutions are so arranged as to maximize accountability to a sovereign people.

Summary

- Electoral systems are not politically neutral, they are designed to promote certain ends.
- While no element of an electoral system can be considered in isolation, the franchise is the most important variable.
- Electoral systems influence the nature of party systems and electoral competition.
- The impact of any particular electoral system is heavily dependent on the socio-political context to which it is applied.

TUTORIAL QUESTIONS

1. **What are the purposes of electoral systems?**

2. **Evaluate the relative importance of the various elements in an electoral system to its operation and outcomes.**

3. **To what extent can one generalize about the consequences of any particular electoral system?**

4. **How important are electoral systems to the determination of party systems?**

5. **How important are electoral systems to the distribution of power and allocation of resources in a liberal democracy?**

6. **'There may not be a best electoral system, but some are better than others.' Discuss with reference to electoral systems in liberal democracies.**

FURTHER READING

A good starting point for the study of electoral systems are David Butler and Vernon Bogdanor (1983) *Democracy and Elections: Electoral Systems and their Political Consequences* (Cambridge: Cambridge University Press); Andrew Carstairs (1980) *A Short History of Electoral Systems in Western Europe* (London: Allen & Unwin); and David Farrell (1997) *Comparing Electoral Systems* (London: Prentice

Hall). All of these texts set electoral systems within their political and cultural contexts.

A reasonably comprehensive, though somewhat polemical overview, is found in Enid Lakeman and James D. Lambert (1974) *How Democracies Vote: a Study of Majority and Proportional Systems* (London: Faber, fourth edition). Similarly, *The Plant Report: a Working Party on Electoral Reform* (London: The Guardian, 1991) and the *Jenkins Report* (London: HMSO, 1998), offer a number of stimulating observations on different types of electoral system, though as with Lakeman one must beware of special pleading. It is also profitable to read Chapters VII–X in John Stuart Mill's *Considerations on Representative Government* (London, 1861) together with Walter Bagehot's response in *The English Constitution* (London, second edition, 1867). Nor, if one is of a polemical disposition, should one ignore Frederick Hermens's classic *Democracy and Anarchy* (New York: Johnson, reprint, 1972).

More analytical approaches are to be found in Douglas Rae (1971) *The Political Consequences of Electoral Laws* (New Haven, CT: Yale University Press, second edition) and Rein Taagepera and Matthew Shugart (1989) *Seats and Votes* (New Haven, CT: Yale University Press). A. Blais (1988) 'The Classification of Electoral Systems', *European Journal of Political Research*, **16**: 99–110 is the best discussion on the classification of electoral systems. Bernard Grofman and Arend Lijphart (1986), *Electoral Laws and their Political Consequences* (New York: Agathon) and Arend Lijphart (1987), *Choosing an Electoral System: Issues and Alternatives* (New York: Praeger) also contain stimulating and essential articles for serious students of the subject. The journals *Electoral Studies* and *Representation* sustain ongoing research and contemporary debate in the subject area.

REFERENCES

Butler, David and Bogdanor, Vernon (eds) (1983) *Democracy and Elections: Electoral Systems and their Political Consequences*. Cambridge: Cambridge University Press.

Carstairs, Andrew (1980) *A Short History of Electoral Systems in Western Europe*. London: Allen & Unwin.

Cole, Alistair and Campbell, Peter (1989) *French Electoral Systems and Elections since 1789* (third edition). Aldershot: Gower.

Craig, Frederick (1974) *British Parliamentary Election Results, 1885–1918*. Chichester: Parliamentary Research Services.

Craig, Frederick (1977) *British Parliamentary Election Results, 1918–1949* (revised edition). Chichester: Parliamentary Research Services.

Duverger, Maurice (1964) *Political Parties: Their Organisation and Activity in the Modern State*. London: Methuen.

Dyer, Michael (1998) 'Why Should Labour Contest the List Seats in Elections to the Scottish Parliament?', *Representation*, **35**: 24–31.

Dyer, Michael (1999) 'Caveat Emptor: Reflections on the Report of the Independent Commission on the Voting System', *Representation*, **36**: 156–66.

Farrell, David (1997) *Comparing Electoral Systems*. London: Prentice Hall.

Farrell, D., Mackerras, M. and McAllister, I. (1996) 'What is STV? Single Transferable Vote

Electoral Systems in Liberal Democracies', *Political Studies*, **44**: 24–43.

Finer, Samuel (1975) *Adversary Politics and Electoral Reform*. London: Wigram.

Gallagher, M. (1980) 'Candidate Selection in Ireland: the Impact of Localism on the Electoral System', *British Journal of Political Science*, **5**: 489–503.

Grofman, Bernard and Lijphart, Arend (eds) (1986) *Electoral Laws and their Political Consequences*. New York: Agathon.

Hermens, Frederick (1972) *Democracy or Anarchy: a Study of Proportional Representation* (reprint). New York: Johnson.

Jenkins, Roy (1998) *The Report of the Independent Commission on the Voting System*. London: HMSO.

Katz, Richard (1980) *A Theory of Parties and Electoral Systems*. Baltimore, MD: Johns Hopkins University Press.

Lijphart, Arend (1987) *Choosing an Electoral System: Issues and Alternatives*. New York: Praeger.

Mackenzie, W.J.M. (1954) 'Representation in Plural Societies', *Political Studies*, **2**: 64–9.

Taagepera, Rein and Shugart, Matthew (1989) *Seats and Votes*. New Haven, CT: Yale University Press.

Zanella, R. (1990) 'The Maltese Electoral System and its Distorting Effects', *Electoral Studies*, **9**: 205–15.

See also chapters

16 Interest Groups

Wyn Grant

Interest groups are sometimes called pressure groups and at other times lobbies. In a classic definition, Mackenzie defines the subject of study as 'the field of organized groups possessing both formal structure and real common interests, in so far as they influence the decisions of public bodies' (Mackenzie, 1975: 397).

The term 'pressure groups' has never been popular with those who organize themselves to influence government, and the term 'lobby' even less so. 'Interest group' has sometimes had a narrower connotation, that of the sectional interest seeking to defend its position. It has been customary to divide groups into two categories: 'sectional' groups and 'promotional' or 'cause' groups. The first type of group appeals to a defined category of members such as workers in a particular industry or profession. Examples include the Confederation of British Industry (CBI), the Transport and General Workers' Union (TGWU) and the British Medical Association (BMA). The second type of group appeals in principle to the whole population who are invited to support a particular cause. Examples include Amnesty International, Greenpeace and the Royal Society for the Protection of Birds (RSPB). Some groups, however, prefer to recruit a more restricted membership, emphasizing quality rather than quantity.

NON-GOVERNMENTAL ORGANIZATIONS

In recent years there has been an increasing use of the term 'non-governmental organization'. The term non-governmental organization (NGO) has been particularly developed within the context of the United Nations (UN), although it has gained a much wider application. Regulation 1996/31 defines NGOs as 'any international organization which is not established by a governmental entity or international agreement'. The UN Charter itself made provision for formal participation of NGOs through the mechanism of consultative status granted through the UN Economic and Social Committee (ECOSOC). However, as the number of organizations grew rapidly in the 1990s, and their significance also increased, the UN felt the need to redefine and clarify the relationship which it did through ECOSOC Resolution 1996/31. There are now about 2000 NGOs with consultative status with the UN organized through the Conference of Non-Governmental Organizations in Consultative Status with the United Nations (CONGO). They can be international, national or sub-national bodies.

To gain consultative status, the aims and purposes of an organization have to be in conformity with the spirit, purposes and principles of the Charter of the United

Nations. For example, a racist organization or one seeking to subordinate women would not qualify. The eligible body has to be a formal organization in the sense that it has an established headquarters, an executive officer and a democratically adopted constitution. There have to be appropriate mechanisms of accountability to its members, although how far this requirement is enforced is open to question. NGOs are divided into those with general and special consultative status.

Organizations that are concerned with most of the activities of ECOSOC and have a considerable membership in a large number of countries can gain general consultative status. Organizations with a more specialist competence, but which still have to show that they are known in the fields for which they seek recognition, can gain special consultative status. Although this second category appears to include a lot more regional or country-based organizations, the way in which the categorization is applied is not entirely clear. For example, one of the leading NGOs, Amnesty International, gets special consultative status while the World Association of Girl Guides and Girl Scouts, no doubt a worthy body, receives the higher-level general category status.

In practice, it is often assumed that the term NGO refers to groups concerned with such issues as the environment, poverty, women's rights, fighting racism, sexual minorities and third world debt, as well as various faith-based organizations. In fact, the UN classifies many sectional groups as NGOs. This includes a number of business groups ranging from the International Chamber of Commerce to more specific organizations. Media use of the term often seems to have the campaigning cause group in mind and to exclude sectional groups. The reality of group interaction at the international level is often rather different. For example, nearly two-thirds of the civic organizations accredited to attend the Singapore Ministerial Conference of the World Trade Organization represented business interests.

The broader significance of the develop-ment of the NGO and civil society terminology is that it confers a greater legitimacy on the groups concerned. Although no one has elected them, and they often lack effective systems of internal democracy, global governance agencies such as the International Monetary Fund and the World Bank are eager to talk to NGOs. A leaked World Bank report proposed continuing engagement with NGOs and noted that they 'are often better trusted on governance issues than the public sector or big business' (*Financial Times*, 16 August 2001). This conclusion is backed up by a study of 500 opinion leaders in five countries carried out by a unit of Edelman Public Relations Worldwide. This found that NGOs are trusted nearly two to one to 'do what is right' compared to government, media or corporations. NGOs were ranked significantly higher as a source of credible information than media outlets or companies on a wide range of issues and 64 per cent of those surveyed said that NGO influence had increased significantly over the last decade.

This lack of scepticism about statements by NGOs, which have sometimes distorted the facts, combined with the willingness of governments and international organizations to listen to them, does raise questions about their accountability. Governments are, after all, usually elected, however imperfect the election process may sometimes be. Justin Forsyth, policy director of Oxfam, commented: 'It is very important that we do not pretend that we are somehow more legitimate than government or that we represent the people. At Oxfam, we represent ourselves. But we are one input, one part of the solution in terms of ideas' (*Financial Times*, 13 July 2001).

PRESSURE GROUPS AND POLITICAL PARTIES

Some analysts have gone 'so far as to say that no meaningful analytical distinction exists among parties, groups and social movements' (Thomas, 2001: 4). Following Thomas

(2001: 5), three conventional distinctions have been made between pressure groups and political parties:

- The major goal of a political party is to win formal control of government to implement its programme (or at least a share in a coalition government). An interest group does not wish to win control of government but simply wishes to influence public policy in its area of concern.
- Parties are broad coalitions that have to adjudicate between policy priorities, a process that facilitates compromise and governance in society as a whole. Interest groups are more narrowly based and are concerned with articulating the interests of their members to government rather than aggregating a range of concerns into an overall policy.
- Parties run candidates in elections whereas interest groups do not.

This last distinction is the most difficult one to maintain and the term 'interest party' has been developed 'to refer to groups that straddle the fence between an interest group and a party'. However, 'the number of groups in the interest party category constitutes a very small percentage of the groups in a society' (Thomas, 2001: 5). Narrowly based interest groupings have contested elections in Britain, for example opponents of abortion. However, the nature of the electoral system in Britain means that they have very little chance of winning a seat. Groups that contest elections in this way are often outsider groups seeking publicity. Where new movements have won seats (at least in elections outside Westminster) there is a clear distinction between the party and group wings of the movement, for example, the Green Party and environmental groups such as Greenpeace.

Social movements tend to be much looser and less formal in terms of their mode of organization than interest groups that usually have constitutions and defined membership. Social movements may not have a headquarters other than on the Internet and tend to be more radical in their aims than interest groups.

BROAD THEORETICAL PERSPECTIVES

Two broad theoretical perspectives have influenced work on interest groups: pluralism and corporatism. Pluralist analyses of interest groups were developed mainly in the United States where, by contrast with Europe, there are many different points at which the decision-making process can be influenced. The existence of more access points reflects the existence of a federal system of government, the considerable influence enjoyed by Congress and the extent to which issues are resolved by the judiciary. Power structures are relatively fluid and differ from one area of policy to another.

Hence, it is no surprise that pluralists assume that there is a dispersal of power and influence with a large number of competing interest groups. If an interest group develops to defend a particular sectional interest or advance a particular cause, another group is likely to appear to 'countervail' it. Government acts as a kind of umpire or arbiter between these competing groups, with decisions reflecting the balance of influence between them.

Corporatism assumes a rather different and more active role for government and a different kind of relationship between it and interest groups. Government determines which organizations are representative of particular categories of interest. In some cases membership may be compulsory if you are engaged in a particular business, trade or profession. A special status is given to particular groups, most typically those representing business, labour and farmers. They are closely involved in the making of policy in return for guaranteeing the consent of their members to the agreements arrived at. They also usually have a role in the implementation of policy.

Such corporatist arrangements have been most highly developed in smaller European countries such as Austria, the Netherlands and Sweden. Accommodation between elites seems to work better where the personal contacts are closer. The economic vulnerability of smaller countries to external economic forces encourages cooperation. Only a weak form of corporatism, known as tripartism, developed in Britain, principally between the years 1960 and 1979. One of the problems in Britain was that organizations such as the trade unions were relatively decentralized and had difficulty in delivering on their side of any bargain with government.

WAYS OF STUDYING INTEREST GROUPS

There have been three important traditions in the study of interest groups. The first of these is the analysis of why individuals or institutions join pressure groups and how they can be mobilized. This has been a lively theoretical debate and was largely started by the work of Mancur Olson (1965). He provided a theoretical model that showed that the normal assumption made in pluralist theories of politics, that groups would be relatively easy to form, was incorrect. It was not in the interests of individuals to join groups that sought to influence public policy as they could 'free ride' and enjoy the benefits of the policy changes brought about by the groups without being members.

Why, then, did groups exist at all? First, Olson did not claim that his theory applied to groups campaigning for causes, an increasingly important category of group. Secondly, there was an incentive to join relatively small groups where whether one person or company participated or not might make a difference to whether the group existed or whether it was effective. An implication of this finding was that it would be relatively easy for business to organize. Thirdly, Olson advanced a by-product theory of interest groups which claimed that individuals would join groups because of the selective incentives available

to members, for example, discounted services or free advice.

Olson's work stimulated a lively debate. Empirical work suggested that given the low costs of group membership, a rational decision about whether to join or not which calculated costs and benefits was often not made. Inertia was an important factor once the initial decision to join had been made. An important contribution to the debate was made by Salisbury (1970), who pointed out that entrepreneur-organizers would bear many of the costs of setting up a group in the first place. In later work (1992) he pointed out that many group members were not individuals but institutions which calculated the cost of membership in a different way. Walker (1991) was able to point out that the income of many groups derived from legacies or grants from foundations. Although this debate about group membership has been vigorous and of long duration, much of what there is to be said probably has been said already.

INTEREST GROUPS AND PUBLIC POLICY

A second important tradition in the study of interest groups has been concerned with the ways in which they seek to influence public policy. This has been concerned both with the choice of decision-makers they seek to influence and the way in which they approach them, although the two issues are to some extent intertwined.

Insider groups and outsider groups

An important distinction in the literature has been between insider groups and outsider groups. Insider groups, as the name implies, enjoy access to key decision-makers. A distinction may be made between core insider groups that have influence over a wide range of public policy issues, for example the CBI, and niche or peripheral insiders that are concerned with a much narrower and more specific range of issues, for example the

Paintmakers' Asssociation. What they have in common is that they are regarded as legitimate participants in the decision-making process by government. What they have to accept in return for this status is a willingness to abide by 'rules of the game' which include a willingness to engage in a constructive dialogue with government and not to resort to excessive criticisms of policies or too much use of direct action. For example, the CBI became increasingly critical of the Blair government in the spring of 2000. Unattributed quotes from senior members of the government appeared in the press indicating that business was behaving increasingly like any other pressure group and that if it wanted to go down that route, that was how it would be treated. In other words, it risked losing its core insider status and its access to ministers at the highest level.

Outsider groups can be divided into two categories, outsider groups by necessity and ideological outsider groups. Groups of the latter type do not consider that their objectives can be achieved by conventional political means and want to avoid becoming ensnared in the compromises of the political system. Insider status offers access to slow and gradual change and for many groups that is simply not enough. Outsider groups by necessity would like to become insider groups but lack the recognition, resources and political sophistication to do so.

Channels of access

Interest groups have to make decisions about which decision-makers they are going to influence. This choice will be influenced by the distribution of power within a given political system. For example, in a country like the United States where the legislature has considerable political importance, much lobbying activity will take place there. In the type of executive-led political system one finds in Europe, ministers and civil servants will be one of the principal targets of interest group activity. Indeed, it has been argued that looking at the institutions at which pres-sure groups direct their lobbying offers a good litmus test of where power is to be found in a political system.

Multi-level government

However, the choices that interest groups have to make have become more complex as systems of multi-level government have developed in Europe. The ability to make decisions is shared at different levels of government:

● International – global governance agencies such as the World Trade Organization (WTO) and the International Monetary Fund (IMF).
● Regional – the European Union (EU).
● National – traditional state structures.
● Sub-national – the Scottish Executive and Parliament and the Welsh Assembly.

What opportunities for exerting influence are available to insider interest groups at each of these levels? Global governance agencies have been relatively impervious to lobbying in the past, with the exception of the United Nations, as noted above. Business groups have generally enjoyed a dialogue with organizations such as the WTO. However, they now think it is increasingly important to enter into a dialogue with a broader range of non-governmental organizations. Many organizations opposed to globalization suspect that these are simply public relations exercises and prefer to engage in what are often violent demonstrations at major international meetings.

Interest groups and the European Union

The European Union has also had a very close relationship with interest groups representing business. Data collected by Justin Greenwood (1997) identifies 1,357 interest groups operating at the European level, of which 918 (68 per cent) are business associations. Some of these organizations, for example the European Round Table, an organization of chief executives of major

European companies, have claimed to exert a substantial influence on major EU policy decisions such as the formation of the single market.

Trade unions are relatively weakly organized at the EU level. The EU has tried to encourage NGOs, for example those concerned with the environment, by providing them with some financial assistance.

Most interest group activity at the EU level has been directed at the European Commission or more specifically at the civil servants in its directorates-general, which are the functional equivalent of ministries. They are responsible for drafting new legislative proposals that can therefore be influenced at a very early stage. Interest groups also sought to influence decisions taken by the Council of Ministers. This has been done both by exerting influence on the member state governments and on their permanent delegations in Brussels. This route has become less relied on since the replacement of unanimity by qualified majority voting. The European Parliament has become more important with the introduction of co-decision in most areas of EU policy that has made it into a co-legislature with the Council of Ministers. This increasing influence has been reflected in increased interest group activity directed at the European Parliament.

Influencing Whitehall, Westminster and Edinburgh

At the national level, the executive branch of government has always been the main target. Most usually this means discussions with civil servants, often at a relatively junior level. Larger groups have 'set piece' discussions with ministers from time to time, but these can be somewhat ritualistic in character, for example submissions to the chancellor of the exchequer about the budget. The proliferation of executive agencies such as the Food Standards Agency has complicated the task of influencing the executive. Such bodies sometimes have less of a tradition of consultation with interest groups which they

might in any case regard as inappropriate if their main task is regulatory.

Once a piece of legislation has reached parliament, the scope for amending it substantially is limited. Detailed amendments, particularly to secondary legislation containing regulations that implement legislation, may be of value to pressure groups. However, these amendments may be obtained in the House of Lords as much as in the House of Commons. In the Commons, the committee stage of bills offers the best chance to obtain detailed amendments. Select committees may provide a useful opportunity to state a group's position on a particular issue and perhaps influence the development of the policy agenda. However, the less well-known specialist back-bench committees within each party may also be important in that respect. Parliament is most likely to be the target of interest group activity when private members' legislation is introduced on a subject on which the government has not taken an explicit position. Abortion law reform and the abolition of capital punishment was obtained in that way. The fiercely debated issue of whether hunting should be permitted to continue, regulated or prohibited will be resolved in parliament.

The courts have become an increasingly important arena in which interest groups can seek to challenge government policy. At one time they took a very restrictive view of their role in relation to matters that concerned the Crown. This has now changed and judicial review is sought on an increasingly wide range of issues. Human rights legislation increases the scope to challenge existing policies and government decisions through the courts.

Devolution to Scotland and Wales (and to Northern Ireland) complicates the decision-making environment in which groups operate. Interest groups with relatively small memberships in Scotland have to decide whether they can afford to set up an office in Edinburgh to lobby the Scottish executive and parliament. However, Scotland may come to play an important agenda-setting role with policies adopted there later copied south of the border.

Direct action

Outsider groups have increasingly resorted to various forms of direct action which have been seen to be increasingly successful. Direct action is not necessarily illegal, although some forms of it are. It ranges from peaceful demonstrations to violence against individuals:

- Protest marches (usually legal).
- Boycotts of firms or products (legal).
- Stunts (usually legal).
- Blockades, occupations and other disruption (open to civil action and increasingly criminalized).
- Destruction of property (illegal).
- Violence against individuals (criminal).

In assessing the effectiveness of direct action, it is important to remember that it is not necessarily designed to influence government policy or public opinion. For example, the protesters who have campaigned against the animal testing firm Huntingdon Life Sciences see it as engaged in a morally wrong activity which they want to bring to a halt. Their tactics have been particularly ingenious as they have sought to exert pressure on the financial services firms, such as bankers and brokers, that provide services to Huntingdon and on the company's customers. When the company came close to bankruptcy as a result of these activities, the government felt impelled to intervene to ensure that it stayed afloat. The battle then became a much more difficult one for the protesters as they were taking on the state itself.

One important arena for direct action has been the anti-globalization movement. It has successfully disrupted a number of gatherings of international leaders such as the World Trade Organization in Seattle and the G-7/8 summit in Genoa. It is a loosely coordinated social movement. Its impact may be blunted by the events of 11 September 2001

with some of its activists moving across to the anti-war movement.

Direct action is highly visible and attracts a considerable amount of media attention. One of the objectives of the protesters is to draw attention to causes or issues about which they are concerned. However, column inches in the press or air time on radio or television do not equate with influence on government policy. Although the road-building programme was slowed down in the 1990s, this was for a variety of reasons apart from anti-road protests. None of the roads which protesters campaigned against was stopped, even if the costs of building them were increased.

Protests by farmers and road hauliers against petrol prices in September 2000 came close to bringing the country to a standstill. However, the reductions in fuel tax they were asking for were not granted. Petrol prices stabilized, but they did not fall by very much and continued to be influenced by world oil prices. Direct action may be dramatic, but it is not necessarily effective.

INTEREST GROUPS AND DEMOCRACY

A third major theme in the study of interest groups has been their part in the democratic process. Do they increase participation? Do they reinforce biases already present in politics?

As the membership of political parties has declined, that of interest groups has increased. The membership of the RSPB now exceeds the combined membership of the three major political parties. It may appear that citizens are selecting new forms of participation in preference to old ones. However, membership of an interest group may not involve any meaningful democratic participation. Many groups are run in an oligarchic or hierarchical fashion with few opportunities for membership participation in decision-making. Members are essentially 'mail order members' whose principal role is to provide a source of funds for the work of the group.

A key difference between political parties and interest groups is that the former are required to aggregate a range of demands in society and make hard choices between different priorities. The task of a single-issue interest group is somewhat easier. For example, consider a group representing people suffering from a particular illness. It may be able to show that the resources available are inadequate in terms of treatment programmes, drugs, support services and rehabilitation, but the resources of the National Health Service are finite. If more money is spent on one condition, less money may be available for other services that have less powerful advocates.

Schnattscheider's observation that '[t]he flaw in the pluralist heaven is that the heavenly chorus sings with a strong upper-class accent' (1960: 365) is as valid as when it was first made. The voices heard are generally those of the included rather than the excluded. Political resources are more readily available to the prosperous and successful than to the socially excluded. Interest group activity may therefore serve to reinforce existing biases in the political process in favour of the 'haves' rather than the 'have nots'. As interest groups become more influential, the normative issues arising from their activities assume a greater importance. Their role needs to be considered in debates about the future of democracy.

Summary

* A range of terms have been used to refer to interest groups, but that of NGO is becoming more popular.
* It is possible to distinguish between interest groups and political parties.
* Pluralism and corporatism have been the most important general theoretical perspectives.
* Where interest groups exert influence is shaped by the structure of the governments they seek to influence.
* Direct action is becoming a more common way of exercising influence.
* There are many unresolved issues about whether interest groups enhance democracy or not.

TUTORIAL QUESTIONS

1. **What do we mean by an interest group? How do interest groups differ from political parties? How useful are the main ways of categorizing them?**

2. **Does the level of government at which interest group activity takes place have a major impact on how groups seek to exert influence or is the nature of the group itself more important?**

3. **Is the rise of single-issue pressure groups healthy for democracy or not?**

FURTHER READING

R. Garner (1993) *Animals, Politics and Morality* (Manchester: Manchester University Press) provides interesting material on the increasingly important animal protection movement.

W. Grant (2000) *Pressure Groups and British Politics* (Basingstoke: Macmillan) is a general text on interest groups.

J. Greenwood (1997) *Representing Interests in the European Union* (London: Macmillan) provides an overview of interest group activity in the European Union.

G. Jordan and W. Maloney (1997) *The Protest Business?* (Manchester: Manchester University Press) examines how environmental and other cause groups act in some respects as 'protest businesses'.

W.J.M. Mackenzie (1975) 'Pressure Groups in British Government', *British Journal of Sociology*, **6**: 133–48 is a classic article on pressure groups.

N. Robinson (2000) *The Politics of Agenda Setting: the Car and the Shaping of Public Policy* (Aldershot: Ashgate) looks critically at the extent to which anti-roads protests changed government policy.

R.H. Salisbury (1970) 'An Exchange Theory of Interest Groups', in R.H. Salisbury (ed.), *Interest Group Politics in America* (New York and London: Harper & Row), pp. 32–67 comprises an important contribution to our understanding of why interest groups are formed.

E.E. Schnattscheider (1960) *The Semisovereign People* (New York: Holt, Rinehart and Winston) is a classic analysis relevant to the normative issues arising from interest group activity.

B. Seel, M. Paterson and B. Doherty, (2000) *Direct Action in British Environmentalism* (London: Routledge) examines new trends in pressure group activity.

C.S. Thomas (ed.) (2001) *Political Parties and Interest Groups* (London: Lynne Rienner) is a key text on the relationship between these two important sets of participants in the democratic process.

J.L. Walker (1991) *Mobilizing Interest Groups in America* (Ann Arbor, MI: University of Michigan Press) emphasizes the importance of external sources of funding for interest groups.

REFERENCES

Greenwood, J. (1997) *Representing Interests in the European Union*. London: Macmillan.

Mackenzie, W.J.M. (1975) 'Pressure Groups in British Government', *British Journal of Sociology,* **6**: 133–48.

Olson, Mancur (1965) *The Logic of Collective Action*. Cambridge: MA: Harvard University Press.

Salisbury, R.H. (1970) 'An Exchange Theory of Interest Groups', in R.H. Salisbury (ed.), *Interest Group Politics in America*. New York and London: Harper & Row, pp. 32–67.

Salisbury, R.H. (1992) *Interests and Institutions. Substance and Structure in American Politics*. Pittsburgh: University of Pittsburgh Press.

Schnattscheider, E.E. (1960) *The Semisovereign People*. New York: Holt, Rinehart and Winston.

Thomas, C.S. (2001) 'Introduction', in C.S. Thomas (ed.), *Political Parties and Interest Groups*. London: Lynne Rienner, pp. 1–23.

Walker, J.L. (1991) *Mobilizing Interest Groups in America*. Ann Arbor, MI: University of Michigan Press.

See also chapters

17 Social Movements

Lynn G. Bennie

> Alongside the 'normal' avenues of political participation – parties, protectional interest groups and even promotional pressure groups – we have a new form of political action, social movements. These movements have radical aims which question some of the core ideals associated with advanced industrial democracies. The motives of their supporters, and the ways in which they pursue these aims, seem to be significantly different from those found in 'mainstream' politics. (Byrne, 1997: 9)

In recent decades sociologists and political scientists have become increasingly interested in social movements. The literature in this field is constantly expanding, and the common theme developed is that social movements are in some way different from traditional, 'mainstream' forms of political participation, including political parties and interest groups like trade unions. On the face of it, the student movement, new religious movements, the women's movement, the peace movement, the environmental movement, and the anti-capitalist movement are all examples of a political activism that is far removed from conventional electoral politics. Furthermore, few people would challenge the suggestion that these social movements have impacted on contemporary politics. For example, in the 1990s it was estimated that as many as five million British people belonged to an environmental group.

An obvious challenge for social scientists is to develop an understanding of these movements. This chapter addresses two broad questions. First, what are the defining characteristics of these movements? Secondly, how do we account for the rise and development of such movements? It will become clear that definitions and theoretical explanations vary considerably.

WHAT IS A SOCIAL MOVEMENT?

The term social movement has its roots in the field of sociology. It has been applied to a wide range of social phenomena, from the working-class movement of the nineteenth century to issue-centred protest and revolutionary movements of the late twentieth century. But does the term have any real meaning? Are definitional boundaries between social movements and traditional forms of political activity clear?

Three decades ago the political scientist Paul Wilkinson stated that 'efforts to define and operationalize a concept of social movement have been beset by extraordinary confusion and difficulty' (Wilkinson, 1971: 15). In his review of the literature, the first of its kind in Britain, Wilkinson argued that attempts to define the concept had been beset by ambiguity and generalization, and he identified a 'complete absence of consensus in the literature' (ibid., 1971: 26). Wilkinson (1971: 26–7) offered the following as the 'quintessential characteristics of social movement':

- A social movement is a deliberate collective endeavour to promote change in any direction and by any means, not excluding violence, illegality, revolution or withdrawal into 'utopian' community.
- A social movement must evince a minimal degree of organization, though this may range from a loose, informal or partial level of organization to the highly institutionalized and bureaucratic movement and the corporate group.
- A social movement's commitment to change and the *raison d'être* of its organization are founded upon the conscious volition, normative commitment to the movement's aims or beliefs, and active participation on the part of the followers or members.

Wilkinson (1971: 23) argued that the central distinguishing feature of a social movement was a commitment to radical changes in society, building on the work of Heberle (1951), who argued that social movements aimed to change socio-economic and political orders. Furthermore, Wilkinson stated that the normative commitment to change and the active nature of movement membership meant that 'the distinction between social movement, political party, pressure group and voluntary association, is therefore a real one, despite many instances of overlap' (Wilkinson, 1971: 31).

As is common among social movement writers, Wilkinson viewed these movements as progressive, democratic forces, describing them as 'creative and constructive elements' (ibid., 1971: 192).

THE BASIC CHARACTERISTICS OF SOCIAL MOVEMENTS

Thirty years after Wilkinson, there is still a lack of consensus on the defining traits of a social movement. However, there have been a number of more recent attempts to outline the main characteristics and to assess the differences between social movements and other forms of political activity, namely interest groups and political parties. The features most commonly attributed to social movements relate to organization, ideology or aims, tactics and members.

Organization

Social movements are said to have an organizational shape in that we are able to identify their existence. However, they are regarded as having informal structures, made up of informal networks of organizations, alliances and individuals. It is often argued that a social movement is less bureaucratic and less hierarchical than a traditional political party or interest group.

Ideology and aims

Many argue that the ideology of social movements makes them distinctive. In this respect, it is assumed that the social movement will have broader, more radical, objectives than the pressure group. In other words, social movements do not focus on single issues, and descriptions like 'single-issue movement' are not very accurate. Instead, social movements focus on a number of issues, often organized around a broad theme, such as the environmental movement or the peace movement.

However, while the social movement is normally concerned with a broad sector of public life, its agenda is not as broad as that of the political party, which addresses a very wide range of issues in detail.

Tactics

One of the most distinctive features of the social movement model is a readiness to employ a wide range of tactics, from conventional lobbying to unconventional forms of direct political action, and an emphasis on changing individual life-styles. The 1990s in Britain saw the phrase 'non-violent direct action' (NVDA) enter public discourse, and social movements have been commonly associated with this high-profile form of political activism. Examples included the Greenpeace occupation of the Brent Spar oil platform, the anti-roads protest at Newbury, and protests against the building of a second runway at Manchester airport.

Members

Some emphasize the ability of social movements to bring together different types of social group. For example, many of the protests against road building in the 1990s involved a combination of local residents and social movement activists. Others, however, point to the middle-class nature of social movement support (see discussion on the 'new middle class' below).

Many writers argue that these characteristics separate the social movement from other forms of political activity. A good illustration is the way in which Byrne (1997: 24) attempts to distinguish between political parties (formal political organizations that participate in elections), protectional interest groups (groups that protect the interests of members, such as trade unions and professional associations), promotional interest groups (groups that campaign for a general cause, such as anti-poverty groups or animal welfare groups), social movements (which include many organizations or groups, such as the women's movement or environmental movement) and riots (spontaneous acts of civil disobedience). It is often argued, for example, that the protectional interest group (such as the British Medical Association) will have reformist demands which will be pursued through traditional political channels, such as lobbying politicians. Social movements (for example, the Green movement), on the other hand, are said to have much more radical objectives and are willing to employ radical, confrontational tactics.

However, attempts to characterize social movements can appear simplistic and at the same time contradictory and confusing. Indeed, a hallmark of the literature is disagreement over what, exactly, constitutes a social movement. Diani (1992: 12–13), for one, takes issue with some of the characteristics normally associated with social movements. He argues, for example, that social movements need not employ anti-system methods or tactics, that is, action displayed outside the institutional sphere. According to this account, they are just as likely to employ traditional tactics as radical, unconventional forms of political protest. Nor does Diani accept that a loose form of organizational structure should be considered a fundamental feature of social movements. The key here is that looseness/informality of organization should relate to the 'system of interaction', not individual movement organizations. Thus a social movement may contain organizations that appear traditionally hierarchical, but overall the movement is informally interconnected. Greenpeace is a good example of an organization that is in fact rather hierarchical but which is widely regarded as part of the environmental movement (Jordan and Maloney, 1997). Fundamentally, as della Porta and Diani argue, 'a single organization, whatever its dominant traits, is not a social movement' (1999: 16). It can form only 'part of' a movement. One of the most common errors in the study of social movements is to equate one organization or group with a movement.

Diani, instead, argues that social movements represent a specific social dynamic: 'A social movement is a network of informal interactions between a plurality of individuals, groups and/or organizations, engaged in a political or cultural conflict, on the basis of a shared collective identity' (Diani, 1992: 3). In this way Diani emphasizes the importance of a network of informal interactions, which can include a range of different actors (a plurality of actors), including individuals, informal groups, formal interest groups and indeed political parties (as with Green parties which are considered part of the environmental movement). The important point is that they share a set of beliefs, broadly defined, and display a sense of solidarity. As Diani expresses it, they have a 'shared definition of themselves as being part of the same side in a social conflict' (1992: 2). In other words, there is a shared identity. However, this approach does allow for a diversity of ideas within social networks. Diani argues that 'a wide spectrum of different conceptions may be present, and factional conflicts may arise at any time' (1992: 9). The identity of the movement, it is assumed, is constantly being 're-negotiated'. The other key aspect, according to Diani (1992: 11), is the social movement's conflictual relations with other actors. He argues that this may involve political or cultural conflicts, and may involve the promotion of change or opposition to change.

THEORETICAL APPROACHES

Theoretical accounts have attempted to address a number of questions. These can be summarized as follows:

- Why do people become involved in social movements, and what kind of people become involved?
- What is the organizational form of social movements?
- What is the relationship between social movements and economic and social changes in modern society?
- What has been the impact of social movements?

From the overview accounts of social movement theory (for example, Scott, 1995; Byrne, 1997; della Porta and Diani, 1999), we can identify a number of approaches that can be categorized as classical perspectives, resource mobilization theory, political process/ political opportunity structure approaches, and European new social movement models. As della Porta and Diani (1999: 3) argue, however, these should not necessarily be viewed as distinct 'schools of thought' because there is considerable variation within each of the traditions. Moreover, social movement scholars often appear to straddle perspectives and have been known to 'transform' their ideas over time.

Classical perspectives

Scholars in the 1940s, 1950s and 1960s tended to view social movements as potentially damaging to democracy and civil society. This rather sceptical view of social movements is commonly interpreted as a response to right-wing movements in Europe and the United States at the time: fascism in Germany and Italy, and McCarthyism in the USA.

The classical social movement theorists conceptualized movements as rather irrational outbursts of frustration or anger. They associated collective behaviour with the rapid pace of post-war economic and social modernization; however, the main unit of analysis was the alienated individual, uprooted and socially dislocated by the pace of change. These classical approaches tended to offer social-psychological explanations for movement support, arguing that modernization had created a pool of isolated individuals who were susceptible to manipulation by movement leaders.

In sum, it was suggested that individuals' participation could be explained by some psychological or pathological attribute that rendered them susceptible to movement recruitment. Collective action was considered a direct response to 'frustration-aggression'. In other words, those who were personally dissatisfied or deprived were regarded as the most likely to take part. 'Relative deprivation' accounts expanded this analysis by arguing that deprivation 'felt' by observing a reference group, as opposed to absolute deprivation, could provide similar motivations to participate in social movements.

Resource mobilization theory

By the 1970s, a new breed of theorists had emerged. They appeared much more sympathetic to the (democratic) objectives of social movements of the time: the civil rights, anti-war and feminist movements. They also argued that social movement actors, rather than being marginal, alienated or deprived, were of a high socio-economic status and were integrated members of society.

The chief theoretical contender to emerge from this second wave of social movement theorizing was the resource mobilization approach. According to these scholars, grievances and discontent were common characteristics of modern societies and these grievances did not, in themselves, cause people to form or join movements. These writers argued that discontent had to be organized. Thus, they focused on organizations within social movements, and how they attracted supporters and other resources. American sociologists examined social movement organizations (SMOs) and the role of movement professionals, or entrepreneurs, who attempted to attract and speak for 'conscious constituents'. Greenpeace was viewed as a good example of an elite-led SMO.

Another important theme of resource mobilization approaches is that participants in social movements are rational, purposeful actors, in pursuit of their own interests. Based on this assumption, there has been widespread discussion of what organizations have to offer potential members in return for their support. Thus rational choice theorists have argued that groups must offer incentives to potential members that outweigh the costs of membership.

'Political opportunity structure' approaches

By the mid-1980s, the political opportunity approach had evolved, sometimes referred to as the political process model. It was argued that broad political circumstances, including the degree of state decentralization, the extent to which political elites were receptive to the demands of movements, and the existence of organizational support groups, had an effect on the development of a social movement.

The basic idea of constraints and opportunities is used to explain the impact of movements, their style of campaigning (strategy) and their mobilization dynamics. However,

two different 'political opportunity structure' approaches are evident. The first of these involves exploring how changes to some aspects of a political system can affect a social movement. These tend to be detailed historical case studies of single movements and are typical of early American approaches. The second approach involves the cross-national study of comparable movements, and explains variations with reference to differences in political systems. These cross-national comparisons characterize most European approaches.

Overall political opportunity structure approaches consider a diverse range of contextual variables. Della Porta and Diani (1999: 224–5) summarize these as: (1) political institutions; (2) political culture; (3) the behaviour of opponents of social movements; and (4) the behaviour of their allies.

'New social movement' approaches

A number of social movement theorists point to 'macro-societal', structural changes in advanced industrial societies, arguing that social movements have resulted from and contributed to these changes. Some argue that social movements exist during all periods of transition and that the movements that emerged after the Second World War constitute yet another 'wave' of movement activity. Others suggest that the movements emerging during this period are a manifestation of a move away from class-based industrialism towards 'post-industrialism', and that they represent something qualitatively different. A common argument is that the development of advanced capitalist societies – based on an active Keynesian state, welfare provision and the expansion of the service sector – has produced a new set of conflicts. The 'old politics' prioritized economic affluence, political order and strong military defence. The 'new' brand of movement politics appears identity-based and is said to involve a very different set of demands: equal rights for minorities; greater democratization;

concern for the environment; military disarmament, and so on.

Central to these developments is the 'new middle class'. The 'old' middle class relates to those who still control the means of production. The 'new' middle class, it is argued, derives its power from knowledge. Partly this is a result of an active welfare state, which creates a new class of non-commercial, professional educationalists, social and health workers, and so on. However, another important new middle-class group is the people with scientific and technical expertise who are increasingly important in modern economies. These new middle-class groups are regarded as the natural constituents of social movements, but the motivations behind new middle-class support for these movements is widely debated. Some interpret this as an instrumental attempt to protect new middle-class interests, others as an act of altruism (see Byrne, 1997: 52–4 for this discussion).

A closely related argument is that developed by Ronald Inglehart (1977), who has conducted extensive empirical investigations of western liberal democracies and argues that these societies are experiencing a 'culture shift', from materialist to 'post-materialist' values. His theory rests on the idea that post-war European societies have been relatively prosperous and, with basic needs satisfied, post-war cohorts have developed a different value system from earlier generations, moving away from material concerns towards 'quality of life' issues, which include a desire for participation and a rejection of traditional hierarchies. In sum, Inglehart points to a pool of potential new social movement supporters, created by structural changes in post-war societies.

These arguments lead a number of writers to make the distinction between old and new forms of social movement (although, as will be argued later, this comparison can be challenged). Frequently, this takes the form of contrasting the labour and trade union movement with the peace, civil rights or environmental movements. Martell (1994: 112–13) summarizes these arguments in the following way:

1   Location: Old social movements are state-oriented and integrated into traditional politics. New social movements (NSMs), on the other hand, are located in civil society, outside conventional political environments.
2   Ideology and aims: Old social movements aim to achieve political representation and legislative reforms mainly associated with economic rights. NSMs, by contrast, are more concerned with culture and civil society, attempting to change individual life-styles.
3   Organization: While old social movements have formal, hierarchical forms of political organization, the NSMs adopt a grassroots-oriented organization.
4   Medium of change: Unlike traditional movements, which focus on political institutions, NSMs employ more innovative forms of direct action in an attempt to change cultural attitudes.

It is worth noting at this point that, while US researchers were the first to utilize social movement theory of any kind, recent US approaches have been dominated by resource mobilization theory. In contrast, European social scientists since the late 1960s have been more concerned with cultural settings and macro-sociological explanations, and have spent a great deal of time attempting to understand the new social movement phenomenon. European scholars are often critical of the American theorists because, it is argued, they underplay the ideological content of movements and neglect their cultural impact. Because the American theorists concentrate on organizational aspects of movement development, they often appear very 'top-down' and appear to neglect demands for change at the grassroots level. The European approaches, however, are more likely to recognize these 'bottom-up' factors.

DEFINITIONAL PROBLEMS AND AREAS OF CONTENTION

Diani (1992: 2) (also see della Porta and Diani, 1999) notes the analytical difficulties associated with the study of social movements, pointing to a 'loss of specificity and theoretical clarity'. This is partly because the term is used so indiscriminately, with reference to such a diverse range of social and political phenomona as political revolutions and single-issue campaign groups. It is certainly the case that attempts to conceptualize social movements are far from consistent. However, social movement scholars would defend themselves by arguing that it is difficult to assess movements precisely because they are 'amorphous entities which resist neat classification' (Byrne, 1997: 11).

A significant problem, however, is that scholars are constantly modifying definitions and introducing new labels to describe a range of social movement 'types'. There is also a tradition of detailed case study approaches, and these tend to lack theoretical rigour. The risk here is a lack of theoretical understanding and a lack of conceptual clarity, when 'types become as numerous as cases' (Wilkinson, 1971: 17).

The focus on cultural change is sometimes difficult for political scientists to take on board, as they are traditionally more concerned with political institutions and policy outputs. One example of this political science perspective is provided by Jordan and Maloney (1997) who challenge the 'uniqueness' of the social movement, highlighting overlaps in the characteristics of movements and interest groups. For example, they highlight the hierarchical organization of Greenpeace, and ultimately resist the idea that one organization constitutes only part of a social movement network.

Certainly, the definitional literature can appear very 'messy'. It is peppered with hybrid terms that attempt to recognize the overlaps between the political party, interest group and social movement: pressure movements, protest movements and movement-parties are only a few. Unfortunately for the student of politics, the end result can be confusion not clarity.

The real problem may lie in attempts to separate 'old' and 'new' social movements. The ideal-type model of a new social movement is of a loosely organized, decentralized network, attempting to challenge traditional values and affect cultural life-style changes. However, is the conceptual dividing line between old and new social movements clear? As Scott (1995: 35) argues, one is forced to recognize the continuity between old and new movements. Many of the so-called new social movements, he argues, including the feminist movement, were revivals of earlier movements. The crux of Scott's argument is that the characteristics normally ascribed to new social movements apply to social movements in general:

> None of the imputed characteristics are confined to new social movements. An emphasis upon democracy and participation, for example, can be viewed as a function of the concern of social movements in general to open up social and political decision-making procedures; it is part of the rhetoric of populism. Participatory demands and ideology belong to the ideological baggage of any movement, the workers' movement just as much as new social movements, which are not yet integrated into decision-making processes, but which would dearly like to be. (Scott, 1995: 154)

THE IMPACT OF SOCIAL MOVEMENTS

While the relative strengths of political parties can be measured by their electoral performance, the strength or influence of social movements is more difficult to quantify. Movement 'success' may take the form of quite tangible policy successes, as in the case of the Greenpeace Brent Spar campaign, when the oil company Shell was persuaded to reverse a policy decision to dispose of the oil platform in the North Atlantic. However, more often than not the relationship between cause and effect is very difficult to determine, especially when we consider that the aim of social movements is to change cultural attitudes, that is they aim to change the behaviour of both elites and ordinary citizens.

Scott argues that social movements may disappear when they become successful, that is when their demands become integrated into the political system. 'Success', he argues, 'takes the form of integrating previously excluded issues and groups into the "normal" political process' (Scott, 1995: 10). Others, however, believe that integration of social movement demands amounts to failure. Furthermore, the apparent successes of social movements can often lead to internal disputes. As della Porta and Diani suggest, 'it is often the case that movements which are judged successful from the outside are considered to have failed by the activists of the movements themselves' (della Porta and Diani, 1999: 230). So, even the meaning of success is contested.

Nevertheless, few people would disagree with the suggestion that social movements *can* affect political issues and the tone of public life. They have encouraged changes in traditional parties, produced changes in public policy and, perhaps most importantly,

affected cultural attitudes and behaviour on a wide range of issues, from the role of women in society to the use of science in food production.

CONCLUSION

For a time it was fashionable to argue that social movements were likely to replace the more traditional forms of political participation. Some commentators argued that the bureaucratic and hierarchical nature of political parties and conventional interest groups would be challenged by movements, because they better reflected the fluid and fragmented nature of post-industrial societies. This perspective was partly fuelled by the massive increase in membership of social movements and the downturn in membership of traditional parties and groups. However, the 'old' forms of participation have proved quite adaptable, attempting to integrate many of the social movement themes: women's rights, protection of the environment, and so on. We appear to have entered a period of more sober reflection that recognizes the co-existence of political parties, groups and social movements.

Summary

- A social movement is a form of collective action.
- Key characteristics include informal networks, shared identities and the promotion of political or cultural change.
- Theories explore a range of questions, from why people join movements to the effects of political systems on the development of these movements.
- The meaning of 'new social movement' is an example of analytical confusion in the literature.
- The impact of social movements is difficult to measure.

TUTORIAL QUESTIONS

1. What are the defining characteristics of a social movement?

2. How 'new' are new social movements?

3. Outline the main theoretical approaches in the social movement literature.

4. Assess the impact of social movements.

FURTHER READING

Paul Byrne (1997) *Social Movements in Britain* (London: Routledge) provides an informative guide to the literature, combined with a case study analysis of movements in Britain.

Mario Diani (1992) 'The Concept of Social Movement', *Sociological Review*, **40**: 1–25 compares different definitions of 'social movement' and offers a synthesis of these approaches.

Donatelli della Porta and Mario Diani (1999) *Social Movements: an Introduction* (Oxford: Blackwell) is a sophisticated, integrated analysis of social movements and approaches.

Rudolf Heberle (1951) *Social Movements: an Introduction to Political Sociology* (New York: Appleton-Century-Crofts Inc.) is an early attempt to define and theorize the social movement phenomenon.

Ronald Inglehart (1977) *The Silent Revolution: Changing Values and Political Styles among Western Publics* (Princeton, NJ: Princeton University Press) is a famous text on post-materialism.

Grant Jordan and William Maloney (1997) *The Protest Business? Mobilizing Campaign Groups* (Manchester and New York: Manchester University Press) contains a critical discussion of social movement approaches and their relationship with the study of interest groups.

Luke Martell (1994) *Ecology and Society: an Introduction* (Cambridge: Polity Press) is a review of alternative explanations for the rise of social movements, with a focus on the environmental movement. It addresses the divide between old and new movements.

Allan Scott (1995) *Ideology and the New Social Movements* (London: Routledge) is a thorough, systematic analysis of the social movement literature. It questions the division between 'old' and 'new' social movements.

Paul Wilkinson (1971) *Social Movement* (London: Macmillan) is a review of traditional approaches and contains a useful discussion on the difficulties of conceptualizing social movement.

REFERENCES

Byrne, P. (1997) *Social Movements in Britain*. London: Routledge.

Della Porta, D. and Diani, M. (1999) *Social Movements: an Introduction*. Oxford: Blackwell.

Diani, M. (1992) 'The Concept of Social Movement', *Sociological Review*, **40**: 1–25.

Herberle, R. (1951) *Social Movements: an Introduction to Political Sociology*. New York: Appleton-Century-Crofts Inc.

Inglehart, R. (1977) *The Silent Revolution: Changing Values and Political Styles among Western Publics*. Princeton, NJ: Princeton University Press.

Jordan, G. and Maloney, W. (1997) *The Protest Business? Mobilizing Campaign Groups*. Manchester and New York: Manchester University Press.

Martell, L. (1994) *Ecology and Society: an Introduction*. Cambridge: Polity Press.

Scott, A. (1995) *Ideology and the New Social Movements*. London: Routledge.

Wilkinson, P. (1971) *Social Movement*. London: Macmillan.

See also chapters

18 Political Participation

George Moyser

Political participation by ordinary people is at the very heart of democracy for without their voice being exercised, there is no real democracy. Democracy, in other words, is substantially about the active engagement of the citizenry in the processes of government policy-making that affect their lives. Such engagement is not, of course, sufficient by itself for democracy because there are other necessary features, such as the presence of competitive political parties and the willingness of governing elites to listen and be responsive to the views of ordinary citizens. Indeed, some argue that elite competition is a more important ingredient of democracy than citizen participation. But certainly, without the provision of regular opportunities for the governed to have a say in how they are governed, opportunities that are then taken up by significant numbers, there is no democracy worth the name.

Verba and Nie put the argument for this close linkage between political participation and democracy in a classic study: 'If democracy is interpreted as rule by the people, then the question of who participates in political decisions becomes the nature of democracy in society. Where few take part in decisions, there is little democracy; the more participation there is in decisions, the more democracy there is' (Verba and Nie, 1972: 1). Of course, this requires considerable amplification, not least as democracy can be considered to be compatible with a rule of periodic accountability of governmental

elites through elections as much as with a rule of direct personal intervention by citizens in the making of governmental decisions. Nevertheless, at some fundamental level, it is true that democracy, whatever precise formula or institutionalization, does require some citizen input that carries with it some exercise of power, either over the rulers or over the decisions, or both.

That this is so can be readily seen from the differences in the role and character of political participation as it typically exists under democratic and non-democratic auspices. In liberal democracies, there are typically a wide variety of opportunities for ordinary citizens to exercise their voice. Whether the citizens avail themselves of these opportunities is, however, normally a voluntary matter. Compulsory voting does exist in some liberal democracies, such as Belgium and Australia. Similarly, the timing of those opportunities, as with elections, may rest more with the governing elites than with the citizenry. And on these, as on other, occasions, elites may play a significant role in mobilizing ordinary citizens to participate, as in the way certain pressure groups engage their members in political campaigns. These are important aspects of democratic participation. But fundamentally, the choice of the level of personal participation, the methods used and the agenda of concern are matters that typically rest with the individual citizen. As a result, there is considerable variation in how active citizens are. By the same token there is also variation in the particular repertoire of actions individuals use to express their concerns.

In non-democratic states, the character and role of political participation is very different. In authoritarian countries as diverse as Cuba, North Korea, China, Iraq and Zimbabwe, political participation by ordinary citizens is highly restricted and controlled. The exercise of voice by the citizens is not to make a choice about policy, or about which political elites should exercise power, but typically to respond to a demand by their rulers to demonstrate their support in public for those rulers or for the policy decisions the rulers have already made. Participation in these contexts, then, tends to be elite-controlled and non-voluntaristic in character. As a result, when elections are held, they tend to be non-competitive, with vote rigging used if necessary to procure a resounding 'victory' for the governing leadership. Opposition, therefore, is subject to intimidation and suppression. A study of political participation in China (Townsend, 1967), for example, described the politics as essentially 'top-down' in nature with the ordinary people cast as compliant subjects mobilized to express support for the dominant Communist Party elites rather than as active choice-making citizens.

If, therefore, political participation in a democracy is more consequential for the exercise of power, we need to consider its nature and political role more carefully by examining a number of key questions:

- What are the ingredients of political participation within a democratic context?
- What range of political activities does the term encompass?
- What are the typical levels of political participation observed in modern democracies?
- How might we explain why ordinary citizens participate? What circumstances or motivations seem to distinguish the more active from the less active?
- As a result, who are 'the activists' among

the citizenry and what difference does their engagement seem to make in the way governing elites operate and public policy decisions are made?

WHAT IS POLITICAL PARTICIPATION IN A DEMOCRACY?

The essence of political participation in a democracy appears to be beguilingly simple – it is about 'taking part in the processes of formulation, passage and implementaton of public policies' (Parry et al., 1992: 16). But there are very different views about what that precisely means. Some require that the taking part be effective and voluntaristic. In other words, political activity that is mobilized by elites, as can be the case with political rallies and demonstrations, would not be considered political participation. Equally, political activity that is ineffective in making a discernible difference to a policy decision would also be excluded. By this view, voting would not count as political participation because a single vote cannot be seen normally to make a discernible difference. On these grounds, for example, Finer sees voters not as participants, but as controllers, controlling who the real participants will be. For Finer, it is the rulers who do the participating, 'sharing in the framing and/or execution of public policies', not the ordinary citizens (Finer, 1972: 59). Under this view, participation requires an expectation of exercising real influence, of having one's voice clearly heard and weighed. Consequently, it leads to the view that most modern forms of representative government are, by this measure, defective democracies. The only 'real' democracy is one based on 'genuine' participation where the role of the citizen is indeed that of direct participant. Advocates of that view point to such practices of 'direct democracy' as referendums and initiatives where legislation is directly decided by popular vote. Similarly, at local level, the New England Town Meeting (Bryan, forthcoming), in which the citizens gather to decide matters of local public policy, is held up as an exemplar of 'genuine' participation and hence 'real' democracy.

Such views are useful in that they point to the requirement that political participation must involve some minimal degree of effectiveness and intentionality in contributing to the making of public policy. But beyond that, what precisely is included or excluded as 'taking part' is a matter of continued debate. For example, there has been debate around the issue of whether or not political participation must involve some form of action by the individual. Is the expression of political interest, or even political discussion among family or friends, an aspect of political participation? Is the expression of verbal support for, or rejection of, a government policy political participation? Is an expression of readiness, or willingness, to undertake some future action a measure of political participation? Is the passive membership of a group whose leaders then seek to influence government sufficient to count? What about action in areas related to, but distinct from, the political arena, such as in the workplace? And, finally, what about actions that seem to violate democratic principles, such as political violence, or that are simply unconventional, like sit-ins? Should they be part of what we take political participation to mean?

There are no easy answers to such questions and different authors have come to different conclusions. Pateman (1970), for example, has argued for including participation in the making of decisions in other nongovernmental arenas. And certainly, as Eckstein (1961) once pointed out, what is learned about participation in those arenas may indeed have an impact upon participation in the political sphere itself. Others, such as Barnes, Kaase and others (1979), recognized that political protest had become a significant part of citizen political activity in advanced industrial democracies in the late 1960s and so brought direct action within the compass of the term. At the same time, however, they also expanded it by commingling various protest activities with measures of

approval and potentiality for protest. Thus gradually the term has come to encompass a relatively wide array of specific activities, far wider today than once was the case.

THE RANGE OF POLITICAL PARTICIPATION IN A DEMOCRACY

Early studies of mass political behaviour focused on the electoral arena and, as a result, political participation was initially associated with involvement in election campaigns (see, for example, Lazarsfeld et al., 1944: especially chapter 5). That this should be so is not perhaps surprising. After all, election is the principal formal way in which citizens are given the opportunity to participate in democracies with representative forms of government – as effectively all are nowadays. In this context, Verba and Nie's 1972 study, which expanded the range of the term to include other types of action outside the electoral arena, has become a classic in the field. While being narrower in its usage than previous studies, like Lazarsfeld's, in excluding expressions of political interest as 'participation', or passive activities like paying attention to an electoral campaign through the mass media, they took a decisive step in recognizing that influence exercised through the ballot box was only one of multiple ways citizens in democracies can seek to take part in influencing public policy. Their formulation of the notion of 'modes of participation' as 'alternative systems by which the citizenry influences the government' (Verba and Nie, 1972: 51) has become very influential indeed in subsequent research.

Their analysis included measures of voting, which they viewed as 'the most widespread and regularized political activity, and in terms of the overall impact of the citizenry on governmental performance it may be the single most important act' (Verba and Nie, 1972: 46). They also included those activities associated with electoral campaigns such as working for a political party or candidate, contributing money, trying to mobilize others to vote and persuading them as to how they should vote. Crucially, however, they recognized that political participation is, in principle at least, something that continues even when an election is not under way. Citizen participation is obviously heightened during elections but, by that token, a more complete picture of the phenomenon requires looking beyond those rather intermittent, somewhat short-lived and atypical periods.

To that end, Verba and Nie added two other modalities. One, called 'citizen-initiated contacting', consisted of contacts made by individual citizens with government officials (local and extra-local) on issues of public policy that the citizen was concerned about, such as a school or a road repair or some environmental matter. The fourth and final mode involved participation through interest groups. Rather than participating as an individual citizen, this mode was characterized by its cooperative character – working with others to raise an issue affecting the entire community, for example. The overall result was a set of four distinct modes of participation, measured by 15 discrete activities. In short, it was, at the time, the most comprehensive study yet undertaken of political participation in a democracy.

Such a broader picture inevitably has made the study of political participation more complicated. No longer could the older 'uni-dimensional' view of participation be sustained whereby citizens were ranked by their activity level on a single scale. The classic and influential picture in this respect put forward by Milbrath and Goel (1977) of 'gladiators' (the most active), 'spectators' (the occasionally active) and 'apathetics' (essentially those who never voted at all) had to be revised. Now, in short, political participation had to be viewed, potentially at least, as a multi-dimensional phenomenon in which there might be gladiators in each modal type of participation.

That this was so became even clearer with the further expansion of the range of political participation to incorporate what Barnes, Kaase and others (1979) called 'unconven-

tional participation', that is, various specific forms of direct action ranging from 'mild' activities such as 'signing a petition', through those that are more challenging like 'lawful demonstrations', 'boycotts' and 'street blockades'. These, in their view, formed yet another mode of participation distinct from the kind of 'conventional' activities covered by Verba and Nie but which had become part of the 'behavioral repertory' of significant numbers of citizens in modern western democracies. As they persuasively put it, 'In the 1960s, demonstrations occurred with sufficient and increasing frequency in the countries of our study (and certainly in other democracies such as France, Sweden and Italy not covered here) to warrant consideration and inclusion in empirical studies of political participation' (Barnes et al., 1979: 35).

Following up on this argument, these modes, now notionally five in number, were then brought together in a more recent British study by Parry, Moyser and Day (1992). In their study, the range of activities used to measure political participation expanded to 23. Even that, however, by no means exhausts what would be a truly comprehensive picture of political participation. Thus, for example, Parry, Moyser and Day also attempted to incorporate what they termed 'output participation' – 'activities which aim to influence the making of policy . . . in its implementation' (Parry et al., 1992: 41). Under this mode they included such activities as service as a special constable in a police force, being a citizen volunteer on a local governmental advisory body or doing jury duty. As it turned out, however, the numbers in their survey who claimed to have participated in this way were too few to analyse. That in itself is substantively significant, of course, but it also points to that fact that there are significant practical problems in encompassing a truly comprehensive picture of political participation in any one study (see also Verba et al., 1995: 32–3).

THE LEVELS OF POLITICAL PARTICIPATION IN A DEMOCRACY

Across the various studies of political participation in democratic states, there are both significant differences in levels of reported citizen participation, but also some broad similarities. Perhaps the key similarity is that it is only the act of voting in national elections which engages a majority, or near majority, of the adult citizen population, virtually all of whom nowadays, in contrast to earlier times, enjoy that right as a matter of law. Dalton (1996: 45) estimates the average rate of turnout across 21 democracies during the 1990s at 76 per cent. This means, of course, that about one-quarter of the adult population does not typically participate by voting in national elections. There are, however, significant variations across different countries, across different types of election and across time.

Cross-nationally, as Dalton shows, rates vary with the United States (53 per cent) and Switzerland (46 per cent) at the low end, with barely half of adults turning out to vote. The Swiss case, however, is untypical of Western Europe in general where turnout is generally in the range of 70 per cent to 90 per cent. In Great Britain, for example, the figure given is 78 per cent, in (West) Germany 77 per cent, and in the National Assembly elections for France 69 per cent.

These rates are, of course, generally higher than those recorded for local (or state) elections or, in the case of Europe, for European elections. In Britain, for example, Chandler (1991: 217) records turnouts of between 36 per cent (for metropolitan districts) and 53 per cent (for Welsh county elections) in local elections held between 1973 and 1978. There have also been low turnout rates for elections to the European Parliament, seen tellingly by George and Bache as 'second order national elections . . . on a par with local government elections' (2001: 268). In the latest election, held in 1999, turnout for the 15 member states averaged 49.9 per cent,

which means that as many European Union citizens stayed at home as bothered to vote. Here, too, though, there were wide national variations. As many as 91 per cent turned out to vote in Belgium, mainly in this case because voting is compulsory and the election happened to coincide with a national election. In Italy (70.8 per cent) and Spain (64.4 per cent), turnout was also quite high, but in both cases below norms for national contests in the 1990s (87 per cent and 76 per cent according to Dalton, 1996: 45). In many other member states, eight in all, turnout was below 50 per cent. In Finland and the Netherlands, the turnout was around 30 per cent, and in the UK, a mere 24 per cent.

What is more alarming for those democratic theorists who see the health of democracy as closely tied to a high level of citizen engagement, is the trend over time in voter turnout. Since the Second World War, this has been downward. In the first elections to the European Parliament in 1979, turnout was 62.5 per cent. Since then it has gone down in each subsequent contest – 61 per cent in 1984, 58.5 per cent in 1989, 56.9 per cent in 1994, and 49.9 per cent in 1999. The same pattern also seems to hold for national elections. Thus, Dalton reports an average turnout for the 1950s of 82 per cent across the 21 democratic states he reviewed. Since then, there has been a modest decline of about six points over the four decades, with little sign of the trend being arrested. In Britain, for example, the first five post-war elections (1945 to 1959) had average turnouts of 79.7 per cent. For the most recent five, the figure was 71.3 per cent, with the 2001 election producing the lowest turnout of all, 59.4 per cent (King, 2002: 197).

While such rates of voter participation obviously fall well below what some would view as ideal in a representative democracy, the levels of participation in other modes are typically far lower still. Although exact cross-national comparisons (even with voting turnout) are difficult because of differences in institutional contexts and survey instrumentation (Parry et al., 1992: 44), Verba et al. (1995: 70) report participation in campaign activities from previous surveys as averaging a mere 5.6 per cent across six countries. Now, there is again some cross-national variation – the US figure is as high as 14 per cent, but such rates are atypically high. Far more common are rates in single figures. In Britain, for example, only 5.2 per cent reported that they had helped with fund-raising, and a mere 3.5 per cent said that they had participated in canvassing or doing clerical work for a political party or candidate (Parry et al., 1992: 44).

This pattern of low levels of participation also applies to the other modes of 'conventional' participation that have been studied – personal contacting of officials and participation in politically active groups (Parry et al., 1992: 44; Verba et al., 1995: 70). It is perhaps not surprising, therefore, that Barnes, Kaase and others should remark that: 'One may be forgiven for speculating a moment about how the business of representative democracy is ever carried out. The "grass-roots" of politics seem shriveled and starved of the nourishment of participation by the citizens' (Barnes et al., 1979: 84). Of course, this assumes that democracy is about the continuous input of an active citizenry – a view not all democratic theorists would share. But it is also true that while in percentage terms few citizens are active gladiators, in absolute terms they represent a substantial 'army' exercising their voices in these various ways, far out-numbering those who might be described as forming the political or governing elite. Furthermore, in the United States, at least, the decline in voter participation over time is not replicated in these other modes. In perhaps the only country where adequate trend data are available, Verba et al. report that 'the falloff in voter turnout may not be part of a general erosion in political participation' (1995: 71).

Indeed, in the mode of political protest, the evidence suggests that there has been a 'growing wave . . . in recent years' (Dalton, 1996: 71). The most common activity by far has been petition-signing, arguably one of the least challenging and most accepted of protest actions. The 1990–91 World Values Survey reported by Dalton, covering 17 democracies, showed that an average of 52 per cent had participated in this way. Again, however, there were wide cross-national variations. Canada topped the list with 77 per cent, a rate over four times that for the lowest, Spain, at 18 per cent. As specific activities become more challenging, and so more unconventional and even illegal, not surprisingly, rates drop to much lower levels. For example, the average reported participation in a lawful demonstration in the USA, Britain, Germany and France in 1990 was 21 per cent, for joining in a boycott 12.8 per cent, and occupying a building (the most challenging) 3 per cent (Dalton, 1996: 76). It is clearly apparent, therefore, that even at these levels they now represent a significant part of the total flow of citizen participation in modern democracies, as significant as some other 'conventional' modes.

What seems to have happened is that the overall shape of the participatory repertoire has changed over the years with a decline in voter turnout but a rise in political protest. That does not, of course, necessarily mean that those who might be described as 'gladiators' have increased much beyond the 5–7 per cent of the adult population originally estimated by Milbrath and Goel (1977: 11). Nor does it necessarily mean much diminution in the large percentage, perhaps 50–60 per cent, who confine their participatory activity to voting. Nor does it probably erode the 25–30 per cent of citizens who are essentially non-participants in the democratic process. Nevertheless, it does mean that there are still substantial numbers who exercise their voice from time to time, and many who do so on a quite regular basis using a variety of methods that challenge governing elites to pay close attention. Rates no doubt remain below what is ideal for those who wish that most citizens would be active participants, but they seem sufficient to reassure those who ponder whether democracy is being seriously undermined by insufficient numbers of ordinary citizens willing to have their say.

WHO ARE THE ACTIVISTS?

Given that citizens participate in different ways, it follows that there is not one homogeneous group of those that are active, but several overlapping yet distinct types of activists (Verba and Nie, 1972: 85–93; Parry et al., 1992: 227–32). This makes it correspondingly more difficult to explain why some are more politically active than others. Some factors and circumstances, in other words, are more crucial in one mode of participation than another. Nevertheless, there are some general factors that help answer the question 'Who are the activists?' These factors can be identified as follows:

- Governmental arrangements and legal requirements.
- Personal characteristics and resources.
- Political attitudes and beliefs.
- Group and media context.

Governmental and legal arrangements exert an influence on levels and patterns of political participation. Thus, democracies differ in the number of formal access points that are provided. In Britain, for example, the advent of direct elections for the European Parliament in 1979 and the creation of elected legislatures for Scotland and Wales in 1998 have increased the opportunities for citizens to vote. On the other hand, burdensome legal requirements and administrative procedures for voter registration, such as are found in the United States, clearly result in lower turnout rates (Crewe, 1981; Powell, 1986). Other factors under this general heading that have been shown to influence participation include mandatory (compulsory) voting laws, electoral arrangements in which 'who governs' is directly at stake and, not least, campaign finance laws (Jackman, 1987; Franklin, 1996; Conway, 1991: 118).

While such factors have been shown to play a significant role, particularly in the arena of electoral participation, it is clear that, even for voter turnout, other factors play an important part in influencing who participates and who does not. One such factor is socio-economic status. As Milbrath and Goel put it, 'No matter how class is measured, studies consistently show that higher class persons are more likely to participate in politics than lower class persons. . . . This proposition has been confirmed in numerous countries' (Milbrath and Goel, 1977: 92). Though this 'SES model' became very influential and widely used, it has been criticized because it 'fails to provide a coherent rationale for the connection between the explanatory socioeconomic variables and participation' (Verba et al., 1995: 281). As a result, the Verba team, and others, have made attempts to provide such a rationale through the concept of resources. In their most recent study, for example, Verba and his colleagues focus on three different kinds of personal resources they consider relevant to political activism: free time, money and civic skills. As they note, 'many forms of political activity – campaign work, informal efforts to solve community problems, even voting – require time' (Verba et al., 1995: 271). Similarly, civic skills, such as the capacity to plan a meeting, write a letter, make a speech, know how to contact an official, at the least lower the barriers to becoming politically active. These are the learned skills that lie behind the regularly reported positive association between formal education and participation whereby those with higher levels of education typically participate at higher levels (Milbrath and Goel, 1977: 98–102).

Money is a somewhat different matter. It clearly is an important resource in the United States where 'contributions to candidates or political causes . . . have grown in relative importance in recent decades' (Verba et al., 1995: 271). And wealth as a personal resource has been shown by Parry, Moyser and Day (1992: 76–84) to be positively related to all modes of participation in Britain, except notably political protest. But in general it would seem that money by itself plays less of a role in contexts other than America. All in all, however, this more sophisticated resource model has enhanced understanding of activism, not least when the picture is then expanded to consider the important ways in which these resources are differentially distributed across significant social groupings defined by class, age, gender and ethnicity. It is this that leads on to pertinent questions about political equality and democracy.

Important though resources are, they need to be augmented by a set of factors some authors refer to as psychological – key political attitudes and beliefs that inform the citizen's propensity to become active. The central concept here is that of 'engagement' or psychological 'involvement' – those beliefs and values through which the citizen views the political world, and her or his place in it. There are potentially many different ingredients that help shape the level and nature of a citizen's sense of political engagement, but most commonly research has consistently found activism to be associated with such factors as:

- Higher levels of interest in political and governmental affairs.
- Feelings of personal efficacy – that the individual can make a difference.
- Sense of civic duty – that citizenship entails being active as a voter or in the community.
- Having a strong identification with a political party and other politically relevant groups.

In addition, heightened levels of political cynicism, alienation and dissatisfaction have been suggested as specific factors associated with political protest. This is the thrust of the deprivation approach that grounds protest and violence in feelings of frustration that leads to aggressive behaviour (Gurr, 1970). While superficially plausible, however, research has shown the linkages to be 'complex and at times convoluted' (Parry et al., 1992: 188). Indeed, Dalton argues that:

> Protest in advanced industrial democracies is not simply an outlet for the . . . alienated and deprived; often just the opposite appears. Protest is better described by the resource

model. Protesters are individuals who have the ability to organize and participate in political activities of all forms, including protest. (Dalton, 1996: 79)

What none of these factors so far outlined explain very well is the substantive agenda of political issues and personal concerns that citizens bring to the public arena when they participate. This brings us to the last group of factors – the social, economic and political environment in which citizen political activity takes place. It is clear that participation has indeed an instrumental quality to it: activists are concerned about specific policy matters and want to influence the direction of public policy about those matters. It is a matter of what Verba et al. call 'issue engagement' or 'the politics of passionate issue commitment' (1995: 392, 398). As a result, it is not surprising that an American study of environmental, social justice and pro-life activists found their activism to be the basis for the construction of their whole identity as self-interested yet also altruistic and moral beings (Teske, 1997). In short, activists have substantial issue agendas, by one estimate four times as long as non-participants (Parry et al., 1992: 251). Some of those issues are undoubtedly personal; most, however, reflect wider concerns – issues surrounding the meeting of basic needs in the community like employment, housing and health care; levels of taxation; the state of the national economy; education; the environment; crime and drugs; and even international concerns like defence policy, terrorism and human rights.

In many of these contexts, citizen concern is heightened, and activism stimulated, by 'external' agencies such as the mass media, political parties and the array of groups with which many citizens are affiliated. The same is also true of more informal networks of family, work colleagues and friends. That political mobilization is an important part of the overall understanding of political activism is clear from studies of the role that such forces play in an individual's decision to participate. Verba et al. (1995: 137), for example, estimate that between 30 per cent and 43 per cent of political activity was mobilized rather than spontaneous. An even higher figure, 57 per cent, was reported for Britain (Parry et al., 1992: 87). From a resource viewpoint, however, such linkages and networks can be seen as yet another set of assets available to individuals. And, like more personal resources, they are not equally distributed across the adult population. On the contrary, it is clear that in most instances, these group-based resources tend to favour those already better off in terms of personal resources (Parry et al., 1992: 93). The result, widely found, is that political activists of whatever mode are not a microcosm of the society from which they spring. On the contrary, they typically reflect a persistent over-representation of dominant social, economic and cultural groups.

CONCLUSION: DOES POLITICAL PARTICIPATION MAKE A DIFFERENCE?

The question of whether political participation makes a difference can be answered at two broad levels. At one level, one may ask what difference it makes for the individual activist. Is political participation educative for the participant and if so, in what ways? Some make this a more important purpose for promoting political participation than any other, believing that it produces the kind of well-informed, responsible citizenry open to the views and interests of other members of society on which a healthy democracy depends (Pateman, 1970: 42; Mill, 1972: 217). The empirical evidence on this, however, is rather mixed. Parry, Moyser and Day (1992: 287–9), for example, find substantial minorities who thought their actions had increased the levels of their political knowledge and most reported high levels of satisfaction. On the other hand, the majority also said that their actions had not made their impressions of politics either more or less favourable. For the minority who did report a change, it

tended to be towards a more negative stance, particularly when the action had been a form of political protest. In America, participation has also been associated with increased levels of political knowledge, but protest too has been shown to decrease political trust (Jennings and Niemi, 1981). Thus while there are some cross-nationally consistent educative effects of political participation, they may not produce quite the kind of 'responsible citizenry' that John Stuart Mill envisaged in the nineteenth century.

The second level at which the impact of political participation may be examined concerns its impact on public policy-making. Here again the evidence is mixed. Obviously, in cases of direct democracy such as in referendums, initiatives and town meetings, the impact is clear. The people, or at least those who choose to participate, decide the outcome. But most public policy decisions are not made directly by the people but by governmental officials. This makes the causal connections between public participation and policy outcome more difficult to substantiate. One approach has been the study of the levels of concurrence, or agreement, between elite and citizen policy agendas. These studies have been suggestive of some influence on the part of activist citizens. As Parry, Moyser and Day put it:

> Participation may only be the work of a minority but, judged by the levels of concurrence on priorities, that minority can make itself count. It can make its weight felt on those issues, such as environment, planning and housing which can have an impact both on particular individuals and on the general public in the locality. There are, therefore, clear signs that elites do respond and that political action can produce results. (Parry et al., 1992: 388; see also Verba and Nie, 1972: 332–3; Conway, 1991: 181–90)

Yet to the extent that political participation can be shown to make a difference, one key question remains – 'different for whom?' As Pizzorno (1970) once pointed out, political participation may enable the economically or culturally disadvantaged to exercise their voice to change public policy in favourable ways. Clearly this has happened, the American civil rights movement of the 1960s being a major example. But political participation may also be used by those already advantaged socially and economically to consolidate their advantages by political means. And certainly activists tend to be drawn from the more privileged sectors of society. The result of enhanced opportunities for political participation may be, paradoxically, to increase political inequality and exacerbate problems of political exclusion. All in all, while political participation is at the heart of democracy, whether it always promotes a more just and equal society is another question.

Summary

- Political participation by ordinary citizens is a central feature of democracy.
- How often, and in what ways, citizens participate in democracies vary widely, reflecting the importance of voluntary choice in such decisions.
- Political participation is about taking part in the making of decisions about public policy, but there are different views about what this should be taken to mean.
- In early studies political participation was taken to mean participation in the electoral arena through voting and campaigning, but over the years the term has gradually expanded to incorporate a relatively diverse set of activities.
- Studies show relatively high though varying levels of participation in voting but otherwise relatively low levels elsewhere.
- Studies show signs of decline in voter turnout, but also a rise in political protest, changing the overall mix of citizen participation over time.
- Levels of political participation are influenced by a number of factors, including governmental and legal arrangements, personal resource levels of individual citizens, their political attitudes and beliefs, and their issue concerns.
- The cumulative result of such influences is a set of political activists who over-represent dominant social, economic and cultural groups.
- Political participation does affect political outlooks, but the effects are not particularly strong, nor are they consistent.
- Political participation also has discernible effects upon public policy-making, but those effects are not always clear, nor is it always obvious whether a more just and equal society is thereby promoted.

TUTORIAL QUESTIONS

1. To what extent is it the case that the more participation there is in the making of decisions the more democracy there is?

2. What are the important differences in the character of political participation as it is observed in democratic and non-democratic regimes?

3. Given the observed levels of political participation, do you think that the grassroots of democratic politics are 'shriveled and starved' (Barnes and Kaase et al., 1979)?

4. Outline and discuss the 'resource model' of political participation. How might this model point to issues of political inequality and exclusion?

5. Does political participation by ordinary citizens make a difference? What are the possible costs and benefits of enhancing opportunities for political participation?

FURTHER READING

Lester Milbrath and M.L. Goel (1977) *Political Participation: How and Why Do People Get Involved in Politics* (Chicago, IL: Rand McNally, second edition) remains a useful, if somewhat dated, compendium of findings about the correlates of political participation.

The classic study is by Sydney Verba and Norman Nie (1972) *Participation in America: Political Democracy and Social Equality* (New York: Harper & Row), developed later in a seven-nation study by Sydney Verba, Norman Nie and Jae-On Kim (1979) *Participation and Political Equality: a Seven-Nation Comparison* (Cambridge: Cambridge University Press).

Political protest was first comprehensively studied by Samuel Barnes, Max Kaase et al. (1979) *Political Action: Mass Participation in Five Western Democracies* (Beverly Hills, CA: Sage Publications) and revisited by M. Kent Jennings and Jan W. van Deth (1989) *Continuities in Political Action* (New York: Walter de Gruyter). It was developed into a study of social and political movements by Russel J. Dalton and M. Kuechler (eds) (1990) *Challenging the Political Order: New Social and*

Political Movements in Western Democracies (Cambridge: Polity Press).

More recently, significant single-country studies have been undertaken in Britain by G. Parry, G. Moyser and N. Day (1992) *Political Participation and Democracy in Britain* (Cambridge: Cambridge University Press) and in America by Sydney Verba et al. (1995) *Voice and Equality: Civic Voluntarism in American Politics* (Cambridge, MA: Harvard University Press). A comprehensive study of the New England town meeting as a form of direct democracy is provided by F.M. Bryan (forthcoming) *Real Democracy: What It Looks Like, How It Works* (Chicago, IL: University of Chicago Press).

REFERENCES

Barnes, Samuel, Kaase, Max et al. (1979) *Political Action: Mass Participation in Five Western Democracies*. Beverly Hills, CA: Sage.

Bryan, Frank M. (forthcoming) *Real Democracy: What It Looks Like, How It Works*. Chicago, IL: University of Chicago Press.

Chandler, J.A. (1991) *Local Government Today*. Manchester: Manchester University Press.

Conway, Margaret (1991) *Political Participation in the United States* (second edition). Washington, DC: CQ Press.

Crewe, Ivor (1981) 'Electoral Participation', in David Butler et al. (eds), *Democracy at the Polls*. Washington, DC: American Enterprise Institute, pp. 216–63.

Dalton, Russell J. (1996) *Citizen Politics*. New York: Chatham House.

Dalton, Russell J. and Kuechler, Manfred (eds) (1990) *Challenging the Political Order: New Social and Political Movements in Western Democracies*. Cambridge: Polity Press.

Eckstein, Harry (1961) *A Theory of Stable Democracy*. Princeton, NJ: Center of International Studies.

Finer, Samuel E. (1972) 'Groups and Political Participation', in Geraint Parry (ed.), *Participation in Politics*. Manchester: Manchester University Press, pp. 41–58.

Franklin, Mark (1996) 'Electoral Participation', in Larry Leduc et al. (eds), *Elections and Voting in Global Perspective*. London: Sage.

George, Stephen and Bache, Ian (2001) *Politics in the European Union*. Oxford: Oxford University Press.

Gurr, Ted Robert (1970) *Why Men Rebel*. Princeton, NJ: Princeton University Press.

Jackman, Robert W. (1987) 'Political Institutions and Voter Turnout in the Industrial Democracies', *American Political Science Review*, **81**: 405–23.

Jennings, M. Kent and van Deth, Jan W. (1989) *Continuities in Political Action*. New York: Walter de Gruyter.

Jennings, M. Kent and Niemi, Richard (1981) *Generations and Politics*. Princeton, NJ: Princeton University Press.

King, Anthony (ed.) (2002) *Britain at the Polls, 2001*. New York: Chatham House.

Lazarsfeld, Paul, Berelson, Bernard and Gaudet, Hazel (1944) *The People's Choice: How the Voter Makes Up His Mind in a Presidential Campaign*. New York: Columbia University Press.

Milbrath, Lester and Goel, M.L. (1977) *Political Participation: How and Why Do People Get Involved in Politics* (second edition). Chicago, IL: Rand McNally.

Mill, John Stuart (1972) *Representative Government* (Everyman edition). London: Dent.

Parry, Geraint, Moyser, George and Day, Neil (1992) *Political Participation and Democracy in Britain*. Cambridge: Cambridge University Press.

Pateman, Carole (1970) *Participation and Democratic Theory*. London: Cambridge University Press.

Pizzorno, Alessandro (1970) 'An Introduction to the Theory of Political Participation', *Social Science Information*, **9**: 29–61.

Powell, G. Bingham (1986) 'American Voting Turnout in Comparative Perspective', *American Political Science Review*, **80**: 17–44.

Teske, Nathan (1997) *Political Activists in America*. Cambridge: Cambridge University Press.

Townsend, James (1967) *Political Participation in Communist China*. Berkeley and Los Angeles, CA: University of California Press.

Verba, Sydney and Nie, Norman (1972) *Participation in America: Political Democracy and Social Equality*. New York: Harper & Row.

Verba, Sydney, Nie, Norman and Kim, Jae-On (1979) *Participation and Political Equality: a Seven-Nation Comparison*. Cambridge: Cambridge University Press.

Verba, Sydney et al. (1995) *Voice and Equality: Civic Voluntarism in American Politics*. Cambridge, MA: Harvard University Press.

See also chapters

1	Sovereignty	16	Interest Groups
6	Representative and Direct Democracy	17	Social Movements
		19	Social Capital
9	Civil Society – National and Global	20	The Welfare State and Democracy
14	Parties and Party Systems	21	Cyber-democracy
15	Elections and Electoral Systems		

19 Social Capital

William A. Maloney and Linda Stevenson

The concept of social capital is *en vogue* and research in this area highlights the central role played by civic networks and information channels, the trustworthiness of relations between actors and institutions, and the norms and effective sanctions in political, social and economic life. While the genealogy of the concept can be traced well before the contributions of Coleman (1988) and Putnam (1993, 2000), these authors are the main tributaries of the contemporary debate. The main, although not exclusive, focus of this chapter, however, is on Robert Putnam's contribution largely because he has popularized the concept and (more significantly) because his approach attempts to synthesize components of Coleman's perspective with de Tocqueville's (nineteenth-century) praise of the positive effects of a vibrant associational life.

DEFINING THE CONCEPT

Social capital is considered to be a productive resource '. . . making possible the achievement of ends that in its absence would not be possible' (Coleman, 1988: 98). It has been suggested that social capital helps to resolve the dilemmas of collective action, that it is necessary for the proper functioning of a democratic political system and that it contributes to *positive* policy outcomes in areas such as education, health, crime, welfare and in stimulating economic growth. Coleman stated that:

Social capital is defined by its function. It is not a single entity but a variety of different entities, with two elements in common: they all consist of some aspect of social structure, and they facilitate certain actions of actors – whether persons or corporate actors – within the structure. . . . Unlike other forms of capital, social capital inheres in the structure of relations between actors and among actors. (Coleman, 1988: 98)

In his exposition of social capital Coleman draws analogies with financial capital, having been influenced by principles of rational action taken from economists (his vision draws on both sociology and economics). In his analysis of social systems, both profit (economic capital) and human capital (friendship, families, colleagues, schools, churches) are taken into consideration. He considered that analysis of social systems should include economic analysis, and that social capital is context-specific: *endogenous* to particular social structural contexts.

On the other hand, Robert Putnam argues from a political science standpoint, drawing on theories of political culture in which norms and values are treated as *exogenous* variables. He defines social capital as entailing, 'features of social life – networks, norms, and trust – that enable participants to act together more effectively to pursue shared objectives. . . . Social capital, in short, refers to social connections and the attendant norms and trust'. He contends that the core idea of social capital theory is that social networks have value: 'Just as a screwdriver (physical capital) or a college education (human capital) can increase productivity (both individual and collective), so too social contacts affect the production of individuals and groups . . . social capital refers to connections among individuals – social networks and the norms of reciprocity and trustworthiness that arise from them' (Putnam, 2000: 18–19).

Putnam argues that networks of civic engagement generate social capital: the denser such networks in the community, the more likely its citizens will be able to cooperate for mutual benefit. And, he suggests, unless civil society is organized around 'horizontal bonds of mutual solidarity' (through face-to-face relations among individuals across society) rather than through 'vertical bonds of dependency and exploitation' (for example social class divisions), trust and cooperation (necessary for the creation of social capital) cannot develop. Norms of reciprocity and civic engagement are to be found, then, in dense horizontal networks of civic engagement, for example in neighbourhood associations, choral societies, cooperatives, arts and cultural societies, hobby and sports clubs, religious and ethnic groups. (Putnam was particularly interested in American Bowling Leagues.)

Associations are considered to have numerous internal and external effects. They help to shape public opinion, provide fora for deliberation, and promote participation (both social and political). In turn they may act as countervailing powers, promoting alternative forms of government, etc. For Putnam, associations are crucial because they act as (de Tocquevillian) 'schools of democracy' where citizens learn to become 'better democrats'. The more citizens participate in a wide and diverse range of associations, the more they will learn important skills such as tolerance, mutual accommodation and trust. In summary, Putnam argued that:

> civil associations contribute to the effectiveness and stability of democratic government . . . both because of their 'internal' effects on individual members and because of their 'external' effects on the wider polity. Internally, associations instill in their members habits of cooperation, solidarity, and public spiritedness. . . . Externally . . . a dense network of secondary associations . . . contributes to effective social collaboration. (Putman, 1993: 89–90)

Putnam maintains that there are positive spill-over effects in a society rich in social capital. For example, a poorly connected individual in a well-connected society may benefit from living in a neighbourhood where the crime rate is depressed because her or his neighbours may maintain a vigilant eye on each other's homes. Social capital can be both a *public* (of benefit to the community as a whole) and a *private* (of personal benefit) good. Sometimes it benefits those who have not contributed to the generation of the good, for example civic amenity trusts run by volunteers operate 'clean up' campaigns and tree planting projects in their community, providing environmental improvements that everyone can enjoy. At other times, it can be exclusionary, primarily benefiting the 'insiders' of an association, for example Alcoholics Anonymous. A key component of social capital, however, is generalized reciprocity, which Putnam (2000: 21) defines as 'I'll do this for you without expecting anything specific back from you, in the confident expectation that someone else will do something for me down the road'.

PROBLEMATIZING THE CONCEPT

How best to measure social capital is a major challenge. There are two main ways: (1) by gathering data relating to associational vibrancy and membership levels (organizational focus); and (2) by acquiring survey data on trust and civic engagement (individual member focus). However, we shall disregard methodological challenges to data gathering and analysis, and shall concentrate on some substantive problems that the concept of social capital raises.

The relationship between different types of involvement

Putnam maintains that a vibrant civil society facilitates and encourages a vibrant political society. Rosenstone and Hansen provide some statistical support for the (Tocquevillian/)Putnam thesis: 'Involvement in associations promotes political activism . . . people who have joined with others to work on a local problem are 12.9 percent more likely to write to national leaders, 22.9 percent more likely to sign a petition, and 28.7 percent more likely to take part in a local political meeting' (Rosenstone and Hansen, 1993: 84). However, it is unclear how social involvement positively enhances the willingness to become politically involved: what is the causal link between participation in sporting and other recreational activities and political activism? In fact some have argued that there is much evidence that the Tocquevillian thesis should be modified, local civic life is not a breeding ground for wider political involvement, but may actually serve as an alternative to it.

A related concern is that the Putnam/Tocqueville perspective suffers from what Rosenblum (1998) terms the 'logic of congruence', that is, the *general* expectation that all associations contribute to society in the same way. In addition to this, it exhibits the misplaced 'liberal expectancy' of the beneficial effects of associational life, that '. . . moral effects generated in one associational context necessarily generalize to other associational contexts' (Rosenblum, 1998: 57). Membership of associations in specific sectors is likely to have a differential effect on social capital: enthusiasm for the ubiquitous 'positive' effects of associational memberships should be tempered.

The dark side of social capital

There can be contradictory qualities to collective action organizations: promoting internal unity and external conflict. In most cases this conflict may not be immediately harmful, but there are many instances where the social capital appropriated or generated can be used to the detriment of specific groups or sections of society. Coleman (1988) acknowledges that social capital is a resource that can be used for both 'positive' *and* 'negative' purposes: it has the potential to be valuable in facilitating certain desirable activities and useless or even harmful for others. Individuals construct 'collective identities', which shape commonalities and act as an adhesive that binds these people together. An important component of this 'gluing' process is the identification of, what Piven and Cloward (1997) term, the *other*. Accordingly, the groups partly define themselves through (in many cases) a negatively constructed juxtaposition. While 'identity politics' can offer people 'protection, comfort and pride, it has also been a bane upon humankind, the source of unending tragedy (Serbs and Muslims and Croats; Protestants and Roman Catholics, Sikhs and Hindus *etc.*)' (Piven and Cloward, 1997: 43). Piven and Cloward (1997: 46) also highlight that identity politics can be liberating and equalizing, for example, the civil rights movement in the USA. A major flaw in Putnam's original formulation of the concept is that he overlooked the difficulty of transferring intra-group social capital to the inter-group setting. Social capital does not necessarily facilitate or foster social or political integration.

In response to such criticisms Putnam has conceded that there can be a 'dark side' to social capital. Accordingly, he has emphasized that social capital can emerge in two forms: *bonding* and *bridging*. Bonding creates strong ties within existing groups ('a kind of sociological superglue'), bridging creates ties between groups ('a sociological WD-40'). Bridges across social or political cleavages may facilitate the development of tolerance, trust, reciprocity, accommodation and cooperation. Bonding social capital can be pernicious because of its intra-group qualities: it may reinforce intolerance within social or political groups. Thus neo-fascist or racist organizations can be strengthened, just as much as charitable or humanitarian aid organizations, through the development of bonding social capital.

Trust

The concept of trust is crucial to the social capital model. Putnam argues that it is an essential component which lubricates co-operation. Putnam's account of the democratic effects of voluntary associations is almost entirely predicated on trust. Yet, Putnam never offers a precise definition of trust. Trust comes in many guises: generalized trust which relates to those we do not know; special trust which is trust in friends and institutions. He places a wide range of relationships and expectations under the universal label of trust. It is clear that when Putnam (and others) refers to trust as a basic measure of social capital, there is little (or no) recognition that its existence should not always be seen in such a positive light. There can be moral and immoral uses of trust and it is not necessarily so that all forms of trust will underpin democratic values.

Putnam also decries declining levels of trust in political institutions as being an important indicator of the declining levels of social capital. In the early 1960s in the USA approximately two-thirds of the population expressed high levels of trust in government, by the mid-1990s less than one-third did. However, this decline is not necessarily a cause for concern. In fact, it may be seen much more positively. Scepticism of government accords with expressed principles that citizens should closely scrutinize government. Schudson (1998) highlighted that such scepticism had important historical roots and provided a significant part of American political culture at the time of the revolution and the formation of the nation. He argued that, 'compared to England, the colonies were renegade, individualistic, and distrustful of authority' (Schudson, 1998: 23). Fukuyama (1995) points out that contemporary Americans have retained that strong anti-statist tradition. Many opinion polls show that

Americans have lower levels of confidence in government than do people in other advanced democracies but, as Fukuyama suggests: 'anti-statism is not the same as hostility to community'. Thus he maintains that while Americans may dislike and distrust 'Big Government', they are 'extraordinarily co-operative and sociable in their companies, voluntary associations, churches, newspapers, universities' (Fukuyama, 1995: 51). The issue is not one of whether or not citizens are anti-statist, but whether they are prepared to place their own individual interests below those of intermediate social groups. Schudson (1998: 300–1) maintains that language of decline in the 1990s is broadly similar to that of the 1950s in the discourses of Robert Dahl, David Riesman and C. Wright Mills, who judged Americans as apathetic, 'inactionary' and 'out of it'. Putnam concedes that the 1950s and 1960s, were hardly a 'golden age' for 'Americans who were marginalized because of their race or gender or social class or sexual orientation' (2000: 17).

Finally, increases in citizens' distrust and alienation from political institutions and the political system generally may be a *rational* response to poor performance in important policy areas. Trust is a relational and experiential concept: if an individual's experience of others is that they can be trusted, then it is likely that he or she will exhibit trusting attitudes in others. If the experience is the reverse, then a less trusting orientation is likely to follow. As Fiorina notes, distrust in government might have been earned by government: 'Vietnam and civil disorders, Watergate, stagflation, and the Ayatolla, $200 billion deficits and Iran-contras, Whitewater, Lewinsky' (Fiorina, 1999: 405). He wryly turns Putnam's argument on its head: 'Rather than 1994 Americans being a bunch of angry cynics, 1964 Americans may have been a bunch of deluded optimists' (Fiorina, 1999: 401).

It should also be borne in mind that measurements of trust in political institutions are in many cases actually surveys of the perceived effectiveness of political office holders.

It would be of great concern if surveys consistently found widespread or growing distrust in political institutions and political regimes, but it is less problematic if citizens exhibit disenchantment or distrust in the performance of office holders. This key distinction is sometimes lost in the debate: citizens may rationally express low levels of trust in office holders and simultaneously exhibit high levels of support for the system of government and democratic values.

To be sure there must be some balance in the institutional trust equation: little or no trust could provide a fertile breeding ground for extremists. However, it is not troubling that citizens are watchful and distrustful of the 'office holders'. In a healthy democracy they should be closely scrutinized and held to account. Schudson (1998) poses the (empirical) question: What would be the optimal level of trust? He maintains that 100 per cent trust in major political, social and economic institutions would be 'deeply troubling': 'But is 75 percent the right level? Or 50 percent? Or 25 percent?' (Schudson, 1998: 307).

ASSOCIATIONAL VITALITY AND GOOD GOVERNMENT

Putnam's correlation between associational vitality and good government has been challenged as oversimplistic. While the idea that a vibrant associational life can be causally related to good government is intuitively appealing, several questions remain unanswered. What is the causal mechanism between civic activity and good governance? How do norms and networks of civic engagement undergird good government? Associational activity may actually be a response to 'poor government'. As Berman (2001) notes: 'A flourishing civil society [may] signal governmental and institutional failure and bodes ill for political stability and democracy'. She maintains that militia movements and home

schooling societies emerge from dissatisfaction with the outputs of public institutions and should be seen as signs of sickness rather than health. Once one looks beyond the sphere of benign social participation (bird watching, choral societies and sports clubs) then we find that social capital may breed social and/or political conflict. It is also the case that 'Poujadism in France, extreme right wing activity in the United States, and Nazism in Germany were all supported by a vibrant civil society. . . . [The Nazis used] choral societies and bird-watching clubs in their infiltration and eventual takeover of German society' (Berman, 2001: 35).

THE ROLE OF POLITICAL INSTITUTIONS

Putnam's argument is that the levels of social capital a society possesses is based on its historical and cultural roots, and that governments and other public agencies can do little to effect the creation or destruction of social capital. Yet public authorities do have a role to play in the creation (and/or destruction) of social capital. Tarrow (1996) is critical of the role assigned to regional government in Putnam's work on Italy: 'the character of the state is external to the model, suffering the results of the region's associational incapacity, but with no responsibility for producing it' (Tarrow, 1996: 395). Skocpol (1999) argued that the structure of political institutions in the USA had a significant influence on form, shape and size of associational life: 'the structure of government served as an organizational model'. She further argues that 'The story of American voluntarism has clearly been one of symbiosis between state and society – not a story of society apart from, or instead of, the state' (Skocpol, 1999: 47). The same picture could be painted of associational life in the UK.

CIVIC EROSION THESIS: 'BOWLING ALONE'

Putnam has famously argued that there has been an erosion of the 'civil community' over the last 30 years or so in the USA: his famous 'Bowling Alone' thesis. While the total number of bowlers in the USA increased by 10 per cent between 1980 and 1993, the number of bowling leagues fell by 40 per cent. Putnam argued that this decline in formal association and rise in individual activities in US bowling alleys was indicative of a general process of disassociation in civil society. In *Bowling Alone* (2000), Putnam lays out a great deal of evidence demonstrating declines in political participation in American political and civic life. For example, in 1960 62.8 per cent of US citizens eligible to vote cast their ballots. In 1996 it was 48.9 per cent. Participation in partisan politics (that is, traditional door-to-door canvassing) is also in decline – increasingly political parties contact citizens via telephone or direct mail marketing. The percentage of those attending a political rally or speech, those working for a political party, those who have held or ran for office, those attending a public meeting on town or school affairs, those who have served as an officer of some club or organization or on a committee for some local organization, have all declined over the last 30 years. He estimated that the USA now has 16 million fewer participants in public meetings about local affairs, eight million fewer committee members and eight million fewer local organizational leaders (Putnam, 2000: 42).

Most commentators have been persuaded by the deluge of evidence which Putman has mobilized in support of the argument about declines in traditional associational life. Nevertheless, there have been disputes over its impact on US democracy and society. Survey data do not always capture newer types of involvement such as parents interacting at their kids' regular sports events, or families and friends bowling together and the growth in private sports/fitness centres. People attend these clubs regularly and are as likely to make acquaintances and friends in these areas as they previously were in what might have been considered more public venues. Fiorina (1999) challenges the 'iron' assumption that high levels of civic engagement are optimal. He cites Tingsten (1937: 225–6), who showed that high voter turnout in Austria and Germany before the Second World War occurred simultaneously with the decay of their democracies, and that these impressive levels of political engagement 'apparently represented anger, desperation, and other motivations that normally are not viewed as things society should maximize' (Fiorina, 1999: 396).

MUTATING ORGANIZATIONAL STRUCTURES

Putnam is also pessimistic about the changing organizational structure of many interest groups and voluntary associations. He decries the decline of 'classic secondary associations' (such as trades unions, professional associations), and the growth of what he terms 'vertically ordered', 'tertiary associations' (such as Greenpeace, the Sierra Club or Friends of the Earth). These organizations may be important in terms of policy-making, however: 'For the vast majority of their members, the only act of membership consists in writing a check for dues or perhaps occasionally reading a newsletter. Few ever attend any meetings of such organizations, and most are unlikely ever (knowingly) to encounter any other member' (Putnam, 1993: 71).

Membership ties within such groups are to 'common symbols, common leaders, and perhaps common ideals, but not to one another'. Putnam sees these organizations as antithetical to the development of social capital with many members being in *not so splendid isolation* from one another. However, critics of Putnam have contended that such tertiary groups may well be a site of social capital creation. Membership of these groups may not be as detrimental to the generation of social capital as the Putnam/Tocqueville model implies. Minkoff (2001) argues that these types of organization provide an infrastructure for collective action and produce a type of symbolic affiliation and social integration: 'For isolated and marginalized constituencies – the disabled, gay men and lesbians, the poor, and others – this sense of collective identity or "we" may literally be life-saving' (Minkoff, 2001: 183–4).

CONCLUSION

Social capital is an important and potentially powerful explanatory concept for the social sciences. Dimensions of social capital, such as networks and information channels, the trustworthiness of relations between actors and institutions, and norms and effective sanctions, are of fundamental importance in shaping political, social and economic life. While problems have been identified with the neo-Tocquevillian/Putnam perspective on social capital, it still retains utility. It invites us to explore the infrastructure of civil society and suggests that within it we may find an explanation of why in some polities political activity (and more broadly social and economic activity) display greater vitality and appear to be more effective.

Summary

- The modern social capital debate can trace its origins back to de Tocqueville and nineteenth-century theoretical debates on democracy. However, it is Coleman and Putnam who are the main contemporary contributors and whose views are most often reviewed, and contested, in current literature.
- As a concept, social capital is difficult to define and to measure. Different disciplines approach the topic from different vantage points, employing different methodologies, resulting in apparently contradictory conclusions. Rival schools of thought suggest, on the one hand, that political activism results from involvement in civil associations, and on the other, that participation in civil associations serves as an alternative to political activism.
- In contrast to the optimistic neo-Tocquevillian view of the benefits of associational life to a stable democracy, there have also been suggestions in more recent literature that social capital can be a negative, as well as a positive, resource. Not all associations contribute in the same way to society, therefore social capital has the potential to be a democratic asset in some situations, but useless or harmful in other situations. As Putnam has conceded, there can be a dark side to social capital.
- Care must also be taken when considering the concept of trust, which Putnam argues is a crucial component in the creation of social capital, but for which he provides no definition. His assumption that trust is always a positive concept has also been questioned, as gaining trust can be used for immoral as well as moral purposes, so not all forms of trust necessarily

underpin democratic values. There are different levels of trust that will lead to different levels of social capital. Levels of trust will vary in different aspects of political and social life.

- Putnam's correlation between associational vitality and good government has also been contested. There is no clear causal mechanism between the two. In fact, the opposite may be true, according to alternative interpretations which suggest that a vibrant associational life may actually be a response to *poor* government and the sign of an *unstable* polity.

- There is also some dispute over Putnam's argument that a society's historical and cultural roots dictate the level of social capital it possesses. His claim that political institutions have little effect on the creation or destruction of social capital has been countered by Skocpol, and others who argue that in America (and in the UK) civic voluntarism and the state are in a symbiotic relationship: mutually dependent.

- Despite the deluge of empirical evidence that Putnam has provided to support his argument, not everyone is convinced that there is a correlation between a decline in civil community activity and a decline in political participation in the USA.

- Changing organizational structures may not be the threat to social capital that Putnam predicts either. Although he expresses concern for the decline of classic secondary organizations (such as trade unions and professional associations) and the increase in 'checkbook' associations (such as Friends of the Earth, and Amnesty International), these groups may contribute to social capital by providing an important sense of collective identity, albeit that affiliation tends to be symbolic.

- Although studies of social capital raise as many questions as they answer, this is to be expected with a concept still in the early stages of development. Social capital is still a useful explanatory framework for the social sciences.

TUTORIAL QUESTIONS

1. **Is social capital a fad or fundamental concept in the social sciences?**

2. **'Bowling Alone': critically assess Robert Putnam's perspective on the concept of social capital?**

3. **Is social capital a panacea for all the ills of the modern world?**

4. **Is there a dark side to social capital?**

5. **'The higher the levels of trust in a society the healthier the democracy.' Discuss.**

FURTHER READING

Robert Putnam (2000) *Bowling Alone: the Collapse and Renewal of American Community* (New York: Simon & Schuster) is a highly detailed and clear account. It is data-rich and accessibly written.

There are two excellent edited volumes with contributions from a wide and diverse range of disciplines: B. Edwards, M.W. Foley and M. Diani (eds) (2001) *Beyond Tocqueville: Civil Society and the Social Capital Debate in Comparative Perspective* (Hanover, NH: University Press of New England) and Theda Skocpol and M.P. Fiorina (eds) (1999) *Civic Engagement in American Democracy* (Washington, DC: Brookings/ Russell Sage Foundation).

REFERENCES

Berman, S. (2001) 'Civil Society and Political Institutionalization', in B. Edwards, M.W. Foley and M. Diani (eds), *Beyond Tocqueville: Civil Society and The Social Capital Debate in Comparative Perspective*. Hanover, NH: University Press of NewEngland, pp. 32–42

Coleman, J.S. (1988) 'Social Capital in the Creation of Human Capital', *American Journal of Sociology*, **94**, Supplement: 95–119.

Fiorina, M. (1999) 'Extreme Voices: a Dark Side of Civic Engagement', in T. Skocpol and M.P. Fiorina (eds), *Civic Engagement in American Democracy*. Washington, DC: Brookings/ Russell Sage Foundation, pp. 395–425.

Fukuyama, F. (1995) *Trust: the Social Virtues and the Creation of Prosperity*. New York: The Free Press.

Minkoff, D.C. (2001) 'Producing Social Capital: National Social Movements and Civil Society', in B. Edwards, M.W. Foley and M. Diani (eds), *Beyond Tocqueville: Civil Society and The Social Capital Debate in Comparative Perspective*. Hanover, NH: University Press of New England, pp. 183–93.

Piven, F.F. and Cloward, R.A. (1997) *The Breaking of the American Social Compact*. New York: The New Press.

Putnam, R.D. (1993) *Making Democracy Work*. Princeton, NJ: Princeton University Press.

Putnam, R.D. (1995) 'Bowling alone: America's declining social capital', *Journal of Democracy*, **6**: 65–78.

Putnam R.D. (2000) *Bowling Alone: the Collapse and Renewal of American Community*. New York: Simon & Schuster.

Rosenblum, N.L. (1998) *Membership and Morals*. Princeton, NJ: Princeton University Press.

Rosenstone, S.J. and Hansen, M. (1993) *Mobilization, Participation and Democracy in America*. New York: Macmillan.

Schudson, M. (1998) *The Good Citizen: a History of American Civic Life*. Cambridge, MA: Harvard University Press.

Skocpol, T. (1999) 'Making Sense of the Civic Engagement Debate', in T. Skocpol and M.P. Fiorina (eds), *Civic Engagement in American Democracy*. Washington, DC: Brookings/ Russell Sage Foundation, pp. 27–80.

Tarrow, C. (1996) 'Making Social Science Work Across Space and Time: a Critical Reflection on Robert Putnam's *Making Democracy Work*', *American Political Science Review*, **90**: 389–97.

Tingsten, H. (1937) *Political Behaviour: Studies in Election Statistics*. London: King and Son.

See also chapters

20 The Welfare State and Democracy

Michael Lister and Daniel Wincott

The Welfare State and Democracy are woven from the same cloth.
(Esping-Andersen, 1999: 8)
[Welfare programmes] instill . . . a feeling of childlike dependence [in beneficiaries]. The capacity of the beneficiaries for independence, for making their own decisions, atrophies through disuse.
(Friedman, 1980: 149)

For some, the welfare state is an essential corollary of mass democracy. Others argue that it corrodes democracy, perhaps even undermining it fatally. Competing conceptions of citizenship are central to each of these positions. In most English language debate, both sides take 'independence' to be a defining quality of the citizen (see Pateman, 1989 for a discussion). Citizens should be able to come to political judgements without having to consider their immediate material circumstances or coming under undue pressure from someone wielding power over them. T.H. Marshall, and the analysts and activists who have followed his lead, understand the success of mass democracy to be predicated on a system of social security. Its purpose or effect was to guarantee for all the independence and security that was once the preserve of property-owning gentlemen.

Milton Friedman and other 'New Right' authors see the welfare state as having quite the opposite consequence. So far from securing the independence of citizens, welfare ben-efits reduce robust independent citizens to a condition of childlike dependence. Worse still they have the addictive qualities of a drug, robbing the dependent 'addict' of the capacity for rational choice. While sometimes used with a wider but looser meaning – referring to the simple act of surviving on benefits – the narrower meaning of dependency – meaning a behavioural or cultural 'condition' – tends to infect the looser usage. Individuals trapped within a 'dependency culture' belong to an 'underclass', cut off from mainstream society (except as a threatening presence), incapable of acting in their own long-term best interests, and neither interested in nor fit for exercising the rights (and duties) of political citizenship. For the New Right the irony of the welfare state is that it is primarily responsible for the condition it seeks to ameli-orate. Moreover, it must coerce the tax-paying public into providing the resources for this folly. Fundamental values and public policy objectives of economic efficiency and freedom as well as liberal democracy are threatened by the welfare state.

In the closing decades of the twentieth century these two positions marked out the boundaries of debate about the relationship between democracy and the welfare state. In their dominant forms, both are problematic. As we shall see in the next section, the 'dependency culture' analysis reveals a profound inconsistency in New Right thinking. Equally, however, much centre-left reaction to it mirrors the problems of the original thesis. It also cuts the left off from its own roots. This deracinated left element sometimes appears almost to deny that social conditions can and do affect adversely individuals' abilities to act as full members of society. Despite its flaws, the dependency thesis has become influential well beyond the ranks of the New Right. Tony Blair's 'Third Way' approach to welfare reform is saturated with references to ending dependency. Yet the strategy of 'activating' welfare is hardly confined to Blairites, finding echoes in many other industrialized capitalist democracies.

Proper evaluation of contemporary reforms in welfare policy (including New Labour's 'Third Way') also must be based on a reappraisal of Marshall's theory of citizenship. In a famous essay first published in 1950, Marshall analysed the relationship between citizenship and social class. He traced the development of citizenship, first in the civil sphere, then in politics and finally as it acquired a social dimension. Although the detailed historical analysis and sequence of development was specific to the British case, Marshall's account can be read as a normative argument about how social, political and civil aspects of citizenship ought to relate to one another in a mass democracy. 'Good' citizens should not have to worry about their basic material well-being.

However, too much contemporary welfare state analysis considers the social dimension of citizenship in isolation from its civil and political aspects. Indeed, we have come to talk of 'social citizenship' as a largely separate concept, neglecting connections between social, political and civil rights (but see King and Waldron, 1988). Indeed, the relationship between democracy and the welfare state can be conceptualized in terms of social and political rights of citizenship. Rather than treating social citizenship as a common, universal ideal achieved only if, say, workers are fully 'decommodified' (see Esping-Andersen, 1990 and the discussion below), instead national social contexts produce diverse forms of (political and social) citizenship corresponding to distinct forms of modern democracy. Moreover, state policies play only a part alongside other social and economic factors in structuring the social quality of citizenship. For example, if full employment is a key factor in the decommodification of workers (see Kalecki, 1943 for a relevant discussion), the question then becomes what was the role of the state in achieving – or perhaps even guaranteeing – full employment?

The perception of a democratic deficit, sparked by falling turnout and a decline in membership of political parties, trade unions and other civic organizations, brings these issues into sharp focus. There is a widespread view that western *democracy* is under strain. Conventional accounts of political participation may pay too little attention to the consequences of political choice and public policy configurations for patterns of political participation (see Parry et al., 1992, for example), but in their different ways both New Right and social citizenship analyses suggest that social welfare provision influences these patterns. For the New Right, welfare, or perhaps more specifically, liberal, permissive welfare is likely to reduce or attenuate political participation, by rendering social benefit recipients passive recipients who are less likely to be active citizens. On the other hand, for left-of-centre arguments, the welfare state may secure individual independence, enabling them to become active or full citizens. Moreover, since the character of welfare states seem to differ significantly, are the various 'regimes' associated with distinctive patterns of democracy and political participation? New Right and social citizenship theories clearly differ in terms of what effects the welfare state, or social citizenship, has upon political activity, but they share the view that there is an effect. However, neither the literature on political participation nor that on the welfare state investigates the social foundations of (political) citizenship, or how social citizenship entitlements impact upon political participation.

DEPENDENCY CULTURE

Conservative and (neo-)liberal streams feed into the New Right. It would be as naïve to expect any political movement to be wholly consistent as to believe that logical inconsistency (or even incoherence) precludes a political movement from achieving considerable popularity. Nevertheless, New Right analysis of dependency culture is larded with inconsistency. Strongly influenced by neo-liberalism and new classical economics, historically the New Right celebrated the vibrancy of the free market based on robust individual instrumental rationality. Within the framework of economic liberalism, we would, of course, expect the welfare state to have an effect on the (rational) choices that individuals make. This impact may well be perverse – some individuals may alter their behaviour so as to qualify for any benefits that may be provided – for example, 'preferring' slightly lower (welfare) income plus additional leisure to a higher income and the inconvenience of paid employment. This is an example of the well-established economic concept of 'moral hazard'.

Persuasive though the logic may be, according to New Right nostrums we might expect the actual effect of such moral hazards to be relatively small. The New Right claims that the benefits to be gained from participating in the free market are large. Why, then, would 'rational' individuals choose a life of welfare-financed 'leisure', which the New Right itself argues leads to impoverishment, over participation in the market economy? Moreover, comparative analysis suggests that the most expensive and generous of welfare states – those of the Nordic countries – can coexist with rates of labour force participation at least as high as in the USA, where welfare provision was most limited. Rational moral hazards hardly provide a powerful threat to economic vibrancy, personal liberty or liberal democracy.

Faced by empirical evidence of considerable squalor and nursing hostility to the welfare state, several New Right authors developed a subtly but significantly different perspective on poverty. Often without seeming to recognize the full importance of the change they were making, these scholars argued that the welfare state created a new condition of behavioural dependency. In certain neighbourhoods, often dominated by public housing, welfare claimants become the dominant cultural force, resulting in the development of a dependency culture or an 'underclass'. Once trapped in a dependency culture, individuals are effectively robbed of their capacity to recognize and pursue their own best interests. Moreover, if those making public policy regard the welfare state as a potential solution to this problem, rather than (one of) its cause(s), they may become caught in a perverse policy spiral. Attempts to solve the problem of poverty by enhancing welfare state effort simply exacerbate the problem, while also sucking up ever-larger quantities of taxpayers' money.

This 'dependency culture' argument rests uneasily with the emphasis on instrumental individual rationality in economic liberal thought – the whole case hinges on accepting that welfare dependency destroys an individual's capacity to behave in ways that maximize his or her best interests. If true, then the welfare state may indeed pose a powerful potential threat to liberal democracy, most starkly by stripping welfare beneficiaries of their capacity to be effective citizens. More generally it may establish a powerfully expansive 'welfare dependency' dynamic as governments exacerbate the problem by trying to solve it. Eventually an 'underclass' is created that menaces the members and potentially undercuts the norms of 'mainstream' society.

In attempting to solve the problem of the dependency culture, New Right authors have usually chosen one of two possible solutions. Those most closely associated with economic liberalism suggest cutting back the welfare state would cure 'dependency'. If state welfare causes the problem, then the solution is to allow people to stand on their own feet. If the caricature of this position – that the welfare state should be wholly dismantled – is rarely if ever advocated (neither Hayek nor Friedman endorse it), a very much slimmed down welfare effort *is* envisaged. While the character of welfare dependency remains somewhat out of keeping with it, this solution to the problem is unimpeachably (neo-)liberal, if potentially punitively so.

The second solution to the problem of dependency culture fits much more easily with the precepts of conservatism than liberalism. It is also based on a somewhat different diagnosis of the problem. Rather than blaming welfare policy *per se*, the responsibility for the development of behavioural dependency is given a particular form of 'liberal' welfarism. When benefits are given as *unconditional entitlements* or *as of right*, they risk producing behavioural dependency. The welfare legacy – at least in the USA and UK – is misguidedly liberal or permissive. The alternative is to restructure welfare policy, placing the emphasis on the obligations or conditions required of welfare beneficiaries, not to dismantle it. Indeed, in principle, the restructured welfare effort may be larger and more expensive than the policy it supersedes.

Lawrence Mead (1985) is perhaps the best known 'New Right' advocate of this kind of welfare reform. The accent on the *desirability* of the state playing a more 'authoritative' role is heavy. That is, the power of the state *can* and *should* be used to prescribe and even impose certain patterns of behaviour within society. The implication is that individuals will (eventually) become socialized into these 'acceptable' patterns of behaviour. Mead's

approach is most easily accommodated within the corpus of (neo)conservatism, at least of a North American variety, with its emphasis on state authority and social norms and hierarchies. Of course, such an approach has some similarities with certain left-of-centre traditions and projects – particularly in its emphasis on the interventionist capacity of the state and – whether fully explored or not – the role played by socialization processes. Neither of these elements sits easily with modern liberalism (on which see Bellamy, 1992; and King, 1999).

Such an approach to welfare policy can be reconciled with liberalism, at least to an extent, by understanding it in *contractual* terms. No one is 'coerced' into claiming benefits, but if they do, then there is no principled problem with clear and well-known conditions or obligations being attached to the benefits claimed. Recall that the 'liberal' alternative is a large-scale dismantling of social policy, so both approaches potentially leave some individuals to face the 'coercion' of poverty unaided by adequate benefits. Although this has not been the subject of much explicit debate, (neo-)liberals are potentially divided between those who find the imposition of social norms through state policy morally objectionable and others who advocate at least some policies of this sort. Although such evaluations inevitably have a subjective quality, over the past 25 years the 'New Right' appears to us gradually to have become less economically focused and neoliberal, but more socially oriented and conservative.

The emphasis on processes of socialization of some (conservative) 'New Right' 'cures' for dependency, begs the question: can other features of the social environment also have an impact on individually rational behaviour? If they can, then the economic logic of neoliberalism begins to unravel. If individual instrumental rationality (or even behaviour that can be explained 'as if' it was rational) can be undercut by a wide variety of environmental or contextual features, then the free market (based on such rationality guided by an invisible hand) becomes chimerical. (At least it loses its liberal gloss as the social norms necessary for its success feel increasingly constraining or need to be coercively imposed.) Some neo-conservatives have become increasingly attracted to the idea that state power and tutelary social and moral persuasion should be used to construct individuals disciplined to the requirements of the (labour) market – particularly at its less attractive end. Although arguably becoming more acute as the conservative case is articulated increasingly clearly, during the 1970s and 1980s these dilemmas were rarely confronted by 'New Right' authors. Instead, the various strands within the 'New Right' were bound together to some extent by their identification of the welfare state as the primary cause of the 'dependency culture'. By focusing on the perverse impact of the welfare state, neo-liberals were able both to quarantine the virus of 'socialization' of individuals into irrational behaviour towards the welfare state and to focus a particularly biting criticism on the welfare state. But the plausibility of the 'New Right'argument suffers as a consequence. For example, Charles Murray (1984) attributes the rise in illegitimacy to welfare dependency, wholly ignoring the fact that 'illegitimacy' was growing rapidly in all western societies and at all levels of each society. This position also sits uneasily with other arguments he makes on the genetic foundations of poverty (on which see Wincott, 2001a). It is hardly plausible to suggest that the rise in cohabitation in the professional classes is a product of the welfare state.

The left has reacted to dependency culture arguments in a variety of ways. Some have repudiated the argument wholesale, arguing that a 'dependent underclass' simply does not exist (Goodin et al., 1999). Even if many people may suffer deprivation in an aspect of their lives, these aspects do not generally reinforce one another to create a multidimensional 'cultural' syndrome. However, such a position also implies the repudiation of a well-established centre-left argument about poverty. Analyses of multiple and relative

deprivation (particularly associated with Peter Townsend) and the notion of 'social exclusion' both agree with the 'underclass' analysis in identifying that a group (or several groups) of people become cut off from mainstream society. The difference is that for the left the welfare state is (part of) the solution to the problem (at least potentially) rather than its cause. In other words, multiple deprivation has multiple causes rather than simply being triggered by 'welfare dependency'. For those on the centre-left the responsibility of the welfare state is secondary – limited to its failure to protect people from social ills whose primary source is generally to be found elsewhere.

SOCIAL AND POLITICAL RIGHTS OF CITIZENSHIP

The centre-left view of the relationship between the welfare state and democracy is quite different. Typically, the two notions are seen as intimately connected, both historically and theoretically. First, the welfare state is often seen as the product of democratization – demanded by the newly enfranchised masses after the introduction of universal suffrage. Whether viewed through the lens of 'modernization' theory or the class struggle, the advent of mass democracy and of the welfare state broadly followed (albeit in some cases it anticipated) the political mobilization of the working class and of women. Is it a coincidence that the post-war period, when mass democracy was at its most 'stable' (Bartolini and Mair, 1990), was also the golden age of the welfare state? During this period the 'affiliation' of the mass public to their national state was achieved, at least in part, through the development of welfare programmes. There are differences of opinion about when the welfare state came into being (from the 1870s or after 1945). Nevertheless, in its 'classic' period after the Second World War the welfare state was instrumental in creating an 'affiliation' between the people and their potentially fragile national states, particularly in Western Europe.

Secondly, for most analysts and activists associated with the centre-left, the connection between the welfare state and democracy is not simply a matter of historical coincidence. Instead, there is a deep theoretical connection between the two, characteristically expressed in terms of citizenship. Interestingly, the social meaning of citizenship and independence seem to have shifted with the rise of mass democracy. Reliance on the labour market, once the apotheosis of dependence, has become the badge of independence and citizenship (see Pateman, 1989 for a feminist critique). It is still a precarious form of independence, in at least two ways. First, because the supply of labour power must involve the presence of the labourer, the possibility of coercive relations within employment marring the independence of the labourer is also present. Of course, such unfreedom in labour relations is not necessarily politically debilitating. Nevertheless, if independence is the normative core of citizenship, then its violation in any form remains undesirable (see Orloff, 1993 for an elaboration of the conditions for independence for women as well as men which both qualifies and goes well beyond decommodification). Arguably more significant, the risk of unemployment – and hence of impoverishment, perhaps even to the point of starvation – hovers over all those who depend on their labour for survival. Penury resulting from unemployment does, of course, potentially provide a serious challenge to individual independence and thus to equal political citizenship in a mass democracy. This challenge may take the form, for example, of the vulnerability of individuals in such a position to unacceptable influence by others, or an incapacity to exercise the kind of deliberation expected of the citizen. Even the fear of unemployment may emaciate citizenship.

A possible normative defence of the welfare state in mass democracy depends upon its capacity to protect individuals from these risks. This is the important insight behind the idea of using the capacity of state policy to *decommodify* labour as the defining quality of a welfare state. As a matter of definition, decommodification would allow individuals to survive independently of the labour market. Yet this concept is often misunderstood. The most influential analyst of the decommodifying welfare state, Gosta Esping-Andersen, explicitly argues that the most fully developed welfare states can exist and/ or survive only if full employment can be sustained. Notwithstanding the decommodifying impact of their social policies, these welfare states are full employment states. What, then, is the significance of decommodification? Rather than removing large numbers of individuals from the labour market, the *possibility* of leaving *any particular job* changes power relations within work in such a way as to reduce and/or eliminate its commodifying qualities. Of course, while generous welfare provision can remove the sting of unemployment, full employment has the same effect, particularly if backed by a strong state commitment. Moreover, full employment itself changes power relations in work, as Kalecki (1943) classically argued.

The argument that citizenship in a mass democracy should have social, as well as civil and political, dimensions is inspired by T.H. Marshall (see also King and Waldron, 1988). *Social citizenship* is often used – at least implicitly and, of course, perfectly legitimately – as a normative concept. Only by meeting whatever standard of social rights is normatively prescribed can a state qualify as a welfare state. For most of these standards, relatively few states meet the criteria specified to qualify as welfare states (Wincott, 2001b). Nevertheless, every western capitalist democratic state provides various kinds of welfare, albeit not always equally to all citizens (Veit-Wilson, 2000). For the purposes of empirical analysis, we could relax the widespread (normative) assumption that citizenship must be a common status. Instead, patterns of stratification within social policy as well as the manner in which social policy interacts with wider patterns of stratification could be the subject of analysis. Rather than beginning with very detailed, normatively prescriptive descriptions of democracy and the welfare state, the historical development of citizenship in particular states could be analysed, considering the links between the cluster of rights and patterns of stratification associated with citizenship and the form and quality of democracy. This approach would also address a second problem with most 'social citizenship' analysis – the lack of research on the relationship between social and political dimensions of citizenship, rather than focusing wholly on the quality of social citizenship.

Esping-Andersen's famous analysis of the *Three Worlds of Welfare Capitalism* (1990) provides the best-developed comparative analysis which links forms of social policy to types of democratic regime. Pitched mostly at a macro-social level, the analysis traces the connections between democratic regime formations, patterns of political mobilization and coalition formation, and the development of (social) policy regimes. While the causation is generally assumed to operate from social 'foundations' to political and policy formations, the analysis does identify feedback from policy to patterns of social organization (see also Pierson, 1994). This approach may implicitly suggest that welfare state development occurred in a number of stages or phases. Patterns of social and political action produce a particular institutional settlement, which in turn transforms the setting for, and content of, subsequent action.

Placed in a more precise historical context, the core claim of power resource analysts is that the particular form of a welfare state reflects the pattern of political mobilization and coalition formation that occurred during the democratization of the end of the nineteenth and start of the twentieth centuries. (In turn, of course, these patterns of mobilization were partially shaped by the institutional legacies left by earlier phases of political development.) Remember that Esping-Andersen uses very broad language to describe his results. They concern not just forms of wel-

fare state, but worlds of welfare capitalism. Thus early institutionalization of social policy under 'conservative' political regimes entrenches a 'conservative welfare state regime'. This regime produces a substantial welfare effort, which remains biased towards state employees and effectively entrenches and reproduces status differentials in an organized labour market. According to the theory, it will produce relatively little redistribution of income across classes. The 'liberal' welfare state regime reflects a weakness of the left and trade unions and relative coherence of the right. It involves a minimal welfare state, with maximum scope for market provision. The third 'social democratic welfare state regime' is largely confined to the Nordic countries and reflects the investment of strong working-class power resources into state social policy. This produces an extensive welfare state which decommodifies labour and produces relatively egalitarian results. In each of his three worlds of welfare capitalism not only social policy, but also (post-industrial) economic trajectories are quite distinct. The conservative, liberal and social democratic welfare state regimes – and by extension types of welfare capitalism – each operates according to its own individual 'logic'. Given the connection between social and political rights of citizenship, suggested by T.H. Marshall (on whom Esping-Andersen relies heavily), we should also expect the quality and form of political democracy to differ substantially and systematically in each 'regime' type. There is some tentative evidence to suggest that we can relate political participation, in terms of electoral turnout, to welfare regimes (see Table 20.1).

It would be foolish to exaggerate the significance of the figures in Table 20.1. There are many complex relationships beyond social policy which relate to these differences. Moreover, the very high turnout in New Zealand (together with compulsory voting in Australia) might suggest that the Antipodes may have a distinctive political tradition (perhaps lending some weight to Castles and Mitchell (1993), who disagree with Esping-

TABLE 20.1 *Average post-war electoral turnout for national assembly elections (excluding countries with compulsory voting)*

New Zealand	89.1%
Netherlands	87.5%
Denmark	86.2%
Sweden	86.1%
Germany	85.5%
Norway	80.4%
Finland	80.0%
France	75.8%
UK	75.2%
Canada	73.8%
Ireland	73.2%
Japan	69.5%
USA	66.5%
Switzerland	56.6%

Source: Institute for Democracy and Electoral Assistance (IDEA) (2001).

Andersen's allocation of these states to the liberal regime cluster). Nevertheless, these figures seem to show a pattern. They indicate that turnout is usually lowest in liberal welfare regimes. Although the pattern is less clear-cut, it may also be higher in socialist than conservative welfare states. At most there may be a correlative relationship between certain generic types, or welfare regimes, and patterns of political participation. In other words, all the countries that we might identify as being social democratic, and hence having more generous welfare provision, are in the top half of the table, whereas the countries that we would identify as possessing liberal welfare characteristics lie towards the bottom. Hence, this table suggests that there is a link between different types of welfare state and political activity, and also casts some doubt upon the 'New Right' analysis. For 'New Right' theorists, we should expect the table to be reversed, with the more generous welfare regimes producing less active participants and liberal-type welfare states linking to a more active cit-

izenry. ('New Right' theorists might argue, with justification, that an active citizenry goes beyond voting and that liberal-type regimes sustain a more engaged civic culture. However, in contrast to Robert Putnam's (2000) work on the decline of such activity, or social capital, in America, Rothstein (2001) argues that Sweden retains high levels of social capital.)

However fruitful this hypothesis may seem, the logic supporting it is not robust. The problem is not (necessarily) that social rights are irrelevant for political citizenship. Instead, each 'world' of welfare capitalism is not a wholly distinct and robust empirical 'type'. Instead, the 'worlds' are ideal types, and every actually existing social policy regime – never mind each state's regime of 'welfare capitalism' – contains important elements of at least one other ideal typical regime. As a consequence, every state contains within its structural legacy the bases for a variety of different subsequent forms of mobilization and other political action. These do not necessarily offer themselves up as coherent political strategies, but skilled political entrepreneurs may construct them.

CONCLUSION

Returning to the idea of the democratic deficit, it is tempting to conclude that the retrenchment of social citizenship rights and the decline in formal political participation are connected. The decline in formal participation and the rise of direct, activist participation (see Norris, 2002) may be partly due to citizens no longer feeling connected to their governments. For the left the welfare state was instrumental in establishing this connection and is now under threat. If social citizenship rights are eroded, the means by which citizens gain independence, and hence the basis for participation, are attenuated. For 'New Right' theorists, the argument runs in the opposite direction. Welfare remains permissive and pervasive. Either further retrenchment should correct the passive dependence of citizens, or welfare needs to be made less permissive and requires further emphasis on obligations. Issues of democracy are not discussed as clearly as they might be in the literature on the welfare state. Left- and right-wing perspectives take opposite views on the direction of the relationship, but in both the future of democracy hinges on developments in the welfare state. However, while it is deeply implicated in the structure of modern democracy, academic analysis of political participation has largely neglected the welfare state.

Summary

- The welfare state plays a central, but contested, role in the image of democracy in key theories of contemporary society.
- 'New Right' and social citizenship theories take diametrically opposed views of the relationship between democracy and the welfare state.
- The 'New Right' sees the welfare state as a major threat to democracy.
- For many 'New Right' theorists 'dependency culture' created by state welfare robs beneficiaries of their capacity for independent rational thought and thus makes them unfit for citizenship.
- Neo-liberals generally advocate welfare retrenchment to eliminate dependency.
- Some neo-conservatives argue that the 'permissive' welfare state should be replaced by 'authoratitive' welfare, imposing heavy obligations on welfare claimants in order to make them into 'good citizens'.
- Social citizenship theories see the welfare state as a necessary precondition for a successful mass democracy.
- Social (welfare) rights to a modicum of welfare bolster the independence of citizens.
- Research on (the crisis of) political participation has generally neglected to examine the impact of the welfare state.
- Different forms of welfare state (liberal, conservative and social democratic) may be associated with different patterns of political participation.

TUTORIAL QUESTIONS

1. **Why is 'dependency culture' a threat to democracy?**

2. **Should citizenship have a social dimension in mass democracy?**

3. **Does welfare retrenchment threaten or renew democracy?**

FURTHER READING

Chris Pierson (1998) *Beyond the Welfare State* (Cambridge: Polity Press, second edition) provides an excellent overview of the welfare state, including a number of different theoretical approaches.

Lawrence Mead (1985) *Beyond Entitlement* (New York: Basic Books) is the key text advocating a more 'directive' welfare state.

Charles Murray (1984) *Losing Ground* (New York: Basic Books) is a key text criticizing the welfare state for creating a dependency culture.

T.H. Marshall (and T. Bottomore) (1992) *Citizenship and Social Class* (London: Pluto) reproduces Marshall's classic 1950 essay on the development on citizenship in Britain.

Gosta Esping-Andersen (1999) *The Social Foundations of Post-Industrial Economies* (Oxford: Oxford University Press) is the most recent analysis by this key welfare state analyst of social citizenship and the different varieties of welfare state.

REFERENCES

Bartolini, S. and Mair, P. (1990) *Identity, Competition and Electoral Availability*. Cambridge: Cambridge University Press.

Bellamy, R. (1992) *Liberalism and Modern Society*. Philadelphia, PA: Pennsylvania State University Press.

Castles, F. and Mitchell, D. (1993) 'Worlds of Welfare and Families of Nations', in F. Castles (ed.), *Families of Nations*. Aldershot: Dartmouth.

Esping-Andersen, G. (1990) *The Three Worlds of Welfare Capitalism*. Cambridge: Polity Press.

Esping-Andersen, G. (1999) *The Social Foundations of Postindustrial Economies*. Oxford: Oxford University Press.

Friedman, M. (1980) *Free To Choose*. London: Penguin.

Goodin, R., Headey, B., Muffels, R. and Dirven, H.J. (1999) *The Real Worlds of Welfare Capitalism*. Cambridge: Cambridge University Press.

IDEA (2001) available at *http://www.idea.int/voter_turnout/parliamentary.html*

Kalecki, M. (1943) 'Political Aspects of Full Employment', *Political Quarterly*, **14**: 322–31.

King, D. (1999) *In the Name of Liberalism*. Oxford: Oxford University Press.

King, D. and Waldron, J. (1988) 'Citizenship, Social Citizenship and the Defence of Welfare Provision', *British Journal of Political Science*, **18**: 415–43.

Marshall, T.H. (1950) 'Citizenship and Social Class', in T.H. Marshall and T. Bottomore (1992) *Citizenship and Social Class*. London: Pluto.

Mead, L. (1985) *Beyond Entitlement*. New York: Basic Books.

Murray, C. (1984) *Losing Ground*. New York: Basic Books.

Norris, P. (2002) *Democratic Phoenix: Political Activism Worldwide*. Cambridge: Cambridge University Press.

Orloff, A. (1993) 'Gender and the Social Rights of Citizenship', *American Sociological Review*, **58**: 303–28.

Parry, G. Moyser, G. and Day, N. (1992) *Political Participation and Democracy in Britain*. Cambridge: Cambridge University Press.

Pateman, C. (1989) 'The Patriarchal Welfare State', in *The Disorder of Women*. Cambridge: Polity Press.

Pierson, P. (1994) *Dismantling the Welfare State?* Cambridge: Cambridge University Press.

Putnam, R. (2000) *Bowling Alone: the Collapse and Revival of American Community*. New York: Simon & Schuster.

Rothstein, B. (2001) 'Social Capital in the Social Democratic Welfare State', *Politics and Society*, **29**: 207–41.

Veit-Wilson, J. (2000) 'Concepts of the Welfare State', *Social Policy and Administration*, **32**: 1–25.

Wincott, D. (2001a) 'The Next Nature/Nurture Debate, or Should Labour Place Mothers and Infants at the Heart of Public Policy?, *Political Quarterly*, **72**: 227–38.

Wincott, D. (2001b) 'Reassessing the Social Foundations of Welfare (State) Regimes', *New Political Economy*, **6**: 409–25.

See also chapters

21 Cyber-democracy

Peter Ferdinand

The term 'cyber-democracy' covers a range of theoretical approaches to the application of computer technology to democracy. At one end of the spectrum are those who argue that through the Internet the computer can enable citizens to realize their full potential of citizenship in a democracy. For them it offers the possibility of combining the ideals of classical Athenian democracy with the technological innovations of interactive communications. This is in the tradition of direct democracy. It rests on the belief that the most democratic forms of government allow the maximum degree of participation by all citizens.

Until the advent of modern mass communications, the Athenian model of democracy, with regular participation in public debate and decision-making, remained unattainable for any except the smallest societies. In states larger than city-states it was impossible to organize mass public deliberation on a regular basis. Referendums are an alternative, but only a partial one. The Internet, for the first time, gave life to the prospect of regularly consulting the whole of the population in large states over policy issues in real time.

Towards the other end of the spectrum lie those who see in computer technology chiefly the opportunity to remedy more specific problems in modern liberal democracy. Rather than looking for a new type of politics, they plan to reform existing democracies. For example, computers offer a new technology for casting votes, hopefully increasing parti-cipation. By the 1980s there was a growing unease about the weaknesses of representative democracy in the United States, as well as elsewhere. Elections seemed to be ever more expensive, the media and advertising seemed to determine who could win elections, and (for some) big business seemed to determine political agendas. Elections, at the national level at any rate, seemed to restrict choice rather than widen it. Turnout declined from one election to the next. Washington seemed to be increasingly grid-locked by competing, largely commercial interests. In the 1990s that anxiety has spread more widely to include a general anxiety about the erosion of the sense of community in the USA, exemplified in Putnam's book *Bowling Alone* (2000).

The attraction of the Internet is that it offers new incentives and opportunities for citizens to fit democratic participation into their busy lives. If politics was becoming more of a minority activity and if the main cause was the sense of political ineffectiveness on the part of individual citizens, then possibly a new technology would revive their enthusiasm. Possibly, too, the Internet could facilitate new forms of community that would replace older ones.

In between new forms of politics and reforms of existing systems there are also proponents of the Internet as a means of spreading democracy in countries where currently it is not practised. This is not so much cyber-democracy as cyber-democratization, but it overlaps with the possible impact of the Internet upon existing democracies too, just as democratization may and should lead to democracy.

CITIZENSHIP, STRONG DEMOCRACY AND ELECTRONIC TOWN MEETINGS

The most articulate expression of the normative view is Benjamin Barber's book *Strong Democracy* (1984). Although this first appeared in 1984 and therefore preceded the Internet, it already looked towards interactive television and electronic balloting as a way of developing a new form of citizenship. As he put it, strong democracy 'rests on the idea of a self-governing community of citizens who are united less by homogeneous interests than by civic education and who are made capable of common purpose and mutual action by virtue of their civic attitudes and participatory institutions rather than their altruism or their good nature'. It looks forward to what Dewey called 'the idea of community itself' and requires institutions 'that will involve individuals at both the neighbourhood and the national level in common talk, common decision-making and political judgement, and common action' (Barber, 1984: 117, 119, 261).

Since then Barber has taken a great interest in the possible applications of the Internet to transform democracy. What he advocates is a 'Jeffersonian scenario', where

technology has made possible a quality and degree of communication among citizens and between citizens and bureaucrats, experts, and their information banks [Jefferson] could not have dreamed of. . . . Left to markets (and that is where it is presently being left), [technology] is likely to augment McWorld's least worthy imperatives, including surveillance over and manipulation of opinion, and the cultivation of artificial needs rooted in lifestyle 'choices' unconnected to real economic, civic, or spiritual needs. (Barber, 1998: 584, 588)

Related to this has been the concept of electronic town meetings. The institution of local town meetings, especially in New England, has long been seen as the kernel of American democracy, but as an effective institution it had seemed to be eclipsed in an era of big government. From the 1980s it was taken up by those who advocated the application of cable television to the political process, so that the town meeting could be reborn for meaningful local debate and decision-making.

Arterton was the first to propose this in his 1987 book *Teledemocracy*, which has the significant sub-title *Can Technology Protect Democracy?* This discussed ways in which governments could consult their citizenry over policies using interactive television. However, the technology at that time was still rather primitive. The only mode of organization seriously envisaged was local cable television networks devoted to discussions on local issues. It launched the idea of 'electronic town meetings'. Yet this technology still favoured the distribution of ideas from the top downwards. Insofar as it allowed consultation, this could take place only when the government or the local authorities chose. There were no more possibilities for citizens to mount their own campaigns from below and there were certainly none for citizens to engage in debate among themselves. They could of course organize themselves to challenge the agenda of the authorities or suggest new items to be put on it, but these needed face-to-face town meetings as well as electronic ones. Above the local level any interactive form of political participation was still impossible.

Nevertheless, debates over 'teledemocracy' led to more thinking about new modes of participation. It created an appetite for innovation. Then the Internet emerged to offer new opportunities for interactive communication, both vertical and horizontal, for individuals as well as for groups and it opened up new vistas for a technologically based Athenian era. More recently these ideas have been eloquently advocated by Becker and

Slaton in *The Future of Teledemocracy* (2000). In addition to the ideas already outlined of electronic town meetings, they stress two additional features of the teledemocracy of the future. The first is the use of more scientific deliberative polling of citizens to establish legitimate public policy preferences without having to wait for occasional general elections. The second is the encouragement of the principle of iterative consultation and mediation rather than one-off votes so as to promote better and much more widely approved policies. They look forward to three improvements on existing systems of democracy. First, like Barber, they expect that it will help to 'temper and tether' the 'forces of rampant, market-based globalization'. Secondly, it will lead to a fairer distribution of wealth and social services, to greater success for environmental groups, and to 'a more stable and less turbulent social dynamic'. Thirdly, again like Barber, they look forward to a system where 'average citizens become more personally involved in suprapersonal affairs of state' and to 'a more socially minded life for everyone in society – toward greater self-esteem through selflessness and making sure citizens are not dwarfed by enormous hierarchies of inaccessible power' (Becker and Slaton, 2000: 211–12).

But beyond the town meetings, such visions of future politics are remarkably thin on the institutions that would still be needed to structure political activity.

CYBER-REFORMS OF LIBERAL DEMOCRACY

By the 1990s most western democracies were beginning to show falls in voter turnout at general elections, except in states where voting was compulsory. Insofar as the causes could be attributed to voter apathy, or the inconvenience of having to fit time to vote into hectic lives, some have proposed the Internet as a means of making voting easier and reviving participation.

California, for example, carried out a study in 1999 to examine the feasibility of voting in state elections through the Internet. This identified a whole series of obstacles that would prevent its early introduction as the only form of voting: voter authentication, ballot secrecy, ballot integrity, reliable transport and storing of votes, prevention of multiple voting, defence against attacks on Internet voting machines and defence against attacks on election computer systems. All of this is in addition to the problem of the 'digital divide', separating those who know how to make use of the Internet and those who do not. For all these reasons the Task Force in California proposed a four-stage process, where one would lead on to the next.

1 Internet voting at the voter's normal, assigned polling place: this would be supervised by election officials and simply replace the existing forms of vote.
2 Internet voting at any polling station in the given constituency: again this would require specially designed Internet voting machines whose use was supervised by election officials, but it would allow voters greater flexibility in choosing the most convenient place to vote.
3 Internet voting from remote computers in any established polling station or location approved for this purpose: this would not require the presence of polling officials, so voting could take place at any time throughout the election period.
4 Internet voting from any computer: this would probably involve the supply of a single-use clean operating system and web browser for voting for every voter for every election.

It clearly will take considerable time for all of these stages to be developed, even in as Internet-friendly a place as California. It would be extremely costly. There are also major question-marks over the ability to design an on-line electronic voting system using PCs in stages three and four that could satisfy three vital requirements by ensuring:

(a) that it was the registered voter who voted and that he or she only did so once; (b) separation of the on-line identification of the voter from the vote itself, so as to preserve anonymous voting; (c) that no outsider could intervene, whether as a hacker or by leaving a 'cookie' dormant on the voter's computer memory until the moment for the vote arrived, to change the vote before it reached the polling centre, for once stage (b) had been completed, it would be almost impossible for the voter to know whether the vote that he or she had cast was the one that actually arrived (Phillips and Jefferson, 2000). This degree of system robustness is essential and as yet unattained.

Nevertheless a poll of Californians in 1999 showed a fairly smooth gradient of increasing age correlating with opposition to Internet voting. At one extreme were those aged 18–24, of whom 60 per cent favoured Internet voting and only 37 per cent opposed. At the other extreme only 20 per cent of those aged 65 and above approved of it while 71 per cent opposed. This suggests that it is seen as the future by those who have most of it in front of them – and in fact in almost all age groups polled, more people approved of Internet voting than currently have access to the Internet or e-mail (California Internet Voting Task Force, 2000).

There are more limited ways in which the Internet has begun to transform the practices of established democracies. Parliaments, for instance, have begun to wake up to the challenges that the Internet poses for their traditional roles. Most have long histories and for them the issue is perceived primarily as one of adaptation. In many cases this has led to accusations that they are simply 'Wiring up the deckchairs on the *Titanic*', trying to find new ways of allowing parliament to communicate its views and debates to the public, rather than taking advantage of the new technology to stimulate wider debate and educate the public in the complexity of issues. The new parliament in Scotland, however, has had to confront alternative possible roles more directly: 'Will the parliament operate as a busy hub of democratic information exchange, a "trading floor" through which all important democratic "transactions" will be routed? Or will the parliament sit as one element (albeit an important one) in a wider polity around which information flows?' (Smith and Gray, 1999: 433). The *Bundestag* in Germany has attempted to stimulate educated public debate over political issues by organizing on-line fora at www.Bundestag.de/forum to debate current issues, which are moderated by representatives of the parties represented in parliament.

Embracing the possibilities of the Internet can also change the relationship between elected representatives, electors and parties. Where previously a member of parliament was heavily dependent upon the research and library services of the parliament or of his or her party for specialized policy-relevant information, now he or she can use the Internet to direct the collection of information by assistants. 'It will become easier for individual Members of Parliament to have his or her own network of people and groups and to maintain it, coordinate research, focus groups, poll people throughout society and coordinate activities in larger groups of people than is possible today. This makes Members of Parliament more independent from central infrastructure, be that from the Parliament or the Party' (Mulder, 1999: 561).

Of course, there is a serious potential problem of information-overload. Already the number of e-mails received at the US Congress rose from 20 million in 1998 to 48 million in 2000 and continues to grow at the rate of 1 million per month – and most members of Congress are already afraid of being swamped with communications, so they try to contain it (Goldschmidt, 2001).

In time the Internet is also likely to challenge the way political parties are organized and operate. Norris suggests that for the moment the main contribution will be to provide e-mail links between the leaders and the grassroots, thus ensuring greater policy consultation (Norris, 2001: 168). But in time parties will face increasing pressures to organize members on the basis of the Internet, either alongside or in competition with the traditional local party organizations. This has already begun in Germany (Bieber, 2000). In the more distant future it is also possible to envisage purely Internet-based 'parties'. There already is one in South Korea, to be found at www.cyberparty.or.kr

Lastly, the Internet will change the relationship between citizens and the media. That will also affect the relationship between the media and politics. The Internet has made it much easier for individuals to set up their own websites and publish articles. What is written there may be much less objective than appears on 'established' channels. It may often be just rumour and prejudice, but it can put alternative information into the public domain. Paradoxically, at a time when newspaper editors and the owners of television channels have never been more influential in framing democratic choices, their pre-eminence is beginning to be challenged by the rise of alternative sources of information. Increasingly, politicians will have to incorporate an Internet strategy as part of their campaigning, if only to rebut false allegations that are made there.

These are some of the possible changes that the Internet may make in democracies in the future. What has been the actual effect to date? Perhaps the best-known success was the election of Jesse Ventura as third-party Governor of Minnesota in 1998. Though fighting against better-known and better-funded representatives of the Democratic and Republican parties in the state, he was able to achieve a stunning victory. He and others largely attributed this to his using the Internet to mobilize support on a low budget – his website cost just $600 – by targeting potential voters on a much more individual basis. It seemed to herald an era when good candidates could again overcome the massed and expensive media campaigns of the established parties.

Another success is claimed for the Arizona state Democratic primary elections of 2000, where the option of on-line voting was allowed. Whereas in 1992 the turnout was less than 40,000 using traditional methods, in 2000 it more than doubled to 85,970. Even if only half of these actually voted on-line, this seemed to confirm the optimism of those who argued that the new technology would revive the commitment of apathetic voters.

Yet although the Internet is changing campaigning styles, especially at the local level, it has not yet made the crucial difference in national elections. In 1992 Ross Perot campaigned heavily on the Internet to attract support for his party and he promised to make electronic town meetings a big feature of his administration if elected president, but he failed and his party subsequently lost all its momentum. In 2000 the wealthy magazine publisher Steve Forbes concentrated heavily on using the Internet to win the presidential nomination of the Republican Party from George W. Bush, but still failed (Milbank, 1999). Although the candidates attempted to use the aura of new technology to burnish the appeal of their other campaign promises, it was not enough to make a breakthrough. This suggests that technological messianism alone cannot win elections. The medium frames the message, but it is not the message itself. Issues like the distribution of values and resources in society, and the fitness of individuals to enjoy popular support are still at the heart of the political process. Furthermore, once alerted to the danger, the established parties have taken advantage of their superior resources to incorporate the Internet into their own campaign strategies. The websites for both of the two main presidential contenders and their parties were enormously more glitzy in 2001 than ever before.

To talk then of the decisive impact of the Internet upon democracy still seems premature. Certainly it does not yet seem as though the call for technologically enhanced democracy is sufficient to turn voter apathy into voter enthusiasm, irrespective of the other features of a candidate's election platform. In any case, Internet penetration of most societies remains limited – in the USA it was estimated at 56 per cent at the end of 2000 (Cyberatlas, 2001) and elsewhere it is still much lower. So the impact of the Internet upon democracies in stimulating wider participation will continue to be restricted for years to come. Rather, it seems safer to accept Bimber's notion of 'accelerated pluralism', that is, it will accelerate trends that are already under way. As he put it, the Internet may speed up a growing fragmentation of interest-based group politics with a shift towards 'a more fluid, issue-based group politics with less institutional coherence' that is already under way, rather than creating it (Bimber, 1998: 133).

CYBER-DEMOCRATIZATION

If the Internet has changed, but not yet transformed, existing democracies, what about its possible role in democratizing authoritarian regimes? In the 1990s very optimistic statements were made about the potential of the Internet for undermining authoritarian regimes and helping to launch movements for democratic change. A report for the Pentagon in 1995 cited *Rolling Stone* magazine: 'The Internet is the censor's biggest challenge and the tyrant's worst nightmare.' It added:

> The Internet is clearly a significant long-term strategic threat to authoritarian regimes, one that they will be unable to counter effectively. News from the outside world brought by the Internet into nations subjugated by such regimes will clash with the distorted versions provided by their governments, eroding the credibility of their positions and encouraging unrest. 'Personal' contact between people living under such governments and people living in the free world, conducted by e-mail, will also help to achieve a more accurate understanding on both ends and further undermine authoritarian controls. Information about violations of human rights and other forms of oppression will be increasingly conveyed to the outside world by the Internet, helping mobilize external political forces on behalf of the oppressed. (Swett, 1995)

This prospect has clearly unnerved some regimes. The government of Singapore, for instance, has devoted considerable attention to strategies for taming the Internet by limiting access to particular sites abroad (Rodan, 1998). The Chinese government has followed their lead with considerable interest, especially as activists abroad have sought to use the Internet to undermine the regime, whether over Tibet or democracy more generally (Bray, 2000; Kalathil and Boas, 2001). They have also followed with nervous interest the effect of the Internet in the downfall of regimes such as those of President Suharto in Indonesia, where critics both at home and abroad were able to keep in touch through the Internet to coordinate their protests (Hill and Sen, 2000).

In practice, the chief importance of the Internet for politics may be the opportunities that it opens up for horizontal communication about political issues between individual citizens, rather than the political websites that are feared by governments such as China's. It may be e-mail that is crucial, not the ability to surf the Web. E-mail allows individuals to organize groups or movements without having to rely upon traditional political 'gatekeepers'. As can be seen from the overthrow of the Suharto regime in Indonesia, opponents both at home and abroad were able to communicate and interact with each other in real time in a way that would have been inconceivable only a few years previously. During the crisis there were times when demonstrators outside the national assembly could be contacted and mobilized directly from inside it, thus making their demonstrations much more effective.

The downfall of President Estrada of the Philippines in January 2001 makes the point. This time, however, it was not the Internet so much as mobile phones that became the crucial technology. As protests grew over official corruption and President Estrada's attempts to evade a full judicial hearing, demonstrators used text messages on mobile phones to mobilize anyone they knew to gather in large public spaces for demonstrations at short notice. On a normal day the mobile phone networks would expect to deal with 50 million text messages from the country's 2.5 million mobile phone subscribers, but in the days before the fall of Estrada, this figure had risen to 80 million. Even if the government had been organized to cope with this sort of challenge, there was no way that it could have traced oppositionists and pressured them into backing down in the short time available. The only alternative would have been to shut down the networks entirely, in which case it would have shown its vulnerability and antagonized those who needed it for other purposes.

This success was achieved with the simpler forms of mobile phones. As newer generations with WAP technology become available, the possibilities for political activists to integrate their messaging capabilities with the Internet will increase dramatically, thus facilitating much more sophisticated citizen activism.

The implication of these examples, therefore, is not that the Internet can seriously undermine the legitimacy of existing institutions – it first took the regional financial crisis to provoke widespread protests in Indonesia – but once a crisis has begun, the Internet and/or new forms of communication technology can catalyse protest much more effectively than ever before, however repressive or authoritarian the regime.

Yet President Estrada had been democratically elected and he was swept away by unconstitutional means. His downfall has implications about the challenges that new communications technologies pose for democratic as well as undemocratic regimes.

CONCLUSION

It is still early to determine the impact of the Internet upon political systems, although it is likely to be considerable in the long term, just as it has already wrought many changes in business. One parallel that is often drawn is with the impact of television and there is no doubt that television has transformed political campaigning and the style of government. Yet the Internet, combined with other new forms of communications technology, has the potential for even more serious change, for it offers the first possibility of regular, direct vertical communication among the 'governors' and the 'governed', as well as direct horizontal communication between the 'governed'. Just as the Internet has begun the process of 'disintermediation' in business, that is, cutting out the middle layers of companies and bureaucracy that stand between producers and consumers, so it challenges not merely the role but the very existence of political intermediaries in representative democracies such as politicians and of institutions such as political parties and parliaments. It has captured the imagination of democratic visionaries.

Yet it is not necessarily a technology that guarantees democracy. Dictators could use it to rule, as in (George Orwell's) *1984*, although they would have to do so without all the benefits that it brings to business and markets. Others such as Barber fear that commercialization is already driving out its potential for realizing true democracy. Whether or not this is true, this is more likely without a conscious effort to make the technology serve the public good. The Internet cannot be uninvented, but it will not automatically promote democracy. Only if enough people and institutions want it to do so and devise appropriate procedures, rules and institutions will the Internet become a force for democracy rather than a force for 'dumbing down' or, at worst, enslavement.

Summary

- The Internet has inspired rethinking of the practicality of Athenian and Jeffersonian ideals of democracy.
- Electronic town meetings have been the only institutional innovation proposed so far.
- Electronic voting may revive the legitimacy of existing democracies, but many problems will need to be solved first for people to have confidence in it.
- Greater use of the Internet will change the scale and forms of interaction between existing institutions such as parliaments, parties and the media, as well as with citizens.
- New forms of horizontal electronic communication, including mobile phones, will facilitate direct action and pose enormous challenges for rule, whether in democracies or authoritarian regimes, especially in crises.
- Much wider reflection, debate and agreement is needed if the Internet is to further democracy.

TUTORIAL QUESTIONS

1. **Do theories of cyber-democracy add anything new to concepts of Athenian democracy?**

2. **Which is more important for the practice of democracy: institutions or the technologies for public deliberation?**

3. **Does the Internet give unfair political advantage to those who can master its technology?**

4. **Has the Internet so far made a greater impact upon established democracies or authoritarian regimes?**

FURTHER READING

Benjamin Barber (1984) *Strong Democracy: Participatory Politics for a New Age* (Berkeley, CA: University of California Press) provides the foundation for thinking about how to use the Internet to make the most of democracy, as well as reminding readers that it should be human values, not technology, that drive changes in it.

Benjamin Barber (1998) 'Three Scenarios for the Future of Technology and Strong Democracy', *Political Science Quarterly*, **113**: 573–89 brings the argument up to date.

Ted Becker and Christa Daryl Slaton (2000) *The Future of Teledemocracy* (Westport, CT: Praeger) outlines earlier experiments at electronic forms of direct democracy and presents a vision of how this can work in the future.

Pippa Norris (2001) *Digital Divide: Civic Engagement, Information Poverty and the Internet Worldwide* (Cambridge: Cambridge University Press) provides the best survey of the current state of the Internet and politics around the world.

The Internet, Democracy and Democratization edited by Peter Ferdinand (London: Frank Cass, 2000, also published as a special issue of *Democratization*, **7**: 1) contains articles on various dimensions of the impact of the Internet, including several on its impact upon authoritarian regimes.

The Democracies Online Newsletter (*www.e-democracy.org/do/*) provides almost daily updates on uses of the Internet to develop democracy around the world.

REFERENCES

Arterton, F. Christopher (1987) *Teledemocracy: Can Technology Protect Democracy?* Beverly Hills, CA: Sage.

Barber, Benjamin R. (1984) *Strong Democracy: Participatory Politics for a New Age*. Berkeley, CA: University of California Press.

Barber, Benjamin R. (1998) 'Three Scenarios for the Future of Technology and Strong Democracy', *Political Science Quarterly*, **113**: 573–89.

Becker, Ted and Slaton, Christa Daryl (2000) *The Future of Teledemocracy*. Westport, CT: Praeger.

Bieber, Christoph (2000) 'Revitalizing the Party System or *Zeitgeist*-on-line? Virtual Party Headquarters and Virtual Party Branches in Germany', in Peter Ferdinand (ed.), *The Internet, Democracy and Democratization*. London: Cass, pp. 59–75.

Bimber, Bruce (1998) 'The Internet and Political Transformation: Populism, Community and Accelerated Pluralism', *Polity*, **XXXI**: 133–60, also at *www.polsci.ucsb.edu/faculty/bimber/research/transformation.html*

Bray, John (2000) 'Tibet, Democracy and the Internet Bazaar', in Peter Ferdinand (ed.), *The Internet, Democracy and Democratization*. London: Cass, pp. 157–73.

California Internet Voting Task Force (2000) *Report on the Feasibility of Internet Voting*, available at *www.ss.ca.gov/executive/ivote*

Cyberatlas (2001) at *www.cyberatlas.internet.com/big_picture/geographics/article/0,,5911_594751,00.html*

Goldschmidt, Cathy (2001) 'E-mail Overload in Congress: Managing a Communications Crisis', at *www.congressonlineproject.org/email. html*

Hill, David T. and Sen, Krishna (2000) 'The Internet in Indonesia's New Democracy', in Peter Ferdinand (ed.), *The Internet, Democracy and Democratization*. London: Cass, pp. 119–36.

Kalathil, Shanthi and Boas, Taylor C. (2001) *The Internet and State Control in Authoritarian Regimes: China, Cuba and the Counterrevolution*. Washington, DC: Carnegie Endowment for

International Peace Global Policy Program Paper No. 21.

Milbank, Dana (1999) 'Virtual Politics: Candidates' Consultants Create the Customized Campaign', at *www.democraciaweb.org/demo2paper10.htm*

Mulder, Bert (1999) 'Parliamentary Futures: Representing the Issue Information, Technology and the Dynamics of Democracy', *Parliamentary Affairs*, **52**: 553–66.

Norris, Pippa (2001) *Digital Divide: Civic Engagement, Information Poverty, and the Internet Worldwide*. Cambridge: Cambridge University Press.

Philips, Deborah M. and Jefferson, David (2000) 'Is Internet Voting Safe?', at *www.votingintegrity.org/text/2000/internetsafe.shtml*

Putnam, Robert D. (2000) *Bowling Alone: the Collapse and Revival of American Community*. New York: Simon & Schuster.

Rodan, Garry (1998) 'The Internet and Political Control in Singapore', *Political Science Quarterly*, **113**: 63–89.

Smith, Colin F. and Gray, Paul (1999) 'The Scottish Parliament: [Re-]Shaping Parliamentary Democracy in the Information Age', in *Parliamentary Affairs*, **52**: 429–41.

Swett, Charles (1995) *Strategic Assessment: the Internet*. Washington, DC: Office of the Assistant Secretary of Defense for Special Operations and Low-Intensity Conflict (Policy Planning), the Pentagon, as posted on the Internet by the Project on Government Secrecy of the Federation of American Scientists, at *www.fas.org/cp/swett.html*

See also chapters

22 Democratic Citizenship in the Age of Globalization

Roland Axtmann

THE NATION-STATE AND CITIZENSHIP

The success of the nation-state in the last 200 years or so as well as its universality and legitimacy were premised on its claim to be able to guarantee the economic well-being, the physical security and the cultural identity of the people who constitute its citizens. In the past, the sovereign nation-state was considered to be the 'ultimate power' that could impose, and enforce, order within a territory. Political rule in general, and the regulatory, steering and coordinating capacities of the state in particular, have been territorially bounded in their reach. Since the nineteenth century, the state endeavoured to shape society by attempting to: address the 'social question', restore order through policing 'deviancy', improve moral life, shape the national economy through state subsidies, eliminate internal trade barriers such as tariffs and the imposition of import duties, and expand the communication infrastructureand education. It also turned its attention increasingly to collecting and collating information about its subjects and citizens. The states' development depended upon effectively distinguishing between citizens/subjects and possible interlopers, and regulating the physical movements of each. The states' monopolization of the legitimate means of movement since the French Revolution has been a cen-

tral feature of their development as states. This process of monopolization was propelled by the fact 'that states must develop the capacity to "embrace" their own citizens in order to extract from them the resources they need to reproduce themselves over time' (Torpey, 2000: 2). States had to define 'who belongs and who does not, who may come and go and who not' (Torpey, 2000: 13). Documents such as passports and identity cards have been critical to regulating population movements. In aiming to make distinctions between nationals and non-nationals, and to track the movements of persons in order to sustain the boundary between these two groups, these regulatory endeavours have also been critical to the states' efforts to construct homogeneous 'nations' (Torpey, 2000: 167).

Through its activities, then, the state became the obvious focus for political activity since the nineteenth century. It became the reference point for most social groups as they had to strive to capture, or influence, the core institutions of the state in order to advance their own objectives. Thus, the state pulled society into its political space at the same time as it was trying to shape society according to its own objectives. In this process, state–society relation was tightened and social relations were 'caged' (Michael Mann) over the national rather than the local–

regional or transnational terrain. The state could no longer be evaded; it therefore became imperative to gain rights of participation in order better to control its activities, share in the benefits it could bring and lessen the negative effects of its policies on the life of individuals, families and communities.

As a result of political struggles in the nineteenth and twentieth centuries, democracy came to be linked to the nation-state through the institution of citizenship for members of the national community. The British sociologist T.H. Marshall (1963) distinguished three types of citizenship rights: civil, political and social. Civil citizenship rights are instrumental in securing 'liberty of the person, freedom of speech, thought and faith, the right to own property and to conclude valid contracts and the right to justice'. The state in which civil rights prevail is a constitutional state. The struggles for democratization in the nineteenth century aimed at institutionalizing political citizenship rights: 'the right to participate in the exercise of political power, as a member of a body invested with political authority or as an elector of the members of such a body'. The state in which such political rights can be exercised is a constitutional parliamentary system. The struggle of the working-class movement since the nineteenth century for social justice and economic security against private property, economic power and concomitant political power of aristocracy and bourgeoisie alike was ultimately a demand for rights to resources, and hence for social rights: 'the whole range from the right to a modicum of economic welfare and security to the right to share to the full in the social heritage and to live the life of a civilised being according to the standards prevailing in the society' (Marshall, 1963: 74). The constitutional state with its parliamentary system was to become a democratic welfare state.

As I have argued in Chapter 1 on 'Sovereignty', in western 'liberal' democracies, individuals must be members of the state, must be its 'nationals', in order to possess citizenship rights. 'Liberal' democracy is premised upon an acceptance of a dual notion of self-determination: the capacity of the individual to govern herself or himself and the capacity of individuals as citizens to govern themselves as a political national community. With social relations becoming bounded by the state's territorial reach, it was only logical that democracy, too, should be 'territorialized' within the confines of the nation-state.

GLOBALIZATION

This connection between the territorial nation-state and democratic citizenship, which has long been considered self-evident, has been queried in recent years as a result of debates on 'globalization'. Despite the voluminous literature on 'globalization' – or possibly because of the outpouring of publications on 'globalization' – there is no agreed-upon understanding of what is meant by 'globalization' (see Held et al., 1999; and Scholte, 2000, as sophisticated expositions of the central issues, themes and debates). At a descriptive level, 'globalization' gestures towards the following developments. We live in an era of ever-increasing interconnectedness of people, places, capital, goods and services. We are witnessing an increase, and an intensification of political, economic, social and cultural interactions across territorial borders. As a result, all states and societies – and, increasingly, individuals as well – have become entangled in a complex (and 'global') system of mutual dependencies. It is this reality of worldwide interdependence, its emergence and its dynamics as well as its effects on states, societies and individuals, that the word 'globalization' aims to sum up.

Globalization is a multifaceted process that manifests itself in such diverse forms as global tourism, mass migration and the global reach of nuclear, environmental and health risks. Arguably, however, it has been economic changes and technological innovations in transport and information systems and their worldwide diffusion that have conjured up visions of a 'global' world. We may not yet have seen the emergence of a global economy which would be institutionalized through global capital markets and globally integrated financial systems as well as through global trade and global productions networks, and in which the patterns of production and consumption in the world would be fully interdependent, and income and employment determined at a global level. Yet, as Manuel Castells has argued, the overall dominant trend points towards

> the increasing interpenetration of markets, particularly after the reasonably successful Uruguay Round of GATT, the birth of the World Trade Organization, the slow but steady progress in European unification, the signing of the North American Free Trade Agreement, the intensification of economic exchanges within Asia, the gradual incorporation of Eastern Europe and Russia [as well as China, R.A.] into the global economy, and the growing role played by trade and foreign investment in economic growth everywhere. Furthermore, the quasi-total integration of capital markets makes all economies globally interdependent. (Castells, 1996: 99)

The globalization of the economy is driven forward by the interpenetration of the advanced capitalist countries and, in particular, by the intensification of transfers among three economic macro-regions: North America, Europe and the Asian Pacific. To the extent that capital is buzzing around the world, most of the time it finds a resting place in advanced capitalist countries. To the extent that international trade is increasing, it is an expression of the growing interdependencies of advanced capitalist countries. And despite processes of de-industrialization in the advanced capitalist countries, most of value-added manufacturing is still taking place there.

The emergence of such a global economy has been premised on the development of a technological infrastructure regarding transportation and the generation and circulation of information. The internationalization of production and the establishment of global production networks has been dependent upon faster and more cost-effective rail, sea and air transportation and on more extensive interconnections between them. The global economy more generally has become infrastructurally dependent upon the spread of global communications networks and the systematic use of radio, television, telephone, telex, fax, computer and satellite facilities for the generation and dissemination of information. These technological innovations and their systematic applications in economic transactions have resulted in the 'shrinking' of distances with faster and improved connection between places.

Communication technologies have also created the conditions for a global system of symbolic interaction and exchange. These new communication media allow the generation and dissemination of economically valuable data, but they make also possible the transfer of mental images, exposing the recipients of these images to similar, 'standardized' ways of thinking and acting. In other words, these media and the images they transport may arguably have an impact on the culture and identity of the societies exposed to them.

To sum up, a reference to 'globalization' contains the hypothesis that there has occurred an increase in the density of contacts between locations worldwide and that, as social life has become embedded in global networks, local events are shaped by events occurring many miles away and vice versa. Furthermore, as a result of innovations in communication technology, many of these connections between locations worldwide have become almost instantaneous so that we experience a temporal immediacy to social events and cultural expressions far away. The 'globalization hypothesis' thus implies that the constraints of space and time on social and cultural arrangements are receding and that we can witness the 'spatial' and 'temporal' shrinking of the world as well as an increasing awareness of the world as 'one place'.

MIGRATION, NATIONALISM AND CITIZENSHIP

One of the hallmarks of the global age has been the rapidly increasing mobility of people across national borders. States are struggling to enforce the regulation of population movements. Owing to the influx of labour migrants and their families, refugees and asylum-seekers and their settlement in nearly all highly developed countries, and in many parts of the less-developed regions, populations have become more heterogeneous and culturally diverse. How do these developments affect conceptions of citizenship? Stephen Castles and Alistair Davidson (2000) have highlighted three key issues. First, in order to deal politically and administratively with second-generation immigrants, many (OECD) states have created systems of quasi-citizenship. Adopting Tomas Hammar's term *denizen* for people 'who are foreign citizens with a legal and permanent residence status' (T. Hammar, 1990), they underline the fact that quasi-citizens enjoy neither political rights nor a complete equality of social rights. However, whereas denizens possess the pivotal right of permanent residence, there is an increasing number of long-term immigrants in many countries who lack secure residence status: 'These include illegal workers, unauthorized family entrants, asylum-seekers, refused asylum-seekers who have not (yet) been deported, former legal residents who have lost this status . . ., the long-term unemployed who may be subject to deportation in some countries, and people classed as temporary workers who are in fact permanently integrated into the workforce' (Castles and Davidson, 2000: 95–6). How to deal with these *margizens* (M. Martiniello, 1994), who are truly living on the margins of prosperous western societies, is as politically fraught a question as that about the political and social inclusion of 'denizens'.

This leads into the second major theme pursued by Castles and Davidson. Typically, there have been three 'routes' to citizenship: by descent, that is, having parents who are already citizens (*ius sanguinis*); by virtue of having been born in the country (*ius soli*); or by petitioning for, and being granted, citizenship. The authors now suggest that the socio-political pressures exerted by immigration will result in yet a further mechanism gaining increasing significance: 'that of *ius domicili* (law of residence), according to which people may gain an entitlement to citizenship through residence in the territory of a country' (Castles and Davidson, 2000: 85). This *ius domicili* provides an option of facilitated naturalization to young people of immigrant origin. They predict that, at least in OECD countries, we are likely to see mixed types of citizenship entitlements combining several of the routes to citizenship.

The third theme is firmly linked to the previous two. To the extent that immigration has led to ethnic community formations, political inclusion of immigrant communities must be achieved without aiming for cultural assimilation: 'Minorities can no longer be assimilated because of the speed and volume of migration, the continual nature of population mobility, the cultural and social diversity of the migrants, the ease with which they can remain in contact with the society of origin, and the situation of rapid economic and cultural change' (Castles and Davidson, 2000: 153–4). It is in this context that the issues of 'dual citizenship', of 'multicultural citizenship' and of identity politics have found their way on to the political agenda and into academic reformulations of democratic theory (see Chapter 8 by Judith Squires in this volume). Yet, these developments do not necessarily support political and academic arguments that posit the rise of a 'postnational citizenship'. Yasemin Soysal had declared that national citizenship was losing ground to a more universal model of membership that was anchored in deterritori-alized notions of persons' rights:

> In the postnational model, universal person-hood replaces nationhood; and universal human rights replace national rights. . . . The rights and claims of individuals are legit-imated by ideologies grounded in a trans-national community, through international codes, conventions, and laws on human rights, independent of their citizenship in a nation-state. Hence, the individual trans-cends the citizen. (Soysal, 1994: 142; see also Jacobson, 1996)

As a result of this process, so the argument goes, the role and character of the state have changed, and the state is now charged with the institutionalization of international human rights.

Of course, we need to recognize the causal significance of human rights regimes for pop-ulation movements (in particular, with regard to refugees and asylum-seekers) and the treatment of immigrants in the 'host' country, and here, above all, in 'liberal democracies'. But universal entitlements are still basically delivered by the nation-state, although they are no longer limited by formal citizenship. Furthermore, it is still the state that is seen as that body that is rightfully and legitimately charged with upholding human rights, both domestically and internationally. National citizenship in their 'host' country matters to many immigrants. Indeed, it matters so much that many would wish to possess dual cit-izenship, both in their 'home' country and in their 'host' country. 'National', not 'post-national', citizenship is a status that many immigrants value and crave. As long as this interest prevails among immigrant popula-tions, and as long as there are no autonomous institutional structures that could enforce entitlements that individuals hold on the basis of human rights, it may be argued that 'postnational' membership is not a viable alternative to national citizenship (Joppke, 1999a, 1999b; Doomernik and Axtmann, 2001).

However, in contrast to the conceptualiza-tion of popular sovereignty as the self-rule of nationals in their capacity as citizens, the 'radical' democratic principle, stipulating that everyone who is permanently subjected to rule and domination in a legal order must have a part in the exercise of that sovereignty that ultimately legitimates that rule, may gain greater institutional saliency as a result of these developments (Dahl, 1989: Chapter 9). Citizenship status would therefore become distinct from nationality and would adhere to all permanent residents, who would be sub-ject to the same qualifications as the 'nation-als'. However, we must remain cognizant of the fact that such a redefinition of citizenship is by no means a foregone conclusion. Indeed, the granting of citizenship status to non-nationals – and their 'social inclusion' into their 'host' country more generally – has become one of the main mobilizing political issues in 'liberal' democracies as the rise and success of extreme right-wing populism across Europe testifies (see Chapter 28 by Anders Widfeldt in this volume).

We may put this 'anti-immigration' effect in a wider context, linking it to political ten-sions generated by globalization. Political legitimacy in the sovereign, democratic nation-state has typically been linked to the state's capacity to deal relatively effectively with the demands and expectations of its cit-izens and with the citizens' democratic rights to exercise control over the ruling elites through elections and other forms of political participation, as well as through the use of law. This legitimacy is strained because policy issues increasingly require interna-tional agreement and collaboration and are therefore no longer open to the 'sovereign' problem-solving capacity of individual nation-states. But once policy issues are no longer susceptible to comprehensive govern-mental control, no one can be held democrat-ically accountable for them. As long as it is possible for states to find acceptance among their citizens for the claim that the global pol-icy interdependence can be confronted through international and intergovernmental arrangements which leave nation-states with a veto, this challenge to political legitimacy will not result in a crisis of legitimacy: the citizens will still maintain that their governments are democratically accountable to them for their policy decisions.

However, when and if it becomes apparent that intergovernmental collaboration is less efficient in addressing and solving global policy issues and that supra- or transnational decision-making bodies would have to be created whose decisions became binding on nation-states, the question of legitimacy would be raised again. One response to the realization of the diminished problem-solving capacity of states both as 'sovereign' and 'autonomous' actors and as participants in international and intergovernmental arrangements is likely to take the form of demands for, in political terms, a 'splendid isolation' and, in economic terms, protectionism, and thus for a policy of 'exiting' from the world-system. The issue of a distinct identity of a political collectivity is likely to resurface as a manifestation of popular disappointments with the ability of democratic regimes to meet the expectations of their citizenry and solve pressing policy issues. As the rise of right-wing extremism in many of the democratic countries of the west in recent years shows, there is a distinct possibility for 'xenophobic nationalism' to function as the mobilizing ideology for the establishment of authoritarian regimes in which the 'ethnos' component of citizenship will marginalize the 'demos' component. Citizens demand political representation, physical protection, economic security and cultural certainty, but in a global system that is made up of states, regions, international and supranational organizations and transnational corporations, and that does not have a clear-cut power hierarchy, the nation-state finds it increasingly difficult to accommodate these interests and mediate between its citizens and the rest of the world.

It is within this structural configuration that nationalism can become a strong political force. And this is so for a variety of reasons. First, nationalism is structurally embedded in the changes of the inter-state system. After the end of the Cold War, the geostrategic interests of the major international powers can no longer be defined as necessitating the perpetuation of the freezing of international borders on the grounds of security. As a result, demands for independence within states can be voiced more persuasively along nationalist lines. Secondly, the formation of regional blocs (such as the European Community/European Union) may make it feasible for 'small' states to conceive of themselves as viable, 'independent' states in a 'Greater Europe'. It thus allows for nationalist mobilization in pursuit of secession and independence. Thirdly, the restructuring of the global economy adds to chances of 'survival' of (at least, some) smaller states: with the increasing importance of high-tech, high-know-how economies, scale and space become less important in economic terms, as Hong Kong and Singapore demonstrate. Even 'city-states' have thus a good chance of establishing themselves in the global system. Finally, globalization, and in particular global capitalism, has brought in its wake regional disparities and economic dislocations. De-industrialization and unemployment, rising prices and declining living standards have intensified the demands by citizens for protection and security. The citizens 'call on governments to act in the national interests at a time when policy tools at the disposal of the nation-state are no longer up to the task' (Horsman and Marshall, 1994: 86). In this situation, extreme nationalism and right-wing extremism can become popular among those social classes and groups most affected by the processes of globalization.

CITIZENSHIP: EUROPEAN AND GLOBAL

Even after more than 40 years of economic and political (West) European integration, politics in this European space remains essentially 'nationalized'. It is around the conflict and cleavage structure within the bounded territory of the nation-state that intermediary institutions such as political parties, interest groups, voluntary associations, trade unions or the mass media have been organized. Citizens still direct their interests, concerns and demands primarily to their national, or sub-national, government, not to 'Brussels'. They tend to avail themselves of the national intermediary institutions as their means of political participation. To put it differently, the role of the citizen has been, and remains, firmly institutionalized at the level of the nation-state. Evidently, since about half of all 'national' legislation in the European Union member states in economic and 'domestic' matters has been initiated at the European level, the question of democratic control by the citizens is of the utmost political importance. There has been much debate on the lack of democratic accountability and legitimacy in the EU, its (alleged) 'democratic deficit' (see, for example, Banckoff and Smith, 1999; Weiler, 1999, Part II; Eriksen and Fossum, 2000; Schmitter, 2000). In the context of the discussion in this chapter, I shall concentrate on the institution of 'European Union' citizenship as a component of its democratic order.

Citizenship of the Union does not replace the citizenship of member states; citizenship status in one of the member states is the pre-requisite for Union citizenship. This Union citizenship gives its holder a limited number of rights. The core and the origin of Union citizenship is the right of free movement. Political citizenship rights in the Union are, however, still underdeveloped. Union citizens are given the right to petition the European Parliament on matters which come within the Community's field of activity. They may also take complaints about possible maladministration in the activities of the Community institutions or bodies to an ombudsman who is elected by the European Parliament and acts independently of any Community institution or national government. The core of the political rights of Union citizenship is, however, the right of citizens of member states to vote and to stand as candidates at municipal and European elections in the country of residence rather than the country of nationality.

The political rights of Union citizenship, however, do not cover national parliamentary elections. Arguably, the exercise of voting rights for national elections would be a much more relevant aspect of Union citizenship, 'given the involvement of (some) national bodies of representation in the framing and implementation of the European legal and political order' and their pivotal role in upholding the principle of democratic accountability for decisions taken in intergovernmental negotiations (d'Oliveira, 1995: 73). Thus, while Union citizenship is premised upon citizenship in a member state, it does not give Union citizens residing 'abroad' necessarily or automatically the same rights, duties, privileges or advantages that are inherent in national citizenship in their country of residence. Hence, non-national EU citizens are second-class citizens in their country of residence. Yet, these limited political citzenship rights set EU citizens not only apart from the nationals of their country of residence, they also separate them from third-country nationals who are still denied any political citizenship although they may have lived and worked in the country often for many years. Their daily experience of marginalization and insecurity is compounded by this new manifestation of discrimination.

A genuine European citizenship will evolve only to the extent that European intermediary institutions are built up that allow citizens political participation in a European political system. But the experience of the development of citizenship rights in the western nation-states also shows that it is premised on the formation of some kind of identity that provides the cognitive, normative and emotive framework for the exercise of citizenship rights. Ultimately, shared citizenship rights presuppose the willingness to live together as a community. Such a *vouloir vivre ensemble* must be reconfirmed in a 'daily plebiscite' (Ernest Renan); it must be a will expressed by all members of the community, not just by a small elite of 'Eurocrats' or self-interested business people. So far, such a European consciousness and social-psychological identification with 'Europe' (that is, the European Union) have not yet formed.

It is now often argued that the very existence of a multiplicity of national and ethnic communities and identities makes it imperative that European citizenship minimalizes the importance of ethno-cultural criteria for determining membership and rights in the political community. The idea of a European citizenship and a European 'demos' in a multinational and multi-ethnic Europe, so it is said, must be based on a common political culture which embraces the universalist meaning of popular sovereignty and human rights; it cannot be based on particularist ethnic criteria. What is warranted, therefore, is the development of a European *political* identity, while *ethno-cultural* identity remains largely at the national level – or even moves down towards micro-national 'regional' identities.

Philippe Schmitter has argued that, for the 'eventual Euro-polity' to succeed, it does not need to reproduce 'on an enlarged scale the same intensity of collective sentiment that was once characteristic of its member nation-states'; rather the problem is 'whether it can reproduce an encompassing system of stable and peaceful political relations without such a passionately shared identity or community of fate' (Schmitter, 2000: 28). What is required is the formation of a 'nonnational citizenship', based on rational interest calculation and instrumental reason, a shift from the emotional to the rational, from being enthralled by one's nation's sacrifices and glories of the past to a cool-headed embrace of the rights and procedures enjoyed in the Euro-polity of the present. How this shift is meant to come about – other than through the activities of Euro-elites – is impossible to deduce from Schmitter's analysis. Still, Schmitter is not a lonely voice in his pleading for a 'cool' citizenship. Bryan Turner, for example, has argued that, whereas the traditional nation-state encouraged 'hot loyalty' and 'thick solidarities', the postnational condition will produce, and privilege, 'cool loyalties' and 'thin' patterns of solidarity:

> [H]ot loyalties and thick solidarities are more likely to be points of conflict and violence in postmodern, ethnically diverse markets. Indifference and distance may be useful personal strategies in a risk society where ambiguity and uncertainty reign. In a more fluid world, the ironic citizen needs to learn how to move on, how to adjust and to adapt to a world of cultural contingency. (Turner, 2000: 29–30)

This argument raises at least two questions. First, while the marginalization on the European level of ethno-cultural criteria for the granting of a European citizenship may be warranted because of the multinationality and multi-ethnicity of Europe, we are currently witnessing developments – discussed in the previous section – that have already led to a recharging of the 'ethnos'-dimension of political life. Loyalties appear to be growing 'hotter' and solidarities are getting 'thicker' again, and one reason for this development would appear to be the accelerated speed of European integration and expansion. Secondly, how 'cool' can a democratic order afford to be? In a democracy, the willingness to listen and to be swayed by an argument put forward by others is influenced by the perception of the interlopers' legitimate membership of the conversational community, by their shared status as fellow citizens. There has to be a sense of belonging together, a sense of loyalty, a sense of identity, even. Here the question arises as to what it is that makes collectives cohere, and which role is played by affective ties and sentiments in this regard. But it is also a question about the affective underpinnings of democracy – a problem that goes beyond nationalistic notions of 'love of country'. Does any conceivable, solely rule-governed, constitutional patriotism ultimately presuppose a hinterland of non-rationalistic assumptions

and sentiments? Are there affective preconditions for social solidarity? Does peaceful co-
existence require grounding in some kind of
affective belonging and compassion? If so,
then through what kind of existential experiences can it be acquired in the postnational
condition?

What has just been said about 'postnational' European citizenship is also pertinent to the debate about 'global' citizenship
(see Dower and Williams, 2002). Rengger's
chapter on 'Cosmopolitanism' (Chapter 32)
and Axtmann's chapter on 'Civil Society'
(Chapter 9) highlight developments and
arguments that have underpinned a global
political and ethical orientation of ever more
non-state actors. The idea of a global moral
responsibility of individuals, societies and
states is gaining ever more adherents. Ever
more people accept the claim that they ought
to work for global goals and that the agendas
of citizens within a state increasingly ought
to include global concerns. Global goals such
as the protection of human rights, peace,
the reduction of poverty or caring for the
environment, and action such as working for
Oxfam, joining an Amnesty International
letter-writing campaign or standing in a vigil
for peace at a time of war, may serve as
examples of global commitment and forms
of action geared towards achieving them
(Dower, 2000).

However, we live in a world of value conflicts. For example, some people may believe
that 'global' capitalism is conducive to reducing world poverty, and that excessive environmental concerns and regulations will not
only unduly restrict economic development
but therefore also result in 'global injustice'.
And even if we accept that there is a 'global'
consensus on certain elements of a 'global
ethic' (such as 'human rights'), there are then
still conflicts over the specific policies necessary (or appropriate) to enact such rights.
Think, for example, in the case of abortion
how the (human) rights of the mother are
best balanced with the (human) rights of the
unborn child. Politics may be about many
things, but it finds one expression in the

authoritative allocation of values for a political community as a whole. Given value conflicts, such allocation is, of necessity,
contentious. Democracy aims to prevent the
authoritarian or dictatorial allocation of such
values by institutionalizing mechanisms of
popular participation in, and control over,
political decision-making.

'Global' citizenship therefore needs an
institutional framework. David Held's model
of 'cosmopolitan democracy' is one attempt
at institutional design. Held argues in favour
of a global and divided authority system, 'a
system of diverse and overlapping power
centres, shaped and delimited by democratic
law' (Held, 1995: 234–5). For Held, cosmopolitan law 'demands the subordination of
regional, national and local "sovereignties" to
an overarching legal framework, but within
this framework associations may be self-
governing at diverse levels' (Held, 1995: 234).
His goal is to strengthen democracy 'within'
communities and civil associations 'by elaborating and reinforcing democracy from
"outside" through a network of regional and
international agencies and assemblies that cut
across spatially delimited locales' (Held,
1995: 237; see also McGrew, 2002).

Philip Resnick (1998) has rightly pointed
out that prospects for global democracy are
held back by uneven development, diverging
political traditions, cultural and ethnic identities and solidarities that are primarily local or
national in character (see also Axtmann,
2002). It is also likely to be held back because
the 'universalist' orientation that must underpin the institutionalization of global democracy is counteracted by the 'particularistic'
nationalisms that are as much the effect of
'globalization' as the cosmopolitan orienta-
tions of 'global citizens'. What tends to be
forgotten in the debates on European and
global citizenship is the affective, psycho-
political component of 'citizenship'. This is
not so much a naïve 'patriotic' notion of 'My
country, right or wrong', but rather a sense of

belonging and rootedness and the existence of a collective memory of shared experiences that enables the build-up of solidarity, trust and 'social capital' that grounds democracy.

Summary

- 'Globalization' refers to processes that have led to a 'spatial' and 'temporal' shrinking of the world as well as to an awareness of a global connectivity of individuals, societies and state.
- In the age of globalization, the connection between the territorial nation-state and democratic citizenship becomes problematic.
- Immigration has made the institution of citizenship a fiercely contested political issue.
- Citizenship presupposes a sense of belonging and loyalty. It is by no means certain that it can be transferred on to a level 'beyond the nation-state'.

TUTORIAL QUESTIONS

1. **How does immigration affect our understanding of citizenship?**

2. **Do you find Turner's argument regarding 'cool loyalties' and 'thin solidarities' in 'post-national' polities convincing?**

3. **How desirable is it to become a 'citizen' of Europe and the world? How difficult do you think it will be to create institutions for the exercise of such citizenship?**

FURTHER READING

Roland Axtmann (ed.) (2001) *Balancing Democracy* (London: Continuum) presents essays on the ideas and ideals that are contained in the concept of democracy. How will democracy and democratic institutions develop or change as the new millennium gets under way?

Jan Aart Scholte (2000) *Globalization: a Critical Introduction* (Basingstoke: Palgrave) offers an excellent overview of key debates surrounding the idea of 'globalization' and presents a crisp empirical account of 'globalization'.

Nigel Dower and John Williams (eds) (2002) *Global Citizenship: a Critical Reader* (Edinburgh: Edinburgh University Press) contains essays on the idea of global citizenship and its institutional manifestations – with most of the essays offering a sympathetic assessment.

Philippe Schmitter (2000) *How to Democratize the European Union . . . and Why Bother?* (Lanham, MD: Rowman and Littlefield) offers a provocative argument about what is needed to build a genuinely democratic Euro-polity.

REFERENCES

Axtmann, Roland (2002) 'What's Wrong with Cosmopolitan Democracy?', in Nigel Dower and John Williams (eds), *Global Citizenship: a Critical Reader*. Edinburgh: Edinburgh University Press, pp. 101–13.

Banckoff, Thomas and Smith, Mitchell P. (eds) (1999) *Legitimacy in the European Union: the Contested Polity*. London: Routledge.

Castells, Manuel (1996) *The Information Age: Economy, Society and Culture, Vol. I: The Rise of the Network Society*. Oxford: Blackwell.

Castles, Stephen and Davidson, Alistair (2000) *Citizenship and Migration. Globalization and the Politics of Belonging*. Basingstoke: Macmillan [now: Palgrave].

Dahl, Robert A. (1989) *Democracy and Its Critics*. New Haven, CT and London: Yale University Press.

Doomernik, Jeroen and Axtmann, Roland (2001) 'Transnational Migration, the Liberal State and Citizenship', in Roland Axtmann (ed.), *Balancing Democracy*. London: Continuum, pp. 76–89.

Dower, Nigel (2000) 'The Idea of Global Citizenship – a Sympathetic Assessment', *Global Society*, **14**: 553–67.

Dower, Nigel and Williams, John (eds) (2002) *Global Citizenship: a Critical Reader*. Edinburgh: Edinburgh University Press.

Eriksen, Erik Odvar and Fossum, John Erik (eds) (2000) *Democracy in the European Union.*

Integration Through Deliberation? London: Routledge.

Hammar, T. (1990) *Democracy and the Nation-state: Aliens, Denizens and Citizens in a World of International Migration*. Aldershot: Avebury.

Held, David (1995) *Democracy and the Global Order: from the Modern State to Cosmopolitan Governance*. Cambridge: Polity Press.

Held, David et al. (1999) *Global Transformations: Politics, Economics, and Culture*. Cambridge: Polity Press.

Horsman, Mathew and Marshall, Andrew (1994) *After the Nation-state: Citizens, Tribalism and the New World Disorder*. London: HarperCollins.

Jacobson, David (1996) *Rights Across Borders: Immigration and the Decline of Citizenship*. Baltimore, MD and London: Johns Hopkins University Press.

Joppke, Christian (1999a) *Immigration and the Nation-state: the United States, Germany and Great Britain*. Oxford: Oxford University Press.

Joppke, Christian (1999b) 'How Immigration is Changing Citizenship: a Comparative View', *Ethnic and Racial Studies*, **22**: 629–52.

Marshall, T.H. (1963) 'Citizenship and Social Class', in T.H. Marshall, *Sociology at the Crossroads and Other Essays*. London: Heinemann, pp. 67–127.

Martiniello, M. (1994) 'Citizenship and the European Union: a critical view, in R. Bauböck (ed.), *From Aliens to Citizens*. Aldershot: Avebury.

McGrew, Anthony (2002) 'Transnational Democracy', in April Carter and Geoffrey Stokes (eds), *Democratic Theory Today*. Cambridge: Polity Press, pp. 269–94.

d'Oliveira, Hans Ulrich Jesserun (1995) 'Union Citizenship: Pie in the Sky?', in A. Rosas and E. Anatola (eds), *A Citizen's Europe: in Search of a New Order*. London: Sage, pp. 58–84.

Resnick, Philip (1998) 'Global Democracy: Ideals and Reality', in Roland Axtmann (ed.), *Globalization and Europe*. London: Pinter, pp. 126–43.

Schmitter, Philippe (2000) *How to Democratize the European Union . . . and Why Bother?* Lanham, MD: Rowman and Littlefield.

Scholte, Jan Aart (2000) *Globalization: a Critical Introduction*. Basingstoke: Palgrave.

Soysal, Yasemin N. (1994) *Limits of Citizenship: Migrants and Postnational Membership in Europe*. Chicago, IL and London: University of Chicago Press.

Torpey, John (2000) *The Invention of the Passport: Surveillance, Citizenship and the State*. Cambridge: Cambridge University Press.

Turner, Bryan S. (2000) 'Liberal Citizenship and Cosmopolitan Virtue', in Andrew Vandenberg (ed.), *Citizenship and Democracy in a Global Era*. Basingstoke: Macmillan [now: Palgrave], pp. 18–32.

Weiler, J.H.H. (1999) *The Constitution of Europe*. Cambridge: Cambridge University Press.

See also chapters

1	Sovereignty	19	Social Capital
2	Constitutionalism	27	Nationalism
3	Human Rights and Democracy	28	Contemporary Right-wing Extremism
8	Pluralism – Difference	32	Cosmopolitanism
9	Civil Society – National and Global		

PART III

Ideologies and Movements

23 Liberalism

Antonino Palumbo

The history of liberalism is the history of an ideology, the ideology of the bourgeoisie. The use of terms like 'ideology' and 'bourgeoisie' are neither meant to be disparaging, nor intended to advocate a Marxist reading. In using these words the intention is to present liberalism as a historical phenomenon: a social and political movement that has shaped the (western) world we inhabit, and supplied the cultural tools for understanding and justifying it. To flourish, the bourgeoisie had first to break with the pre-existing social and political order and then to build a new one on different foundations. The relationship between liberalism and democracy reflects this twin enterprise. In its revolutionary phase, liberalism was a force for liberalization and democratization that contributed to the development and grounding of the values of individual autonomy and political self-determination. Once established as the dominant social and political class, the bourgeoisie developed a protective liberalism to curb the strength of those same values and institutions it had originally promoted. Culturally, the passage from *revolutionary* to *protective* liberalism is also the passage from a sceptical – but tolerant – political philosophy to a far-reaching natural philosophy. For this naturalized liberalism, democratic politics was no longer concerned with engendering the values of autonomy and self-determination. Democratic politics was simply the tool with which irrational and greedy masses could periodically sanction elites

whose political agenda had been rigidly limited from without.

This chapter is divided into three sections. The first gives a historical account of the process through which a revolutionary bourgeoisie succeeded in shaping political and social institutions in accordance with individualistic principles. Here the main claim is that the liberal challenge to the pre-existing social and political order rested on an appeal to both universal individual liberties and a political right to representation and participation. The second section focuses on the relationship between the liberal state and democracy. Here it is argued that, once in power, the bourgeoisie developed a method of government (liberal democracy) which, while recognizing formal universal principles, in reality denied an active involvement to the lower classes. The third section looks at the relationship between liberalism and democracy in analytical terms. After comparing liberal strategies of justification and ideal-types of democracy, I end by claiming that liberalism is compatible only with procedural and aggregative forms.

THE LIBERAL REVOLUTION

Liberalism has its roots in the sceptical philosophy of the seventeenth century and the political theories advocating a *modus vivendi* which could put an end to the religious wars that had racked Europe since the Reformation. The champions of this proto-liberalism were mainly intellectuals educated in the secular universities and those reformist splinter-groups that lacked the protection of a powerful prince. Although these proto-liberals belonged to the urban middle classes, at this stage the bourgeoisie as an economic and social class was still in the making. In Britain the events that kick-started the development of the bourgeoisie are related to the Agrarian Revolution which followed the enclosures of commons and the establishment of the constitutional monarchy of William and Mary (1688). The appropriation of common lands by the landed gentry had already started before the Civil War. Cromwell's Commonwealth and the constitutional regime that emerged after the Glorious Revolution accelerated the process by depriving cottagers, yeomen and rural communities of the scanty protection previously offered to them by the Crown. As a result, the enclosure movement gathered pace and was carried out by means of parliamentary acts under the protection of the law. The enclosures not only favoured the big landlords and their tenants, they also brought significant benefits to the urban commercial classes. For them, the rationalization of the land meant three things: better food for their households; raw wool for their textile industry; and an almost inexhaustible supply of cheap labour. If the rural revolution 'broke the back of the English peasantry' (Moore, 1967: 28), it also led to a rise in the standard of living of the middle classes and paved the way for the Industrial Revolution.

The Glorious Revolution is a turning point in the history of liberalism, for it marks the entry of the bourgeoisie on to the political stage on an equal footing with the monarchy and the aristocracy. This achievement was witnessed by a new constitutional arrangement which established a division of powers that set effective limits to the sovereign authority, while creating social checks and balances between the monarchy, aristocracy and bourgeoisie that prevented any one of

them from monopolizing political power. The spokesman for this liberal revolutionary vanguard was John Locke, who supplied a moral justification for the claims of the bourgeoisie which rested on three tenets: the natural rights of men as opposed to the natural rights of kings; the priority of the social over the political; the rule of law and balancing of powers as a safeguard against tyranny.

In contrast to thinkers like Robert Filmer, who argued that the authority of kings rested on their being the direct heirs of Adam and therefore descended from God, Locke showed that such claims were groundless, and that the idea of a rational and benevolent God implied an equal right to liberty for all men. 'The *Natural Liberty* of man is to be free from any Superior Power on Earth, and not to be under the Will or Legislative Authority of Man, but to have only the Law of Nature for his Rule' (Locke, 1690/1988, § 22: 283). In disagreement with those who subscribed to the claim that the natural condition of humankind was political, Locke maintained that political authority rested on individual consent and was justified only insofar as the individual's pre-political rights and liberties were protected. 'The *Liberty of Man, in Society*, is to be under no other Legislative Power, but that established, by consent, in the Commonwealth, nor under the Dominion of any Will, or Restraint of any Law, but what that Legislative shall enact, according to the Trust put in it' (Locke, 1690/1988, § 22: 283). Finally, to prevent the arbitrary use of political power or to resist the temptation to abuse it, Locke argued for the rule of law and the division of powers as 'methods of restraining any exorbitances of those to whom they [the people] had given the authority over them, and of balancing the power of government' (Locke, 1690/1988, § 107: 338).

At the outset, the social costs of the Agrarian Revolution were offset by the job opportunities created by both the structural investments required by the new system of private ownership and the expansion of the textile industry. It is worth noting that, at this stage, industrial production was still decentralized and carried on by a myriad of independent artisans on the basis of bilateral contracts with capitalist entrepreneurs. This is the horizontal division of labour celebrated by Adam Smith. According to Smith, this social division of labour not only assured the just remuneration of the factors of production, but it also guaranteed that 'the accommodation of a European prince does not always so much exceed that of an industrious and frugal peasant as the accommodation of the latter exceeds that of many an African king, the absolute master of the lives and liberties of ten thousand naked savages' (Smith, 1776/1983: 117). As a result, Smith puts forward the most enduring apology for a capitalist economy: a naturalistic justification that depicts markets as both moral-free areas and the best means for allocating social resources, while supplying an instrumental defence of property which, unlike Locke's, did not rest on the controversial theological assumptions of a benevolent and rational God.

As the Industrial Revolution unfolded, Smith's theories were not vindicated by events. First, the system of production underwent a process of vertical integration which forced the independent artisans to become a salaried workforce and turned employment contracts into relationships of authority. Unlike the network of small producers celebrated by Smith, the modern capitalist firm came to be characterized by a hierarchical structure and a well-defined system of authority. The different stages of production were concentrated under one roof and carried out under the strict supervision of the 'boss'. Industrial relations mirrored this set-up. Employment contracts established a relationship of authority where it was left to the boss to decide how work had to be carried out. The worker was left little or no managerial autonomy, thus promoting what Marx called a process of alienation. Secondly, industrial capitalists pushed the various governments to adopt free-market policies that outlawed the medieval system of corporations and guilds. The outcomes of these policies were

similar to those noted above with regard to the rationalization of rural economy. If the abolition of guilds freed the individual workers from the tyranny of the master, and the professions from many artificial barriers to entry, it also removed the safety nets that protected workers from market fluctuations. Thus, many skilled workers rapidly became exposed to the cyclical crises that affected the various sectors of the manufacturing industry and they ended up joining the growing number of impoverished labourers crowding the English cities.

The Industrial Revolution not only stripped the worker of any autonomy in production matters, but also turned the life of the working classes into an endless struggle for job and income. Evidently, such a state of affairs led to social unrest and turmoil. The poor demonstrated against the protectionist laws that kept food prices up; skilled weavers turned against the newly introduced machines they held responsible for losing their jobs; industrial workers rioted against working conditions and low salaries and attempted to reorganize the old system of corporations and guilds in the form of trade unions. Up to the 1760s the plight of the working classes had met with some sympathy from the ruling classes and this made state repression relatively lenient. After that date confrontations became more radicalized and turned into political class struggles. From this perspective the French Revolution represents a second turning point in the history of liberalism; it brought to the fore the liberal perplexities about democracy and changed liberal thought into a protective political ideology concerned with law and order.

In his *Reflections on the French Revolution* (1790), Edmund Burke exposed the danger of the universalistic liberalism advocated by natural rights theorists since Locke: 'The pretended rights of these theorists are all extremes; and in proportion as they are metaphysically true, they are morally and politically false' (Burke, 1790/1993: 62). For him, the rights of man represented 'a mine that will blow up at one grand explosion all examples of antiquity, all precedents, charters, and acts of parliament' (1790/1993: 58). As for democracy, Burke questioned the 'consistency of those democrats, who, when they are not on their guard, treat the humbler part of community with the greatest contempt, whilst, at the same time they pretend to make them the depositaries of all power' (1790/1993: 56). He pointed out that 'if popular representation, or choice is necessary to the legitimacy of all government', then not only the Crown and the House of Lords, but the House of Commons as well was 'no representative of the people at all, even in "semblance or in form"' (1790/1993: 57). Hence, Burke made it clear that, to express the will of society, there was no need to consult the people. A better job could be done by restricted representative bodies composed of people whose intellectual skills and social rank made them apt to understand and appreciate the value of tradition. To avoid any interference with legislation, Burke also spelled out that the links between representatives and represented had to be indirect and could not take the form of an imperative mandate.

Two things are worth noting about Burke's position. The first concerns the audience he was addressing. Burke's argument was directed against those sectors of the English bourgeoisie who blamed the system of tariffs imposed by the landed gentry for keeping prices up and worsening the conditions of the working classes. The mercantile bourgeoisie and its intellectuals were reminded of the benefits they derived from the political accommodation reached in 1688 and warned that any instrumental support given to democracy could end up undermining not only the status of the House of Lords and its social referent, the landed gentry, but also the overall legitimacy of the institution of property. The second thread in Burke's argument pertains to the justification of the liberal order. Following Smith, Burke advanced a naturalistic account of the liberal order that dismissed Locke's references to a divine

rational artificer. Individual entitlements were the outcome of an evolutionary historical process which led to the development of those social arrangements that best fitted human nature. Within this naturalistic framework, the role of democratic politics was restricted to 'acknowledging' the normative priority of inherited laws and 'applying' them against any appeal to spurious human rights. With Burke, liberalism turned into a protective ideology ready to use the power of the state against the radicals who longed for a more democratic and egalitarian society, and willing to show that the latter's ideals were either utopian or totalitarian or both. The keyword of this naturalized liberalism was 'feasibility', a concept which occupied Immanuel Kant long before John Rawls gave it the philosophical prominence it has today.

LIBERALISM AS A METHOD OF GOVERNMENT

In the decades that followed the French Revolution, the challenge for liberalism was to consolidate the power achieved by the bourgeoisie. The result was 'principled pragmatism', a characteristic method of government the aim of which was to neutralize the threats coming from the radicals and conservatives while advancing the cause of the bourgeoisie. Once again, Britain led the way. After the Napoleonic wars, Britain withdrew from continental politics and concentrated on internal affairs and the expansion of the Empire. Legislation was passed to contain social discontent and the threat of revolution. 'Law had shifted into a class pattern. Working men, accustomed to fight disabilities in the courts, lost traditional rights and had their independent action constrained' (Harvie, 2001: 491). By the middle of the century the balance of power had shifted in a different direction: the industrial bourgeoisie moved to the left and established close ties with sectors of the labour movement. This shift led to the expansion of the franchise to the top end of the working classes (1832) and the Repeal of the Corn Laws (1846). The change of front worked wonders. On the one hand, it drained support from the labour movement and made Britain immune from the revolution that stormed the continent in 1848. On the other hand, it brought to the liberals a larger electoral base, thus putting the Tories out of power for decades to come.

The success of the liberal state in establishing an effective pattern of governance without tackling the inequalities generated by a free market economy was in great part due to the benefits brought about by empire. By the middle of the nineteenth century the British Empire was the most extended trade area of the world. The resources generated by such a vast empire resulted in a steady improvement of social conditions which offset the rising inequalities. Thus, the negative effects of a highly exploitative economic system were defused by the spill-overs generated by a parallel, but equally exploitative, colonial system. In spite of this, the liberal age came to be celebrated as an era of freedom and prosperity, when an unbounded market economy was producing sufficient wealth to make everybody better-off and the state was safely within the rule of law. Unfortunately, once other continental nations set out along the colonial path traced by Britain, the result was a policy of confrontation which eventually erupted into the First World War and brought to an end both the liberal age and Arcadian capitalism.

The liberal state established the template for a system of government that in the twentieth century would spread worldwide: liberal democracy. This system combines three things: constitutionalism, representation and citizenship. 'A constitution is not the act of a government, but of a people constituting a government; and government without a constitution, is power without a right' (Paine, 1792/1984: 185). Constitutions clarified the set of values and institutions upon which the legitimacy of the political system rested, and established side-constraints on the exercise of legislative power. Also, constitutions pro-

vided the opportunity for applying the theory of separation of powers to the national context and defining the criteria of representation and citizenship. 'Representation was a thing unknown in the ancient democracy', wrote Thomas Paine. 'Had the system of representation been understood, as it now is, there is no reason to believe that those forms of government, now called monarchical or aristocratical, would ever have taken place' (Paine, 1792/1984: 177). Representation made democracy a feasible form of government for the nation-state and granted the bourgeoisie the leadership of the productive sectors of society. In practice, this meant keeping the masses at a distance from a direct involvement in the political process. The third and more controversial achievement of liberal democracy was the redefinition of citizenship. If the *ancien régime* attributed full citizenship in relation to birth and status, the liberal state made citizenship accessible to all those capable of succeeding in the economic struggle. Liberal citizenship 'did not confer a right, but it recognized a capacity. No sane and law-abiding citizen was debarred by personal status from acquiring and recording a vote. He was free to earn, to save, to buy property or rent a house, and to enjoy whatever political rights were attached to those economic achievements' (Marshall, 1950: 20).

There are two important things to note about liberal democracy. The first concerns the value of individual autonomy, the second pertains to the principle of self-determination. Liberal thought treated political rights as a by-product of civil rights. As Benjamin Constant explains, 'individual independence is the first need of the moderns: consequently one must never require from them any sacrifices to establish political liberty' (Constant, 1819/1988: 321). Individual autonomy represents the sphere where the individual is free to do what he or she wants. As a result, it is identified with pre-political rights that set strict limits to what a legitimate political authority can do. This means that the definition of individual entitlements is independent from politics and the task of political institutions is to maximize the sphere of autonomy to which each individual is entitled. Consistent with this conception of autonomy, liberals view constitutions as external to the political process and resting on philosophical tenets rather than actual consent. The implication for the principle of self-determination is unambiguous. A community of autonomous individuals requires universal formal procedures that can combine individual entitlements so as to maximize the total sum of liberties enjoyed by all. Democratic politics is, therefore, a means of 'aggregating' pre-political entitlements rather than promoting participation and deliberation.

This reading of democracy as an aggregative mechanism explains the deep appeal exerted by utilitarianism and welfarism on liberal thought. According to utilitarianism, individual preferences rather than rights represent fundamental individual entitlements upon which to establish a principle of political morality. Consequently, it claims that democratic politics ought to endorse those courses of action that maximize the total sum of preferences of the greatest number of people. This maxim is consistent with liberal democratic principles on three counts: it attributes equal consideration to all individual preferences, aggregates individual preferences impartially and advances a notion of the public good that is both objective and morally neutral. Originally, utilitarianism also assumed the existence of a 'law of decreasing marginal utility', a naturalized version of Locke's provisos, which reduced the likelihood of inconsistencies between the attempt to maximize the preferences of the individual and those of the greatest number of people. Thus, in the English-speaking world liberals came to believe that utilitarianism could represent the basis for a scientific liberalism, and that the application of utilitarian principles would lead to equilibria that allocated social resources efficiently while satisfying the basic needs of the worst-off members of society. The 1930s depression undermined people's faith in both the self-

regulating ability of market forces and the self-balancing mechanism of preferences, and promoted the progressive recognition of universal social rights. However, the way in which liberal states granted social rights to their citizens resembled that in which nineteenth-century monarchies conceded constitutional charters to their subjects. Not only did citizens have a very remote and indirect say in the definition of social rights, but the management of welfare provision was delegated to monopolistic bureaucratic structures over which even representative bodies had limited control. Likewise, the redefinition of social rights and the partial withdrawal of welfare provision that has taken place since the 1980s has been carried out without a clear political mandate and in spite of widespread social opposition.

The development of mass political parties and the twentieth-century recognition of universal franchise have had virtually no effect on this aggregative attitude of liberal democracy. The main liberal schools of thought have taken 'for granted the view that just as economics is concerned with individuals maximizing their self-interests, politics is concerned with sets of individuals maximizing their common interests' (Held, 1987: 188). Elitists have insisted in purporting democracy to be a method of government which allows the electorate to sanction its political leadership at periodical intervals. Between elections, however, it is left to those in charge to carry out the business of government and maximize the public good. Similarly, pluralists have defined democracy as a 'polyarchy' where a number of social elites are continuously bargaining so as to reach political compromises capable of reducing social conflicts while satisfying people's needs and entitlements. Here, political parties are delegated full responsibility for collecting and refining individual preferences and for mediating between conflicting claims concerning the common good. Although elitists and pluralists regard the electorate as lacking the time, competence and expertise to express reasonable political judgements, they view democracy as a mechanism of government capable of leading to optimal social equilibria. This optimism is not shared by rational-choice theorists for whom democracy amounts to a game 'in which many players with quite disparate objectives interact so as to generate a set of outcomes that may not be either internally consistent or efficient by any standards' (Buchanan, 1984: 20). Hence, they advocate a neutered democracy where decision-making is limited by constitutional rules requiring strict unanimity and major functions of government are devolved to the market, in their view, the only mechanism capable of leading to efficient social choices.

LIBERALISM AND DEMOCRACY: THE BIG TRADE-OFF

The discussion carried out in the first section of this chapter portrays liberalism as a complex and pluralist tradition of thought; that is, a tradition where appeals to fundamental principles and to justificatory strategies combine. Table 23.1 supplies a taxonomy of liberal positions along two main dimensions: the domain upon which liberal values are grounded and the nature of the core elements upon which liberalism allegedly rests.

Liberalism's first incarnation rests on a sceptical philosophy committed to the value of tolerance and the search for a *modus vivendi* capable of establishing a ceasefire between groups subscribing to alternative world-views. Philosophically, this is the weakest form of liberalism, for it does not supply overriding reasons for justifying tolerance *vis-à-vis* other fundamental principles, or for

preferring a political accommodation to the 'conversion by the sword' advocated by religious doctrines. The confident liberalism that emerged with a victorious revolutionary bourgeoisie grounded its political claims on ethics rather than politics. Following Locke, liberalism has developed rights-based theories that establish what people are entitled to and set clear and strict limits to what 'person[s] or group[s] may do to them (without violating their rights)' (Nozick, 1974: ix). The controversial theological grounds upon which Locke erected individual rights and the shallow foundations upon which his more secular followers, like Nozick, ground theirs have pushed liberal theory towards a Kantian notion of individual autonomy. According to this, 'the ground of obligation . . . must . . . be sought not in the nature of man nor in the circumstances of the world in which man is placed, but must be sought a priori solely in the concepts of pure reason' (Kant, 1785/1993: 2). This implies devising universal formal procedures for assessing the validity of alternative moral claims; procedures that are based on the assumption that moral principles ought to take the form of categorical imperatives, or be the outcome of a hypothetical rational agreement.

The most accomplished attempt in this direction is that carried out by John Rawls. Following Kant, Rawls maintains that the principles of justice that have to underpin a well-ordered society are those that 'mutually self-interested and rational persons, when similarly situated and when required to make a firm commitment in advance, would acknowledge as restrictions governing the assignment of rights and duties in their common practices, and would thereby accept as

TABLE 23.1 *Analytical liberal models*

	Politics	**Ethics**	**Epistemology**
Principles	Toleration	Rights	Liberty
Procedures	Modus vivendi	Autonomy	Rule of law

limiting their rights against one another' (Rawls, [1971] 1999: 191–2). Rawls's theory of justice pursues two main goals. On the one hand, it attributes to the individual basic entitlements and thus sets moral limits to any utilitarian attempt to maximize the public good. On the other hand, Rawls's contractarianism does not assume the existence of rights as primordial moral facts and thus supplies the grounding that rights-based theories lack. The doubts raised by Rawls's enterprise have led to the flourishing of naturalistic approaches to norms. Here, moral claims about what is 'good', 'right' or 'just' are grounded on epistemic theories that avoid any reference to controversial moral agreements or appeal to spurious individual rights. As for Burke, these epistemologies endeavour to highlight the utopian spirit vitiating normative theories of the type advocated by Rawls by showing that positive conceptions of liberty are either logically incoherent or incompatible with the rule of law. Hence, they are committed to define objective criteria of *feasibility* for assessing the practicality of 'any worthwhile proposals for the reform of existing moral attitudes and ideas' (Mackie, [1982] 1985: 153).

These objections have pushed Rawls to recast his theory of justice into a less demanding 'political liberalism'. For it, a society which promotes and values pluralism can be stable if, and only if, its political institutions work according to constitutional principles that could be the outcome of a 'reasonable' agreement. The notion of reasonable, as opposed to rational, is used to identify principles and institutions that could promote the allegiance of a plurality of individuals and groups subscribing to different moral, philosophical and religious viewpoints, thus achieving an 'overlapping consensus'. Consistent with liberal tenets, in Rawls's political liberalism, 'the idea of right and just constitutions and basic laws is always ascertained by the most reasonable political conception and not by the result of an actual political process'

(Rawls, 1993: 233). Thus, it exalts the role of unelected and unrepresentative bodies like the Supreme Court for interpreting and implementing constitutional principles arrived at through philosophical reasoning, and whose primary concern is to check the *demos*.

This taxonomy shows that, if there is a common denominator between these liberalisms, it resides in the advocacy of an 'externalist' approach to politics; that is, an attempt to justify constraints on political action that are derived from non-political domains. The implication of this (distinctively liberal) externalist attitude for democratic politics can be fully appreciated when we compare this taxonomy with the representation of democratic thought given in Figure 23.1.

Figure 23.1 combines two dimensions along which democracy has been justified. The first pertains to the nature of democracy whereas the second concerns the aims of democracy. Following Schumpeter (1943), political theorists have put forward a clear-cut separation between democracy as a method of government based on periodical elections aiming at selecting people's representatives and as an activity granting people a direct voice in decision-making. Alternatively, political philosophers have justified

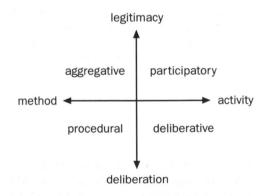

FIGURE 23:1 *Models of democracy*

democracy as supplying some form of legitimacy to the state or as a device for collective deliberation. Criss-crossing these two dimensions, we can identify four ideal types of democracy: aggregative, procedural, participatory and deliberative.

Of these four models, only the aggregative type is fully consistent with liberal democracy. Procedural and participatory models of democracy are compatible with liberal democracy only insofar as deliberation does not encompass individual entitlements or participation undermines the principle of representation. Beyond these limits they tend to be inconsistent with liberal tenets. For example, a procedural approach which, unlike Rawls's, views constitutional essentials simply as the outcome of political deliberations aimed at establishing self-limits would be seen by liberals as resting on a political compromise without any moral force, that is, it would be a *modus vivendi* rather than an 'overlapping consensus' (Rawls, 1993: 170ff). Similarly, a participatory model of democracy that establishes a system where citizens have a direct role in decision-making, or a tight control on their representatives, would raise not only practical questions concerning its applicability, but fears about

the possibility of a tyranny of the majority. Even more frightening would be the idea of expanding democratic decision-making to managerial issues through forms of partnership that set limits to the exercise of property rights.

Particularly evident is the tension between a deliberative model of democracy and liberal democracy. Here, not only are people required to have some direct part in decision-making, but the constitutional essentials that regulate deliberation are internal to the political process itself. This means that 'egalitarian and liberal political values emerge . . . as elements of democracy rather than constraints upon it' (Cohen, 1998: 187), and that the limits on the exercise of political power are self-imposed and, therefore, revisable. In short, substantive models of democracy that reject the quest for 'external' limits on the exercise of political power and do not perceive decision-making as a mechanism for 'aggregating' pre-political individual entitlements turn out to be deeply problematic for, if not incompatible with, liberalism as both a system of ideas and a method of government.

Summary

- Historically, liberalism and democracy are two movements of thought that share similar concerns about individual rights and political participation and have promoted constitutional arrangements that embody and foster those values.
- Theoretically, the relationship between liberalism and democracy is more complex and conflictual.
- Liberal thought has systematically attempted to define external constraints on collective decision-making, whereas democratic theory has attributed to it both moral and political value.

- Also, liberals have purported to show the inherent shortcomings of political intervention, whereas democrats have championed it as a means for achieving social justice and/or social efficiency.
- The chapter supports the claim that liberalism is compatible only with procedural and aggregative, rather than substantive, models of democracy.

TUTORIAL QUESTIONS

1. **Is individual liberty more important than political self-determination?**

2. **Should democracy be limited to aggregating pre-political entitlements?**

3. **Can liberalism tackle the question of social justice without making it a global issue?**

FURTHER READING

Richard Bellamy (1992) *Liberalism and Modern Society* (Cambridge: Polity Press) offers a thorough historical account of liberalism.

John Dryzek (2000) *Deliberative Democracy and Beyond* (Oxford: Oxford University Press) is a forthright defence of deliberative democracy by one of its more radical proponent.

Sheldon Wolin (1960) *Politics and Vision* (Boston, MA: Little, Brown & Co.) contains an outstanding cultural history of liberalism and utilitarianism that anticipates current republican criticisms.

REFERENCES

Buchanan, James (1984) 'Politics without Romance: a Sketch of Positive Public Choice Theory and Its Normative Implications', in J.M. Buchanan and R.D. Tollison (eds), *The Theory of Public Choice. Vol. II*. Ann Arbor, MI: The University of Michigan Press, pp. 11–22.

Burke, Edmund (1790/1993) *Reflections on the Revolution in France*. Ed. L.G. Mitchell. Oxford: Oxford University Press.

Cohen, Joshua (1998) 'Democracy and Liberty', in J. Elster (ed.), *Deliberative Democracy*. Cambridge: Cambridge University Press, pp. 185–231.

Constant, Benjamin (1819/1988) 'The Liberty of the Ancients Compared with that of the Moderns', in B. Fontana (ed.), *Political Writings*. Cambridge: Cambridge University Press, pp. 309–28.

Harvie, Christopher (2001) 'Revolution and the Rule of Law', in K.O. Morgan (ed.), *The Oxford*

History of Britain. Oxford: Oxford University Press, pp. 470–517.

Held, David (1987) *Models of Democracy*. Cambridge: Polity Press.

Kant, Immanuel (1785/1993) *Grounding for the Metaphysics of Morals*. Indianapolis, IN: Hackett.

Locke, John (1690/1988) *Two Treatises of Government*. Ed. P. Laslett. Cambridge: Cambridge University Press.

Mackie, John ([1982] 1985) 'Cooperation, Competition and Moral Philosophy', in J. and P. Mackie (eds), *Persons and Values*. Oxford: Clarendon Press, pp. 152–69.

Marshall, T.H. (1950) *Citizenship and Social Class*. Cambridge: Cambridge University Press.

Moore, Barrington J.R. (1967) *Social Origins of Dictatorship and Democracy*. London: Allen Lane.

Nozick, Robert (1974) *Anarchy, State, and Utopia*. Oxford: Blackwell.

Paine, Thomas (1792/1984) *Rights of Man*. London: Penguin.

Rawls, John ([1971] 1999) 'Justice as Reciprocity', in John Rawls, *Collected Papers*. Cambridge, MA: Harvard University Press, pp. 190–224.

Rawls, John (1993) *Political Liberalism*. New York: Columbia University Press.

Schumpeter, Joseph (1943) *Capitalism, Socialism and Democracy*. New York: Harper & Row.

Smith, Adam (1776/1983) *The Wealth of Nations*. Harmondsworth: Penguin.

See also chapters

1	Sovereignty	7	Majoritarianism – Consociationalism
2	Constitutionalism	8	Pluralism – Difference
3	Human Rights and Democracy	9	Civil Society – National and Global
4	Justice, Equality, Liberty	13	Parliaments
5	Power, Authority, Legitimacy	18	Political Participation
6	Representative and Direct Democracy	20	The Welfare State and Democracy
		31	Democracy and the Islamist Paradox

24 Conservatism

Arthur Aughey

DEFINING CONSERVATISM

There are contending definitions of conservatism. There is even a definition of conservatism which holds that it is incapable of definition. In the literature three general approaches to the subject may be identified.

- The first defines conservatism as a recognizable *habit of mind*. It is the condition of being set in one's ways and of preferring the familiar to the unknown. It is a characteristic of human nature and this is often attached to some larger conception such as 'natural law' or the 'organic society'.
- The second defines conservatism as the *ideology of a ruling class*. It is a rationalization of the position of those who hold wealth and power in society and who want things to remain that way. Certain classes are 'carriers' of this ideology (aristocracy), certain institutions embody it (the Church) and other institutions are potential vehicles of it (bureaucracy).
- The third defines conservatism as a set of propositions about *the activity of governing*, one which defined itself against the radical ideologies and movements of the nineteenth and twentieth centuries. It defends a limited style of politics, is opposed to grand schemes for the emancipation of humankind and emphasizes the importance of continuity in the state.

The first two definitions have some force and

are held, mainly, by those on the right and left of politics respectively. The third definition attempts to give historical and principled focus to a large and diverse body of thought and, for that reason, appears more adequate than the other two. The history and values of conservatism are relatively recent. Conservatism is a product of the modern age.

CONSERVATISM AND MODERNITY

There is a simple picture of political life, held by Tony Blair among others, in which the 'forces of conservatism' struggle against the 'forces of modernization'. In this view, conservatism and modernization (meaning change) are antithetical. This is a questionable assumption not only because of its limited perspective on what constitutes change but also because of its limited view of conservatism. It assumes history to be linear, the march of progress from ignorance to reason, from oppression to justice. The objective is human emancipation, a radical vision of politics which is synonymous with democratization. It involves vanquishing those conservative interests which stand in the way of emancipation and democratization. It is an audacious concept of destiny with quite dramatic consequences for politics. That is why the French Revolution remains such a vital event in this view of politics. It was the vortex into which the contesting currents of European intellectual life were drawn and out of which emerged political debate aligned along a historical axis of progression and regression. Two broad movements of thought emerged from the French Revolution and together help us identify what is distinctive about conservatism. The first was *revolutionary*. To be revolutionary was to desire the transformation of the present in terms of an ideal future. People, it was thought, had the power to make the world over again to achieve complete democracy. The second was *reactionary*. To be reactionary was not just to resist revolution but to desire the re-creation of the past in the present. People needed to return to true allegiances, to respect the authority of the *ancien régime* and enter again into the realm of legitimacy which had no place for democracy. Both of these movements are radical, albeit radical with diametrically opposed objectives. This may appear a contradictory conclusion since we have come to associate radicalism exclusively with those on the side of progress and not with those opposed to it (an association which reveals the triumph of modernist thinking). What is common to revolutionary and reactionary thought?

Both make an absolute distinction between what is real, true or rational and what exists. Both identify a fracture between the legal and political structures of a country and the social reality, spiritual truth or historic destiny of its people. In other words, what is at the heart of both forms of thought is *alienation*. It is the common objective to remove alienation and to achieve either a future democratic harmony (the revolutionary goal) or a lost hierarchical harmony (the reactionary goal). This is also a question of legitimacy. A legitimate political association will be achieved only when alienation is removed. For the *Marxist revolutionary*, for instance, legitimacy lies in the historic task of the proletariat to achieve the realm of freedom which is also the realm of equality and fraternity. This task involves not the seizure of power alone but the complete transformation of politics in which the alienation of class will be abolished. For the *reactionary*, legitimacy is to be found only in a

return to the values of the old order. Time and change are irrelevant. The right of those who have usurped legitimate authority can never be secure no matter how long they have held power. The task of reactionary politics is to recall people to their true allegiance, to reveal radical democracy as a foul and corrupt illusion.

CONSERVATISM AND CONTINUITY

The starting point for reflection on conservatism may be found here. It is not a case of positioning it at the half-way point of a mental line which stretches from reaction at one end to revolution at another. Rather, the starting point of conservative politics is a rejection of this simple linear model of history and what it implies about modernity. Conservatism also rejects the theory of alienation in both its reactionary and revolutionary expressions. It does so because alienation is subversive of constitutional order and encourages the search for anti-constitutional solutions to political problems. In their turn, these rejections help to explain the conservative understanding of democracy.

The initial conservative sympathy, then, is with the historic achievements of a political association. It displays a certain reverence for enduring institutions and for the principles which those institutions are held to embody. Where both revolutionary and reactionary politics proclaim a profound incompatibility between the values of the social order (or 'the people') and the principles of the political order (or the state), conservatism proclaims a deep congruence. The motivation of conservatism is to secure continuity rather than to create discontinuity. Tradition, which is shorthand for a politics of continuity, emerges as an important value in traditional conservative politics. It would be an error, though, to confuse conservatism with traditionalism.

Traditionalism is unreflective and immediate. It has no need for intellectual formulation for it finds sufficient justification in symbol and ceremony. Conservatism, by contrast, is an ideological apology for tradition and puts the idea of tradition to work in defence of the political order. It asserts that practical wisdom, found in the inherited practices of contemporary political life, is to be preferred to a reactionary (and romantic) longing for an ideal past or to a revolutionary (and equally romantic) longing for an ideal future. These longings are the source of alienation. The object of conservatism is to encourage people to feel at home in the world. It may not be the best of all possible worlds (here the revolutionary is right). Everything in it may not be a necessary evil (here the reactionary is right). It is, however, the world in which we *do* live and it sets limits to democratic power while providing opportunities for democratic improvement.

If the starting point of radical politics is the disassociation of liberty and order, of legitimacy and power, of democracy and government, then the starting point of conservatism is the reconciliation of ordered liberty, of legitimate power, of constitutional stability. It is the starting point but not the conclusion, for experience may not be as the ideology posits it. The reconciliation is a reconciliation within the ideology itself and not necessarily a reconciliation in reality. Conservative politics involves a constant quest to sustain legitimacy in the state and there will always be tensions to be resolved and difficulties to be surmounted. The question of democracy is only one of these. The ideology, though, does help to specify how those tensions and difficulties are to be addressed.

CONSERVATISM AND REFORM

The suspicion of progress, at least as radicals have understood it, lies in a concern that it mortgages the present to the future (whereas reactionaries are willing to sacrifice the present to the past). Seen in this light, the ideology of progress represents another species of alienation, a restless and limitless ambition for change, albeit on a rather abstract model of human experience. Conservative scepticism about progress, a scepticism which also applies to democratization, has required a rather subtle explication of what constitutes legitimate reform. This has found a number of expressions, the common feature of which is the connection between past, present and future.

* Edmund Burke (1968) argued in the eighteenth century that a state without the means of reform is without the means of its own conservation. In the process of reform, improvements are never wholly new and what is retained is never wholly obsolete.
* Benjamin Disraeli proposed in the nineteenth century that reforms should take place only according to the manners, customs, laws and traditions of the people whom those reforms affect. Abstract principles, like democracy, are a poor guide to sensible policy (see Vincent, 1990).
* Lord Hailsham (1947) supported what he called natural change, that is change according to the acquired and inherited character of a society. An ounce of such practical knowledge is worth a ton of theory.
* Michael Oakeshott (1974), the most subtle of all, described reform as the 'pursuit of intimations', that is attending to the general arrangements of a state which is aware of a past, a present and a future. Governance is the politics of repair and not the politics of rational reconstruction.

These formulations confront modernization by associating acceptable change with the reasonableness of existing traditions of behaviour. Conservatism, then, does not entail a passive acceptance of the *status quo*. It entails a critical encounter with what exists, for what exists may not always be favourable to the conservative interest.

The demand for democratic modernization had intensified in the course of the nineteenth century as the *people* jostled for their place on the political stage. Political legitimation demanded some acknowledgement that the state was an expression of the people. These democratic demands posed serious problems for conservatism. Opposition to egalitarianism, for example, and defence of historic inequalities, made it vulnerable to radical appeals to social justice. Equally, its view that liberty could be threatened by democracy seemed like special pleading for particular privilege against the general interest. Some of these criticisms of conservatism were and are fully justified. In the history of conservative thought two responses to the challenge of democracy may be specified. These are the *patrician* and the *populist* responses.

THE PATRICIAN VIEW

Fear of what was to become known as 'mass society' informed the patrician response. It was a product of two related possibilities. The first was the disintegration of traditional allegiances as a consequence of urbanization and industrialization. The second was the manipulation of that disintegration by demagogues who would promise material salvation in return for absolute political power. On the one hand, in the pursuit of emancipation from social convention, people would be left without values or guidance. On the other hand, in the pursuit of equality, mediocrity would triumph over excellence. The consequence would be the rise of a centralized state secured by popular envy against private property. Democracy, in other words, could threaten all institutional obstacles, civil and political, to overweening state power. Conservatism, therefore, has been disposed to defend the authority of those institutions such as property, Church and family which provide a bulwark against the drift to 'mass' society. It has also been disposed to limit the effect of democracy on the affairs of government. As Lord Salisbury candidly put it in the nineteenth century, for a conservative the best form of government in a democratic age is one where the masses have little power, and seem to have a great deal.

Such views can still be detected in contem-porary conservative argument suspicious of the effect of popular culture on social discipline. They also inform criticisms of the vulgarization of the mass media and its effect, the 'dumbing down' of public values. Democracy is far from an unmixed blessing and, in this view, can corrupt public life by turning it into a competition in which popular sentimentalism substitutes for reasoned judgement. The tone of the patrician style is frequently suggestive of an approaching apocalypse in which the decencies of civilized life will be subverted by popular barbarism. At times it comes close to embracing the central idea of its historic opponents – alienation.

THE POPULIST VIEW

One form of populist politics, to which conservatism not only adapted but also helped to define, has been nationalism. The nation, though, had a quite distinctive meaning in conservative politics. It was understood to be a political community united in acceptance of the legitimacy of traditional political arrangements. Conservatism assumed a distinctive sort of populism in which 'popular' did not entail the sort of social equality feared by patricians. Snobbery was an important aspect of this populism, the sort of snobbery which crossed class boundaries. This was, and in some cases remains, the case for those many working-class and lower middle-class conservatives who thought it best to maintain distinctions of social rank. Conservative argument, then, was concerned to justify social rank to the new democracy. Here the people was not some abstract sociological category but the historic nation in its regional and social variety, a people with traditional beliefs, particular affections and long-standing prejudices.

That populist style permitted conservatism to adjust more easily to democratic politics. Conservatism could move relatively at ease in a world where deference was second nature. Moreover, populist conservatism put practical common sense on a par with revolutionary intellectualism and assumed that the common sense of the masses was more likely to be conservative than the rationalism of the educated elite. It was also more likely to be loyal. Populism (the demands of democratic politics) and patriotism (upholding established institutions) were not contradictory but complementary. Conservative politics was to be educative, making the democratic citizenry conscious of a responsibility to limit collective power (the arena of the regulatory state) in order to enjoy civil liberty (the arena of personal freedom).

This view remains recognizably strong in contemporary conservatism. The parties of conservatism lay claim to being the real representatives of the people whose adversary today is called 'political correctness', a term which conjures up a conspiracy of petty tyrannies conducted by unrepresentative metropolitan elites against popular common sense. The lineage of this style goes back at least as far as Edmund Burke, who denounced the self-serving sophistry of the French revolutionaries. However, there are clear problems today. Conservatism can no longer rely on social deference. It can no longer refer unproblematically to tradition. The authority of institutions is not secure in a less reverential age. Moreover, the claims of multiculturalism have made it more difficult, but not impossible, for conservatives to speak with certainty and conviction about the values of the nation. These are the problems of what has become known as the 'postmodern' age.

CONSERVATISM AND POSTMODERNITY

At first glance, postmodernism would appear to have little in common with conservatism. Its aim to de-construct established values and its desire to unmask authority would fit uneasily into any catalogue of conservative virtues. Yet, postmodernism's rejection of the 'grand narratives' of the last two centuries also constitutes disillusion with such radical narratives as Marxism, liberal rationalism and other emancipatory ideals. Such a critique, when disengaged from some of the modish discourse of the academy, is, as we have seen, a long-standing conservative theme. Insofar as conservatism never subscribed to the grosser forms of modernism, then the sceptical revelations of postmodernism come as no surprise. If postmodernism is an admission that revolutionary ideologies like Marxism have been a failure in both theory and practice, then conservatives can feel some sort of vindication, especially after the fall of the Berlin Wall in 1989. The 'people power' revealed then appeared to confound the revolutionary myth. There has been, however, little sense of the political argument being over.

Conservatism now feels challenged by a radical interpretation of postmodern democracy. Formerly, democratic egalitarianism was to have been the outcome of a politics in which economic resources were redistributed between the social classes. Today that view is replaced by a politics of inclusion which demands recognition of 'difference' and redistribution of 'worth' between social groups. Parity of esteem is the key principle which apportions rights to categories of individuals such as women, gays and ethnic minorities. The dynamic of this principle is towards the removal of all the obstacles which stand in the way of the achievement of equal worth. This has alarmed conservatives for a number of reasons. They believe that:

- This new politics of rights is yet another strategy to achieve an old objective, the utopian objective of perfect democracy.
- The only way this objective can be realized is by calling on the state to implement an ever expanding body of rights. The new moral agenda will lead to an even greater growth of government than the old economic agenda.
- The emphasis on group identities and group rights will weaken the informal bonds of association in a society and

encourage not a limited but an assertive style of politics.

- The state will, on that basis, become dangerously intrusive in the life of citizens, destroying the distinction between public and private.

When Edmund Burke attacked the philosophy of the French revolutionaries he argued that in the groves of their academy, at the end of every vista, one caught a glimpse of the gallows. In the groves of the new radical postmodern academy conservatism now catches a glimpse of the meddling bureaucrat. In the name of democratization the liberties of individuals will be invaded.

One interesting response to this concern has been the attempt to develop an ideal of *civic conservatism*. This owes much to the legacy of Michael Oakeshott (1975), especially his reflections on civil association. Civic conservatism holds that the problem with radical postmodern democracy is the same problem with radical modernist democracy. It promises emancipation and freedom but imposes uniformity of purpose. It celebrates diversity but is suspicious of people acting or thinking independently. This sort of 'therapeutic authoritarianism' wants to make (or force) people to be 'good'. The criticism is as old as the criticism of Rousseau. The general will triumphs over personal freedom.

Civic conservatism, by contrast, proposes that citizens do not need to accept a common purpose or subscribe to a common good. In other words, they do not need to be agreed about the *ends* of politics. Agreement about ends is not the condition of diversity or even democracy. What is essential is agreement about the *means* of politics. Government should be constitutional, operate within the rule of law and be representative of, and accountable to, its citizens. Its goal ought not to be the direction, management or planning of the lives of citizens. Nor ought it to be an instrument of their collective enlightenment. Its goal, rather, is to secure the liberty of individuals and the diversity of their culture by upholding a framework of law. The freedoms of civil society are not to be valued as claims on public expenditure. They are to be valued because they are the condition of independence, self-reliance and creativity. The changing variety and social experimentation so favoured by postmodernism may be found there. Limited – but authoritative – government is the proper complement to a society of 'difference'. Democracy is one of the values of civil association. It is not the exclusive value.

This represents an imaginative reworking of traditional conservative themes though it may be argued that conservatism in this mode is little different from traditional liberalism. There is obvious similarity but there are two major distinctions. First, individual freedom, for civic conservatives, cannot be conceived of separately from the legitimate authority of government. Secondly, both individual freedom and authoritative government are not conceived of abstractly. They are the historically achieved conditions of a way of life captured by a term like 'British democracy'.

CONSERVATISM AND GLOBALIZATION

The term 'globalization' is an attempt to capture the significance of contemporary political changes which are blurring the boundaries between the national and the international. Relations between states are in the process of change, as are relations within states. Some have argued that the consequence of this post-industrial revolution, and the impact of the computerized, information economy, will be the end of the nation-state and the emergence of a global, consumerist civilization. Globalization theory, some would argue, puts in doubt some traditional conservative assumptions about connections between the social, the cultural and the political. Nevertheless, the prospects are ambiguous. On the one hand, globalization may have a destabilizing effect on national identity, weakening state institutions and their sovereignty. On the other hand, national identity may be strengthened as people seek some insurance against the power of the global market and protection against a global civilization which values culture only for its marketing potential. Consequently, the conservative response itself has been rather ambiguous. The debate may be said to range between the perspectives of cultural and civic conservatism.

For *cultural conservatives*, global trends do threaten the integrity of the nation-state. This has encouraged an emphasis on a more authentic form of identity in reaction not only to the world market, but to larger political associations like the European Union. The temptation has arisen to defend the hard-won democratic legitimacy of the nation-state on a cultural rather than on a civic basis. For some British conservative thinkers like Roger Scruton (1990), the most articulate exponent of this view, unity is a cultural rather than a political product and it ought to be national. The model of procedural constitutionalism favoured by civic conservatives is thus too abstract to engage the loyalty of its citizens. The more abstract it becomes under global market pressures the more it detaches itself from public sentiment. The danger is that national governments will exhaust their own legitimacy.

Civic conservatives are implicitly criticized for detaching the question of legitimacy from the question of political unity. Cultural conservatives, by contrast, assume that unity is a prerequisite of legitimacy. Democracy needs roots in the stable ground of national identity. Far from diminishing the values of such an identity, globalizing tendencies actually intensify them. They become prime assets in enabling a state not only to adjust to the requirements of the global market, but also to moderate the impact of those markets on its citizens. These assets ought not to be squandered in dubious pursuit of, for example, a European superstate. Suspicion of the European Union lies not in its collective capacity to enhance the effectiveness of member states. It lies in its potential to de-legitimize the democratic institutions of member states

by frustrating their ability to act in the national interest. Indeed, the form which this globalist/Europeanist critique takes has strong echoes once again of Edmund Burke's hostility to the 'rational despotism' of the French revolutionaries of 1789.

Civic conservatism also has problems with globalization and with the project of European Union. However, it dissents from cultural conservatism's stress on unity. It shares the view that citizens are not abstract political beings, but it does not subscribe to the view that democratic legitimacy requires membership of a single, cultural community. From this perspective, it is common political authority which fosters community and not *vice versa*. The sort of securely homogeneous national community which cultural conservatism assumes to be the basis of legitimate government is no longer available (if it ever were). While it may be emotionally attractive in an era of rapid change to stress national integrity, it is at odds with a postmodern democracy of difference. The irony is that, if taken to its logical conclusion in a state like the United Kingdom, the result of cultural conservatism would be not a strengthening of the state but disintegration into its component national parts. Moreover, the immigration necessary to sustain the economic prosperity of West European states, because of falling national birth rates, attenuates further the notion of a homogeneous cultural identity (the very reason why cultural conservatism often questions the priority of economic growth). In these circumstances, civic conservatism suggests a method of securing democratic legitimacy in an increasingly multicultural and multi-ethnic society.

CONCLUSION

Conservatism is a philosophy of modesty, suspicious of grand enthusiasm. It advocates caution and limitation and identifies with the accumulated achievements of a political association even though it may not share all of its contemporary fashions. In heroic mood, conservatism presents itself as a defence of civilized values. In prosaic mood, it presents itself as a set of principles concerned to preserve continuity in the state. If it were possible to identify a distinctive desire uniting all forms of conservatism, it would be the desire to be left alone to enjoy the benefits of a free society. As Lord Salisbury once argued, conservatism is rather like a policeman: if there were no (ideological) criminals around there would be no need for it. However, conservatives will not be left alone.

If revolutionary ideologies like communism have been seen off, arguments in favour of egalitarianism and the aggrandizing state have taken on a new shape. Conservatism is also required to take on a new shape as it engages with discourses such as postmodernism, globalization, human rights and multiculturalism. These supposed 'forces of modernization' are once more intent on defeat of the supposed 'forces of conservatism'. This is a battle which, if history is our guide, is likely to prove unwinnable.

Summary

- Conservatism is an ideology which confronts the common radicalism of revolutionary and reactionary politics.
- In place of a romantic politics of alienation it proposes a politics of modesty which seeks to secure continuity in the state.
- Democratization, especially the radical quest for social egalitarianism, posed significant challenges for traditional conservatism which has inspired two responses: the *patrician* and the *populist*. The lineage of these responses is still apparent in contemporary politics, especially in a common hostility to the 'therapeutic' state.
- As a consequence of a postmodern politics of difference and the effects of globalization two distinctive styles of conservatism can be identified today. The first of these styles, *civic conservatism*, emphasizes agreement on the authoritative democratic means of politics. The second, *cultural conservatism*, emphasizes national integrity as the foundation of democratic legitimacy.

TUTORIAL QUESTIONS

1. **What do conservatives want to conserve?**

2. **What reservations do conservatives have about democracy?**

3. **What is the significance of tradition in conservative political thought?**

FURTHER READING

Noël O'Sullivan (1976) *Conservatism* (London: Dent) remains a good general introduction and provides a comparative assessment of the conservative tradition in Britain, France and Germany.

Robert Nisbet (1986) *Conservatism: Dream and Reality* (Milton Keynes: Open University Press) is also a useful introduction to traditional conservative thought.

Arthur Aughey, Greta Jones and William T. Riches (1992) *The Conservative Political Tradition in Britain and the United States* (London: Pinter) provides a survey of political themes.

The most concise statement of cultural conservatism can be found in Roger Scruton (2001) *The Meaning of Conservatism* (Basingstoke: Palgrave, third edition).

Michael Oakeshott's (1974) essay 'On Being Conservative' in *Rationalism in Politics and other Essays*, (London: Methuen, second edition) sets out eloquently the principles of the civic conservative case.

Charles Covell (1986) *The Redefinition of Conservatism: Politics and Doctrine* (Basingstoke: Macmillan) and Robert Devigne (1996) *Recasting Conservatism: Oakeshott, Strauss, and the Response to Postmodernism* (New Haven, CT: Yale University Press, second edition) both deal with contemporary challenges to conservatism.

REFERENCES

Burke, Edmund (1968) *Reflections on the Revolution in France*. Harmondsworth: Penguin.

Lord Hailsham (1947) *The Case for Conservatism*. Harmondsworth: Penguin.

Oakeshott, Michael (1974) 'Political Education', in *Rationalism and Politics and Other Essays* (second edition). London: Methuen, pp. 111–36.

Oakeshott, Michael (1975) *On Human Conduct*. Oxford: Oxford University Press.

Scruton, Roger (1990) 'In Defence of the Nation', in J.C.D. Clark (ed.), *Ideas and Politics in Modern Britain*. Basingstoke: Macmillan, pp. 53–86.

Vincent, J. (1990) *Disraeli*. Oxford: Oxford University Press.

See also chapters

1 Sovereignty
2 Constitutionalism
3 Human Rights and Democracy
4 Justice, Equality, Liberty

5 Power, Authority, Legitimacy
9 Civil Society – National and Global
27 Nationalism

25 Socialism – Marxism

Terrell Carver

> [T]here is a sense in which socialism, like democracy (from which it stems), is rooted in sentiments as ancient and permanent as human society itself. To put the matter simply, men [and women] have always lived in communities and experienced the need to cooperate.
>
> (Lichtheim, 1975: 11)

While there may be features of human society that are ancient and permanent, it is important to remember that the concepts and terms of any political movements, such as socialism and Marxism, come from perceived differences within the human linguistic community. Rather than seeing this terminology as categorizing and classifying along the lines of neat distinctions, it is probably better to remember that these concepts are 'fighting talk' and have figured in actual struggles. Though it is helpful and informative to trace out intellectual genealogies and to clarify the overlaps and differences between democracy, socialism and Marxism (and allied terms like collectivism, cooperation and communism), my purpose in this chapter is to capture some sense of political conflict and the way that these terms have functioned within it. History has not ended, and political struggle will continue. Indeed, within a democratic framework it will flourish, and these ideas will be recycled.

COMMUNITIES AND RESOURCES

Perhaps the most effective way of getting to grips with the socialist tradition is to work from an instructive point of contrast, albeit an imaginary one. As it happens, this kind of 'imaginary' figures in much of the literature that has come to count as socialist, although the term 'socialism' in English dates only from the 1820s. The socialist 'imaginary' is not, however, a vision on its own, divorced from an opposing view or 'other'. The 'other' to socialism is a notion or practice of economic individualism, and in particular individualized or 'private' ownership of resources within a pre-existing community. This, in turn, presupposes an economic surplus beyond the reproduction of material subsistence. Economic individualism becomes particularly noticeable in societies where money has been introduced, as this makes accumulation of wealth and power more significant.

Socialism as a concept thus arises in a literature of critique that has its origins in ideas and schemes that oppose, at least to some significant degree, the supposed intrusions of economic individualism, private property and monetary exchange into societies based on other principles. This view may, of course, be founded on nostalgia or conservatism related to real or imagined pre-existing societies, but it can also be forward-looking and progressive-minded, calling for changes in human nature or behaviour to bring about transformed and superior modes of existence.

Socialists thus typically subscribe to views of humanity that emphasize sharing resources, rather than competitive accumulation; common ownership of goods, especially those involved in the production of essentials, rather than ownership by individual or incorporated bodies; voluntary or responsible cooperation in producing goods and services, rather than disciplines or pressures arising from necessity and scarcity; schemes of distribution that eliminate money or at least severely curtail the accumulation of capital, rather than reliance on markets and private trading; collective decision-making and planning, rather than letting individual decisions and market outcomes determine what happens in society.

The 'other', against which socialism is constructed, is thus one of adult individuals who are legally free to own property, and legally protected in that ownership, whose interests are defined and pursued as a matter of individualized thinking, and who are thus responsible for their own welfare, or lack of it (or belong to some status of dependency which makes them less than an adult male 'individual', typically a child, woman, servant, slave or foreigner).

The outlines of these concepts can be seen just as clearly in Plato's *Republic* (*c.* 379–370 BC) and Thomas More's *Utopia* (1516), as in more modern schemes (Lichtheim, 1975: 10–11). While there are major questions about the personal views and political intentions of both those writers, and no suggestion of any socialist movement around them or their writings, there is nevertheless a clear sense of controversy and critique in their thought. Both portray a conjunction of individual greed with commercialism and monetary gain, the links between that and militarized cultures and wars of aggrandizement, and the sense that the common interests of all those within a community are thus generally ill-served.

POWER AND GOVERNANCE

This programmatic confrontation between 'imaginaries' has thus far not addressed the quintessential political issues of power and governance. And indeed the socialist 'imaginary' is compatible with any number of political systems, not just democracy. To qualify as at least on the way to becoming minimally democratic, a political system must share out the decision-making among 'the many', among whom there needs to be a high degree of equality in terms of civil status, that is choosing office holders and holding office. The better of the two imaginary cities in Plato's *Republic* had hardly any politics because there was hardly anything to decide, given that there was no surplus production. The 'second best' city had surplus production and a benevolent dictatorship of 'philosopher kings', meritocratically selected and educated for the role of selfless and community-regarding rulers (and kept strictly free of private property and other selfish temptations). Intriguingly, women were said to be admissible to this order of rulers on an equal basis with men, and indeed the principle of equality between the sexes was aired more generally for the society as a whole. However, there is no doubt that the qualities associated with ruling are those intellectual skills cultivated by only the most highly trained and educated intellectuals. While there are numerous ambiguities of authorial and political interpretation here, there is no way that this can constitute government by 'the many', nor is any political role for non-philosophers ever countenanced, other than as 'interference' and thus decline from an ideal.

More's *Utopia* is rather similarly undemocratic in that decisions for the community are entrusted to male heads of household, who are assumed to be selfless and kindly enough to rule for the benefit of all and not just for the benefit of their group. As with the Platonic system, anyone within the ruling group parting company with those values would be subject to expulsion. The Utopian community is in some respects closer to the 'first city' of the *Republic* in its material austerity and outright rejection (indeed mockery) of gold as the monetary commodity. Equality in civil obligations and privileges among a minority group, however selected, hardly qualifies as democracy (though there are, perhaps, connections with the democratic institutions of an independent judiciary, judicial review and an incorruptible final judgement on political and constitutional matters).

Putting the relationship between socialism and democracy that way round leads to the rather interesting question of the relationship between democracy and economic individualism, that is, the individualism of private ownership and accumulation of wealth. Some theorists of democracy have made very strong claims that the two necessarily go together logically and historically (Hayek, 1991; Gray, 1998). This is a claim that democratization and marketization are two inseparable sides of individualism, and that both liberate individuals from collectivisms, whether pre-modern communalisms or modern totalitarianisms. On that view only capitalist societies can be genuinely democratic, and democratic societies can be based only on capitalist economies. There is thus a putative analogy between individual 'ownership' of votes and capital and of politics as a process of mutual exchange based on a standard of equality (anyone's vote or pound sterling or dollar or euro is worth the same as anyone else's). There is also an exclusion of other criteria from these transactions, such as a collective or general interest, status or seniority

considerations, and selection procedures other than by elections or market exchange.

Capitalist societies, of course, are not necessarily democratic, and within the firm or household decisions are not necessarily democratic either. Nevertheless, so it is claimed, democratization proceeds as societies conform more directly to institutions of competitive partisan elections and market competition among economic actors, and in both cases, the bedrock principle is that of an economic individualism promoting self-determined and self-determining interests. Since the development of capitalist societies, and the development of modern institutions of representative democracy, socialists have disputed this claim. To do so they have had to drive a wedge between democracy and capitalism, and in some cases socialists have argued that the two are antithetical.

INDIVIDUALISM AND EQUALITY

Re-arranging power among 'one', 'few' or 'many' was a classical preoccupation, and also a medieval one, though on rather different principles. The peculiarly modern impetus to democratization comes with republican forms of government (that is, non-monarchical and non-priestly forms of rulership) that were developed by aspiring commercial classes (including, on occasion, aristocrats aspiring to commercial wealth). This, of course, was a form of government where 'the many', though generally equal to each other in ruling and being ruled, were 'the few' in relation to the population as a whole. It should not be assumed, in any case, that the line between one community and another could always, or indeed ever, be drawn, given the exigencies of empire, colonization, ecclesiastical authorities and local aggrandizement. Nevertheless as a movement, democratization represented a revolutionary (and therefore treasonous and often violent) attack on monarchy and other forms of authoritarian rule. There is a clear connection between this political programme and the broader one of promoting the commercialization of goods and services and the accumulation of capital in proto-industrial forms of production. 'Power to the people' is not an obvious good in itself. What did 'the people' actually want power for?

In many cases those who were in some sense 'of the people' wanted power to clear away laws, traditions, boundaries and other barriers to trade, so as to further a regime of monetary exchange at the expense of subsistence and barter economies in which individual ownership of resources, and the purchase and sale of individuals' own labour and skills, were not as yet the norm. In terms of raising these issues in a European and ultimately world context, the French Revolution (1789–99) is rightly regarded as an iconic event (Lichtheim, 1969: 17–25). Modern socialisms, and indeed the communist and Marxist traditions that are part of it, all look back to the ideas and thinkers of the immediate post-revolutionary generations. These are also the generations who experienced the earliest cataclysms of the Industrial Revolution. This involved the large-scale mechanization of manufacturing processes and transport made possible with the change from waterpower to steam, from horse transport to the railway. Those changes were possible only because peasant production gave way to more productive forms of agriculture, and so more people, and a higher percentage of the total population, moved into towns and cities. Thus more people came into closer contact with the means through which political ideas could be developed, publicized and incorporated into organized movements (rather than mob violence or riotous rebellion).

Broadening access to political power from kings or priests to aristocracies or republican 'burghers' was one thing. Widening participation in politics to 'the many' as a genuine majority of the adult male community, and eventually to a majority of the adult citizenry regardless of sex, race or other such unwarranted discrimination, was a much larger project. It has taken most of two centuries to secure at least some degree of this expansion of civil rights, and thus some degree of democratization, for the benefit of substantial groups of the human global population. Socialists have unambiguously aligned themselves against the 'excesses' of capitalism, or against capitalism and the money economy itself. On the question of democracy, though, there has been outright rejection in some cases, ambiguity and redefinition in others, and in some socialist thought a commitment to ever more radical devolutions of power to majoritarian community decision-making. While there are undemocratic socialisms, there are no grounds for saying that socialism is itself inherently undemocratic. Rather it is the status of capitalism within democracy, as a matter of theory and as a matter of constitutional and political practice, that requires clarification before the relationship between socialism and democracy can be accurately traced.

INTERESTS AND DECISIONS

Early nineteenth-century socialism, before the 1840s, was more a literary genre than a political movement, albeit one in which books led rather quickly to experiments, and experiments sometimes resulted in large-scale movements. Cross-cutting the authoritarian/democratic fracture within the basic socialist premise (hostility to thorough-going economic individualism) there was also the small-scale/large-scale or utopian/practical divide, and furthermore another split in terms of pre-modern/modern technologies, and yet another cleavage along religious/non-religious lines. Some socialists were system-builders with well-worked-out philosophies of human nature, either nostalgic for a return to a pre-modern state of sincerity and goodness, or developmental in encouraging reform or conversion to a new order of humanity, or a bit of both, like François-Charles Fourier (1772–1837). Others, like Robert Owen (1771–1858), were actually industrial entrepreneurs, concerned to promote the welfare of the working poor by moral and practical example, reconciling the profit motive, economic innovation and collective good through enlightened paternalism. Still others promoted an industrial regime of strict equality, like Étienne Cabet (1788–1856), whose utopia resembled More's. Secular socialists, like Saint-Simon (1760–1825), could promote universal reason as a guarantee that elite decision-making would ensure harmony, and Christian ones could appeal to gospel faith to guide the community to a divinely sanctioned plan for human life on earth, like the Shaker communities. There is probably a writer in the tradition for every possibility in the matrix (Lichtheim, 1969: 26–59).

Socialism as a later nineteenth-century mass movement took democracy seriously and fought hard for every extension of the franchise throughout Europe and elsewhere. It also promoted the powers of the democratic state with regard to the economy, that is, arguing for restrictions on the rights of those owning resources to do as they liked. This identified socialism with the 'social question' of wealth and poverty. Economic liberals argued that there were few, if any, questions for 'society' to consider other than the sanctity of private property, maintenance of a sound currency, and selective attention to public decency and morals. For socialists, solving the 'social question' entailed struggling for legislation guaranteeing limited hours and safe conditions at workplaces, state funding or guarantees for the unemployed and their dependants, publicly funded and supervised educational systems, progressive taxation of income and wealth, and encouragement for cooperatives and other systems of public, rather than 'private', ownership of economic resources. Within this mass movement – which was at first a movement of groups like the English 'Chartists' rather than political parties, which came later – there were a number of important points of division.

The first was of course the issue of whether to work within an existing system for further political democratization and curtailment of capitalist industry, or whether instead to organize an open or conspiratorial rebellion and usher in a revolutionary regime of rapid change. The second was whether to push for the abolition of the money economy entirely or merely to reform or restrict the capitalist system while retaining money as a useful rationing or, in some cases, incentivizing device. Broadly speaking, communists were those who were more likely to opt for revolutionary action, albeit of different kinds, and to reject, at least in principle, the money economy. Social democrats were those more likely to opt for gradualist or evolutionary strategies, and to see some virtues in economic individualism, or at least a realm of necessary or even productive compromise with self-interested accumulation. It should be remembered, of course, that virtually all democratic regimes were established through revolutionary processes involving force of arms, and that the process of democratizing these regimes further was itself often violent and occasionally revolutionary (Wright, 1996; Sassoon, 1997).

The political regimes that self-identified most successfully and long-lastingly as communist were the Soviet Union and its satellites, as well as the People's Republic of China, and a number of smaller countries (North Korea, Cuba, Vietnam). Curiously, these have been highly authoritarian regimes rather than obvious outgrowths of the socialist struggles for broadening the franchise within democracies and, oddly, none really had much dedication to abolishing the money economy in practice, even though they institutionalized planned economies that did not rely on market disciplines. There is thus a lively literature of debate on the extent to which those regimes are the rightful heirs of a tradition of revolutionary socialism, given the extent to which the goals of both radical democracy and non-monetary economics were discarded (Lane, 1996).

MARXISM AND SOCIALISM

Of the nineteenth-century socialisms by far the most widely known, politically successful and intellectually dominant was Marxism. Since the 1890s other forms of socialism have been forced to locate themselves against this backdrop, and thus to explain their similarities and differences. As with socialism, though, Marxism contains a number of ambiguities and thus points of potential division. These arise from the writings of Karl Marx (1818–83), those of his friend and colleague Friedrich Engels (1820–95), and the character of the politics that they did and recommended in their lifetimes (versus what others made of these things at later dates).

As young men Marx and Engels had a dedicated but critical attitude to previously existing socialisms and socialists, both purveying in their political journalism a corrected vision of the way to progress. Both aligned themselves with non-utopian, democratizing writers and movements, supporting revolutionary action against non-democratic regimes. They were thus in broad alliance with anti-monarchical and anti-authoritarian forces in the European societies where they were resident or had interests: the German states, Belgium, France, Britain, the Austro-Hungarian Empire, and the like. Both started out on the literary and philosophical side of political commentary, partly because of censorship and repression of any politics that smacked of the 'social question' or class unrest, and partly because that type of writing suited their interests and background. Both tutored themselves in political economy, the economics of the day, and in that way they distinguished their 'outlook', as they called it, from that of other socialists, who took economic matters less seriously and less professionally than they did, or so they claimed.

When Marx and Engels began working together in earnest in 1845 they composed a manuscript critique of other socialists in Germany, *The German Ideology.* Unpublished in their lifetime, this work contains ideas that were nevertheless recycled and refined in further publications. In the jointly authored *Communist Manifesto* of 1848, published anonymously before the revolutionary events broke out, Marx and Engels recounted this view of history, which linked the political and social relationships within any society to a defining mode of production, conceptualized as a particular technology together with its necessarily associated property relations. Those modes of production were in turn presented in a chronological and ultimately developmental sequence, working from classical cities and empires, with slave-holding production and simple tools, through feudal relationships of dependency and decentralization, and on to modern forms of large-scale production, capital accumulation and sharp class differentiation between exploiter and exploited (Carver, 1983).

While Marx and Engels took care to say little about the specifics of socialism (or communism, as they sometimes described its putative culmination), they did indicate that revolutionary violence could be expected (because of the resistance of the possessing classes), that socialists could move from immediate demands for nationalization of productive resources on to the abolition of the money economy, a system of planned production for consumption, and 'from each according to his [*sic*] abilities, to each according to his [*sic*] needs', a slogan borrowed from Louis Blanc (1811–82). Neither Marx nor Engels, however, favoured conspiratorial or vanguardist political parties, but rather had a vision of mass action by the armed people, just as they imagined had taken place in the French Revolution. Marx in particular sketched out a political structure for socialism later in life when he took the position, unpopular in England, of defending the actions of the Paris communards of 1870–71, who were said to be experimenting with spontaneous forms of self-government by mandated representatives responsive to the popular will. Marx envisaged a hierarchy of such assemblies, each responsible to the ones below for accurately reflecting and appropriately implementing resolutions arising from the local level (Avineri, 1968; Levin, 1989).

By the 1880s there were 'Marxists', that is, socialists who identified themselves with the increasingly influential writings of Marx and Engels, particularly the latter, who had since 1859 taken on the task of introducing, popularizing and ultimately editing Marx's *magnum opus, Capital,* a formidable critique of the principles of capitalism and monetary exchange. That work was socialist or communist only by implication, rather than by overt declaration (beyond a hurried conclusion that capitalist economic collapse would spark a socialist revolution arising from working-class forces). Moreover, by that time Engels had himself published systematizations of Marx's work, as he understood it, arguing that in Marx socialism had found its Hegel and its Darwin, by which he meant that Marx had produced a comprehensive science of nature, history and 'thought' such that the historical necessity of socialism (and its final stage, communism) was factually established. With this, Engels inaugurated 'scientific socialism' and created Marxism as an intellectual, rather than straightforwardly political, force to be reckoned with (Carver, 1991).

REVOLUTION AND EVOLUTION

Twentieth-century socialism is thus marked by an encounter, one way or another, with the professed revolutionary means and sweeping goals (for example, abolition of money) of Marxist doctrine, and other more gradualist or 'evolutionary' schemes, including that of Eduard Bernstein (1850–1932). In his work the programmatic content of socialism virtually disappeared within the democratic process of extending popular control over resources and processes in national economies (Steger, 1997). Moreover, nationalistic and anti-colonial politics provided a spectacular arena for democratizing struggles in which Marxists and other socialists competed with one another, and with democrats committed instead to the principles and institutions of economic individualism. Marx and Engels had had little success as political actors in practical politics, and the revolutionary movement in which they had participated personally (German revolutionary liberalism of 1848–49) had ended in what seemed to be a rout and a decade of conservative reaction.

By contrast, later self-defined 'Marxists', such as V.I. Lenin (1870–1924), Joseph Stalin (1879–1953) and Mao Zedong (1893–1976), took political success much more seriously, and took charge personally, creating disciplined party structures, and disciplining party doctrines, that promoted new power structures. Those power structures became infamous for harsh methods and terror (though democracies, and democrats, when under threat, are not immune from very uncivil actions). Forced collectivizations of agriculture and industry in national settings produced a form of modernization at great cost, not least to those involved, but also to the content and reputation of Marxism and socialism. Whatever the justification involved in war and civil war, none of those regimes made a transition to democracy as Marx, or as democratic socialists, had envisaged it, and none fulfilled the high standards of welfare and productivity that Marx and the 'industrializing' socialists had promised (McLellan, 1998).

The non-Marxist field has been rather more successful, and rather less compromised, in terms of the socialist tradition. Social democratic parties and politics have been an important feature of democratic politics and policy-making (with the rather notable exception of the United States). Social democrats have thus pursued a strategy of working within the democratic structures established by and for economic individualists, yet finding or inventing powers of regulation, control and management that have forged compromises. Those compromises have been between ruthless capitalist competition, promoting productivity and innovation, and tax-driven redistribution in terms of disposable income and public services for the broad mass of the population. While it may seem strange now to look back on Keynesian economic management and populist programmes for pensions and welfare as 'socialist', nonetheless in their time these inspired fierce resistance for just that reason, even though many of those involved in this political process would not have identified themselves as 'socialist'. In terms of the early-nineteenth-century goals that socialists commonly identified (material security from birth to death, access to work with dignity and safety, political leadership responsive to the demands of the worse-off in society, etc.), an enormous amount has been achieved (Padgett and Paterson, 1991).

On the other hand, those achievements are obviously the result of compromise between classes, and compromise about class politics, to the point where class has become a political issue that is hard to identify and one lacking a mass political following. While there are 'market socialists' and advocates of 'cooperative decentralization' claiming kinship with the socialist tradition, these are not mass movements, nor particularly influential with elites (Pierson, 1995). Socialists may have won the battles, but at the cost of a political identity and ideology. However, they still retain a powerful critical purchase on global issues of inequality and exploitation. This is because class can still be discerned beneath the trappings of nationalism and ethnicity, and because the ravages and corruption entailed by largely unchecked and globalized capitalist industry are sometimes exposed by academic and media inquiry (Panitch and Leys, 1999). Those lines of critique and of political action do not perhaps gain today from self-identifications with socialism, Marxism or communism, but possibly it is as well to leave those labels aside, and focus instead on the issues that are still unresolved (Nove, 1991).

Summary

- Socialism is a literature and practice of ideological critique and political struggle.
- The object of socialist critique is the theory and practice of economic individualism.
- Economic individualism is the view that 'private' property, and the monetary economy, are necessary conditions for maximizing freedom and maintaining democracy.
- Some socialisms are authoritarian and some democratic, so there is no necessary connection between socialism and democracy.
- Democratic socialists argue that a capitalist economy, founded on economic individualism, is not necessary for democracy.
- Some democratic socialists argue that capitalism, and indeed the money economy, are inimical to democracy.
- Some democratic socialists, such as Marx and Engels, have pursued revolutionary struggles to resolve the 'social question' of wealth and poverty.

- Other democratic socialists, such as Bernstein, have pursued gradualist strategies within existing political and economic frameworks.
- Marx, Engels and subsequent Marxists have distinguished themselves from other socialists by developing an 'outlook' on history which links political change to economic structures.
- The leaders and ideologists of the Soviet Union, its satellites, and other 'communist' countries promoted authoritarian rather than democratic political structures, and did not fulfil the Marxist goal of abolishing money.
- Socialist ideas about the tensions between capitalism and democracy are increasingly influential in analysing the globalized economy and working to reduce poverty.

TUTORIAL QUESTIONS

1. **How and why do socialists and economic individualists differ in their assessments of 'human nature'?**

2. **Where is the line between 'utopian' and 'practical' socialism?**

3. **Did Marx and Engels, and subsequent Marxists, fulfil or betray the promise of socialism?**

FURTHER READING

Anthony Wright (1996) *Socialisms: Theories and Practices* (Oxford: Oxford University Press, second edition) offers a basic introductory account of socialist history and the principal political debates.

Another more detailed, yet easily accessible historical account of the socialist tradition is Donald Sassoon (1997) *One Hundred Years of Socialism: the West European Left in the Twentieth Century* (London: Fontana).

For shorter introductory surveys, see the chapters 'Social Democracy and Democratic Socialism' and 'Marxism and Communism' in Roger Eatwell and Anthony Wright (eds) (1999) *Contemporary Political Ideologies* (London: Pinter), pp. 80–103 and 104–30.

Another very helpful, longer chapter is 'Socialism' in Andrew Heywood (1998) *Political Ideologies* (Basingstoke: Macmillan, second edition), pp. 103–51.

Michael Levin (1989) *Marx, Engels and Liberal Democracy* (Basingstoke: Macmillan) stands out for the brevity and clarity with which it addresses the relationship between Marx, Marxism and democracy.

A full range of writings from the young Marx to the late works of both Marx and Engels can be found in Robert C. Tucker (ed.) (1978) *The Marx-Engels-Reader* (New York and London: Norton, second edition). This volume contains extracts from 'The German Ideology' and the full text of the 'Communist Manifesto'.

Jules Townshend (1996) *The Politics of Marxism: the Critical Debates* (London: Leicester University Press) covers twentieth-century Marxisms, both theory and practice, from a post-1989 'Fall of the Wall' perspective.

REFERENCES

Avineri, Shlomo (1968) *The Social and Political Thought of Karl Marx*. Cambridge: Cambridge University Press.

Carver, Terrell (1983) *Marx and Engels: the Intellectual Relationship*. Brighton: Harvester Wheatsheaf.

Carver, Terrell (1991) *Engels*. Oxford: Oxford University Press.

Gray, John (1998) *Hayek on Liberty* (third edition). London: Routledge.

Hayek, Friedrich A. (1991) *Economic Freedom*. Oxford: Blackwell.

Lane, David (1996) *The Rise and Fall of State Socialism: Industrial Society and the Socialist State*. Cambridge: Polity Press.

Levin, Michael (1989) *Marx, Engels and Liberal Democracy*. Basingstoke: Macmillan.

Lichtheim, George (1969) *The Origins of Socialism*. London: Weidenfeld & Nicolson.

Lichtheim, George (1975) *A Short History of Socialism*. Glasgow: Fontana/Collins.

McLellan, David (1998) *Marxism after Marx: an Introduction* (third edition). Basingstoke: Macmillan.

Nove, Alec (1991) *The Economics of Feasible Socialism Revisited* (second edition). London: HarperCollins.

Padgett, Stephen and Paterson, William (1991) *A History of Social Democracy in Postwar Europe*. London: Longman.

Panitch, Leo and Leys, Colin (eds) (1999) *Global Capitalism versus Democracy: The Socialist Register 1999*. New York: Monthly Review.

Pierson, Christopher (1995) *Socialism after Communism: the New Market Socialism*. Cambridge: Polity Press.

Sassoon, Donald (1997) *One Hundred Years of Socialism: the West European Left in the Twentieth Century*. London: Fontana.

Steger, Manfred B. (1997) *The Quest for Evolutionary Socialism: Eduard Bernstein and Social Democracy*. Cambridge: Cambridge University Press.

Wright, Anthony (1996) *Socialisms: Theories and Practices* (second edition). Oxford: Oxford University Press.

See also chapters

1	Sovereignty	10	Class – Elites
4	Justice, Equality, Liberty	16	Interest Groups
5	Power, Authority, Legitimacy	20	The Welfare State and Democracy
8	Pluralism – Difference	26	Anarchism and Democracy
9	Civil Society – National and Global		

26 Anarchism and Democracy

Patricia Clark and Sharif Gemie

WHAT IS ANARCHISM?

For most of human history people have lived without the state. Indeed, the modern nation-state is a comparatively recent invention, born with the emergence of capitalism. Liberal democracy is one reaction to these evolutions; anarchism, developing at about the same time as liberalism, is a second, radically different reaction.

Anarchists make a distinction between society and the state. Society is natural: people are social beings and habitually live in communities. Anarchists see the state, however, as an oppressive entity which is set up over society and which usurps functions that properly belong to autonomous communities and individuals. Rather than allowing people to flourish and develop their own ways of meeting challenges and fulfilling needs, the state is coercive and asserts its monopoly over law-making and government, punishing those who refuse its dictates and conditioning citizens into quiescence and obedience. Therefore, anarchists want to abolish the state and replace it with autonomous, small-scale communities which empower and liberate citizens, so that their cooperative and creative faculties flourish in a non-hierarchical setting.

While anarchists have been less successful than Marxists in developing their political philosophies, their various initiatives and campaigns have been sustained by common political cultures and political ideals. These have certainly varied in their applications from century to century and country to country, but there remains an irreducible core of anarchist practice that marks it out from other political movements. At the heart of anarchism is a deep commitment to a full, demanding interpretation of democratic practice. Indeed, it is perhaps this combination of insurrectionary zeal and democratic practice which has made anarchism so difficult for academic political philosophers to categorize and therefore so tempting to ignore.

Unlike liberalism, anarchist democracy is squarely rooted in a sense of lived community, rather than in the abstract individual person. This democracy is not a right which can be established by a particular government, and then modified, limited or extended as succeeding governments see fit: instead, this form of democracy is a practice which certain communities have the ability to implement for themselves. There is clearly some similarity between these ideals of democracy as lived practice, and our impressions of some ancient Greek practices where, significantly, there was no clear division between concepts of government, people and society. The people *were* the government, the government *was* the people.

Distinctions

Anarchists have occasionally been confused with liberal libertarians. Liberal libertarians, however, normally approve of a minimal state. For example, Locke proposed a 'night watchman' state whose function was solely to protect citizens' rights to 'life, liberty and property'. In the twentieth century, Robert Nozick (in *Anarchy, State and Utopia*, 1974), arguing from a Lockean perspective, claims that one can justify a minimal state to protect these rights but that anything further is an encroachment on individual liberty. This strand of thinking differs from anarchism simply because it tolerates the state.

There is another distinction that can be made between two forms of anarchism, namely individualists and collectivists. Individualist anarchists, for example Stirner (1844), start from the perspective of the individual, hence his statement: (in *The Ego and His Own*), 'I hold nothing higher than I' (Stirner, 1963: 5). By this he meant that one can see the world only from one's own point of view. Attempts to impose an external perspective are inherently oppressive. This was not a celebration of selfishness. Rather, it meant that one must first liberate oneself before choosing whether (and if so, how) to link with others. On the other hand, collectivists such as Kropotkin (in *Mutual Aid*, 1902) see the community as the basic building-block. This distinction clearly represents a difference in emphasis, but in practice both individualist and collectivist anarchists have significant features in common: a hostility to authoritarian institutions and a common stress on the values of autonomy and liberation.

ANARCHIST CRITICISMS OF LIBERAL DEMOCRACY

Anarchists have made a number of criticisms of liberal democracy.

Tyranny of the majority

First, liberal democracy is representative democracy. This means that minority views can consistently be out-voted. Anarchists find this unpalatable, as do some liberal thinkers such as John Stuart Mill who, in *On Liberty* (1859/1991), pointed out the danger of a 'tyranny of the majority' who could impose their views on minorities, imposing a social homogeneity which stifled freedom of expression.

Unrepresentative government?

In addition, many so-called representative democracies do not genuinely represent the will of the majority of the electorate. No post-war British government has won the votes of a majority of those entitled to vote. And some states make it very hard for even second- or third-generation immigrants to obtain citizenship.

Danger of bureaucracy

Anarchists agree with the sociologist Max Weber that bureaucracies have built-in oligarchical tendencies. Modern governments need a civil service to execute their decisions efficiently. But, over time, the bureaucrats in the civil service can acquire some of the politicians' decision-making powers (though anarchists would claim that these powers properly belong to the people). This is because the bureaucrats tend to be specialists and gradually acquire more experience and expertise than government ministers who change fairly frequently. A new and inexperienced minister may rely on expert bureaucrats for guidance and, gradually, the bureaucracy usurps the functions of government.

Globalization and multinational companies

Anarchists point to a new danger from multinational companies. Many large corporations cross national boundaries and grow so large and economically powerful that they exercise undue influence on individual governments.

Thus, a government which imposed stringent anti-pollution laws might find that a multinational company merely switched production operations to a (usually third world) state with no such legislation. This means a loss of jobs and economic activity in the first country and a risk of serious pollution in the second. The same thing could happen to a state which passed legislation in favour of a high minimum wage and strong health and safety legislation. Production might survive in specialist areas of expertise where highly trained workers are needed, but trades such as garment or footwear manufacture are likely to relocate to less developed economies where wages are cheaper.

It is undeniable that large transnational corporations have immense economic power: states regularly compete to attract business if they hear that, say, a vehicle manufacturer intends to set up a new plant. Because of this economic clout, multinationals unduly influence governments to refrain from legislation that is actually desired by the majority of the people. Meanwhile, unpleasant, routine or potentially unsafe production is carried out by people in less developed countries who are denied any real choice about their work.

Even on an individual level there is a significant difference between the executive of a multinational and an ordinary citizen. Both have formal equality – one vote each – but if the individual wants to be heard about an issue, then he or she may lobby his or her member of parliament and hope the MP is sympathetic, or write a letter to the local paper and hope it is published. Powerful business people, however, have the ear of politicians and the media.

In their defence, supporters of the free market claim that it maximizes the amount of choice available to consumers and allows them to buy cheap goods. However, the anarchist supporters of anti-globalization movements are unimpressed, suggesting that it is unjust and parasitic for western consumers to benefit from third world poverty, also pointing to the unacceptable influence of

unaccountable corporations over individual states.

Passivity

Some versions of liberal democracy see the voter as a consumer. This is especially noticeable in the writings of Joseph Schumpeter, particularly in *Capitalism, Socialism and Democracy* (1942/1962). During elections a variety of political elites compete for the elector's vote. The voter is choosing the politicians who will govern until the next election. The fact that there will be another election protects the voter from tyranny. The whole procedure of selecting a government is similar to buying goods or services in the market. It is an extension of the free market into the political sphere.

Anarchists considering this perspective on liberal democracy claim that it encourages passivity in the electorate. While politicians become extremely sensitive to the views of voters during election campaigns, they often prefer a quiescent and passive electorate the rest of the time. This may well account for the low turnout figures in countries like Britain (where voting is not compulsory). There is an increasing cynicism among voters about the promises and general integrity of politicians and this may account for the apathy and alienation felt, especially by minority groups who are alternately courted then ignored.

The passivity inherent in liberal democracy has been represented by one of the starkest political caricatures ever produced – an anarchist poster which simply shows:

XXXXX

XXXXX

The slogan beneath the ten crosses reads: 'Here is your lifetime's supply of democracy.'

Again, one frequently hears neighbours grumbling about poor street lighting, unsatisfactory street cleaning or the like, and saying: '*They* ought to do something about it.' Anarchists point out that in an autonomous society people would say: '*We* must do something about it'. Government should not be something done by an elite but is rightfully something a community organizes for itself to meet its own needs.

WHAT HAS GONE WRONG WITH DEMOCRACY?

These criticisms point to a central failing. At first sight, the anarchist criticism may seem to be directed simply against the idea of voting for representatives. But the matter is more complex. On some occasions, practices of representation have excited interest, even enthusiasm, if not exactly empowerment. During the nineteenth century, as wider electorates, based on a large proportion of the male population, became more common in Europe and the USA, electoral turnout was frequently over 80 per cent, even over 90 per cent. The growth in abstention can be dated to recent decades. The technical process of voting has not changed. Indeed, conditions have actually improved for the individual voter over the past century and a half, with greater rights to secrecy when voting, less likelihood of bribery or intimidation and greater access to information concerning the political issues debated. Instead, the significant factor that has changed has been the decline of any sense, real or imagined, of a participatory electoral culture. Significantly, the Zapatista Army of National Liberation in today's Mexico does not call for different forms of electoral procedure, but a different type of *participatory* political culture, one in which 'those that command are thoughtful people who command by obeying' (Marcos, 1995: 163).

Politics has become the business of experts who fear or despise the electorate's opinion and who see their task as the paternal one of setting limits. Political parties are ruled by conventions as strict as those governing an absolutist royal court: dissent, disobedience and creativity are all seen as heresies to be repressed with the utmost vigour.

Anarchist critics argue that such develop-ments are inevitable within the framework provided by liberal parliamentary democracy. Without any firm basis in any 'lived' form of democratic practice which relates directly to people's lives, liberal democracy is an artificial construct, imposed over the divisions and diversity of a growing society. Anarchist democracy, instead, grows from where practices of self-empowerment and self-management are strongest. The zones and forms which have interested anarchists have varied, from the factory and workshop, through the neighbourhood community and peasant village, to the sense of community felt by avant-garde artists and, more recently, the virtual communities formed over the Internet.

DIRECT DEMOCRACY

Anarchists have drawn inspiration from the direct democracy of classical Athens. Greek democracy theoretically went a fair way to removing the dichotomy between governors and governed. Any citizen could attend the democratic Assembly and speak, vote or be chosen for office. Bureaucracy was minimized: the administration was chosen by lot and often bureaucratic posts were rotated between notional 'tribes' to ensure a power balance; before military campaigns were fought, a vote was taken; generals were elected by the Assembly and the army was a citizen militia.

One might think that with a few modern amendments anarchists would propose a contemporary version of direct democracy, including all adult inhabitants as full citizens (which the Athenians failed to do), perhaps having Internet or televised debates in place of an Assembly where citizens were physically present. But this would not go far enough, for there would still be an important distinction between citizens – that of economic power. Greek democracy operated only in the political sphere. For anarchists, such democracy needs to be extended into the economic sphere. Only then can one dissolve the distinction between governed and governing so that each citizen can be autonomous and empowered. Issues would be decided by the people who are affected by them, thus avoiding apathy and alienation. So workers would decide on production methods in their factory and elect the necessary administrators, or rotate the tasks so that everyone develops experience. Instead of local government deciding what sort of new public facility should be provided, the users decide.

For this to work, society would be organized differently from the way it is now. Communities would be on a relatively small scale so that individuals would need to be involved in their community and would have their voice heard. If everyone has a stake, then apathy and alienation would vanish. Moreover, it is a myth that anarchists are against organization. They are against hierarchical forms of government, but accept organization and administration that does not develop into bureaucracy. In order to prevent this, administrative tasks might be voluntary and based around a single function. Post-holders might be volunteers, or chosen by lot, or posts might be rotated among members of the community so that everyone interested takes a turn and gains experience. This would develop the capacities and potentials of individual citizens, so that they become more autonomous and empowered. Anarchists deny that government is a specialized area which only experts can manage successfully. On a larger scale, there would be federal coordination between different communities, to exchange resources and the like.

ANARCHIST DIRECT DEMOCRACY AND CONSENSUS

Some people might be satisfied with the introduction of direct democracy in all areas of public life. However, it would not be absolutely coherent: minorities could still be overlooked. And majorities are not always right:

they can be ignorant or prejudiced. Anarchists recognize this and say that in a non-hierarchical society it would be wrong for a majority to impose its will on a minority. This would coerce members of the minority into accepting obligations and so infringe their autonomy. So what is to be done when disagreements arise? The answer depends on the nature of the disagreement.

With relatively minor disagreements, dissenters might concede the issue. Malatesta, the Italian anarchist, notes that:

> Certainly anarchists recognize that where life is lived in common it is often necessary for the minority to come to accept the opinion of the majority. When there is an obvious need or usefulness in doing something and to do it requires the agreement of all, the few should feel the need to adapt to the wishes of the many. . . . But such adaptation . . . by one group must . . . be reciprocal, voluntary and must stem from an awareness of need and goodwill to prevent the running of social affairs from being paralysed by obstinacy. It cannot be imposed as a . . . statutory norm. (Malatesta, 1965: 100)

In the case of more serious and important disagreements, it is inappropriate to expect dissenters to give way. As Malatesta pointed out:

> One cannot expect, or even wish, that someone who is firmly convinced that the course taken by the majority leads to disaster, should sacrifice his convictions and passively look on, or even worse, should support a policy he considers wrong. (Malatesta, 1965: 132)

So, given that majority decisions are not binding on dissenters, they can either remain in the association (the workplace, community or whatever), protesting and attempting to persuade the majority of its error, or, as a last resort, they can secede and do things their own way.

Some critics will see this sort of democracy as unrealistic, but in family life, where there is a spirit of goodwill, disagreements are often solved with this sort of 'give and take'.

The same spirit and practice applies in some offices and staff-rooms when there is a sense of respect for others. If this version of democracy can work at one level, then why not at another?

Finally, some anarchists argue that even this sort of democracy is not sufficient. They demand consensus: the unanimous agreement of all involved. All anarchists agree that this is the ideal, though many doubt whether it is practicable. In families and small groups where there is mutual trust this ideal can often be achieved. But in larger groups the resulting agreements tend to be mediocre, lowest-possible-denominator compromises. Alternatively, dissenters feel obliged to keep quiet and stifle their misgivings, so that consensus can actually turn into a sort of authoritarianism masquerading as unanimity. Murray Bookchin has warned of these dangers:

> [I]n order . . . to create full consensus on a decision, minority dissenters were often subtly urged or psychologically coerced to decline to vote on a certain issue, inasmuch as their dissent would essentially amount to a one-person veto. This practice, called 'standing aside' in American consensus processes, all too often involved intimidation of the dissenters, to the point that they completely withdrew from the decision-making process, rather than make an honourable and continuing expression of their dissent by voting, even as a minority, in accordance with their views. Having withdrawn, they ceased to be political beings – so a decision could be made. . . . On a more theoretical level, consensus silenced that most vital aspect of all dialogue: *dissensus*. The ongoing dissent, the passionate dialogue that still persists even after a minority accedes temporarily to a majority decision, . . . [may be] replaced . . . by dull monologues – and the uncontroverted and deadening tone of consensus. In majority decision-making, the defeated minority can resolve to overturn a decision on which they have been defeated – they are free to openly and persistently articulate reasoned and potentially persuasive disagreements. Consensus, for its part, honours no minorities, but mutes them in favour of the metaphysical 'one' of the 'consensus' group. (Bookchin, 1997: 8)

ANARCHIST PRACTICES

Forms of anarchism

While there are still relatively few academic studies of anarchism, anarchist movements have been extremely influential in recent history. The first trade union movements in countries such as Italy, France, Spain, Argentina and Mexico were begun by anarchists. While the revolutionary wave in northeast Spain, particularly in Catalonia, in 1936–37 probably constitutes the single example of a genuinely anarchist revolution, anarchists contributed significantly to revolutions in Russia in 1905 and 1917 (and were prominent in the first rebellion against the Soviet regime in 1921), in Mexico (1910), and in Paris (1871 and 1968). Anarchism has also exercised a wide cultural influence, inspiring artists such as Camille Pissarro, novelists such as Tolstoy, and writers such as Oscar Wilde. More recently, both Noam Chomsky and Ursula Le Guin have been encouraged by anarchist ideas.

Aside from these headline-grabbing revolutionary movements, anarchists have also been prominent in more subtle, small-scale activities. During the late nineteenth century anarchists began a series of debates on the nature of schooling, initiating a tradition of 'free schooling' which stretches through to A.S. Neill's Summerhill school and radical experiments in pedagogy. In France, Spain and Italy, anarchists were among the first groups to campaign for contraceptive rights. In Britain, anarchists such as Colin Ward have inspired critical reflections of housing and the urban context, and encouraged an appreciation of the values of autonomy and self-management in this context.

These points add up to a movement which is far wider and deeper than the popular stereotype of evil anarchist terrorists, who take the bomb as their sole political weapon.

While certainly there have been outbreaks of anarchist terrorism (principally in Europe in the early 1890s), it would be extremely misleading to present this current as the dominant one within modern anarchism.

Anarchism in practice

To date, the most influential of anarchist models has been the working-class community gathered together by the factory and workshop, and it was among such groups that the first anarchist trade unions were formed in the 1880s. This was known as 'anarcho-syndicalism' – an anarchism based among syndicates (the French and Spanish term for trade unions). Such bodies differed radically from the now-standard model of an institution to negotiate rates of pay and conditions of work with management. To cite an anarchist slogan, anarchist unions were not looking for a bigger slice of the cake; they wanted to take over the whole bakery. As well as defending their members' immediate interests, they aimed at the deeper goal of the revolutionary seizure of production from the management.

From the start, such militants were suspicious of bureaucracies. As in the example of the Greek Assembly, their ideal was that there should be no difference between the body of workers and the union. In a sense, they remained true to this ideal: in 1936, the Spanish anarcho-syndicalist CNT (National Confederation of Labour) had between half a million and a million members, and could boast that there was only one paid union official. The CNT depended on the voluntary activities of its members rather than on the specialized knowledge of a few experts. However, economic conditions worked against these anarchist principles. In late nineteenth-century and early twentieth-century Europe, any known union activist could expect trouble from the boss. Where possible, bosses would simply fire activists. This meant that simply in order to survive, union activists needed some alternative source of income. In some cases they might set up pubs and cafés;

elsewhere a salaried position, paid for by the union was considered. The CNT remained true to its opposition to paid bureaucracy by finding jobs for activists within the anarcho-syndicalist press.

Anarcho-syndicalist unions reflected the entirety of their members' lives. As well as fighting for better rates of pay, they also sponsored campaigns on housing conditions (leading bitterly fought rent strikes in Barcelona). They encouraged learning, often beginning by teaching their members to read and write, and then introducing them to as broad a range of cultural influences as possible. Poetry readings, theatre groups and choirs formed by the workers themselves were promoted. Anarcho-syndicalist unions would attempt to provide their members with medical and contraceptive advice where possible. Concern for the quality of food consumed by workers led to the foundation of cooperative stores, which guaranteed the quality of their produce, and sometimes led to campaigns against alcoholism, occasionally even vegetarianism and teetotalism.

All of these concerns suggest a quite different approach to the substance of democracy: anarchist democracy is rooted in the concerns of daily life. Beyond the most fundamental principle of opposition to an elite of experts, anarchism cannot be reduced to particular techniques – often because repression by state, church and party never allowed anarchist militants the space to put their ideas into practice. Anarchist democracy, instead, depends on the existence of a broad culture which supports and encourages individual empowerment within a collective setting.

CRITICISMS OF THE ANARCHIST VIEW OF DEMOCRACY

There are many largely ill-informed criticisms of anarchism depicting it as violent and chaotic. These arose in reaction to the small minority of late nineteenth-century anarchists who adopted terrorist tactics. Their successors can be seen in the minority of contemporary anarchist anti-globalization protesters who use violence to make their point. However, the majority of anarchists today believe in peaceful approaches, campaigning for libertarian issues to raise people's awareness.

The central criticism of anarchist views of democracy focuses on the question of human nature. It is difficult for anarchists to prove their central claims about the human potential for cooperation. This leaves the way open for other theorists to present different views. Thus elite theorists, such as Pareto and Mosca, claim that it is natural for elites to occur in social groupings, and so a non-hierarchical society is both unnatural and impossible. Others suggest that it is unrealistic to expect everyone to participate in decision-making: some people are just apathetic. Diehard capitalists argue that human beings are naturally acquisitive and selfish.

Anarchists hold that human beings have a number of potentials and capacities and the best ones (for cooperation and creativity) will flourish in a non-hierarchical society of autonomous individuals. Western capitalism only encourages people's capacities for greed and selfishness. However, it is difficult, if not impossible, to say what human nature is 'really' like, particularly if we see it only through the distorting mirror of the state. Anthropological studies of indigenous peoples who organize themselves without reference to a state might be useful but, given that the whole surface of the globe (with the partial exception of Antarctica) has been divided into states which attempt to impose their mandate on these nominal citizens, together with the pervasive influence of business, such as Brazilian logging companies, such evidence is both scanty and tainted.

CONCLUSION

Anarchism stands for a demanding and far-reaching concept of democracy. To date, it has represented a minority current. Yet, in the context of massive public alienation from the dominant forms of liberal, representative democracy and the collapse of authoritarian Marxism as a practical alternative, it seems probable that anarchist ideas and themes will inspire a growing number of people in the twenty-first century.

Summary

- Anarchists see the state as an oppressive and alienating institution, which should be abolished.
- Anarchists criticize liberal representative democracy because:

  - Minorities can consistently be outvoted.
  - An allegedly democratic state may not represent the will of the majority.
  - There is a danger of bureaucracy usurping decision-making powers.
  - Real power can leach from governments to unaccountable multinational companies.
  - Most importantly, representative government encourages passivity in the electorate.

- Anarchist critics of liberal democracy believe that:

  - Democracy is something that must relate to people in their everyday lives.
  - Democracy grows from life in a community.
  - Democracy should not be an artificial construct imposed from above.

- Anarchists hold that direct democracy is a good thing but does not go far enough. All areas of public life should be democratic. This would involve major changes to the economic structure of western society, particularly the end of the free market system.
- Regarding consensus, democracy is a tool for discovering what people want and feel. This is a starting point for the search for a creative solution that everyone involved can live with. A genuine consensus is an ideal, not always practicable.
- In practice, anarchism can take a number of different forms as it responds to people's needs in a given situation.
- Anarchist democratic theory rests on a view of human nature which is largely unprovable. However, this is also true of other theories.

TUTORIAL QUESTIONS

1. Is the modern state an oppressive institution? Even if the modern state is oppressive, is anarchism the best solution? Is it possible to live without the modern state?

2. Is anarchism based on an unrealistic view of human nature? Are people naturally cooperative and responsible? Can we tell what people are 'naturally' like? Why are many people apathetic or cynical about politics today? Is it realistic to expect mass participation in an anarchist society?

FURTHER READING

Peter Marshall (1993) *Demanding the Impossible: the History of Anarchism* (London: Fontana) is a lively, encyclopaedic survey of anarchist movements, thinkers and militants.

Murray Bookchin (1982) *The Ecology of Freedom: the Emergence and Dissolution of Hierarchy* (Palo Alto, CA: Cheshire) provides a rich and sustained philosophical statement of eco-anarchism.

Jerome Mintz (1982) *The Anarchists of Casa Viejas* (Bloomington and Indianapolis, IN: Indiana University Press) offers a well-written oral history. Set in one village, it gives a rounded picture of early twentieth-century anarchist organization.

Jon Purkis and James Bowen (eds) (1997) *Twenty-first Century Anarchism: Unorthodox Ideas for a New Millennium* (London: Cassell) contains a thought-provoking set of essays on a wide range of cultural, political and social themes.

Ursula Le Guin (1974) *The Dispossessed* (London: Grafton), offers an imaginative fictional account of dilemmas in an anarchist society.

Anarchist Studies is a six-monthly journal, encouraging academic debate on anarchist history, culture and politics (from 1992 onwards).

REFERENCES

Bookchin, Murray (1997) 'Communalism: the Democratic Dimension of Anarchism', *Democracy and Nature*, **3**, available at: http://www.democracynature.org/dn/vol3/bookchin_communalism.htm

Kropotkin, Peter (1902) *Mutual Aid*. London: Heinemann.

Malatesta, E. (1965) *Life and Ideas*. Ed. Vernon Richards. London: Freedom.

Marcos, Subcomandante (1995) *Shadows of Tender Fury*. New York: Monthly Review Press.

Mill, John Stuart (1859/1991) 'On Liberty', in John Gray (ed.), *John Stuart Mill: On Liberty and Other Essays*. Oxford: Oxford University Press, pp. 1–128.

Nozick, Robert (1974) *Anarchy, State and Utopia*. New York: Basic Books.

Schumpeter, Joseph (1942/1962) *Capitalism, Socialism and Democracy*. New York: Harper and Row.

Stirner, M. (1963) *The Ego and His Own: The Case of the Individual Against Authority*. Translated by Steven T. Byrington. New York: Libertarian Book Club.

See also chapters

27 Nationalism

Alain Dieckhoff

While democracy has not become a universal political reality, it has become so positively valued that even authoritarian regimes feel bound to assert their democratic credentials. Thus, we had in Eastern Europe for more than 40 years so-called 'popular democracies' where the rule of the Communist Party was presented as the realization of 'true democracy'. This was not just a ruse but the expression of the normative attractiveness of democracy which compelled even obviously non-democratic leaders to claim they governed with the consent of the people. Such a positive evaluation is obviously not given to the term 'nationalism', at least in the western world. Here nationalism is spontaneously associated with narrow ethnic ties and violent upsurges. Indeed, the dramatic break-up of Yugoslavia helped to spread the idea that nationalism was an atavistic force, glorifying blood, deadly set against democracy and individual rights. The heavy fighting in Chechnya, the ethnic cleansing of Albanians in Kosovo, the assassinations of journalists and political opponents by the radical ETA in the Basque Country have also helped to 'demonise nationality' (Nairn, 1997: 57). But should nationalism be equated only with these negative features? Is it only a harmful feature that has to be overcome as soon as possible? Is it totally in contradiction with democratic freedom?

NATIONALISM AND SOVEREIGNTY

Nationalism is both an ideology and a political movement which mobilizes a nation. But, to use Ernest Renan's very well-known question: what is a nation? Answering this question has given rise to a huge amount of theoretical literature but in the end finding empirical characteristics in order to get a generic definition of the nation has generally proved disappointing. Rather than isolating the nation's putative contents (for example, political bond, language, religion, common history, sense of belonging), it is better to trace the evolution of the concept. The major shift occurs when 'nation' loses its original sense (community of origin) and gets its modern meaning (a sovereign people). This qualitative transformation has been located at different points in history, with some authors saying that it occurred in early sixteenth-century England (Greenfeld, 1992), others that it came about in the second half of the eighteenth century with the American Declaration of Independence (1776) and, even more so, the French Revolution (1789) (Best, 1988). Whatever the turning point, by making the whole people in a given territory the bearer of sovereignty, nationalism is clearly linked with the advent of democracy as the rule of the people. Thus nationalism was, in its initial phase, an emancipating force; and the Germans, the Poles, the Italians and the Greeks who fought for their independence during the first half of the nineteenth century conceived it as such. The nationalism of Mazzini, Mickiewicz and others longed for the political sovereignty of their country but those leaders did not think that it should come at the expense of other peoples. Instead, they hoped to build a genuine solidarity between democratic nations. This original nationalism, frequently called 'liberal', gave way, after the failure of the 1848 revolutions, to a new form of nationalism which challenged political liberalism and defended a closed conception of the nation based on ascriptive qualities and shared ethnicity. This nationalism had a strong cultural component because in Eastern Europe, where it took shape, culture (especially language) was very often the only resource available in order to give national coherence to ethnic groups which claimed to be nations. The strong ethnic dimension was all the more important because it gave an indigenous content to a foreign framework, the national model, which was imported from Western Europe (Greenfeld, 1992: 14–17). Its aim was first and foremost to protect the national particularism within an independent political framework, not to build a democratic polity. Nationalism assumed the character of a political opposition which claimed to represent the (true) nation against the state. The basic aim was to lead a successful separatist movement, that is, to create a state for the Czechs, the Romanians or the Poles carved out from an imperial order (Austria-Hungary, Ottoman Empire, Tsarist Russia). Nevertheless, this protest nationalism was not directed only towards secession from existing political structures; it also took the call for internal reform within more or less old nation-states (Breuilly, 1982). Italian Fascism, German Nazism or far-right nationalism in Third Republic France were such attempts to rebuild the nation on an organic basis through exclusion of all 'foreigners', first of all Jews. This radical nationalism based on an explicit rejection of democratic rule signalled clearly that, although the modern nation was born as a community of equal citizens partaking in the expression of sovereignty, this link was not a logical necessity. Thus nationalism has two contending faces: it is a truly emancipating force when it gives the power to a nation of free individuals; it is an oppressive force when it promotes the nation as an absolute.

THE NATION-STATE AND DEMOCRACY

Historically, democracy took root in the western world in a very specific political setting: the nation-state whose paradigm remains France. In this model, which became a universal reference, the state as the legal supreme organization has to be linked to the population living within its boundaries which is defined as a nation. According to Gellner, that is precisely what nationalism is all about: giving one political roof to a culture (Gellner, 1983). Every nation should have its state to accommodate democracy because the nation-state fosters a feeling of brotherhood which renders the development of a common citizenship easier. Such an idea has found many talented advocates among philosophers. John Stuart Mill argues in *Consideration on Representative Government* that 'free institutions are next to impossible in a country made up of different nationalities . . . the boundaries of governments should coincide in the main with those of nationalities' (Mill, 1977: 547). Jean-Jacques Rousseau, too, called upon the Poles to protect their liberties by taking care of their national distinctiveness. They should relentlessly 'shape their minds and hearts in a national pattern that will set them apart from other peoples' (Rousseau, 1972: 12). Democracy could thrive, so the argument goes, only with a common national culture. Why? Because it will be easier to organize a democratic space if the people are using the same print-language. To use Benedict Anderson's image, one hundred thousand people who are reading the same newspaper will never know each other directly, but by sharing the same news, printed in the same language, they feel that they are members of the same imagined community (Anderson, 1991). But the nation is not an entity which is just there; it has to be built, and in that endeavour the state plays a crucial role. Already during the fourteenth and fifteenth centuries, in the first modern states (England, France, Spain), the kings strengthened their political power while doing their utmost to spread the language of the court. In all three countries, the authorities prescribed the use of the vernacular for all administrative deeds. The aim was to have one unified state language. Nevertheless, the rulers did not care much whether the people spoke different languages. This indifference towards linguistic plurality changed with the advent of the modern democratic principle that vested sovereignty in the people. It is not by chance that the French revolutionaries who declared the Republic to be one and indivisible were also firmly set against the so-called *patois* (Breton, Basque, Occitan, Alsatian). In the name of national unity, it was better that those regional languages should fade away, with the active help of the state which pursued policies of nationalization – in which the school system played a central role – in order to increase cultural contiguity among the citizenry. In a genuine nation-state, cultural homogeneity is a requisite because everybody should experience the nation as a concrete fact. A national community is thus not only a political association based on citizenship, but also a communal relationship based on a common culture that gives to its members a subjective feeling of belonging (Weber, 1968: 40–2).

The idea that the nation-state is best suited to a well-functioning democracy has been widely shared by political scientists. In the 1960s, the theorists of political development tried, in the wake of decolonization, to understand how the new states could stabilize their political systems and consolidate democracy. They saw the great variety of cultural, ethnic and geographical sub-units in those states as a major hindrance in the building of national loyalty (Almond and Powell, 1966). The consolidation of a democratic system was considered to need a sufficiently strong national identity, otherwise the polity would be torn apart by centrifugal forces. The new states were thus seen to face a double challenge: state-building and nation-building. The first task required the increase of the regulative and extractive capacities of the political system through the development of a bureaucracy and the fostering of attitudes of compliance in the population. The second task required the transfer of the people's commitment and loyalty from sectorial groups to the national unit. Political development could succeed, so it was argued, only if the new states were able to overcome this crisis of identity.

Although developmentalism has faded away, the argument, which makes national integration a requisite for a genuine democratic participation, is still powerful. In the 1990s, after the breakdown of the communist regimes, among the conditions identified for consolidating democracy after an authoritarian experience, the formation of a stable national identity has often been stressed. The transition in Eastern Europe gives undeniably some credit to this theory. Countries which were solid nation-states with small ethnic minorities (Poland, Hungary, the Czech Republic) were more successful in their democratic transition than countries which were deeply divided along ethnic lines (Slovakia, Romania, Bulgaria, former Yugoslavia). Precisely because national unity was shaky, political leaders in those states often used a militant nationalist discourse and practices which were directed against their own minorities (for example, Hungarians, Turks, Albanians). Ethnic cleavages appear thus as a liability for the quick consolidation of democracy. What is more, in deeply divided societies democracy often reinforces those divisions rather than overcomes them. Indeed, political mobilization occurs around narrow communitarian dynamics rather than on the basis of individualistic political choices. Thus, in Bosnia, Muslims, Serbs and Croats overwhelmingly tend to give their support to three nationalist parties, the Democratic Action Party, the

Serbian Democratic Party and the Croatian Democratic Union, and not to 'catch-all' parties. All this would appear to support the strong case for the nation-state and its striving towards cultural homogeneity, and to disparage multi-ethnic states which are depicted as condemned to fragmentation because narrow ethnic preferences will always prevail over the general interest (Rabushka and Shepsle, 1972). Nevertheless, if it may be easier to uphold democratic institutions in a nation-state, where the people share a 'basic sameness', we should not overstate the case. Indeed, three things should be stressed. First, national identity is always relative. For instance, China seems quite homogeneous, having a 90 per cent Han majority which shares the same ideographic scripture. Nevertheless, diversity comes back with spoken language, which varies substantially from region to region, rendering mutual understanding difficult and making the Chinese far less culturally uniform than it would appear at first sight. Secondly, a strong sense of national identity is not by itself conducive to democratization. Japan has a well-defined territory, a unifying language, a shared ethnicity and a specific amalgam of an indigenous religion (Shinto) and an imported one (Buddhism). Nevertheless, although modernization started with the Meiji era (1868), democracy was only fully implemented after Japan's defeat in 1945 under American patronage. Thirdly, even if there is a visible cultural commonality and a shared legacy of memories, this is not a guarantee that other cleavages (of a social, ideological or cultural nature) cannot tear the nation apart and weaken democracy. This was exactly the case with the American Civil War (1861–65) when the Confederates fought the Unionists, despite what they had in common, because they disagreed on the question of slavery which was part of a larger economic dispute.

Clearly, just as the linkage between nation-state and democracy is a complex one, so also is the one between a multinational or multicultural state and democracy. Is it really so obvious that 'the more the population of the territory of the state is composed of plurinational, lingual, religious or cultural societies, the more complex politics becomes because an agreement on the fundamentals of a democracy will be more difficult' (Linz and Stepan, 1996: 29)? I should wish to argue that in divided societies it is vital to dismiss the culture–state congruence and to recognize a constitutive plurality in order to achieve a working democracy.

MULTINATIONAL STATES AND DEMOCRACY

Against those who advocated the principle of unity which seeks to make state and nation commensurate with each other, Lord Acton, professor of history at Cambridge, defended already in the middle of the nineteenth century the principle of diversity: 'The co-existence of several nations under the same State is a test, as well as the best security of its freedom. It is also one of the chief instruments of civilization . . . those states are substantially the most perfect which include various distinct nationalities without oppressing them' (Lord Acton, 1862/1996: 31 and 36). This call for the 'respect' of national plurality has been an essential feature of a number of multinational democracies, that is, states which contain at least two nations, like Canada, Spain or Belgium. In all those cases democracy is premised on the recognition of diversity.

Such recognition is mainly achieved through two institutional means (Dieckhoff, 2000). One is consociationalism, a model first developed in reference to the Netherlands where political stability was intrinsically linked with the overt recognition of internal cleavages between four groups (Catholics, Calvinists, socialists, liberals) (Lijphart, 1968). Consociationalism is based on two guiding principles. The first is the segmental autonomy granted to the constitutive groups. The autonomy can be non-territorial: every individual, wherever he or she lives, is affiliated to a community with its own political parties, trade unions, schools, hospitals, mass media, etc. It can also be territorial, as in Switzerland which is divided into 26 cantons which, together with the communes, are the basic locus of identity. The second feature is a power-sharing mechanism between the elites of each subculture. Political representation is always based on proportionality and governments are made up of large coalitions. The Swiss executive is a skilful mixing of political affiliations, cantonal membership, languages and religions.

Consociationalism is optimal when societies are crossed by ideological, religious and social cleavages. It is far less suited when the dividing line is ethno-national. Thus Belgium had from the start a strong consociational component but the latter became clearly inadequate with the growing salience of the language question between Flemings and francophones. Furthermore, the model is more efficient when the constitutive groups acknowledge the full legitimacy of the general political framework. Undeniably, a shared patriotism moderates the acuteness of the cleavages, both in the Netherlands and in Switzerland, but as soon as sub-nationalisms are growing (as in the case of Belgium), political loyalty to the centre tends to weaken and thus to impede the elaboration of compromises between elites. Almost unavoidably a second means to accommodate diversity seems necessary: federalism.

It is not by chance that democracy in multinational states is often seen as enhanced by federalism. Indeed, federalism is based on shared sovereignty, with central government and the federated states being both supreme in their respective fields, which are constitutionally defined. Within this framework, a sub-unit with historical and cultural peculiarities may possess considerable autonomy, which may be useful for the defence of its collective identity. Thanks to federalism, Flanders and Walloonia in Belgium, the Quebecois in Canada, the 'historical nationalities' (Basque Country, Catalonia and Galicia) in Spain were, for instance, able to take various measures in order to protect their languages. The Spanish case is also noticeable because it shows that in a multinational setting the transition to democracy has to move forward on two legs – the guarantee of civil and political rights to the citizens had to be complemented by the devolution of power to autonomous sub-units. Ignoring the problem of stateness by keeping a unitary state organization would have surely hindered the democratic stabilization of the country. Federalism is a good mechanism for managing nationalist dynamics in multinational states, although it will never quell clearly separatist trends. Thus, in the Basque Country, despite a very generous statute of autonomy, the armed organization ETA never stopped using political violence to enforce its aim, namely, the creation of an independent state.

To sum up, without federal arrangements, a democratic multinational state is doomed to split quickly along its internal cleavages. However, setting up a federal framework does not guarantee that the state will remain forever a united polity. When renegotiations of the federal compact are no longer possible, secession becomes a tangible outcome, thus indicating the triumph of nationalism as a movement of separation.

SECESSION AND DEMOCRACY

Secession is generally justified on the basis of the right of peoples to self-determination. However, for international law, this last principle is valid only in cases of decolonization and within the limits of the colonial boundaries. This means that once a new state is created, no people within it can claim national self-determination in order to set up its own state. The international community was thus very reluctant to back secessionist movements: from 1945 to 1991, there was only one instance of successful secession – Eastern Pakistan that became Bangladesh in 1971. Things have changed a little bit in the

1990s when the break-up of the three communist federations (Soviet Union, Yugoslavia, Czechoslovakia) led to the emergence of
an array of new states. This process was
endorsed by the United Nations and gave
legitimacy to national self-determination for
people within internationally recognized
states. Is this tendency to be applauded from
a democratic point of view? An answer
depends on how the right to secede is understood. Indeed, there are two theories of
secession (Buchanan, 1997). For the first
school, secession is an absolute right given to
any territorialized group which chooses by a
majoritarian vote to leave the common state.
For some, the group has to share a common pervasive culture, which encompasses
important aspects of life and marks the character of the life of its members. For others, the
group does not need to be defined by ascriptive characteristics (such as speaking the
same language or sharing a specific history):
the group is made up of all those who choose
voluntarily to break the political association
with their fellow citizens and decide by a
majority to create a new political bond. This
primary right to secession seems at first
glance to fit in with a true concern for democracy. First, because keeping a group within a
state which it wishes to leave looks like a
coercive, and thus an un-democratic, measure. Secondly, because the realization of
national self-determination will unite the
people with a new political identity that will
strengthen its democratic autonomy. Self-
determination understood in a liberal way is
part and parcel of democracy. To this line of
arguments, two main objections can be made.
The first objection has to do with democratic
theory. The partitioning of multi-ethnic/
multinational states should not become an
ordinary way to settle national questions
because it will lead to the development of
states with a strong ethnic base, a situation
which is conducive to the narrowing of political debate. The trend towards homogeniza-
tion is noticeable, for instance, in Eastern
Europe. After the separation from Slovakia,
the Czech Republic has become a mono-

national state and all the successor states in
ex-Yugoslavia have now a thick core identity
(Slovenian, Croatian, Serbian). Is this necessarily an improvement for democracy? Even
if this principle of likeness can – from a functional perspective – make the day-to-day
working of democracy easier since the people
share the same cultural code, it is not a prerequisite for democracy. On the contrary, we
may argue that democracy means 'learning to
make decisions with others who are not like
oneself and who may deeply disagree with
one. . . . Democratic decision-making and the
institutions they support take diversity as a
given and are designed to use it construc-
tively, not to banish diversity by reconfigur-
ing the political map' (Buchanan, 1998: 23).

The second objection stresses the perverse
effect of secession. Although the redrawing of
boundaries tends to lead to more homogeneous states, the outcome is either uncertain or
highly costly. The division in two states may
attenuate some lines of cleavages but will put
new ones in the foreground. It may also
deepen the previous cleavages (Horowitz,
1985: 588–92). Both of these developments
have occurred in the partition of British India.
Not only did the Muslim/Hindu divide not
weaken, but the national unity of Pakistan,
based on a shared Islam, became quickly
apparent as a pure illusion as the country was
subjected to centrifugal ethnic dynamics
(secession of Bangladesh, regionalisms within
the rump state of Pakistan). In addition, even
if partitioned states display more homogeneity, this outcome is often the result of violent
measures: slaughters, population transfers or
ethnic cleansing. In practice, secession does
not sit easily with the promotion of
democracy.

All these major shortcomings give a clear
advantage to the second theory of secession
which sees it as grounded in a remedial right.
Thus secession is a legitimate solution in only
two cases: if the physical survival of the
group is in jeopardy (by the permanent discriminatory redistribution of economics
goods, the undermining of its culture, a direct
lethal threat against its survival) or if its

previously sovereign territory was unjustly occupied by a foreign state. Without a just cause, secession should be discarded.

This assumption expresses a sound rule: in the modern world, the nationalist principle which assumes that within a given territory, the people is the bearer of sovereignty, remains a powerful one, which cannot be pushed aside. Undeniably, the nation-state was and still is an effective model for accommodating democracy because the sharing of the same national culture renders the development of a common citizenship easier.

Nevertheless, in contemporary societies which are ever more culturally diverse, a working democracy needs to recognize its constitutive plurality: states will increasingly have to take into account their multinational nature. Consociationalism, and even more so, federalism, are two essential means of coping with ethno-national diversity. However, this legitimate concern needs to be articulated with the preservation of the bond of citizenship. The balance is a delicate one but in the twenty-first century democracy needs such an equilibrium in order to thrive.

Summary

- Nationalism is both an ideology and a political movement which mobilizes a nation and sees it as the bearer of sovereignty. Thus it is linked with the advent of democracy as the rule of the people.
- The nation-state, based on a common culture, is well suited to the working of a shared democratic citizenship.
- However, cultural homogeneity is neither sufficient nor necessary for a democratic order which can also thrive within multinational states.
- Consociationalism and federalism are two ways of accommodating diversity in multinational democracies.
- Secession of national groups is democratically acceptable only as a remedial right in the case of outright injustice.

TUTORIAL QUESTIONS

1. **How is nationalism, as a political concept, linked to popular sovereignty?**

2. **Is the nation-state more in tune with democracy than the multinational state?**

3. **Should secessionist movements be withstood or supported in the name of democratic principles?**

FURTHER READING

John Hutchinson and Anthony Smith (eds) (1994) *Nationalism* (Oxford: Oxford University Press) is a useful reader which gives a good insight both into the theories of nationalism and its historical occurrence.

Craig Calhoun (1997) *Nationalism* (Buckingham: Open University Press) offers a stimulating analysis of the modernity of nationalism by comparing it to kinship and ethnicity and by linking it with the rise of the modern state.

Alain Gagnon and James Tully (eds) (2001) *Multinational Democracies* (Cambridge: Cambridge University Press) clarifies the challenges faced by those states which comprise two or more nations while abiding by democratic procedures.

Liah Greenfeld (1992) in her now classical book *Nationalism: Five Roads to Modernity* (Cambridge, MA: Harvard University Press) gives, through a comparative socio-historical analysis of five countries (England, France, Germany, Russia, United States), a very complete account of the complex relationship between nationalism and democracy.

REFERENCES

Acton, Lord (1862/1996) 'On Nationality', in Gopal Balakrishnan (ed.), *Mapping the Nation*. London: Verso.

Almond, Gabriel and Powell, G. Bingham (1966) *Comparative Politics. a Developmental Approach*. Boston, MA and Toronto: Little, Brown and Company.

Anderson, Benedict (1991) *Imagined Communities*. London, Verso.

Best, Geoffrey (1988) *The Permanent Revolution: the French Revolution and Its Legacy*. Chicago, IL: Chicago University Press.

Breuilly, John (1982) *Nationalism and the State*. Manchester: Manchester University Press.

Buchanan, Allen (1997) 'Theories of Secession', *Philosophy and Public Affairs*, **26**: 31–61.

Buchanan, Allen (1998) 'Democracy and Secession', in Margaret Moore (ed.), *National Self-Determination and Secession*. Oxford: Oxford University Press, pp. 14–33.

Dieckhoff, Alain (2000) *La nation dans tous ses états. Les identités nationales en mouvement*. Paris: Flammarion.

Gellner, Ernest (1983) *Nations and Nationalism*. Oxford: Blackwell.

Greenfeld, Liah (1992) *Nationalism: Five Roads to Modernity*. Cambridge, MA: Harvard University Press.

Horowitz, Donald (1985) *Ethnic Groups in Conflict*. Berkeley, CA: University of California Press.

Lijphart, Arend (1968) *The Politics of Accommodation. Pluralism and Democracy in the Netherlands*. Berkeley, CA: University of California Press.

Linz, Juan and Stepan, Alfred (1996) *Problems of Democratic Transition and Consolidation. Southern Europe, South America and Post-Communist Europe*. Baltimore, MD and London: Johns Hopkins University Press.

Mill, John Stuart (1977) 'Considerations on Representative Government', in John Stuart Mill,

Essays on Politics and Society. Toronto and London: University of Toronto Press/Routledge & Kegan Paul.

Nairn, Tom (1997) *Faces of Nationalism. Janus Revisited.* London and New York: Verso.

Rabushka, Alvin and Shepsle, Kenneth (1972)

Politics in Plural Societies: a Theory of Political Instability. Columbus, OH: Merrill.

Rousseau, Jean-Jacques (1972) *The Government of Poland.* Indianapolis, IN: Bobbs-Merrill.

Weber, Max (1968) *Economy and Society.* New York: Bedminster Press.

See also chapters

28 Contemporary Right-wing Extremism

Anders Widfeldt

THE EXTREME RIGHT – A GROWING POLITICAL FORCE

The 1990s saw a surge in the support and political significance of the extreme right. By the year 2001, parties regarded as belonging to the extreme right family are more important than ever in several West European countries. In Italy, the Alleanza Nazionale and the Lega Nord are members of a coalition government. In Austria, the Freedom Party is part of a two-party coalition government. In Norway, the Progress Party played a key role in allowing the formation of a three-party minority coalition government after the 2001 election. The Danish People's Party played a similar role when a non-socialist coalition government was formed after the election in November 2001, after its anti-immigration policies had influenced the preceding election campaign. In the Flemish-speaking part of Belgium, the Vlaams Blok is supported by around 15 per cent of the voters. Thus, while extreme right parties are not equally successful throughout Western Europe, they are a political force to be reckoned with. At the end of 2001 the extreme right was represented in the national parliaments of Austria, Belgium, Denmark, Finland, Italy, Norway and Switzerland.

But what are these parties? What do they believe in? The focus in this chapter will be on two issues. First is the ideology of the extreme right parties. A number of core features in the extreme right ideology will be discussed. It will be argued that it is possible to identify an ideological core of the extreme right. The second issue is conceptual. There is some considerable debate about the label 'extreme right', its appropriateness and whether there are better alternatives. However, it will be argued that 'extreme right' is the most suitable, or least unsuitable, designation. In connection with this, it will be argued that the inclusion of the word 'populist' in the label offers no extra clarification or precision, and that the links to traditional fascism and Nazism are too weak to justify the label neo-fascist, or neo-Nazi.

The growth of the extreme right as a political force has led to a large number of publications. However, for the purposes of this chapter, the work of the Dutch political scientist Cas Mudde is of primary importance. Mudde has discussed the problems of defining and labelling the extreme right party family. He has also made a number of comparative studies, which deal with theoretical as well as empirical aspects of the extreme right ideology. Therefore, this chapter will draw heavily, although not exclusively, on Mudde's work.

Before we continue, however, a few brief clarifications are needed. The chapter deals with the *ideology* of extreme right *parties*. The concept of ideology is multifaceted and subject to much academic debate. What we are dealing with here is *party ideology*, which will be understood as: 'A party's body of normative(-related) ideas about the nature of man and society as well as the organisation and purposes of society' (Mudde, 2000: 19).

Secondly, the chapter deals with extreme right *parties*. Political parties will be understood as groups that participate in elections with a serious ambition to get representatives elected (Sartori, 1976: 64). Thus, militant racist and neo-Nazi/fascist groups will not be taken into account. The chapter focuses on Western Europe and the situation as of the late 1990s and early 2000s.

THE CORE FEATURES OF THE MODERN EXTREME RIGHT IDEOLOGY

According to Mudde, the extreme right can be defined as a political ideology that contains a number of core features, namely nationalism, racism, xenophobia, anti-democracy and the advocacy of a strong state (Mudde, 1995: 206; Mudde, 2000: 178). These five features, which are derived from literature and not directly from programmes or other material from the extreme right parties themselves, provide a useful point of departure. *Nationalism* is the first, and perhaps most obvious, feature. In Roger Eatwell's words, nationalism is the 'common core doctrine' of the extreme right party family (Eatwell, 2000: 412). Mudde defines nationalism as '[t]he belief that the political unit (the state) and the cultural unit (the nation or ethnic community) should be congruent' (Mudde, 2000: 187).

Eatwell (2000: 412–13) makes the distinction between *liberal nationalism* and *holistic nationalism*. Liberal nationalism is tolerant, individualist, pluralist and based on citizenship and rights. Holistic nationalism is the opposite. It is often, although not always, based on the notion of an ethnic community,

which entails conversion or expulsion of those considered not to belong there. Eatwell argues that it is the holistic form of nationalism that can be found in the extreme right. In fact, according to Eatwell, this is what extreme right parties have in common.

Mudde's distinction between *state* (or *civic*) *nationalism*, on the one hand, and *ethnic nationalism*, on the other, is used as a criterion for separating extreme right parties into two sub-categories (Mudde, 2000: 180–2, 187). State nationalism is the more moderate variant, where membership of the nation is based on citizenship. It is possible for newcomers to enter the nation, and be converted into citizens. This is not possible according to ethnic nationalism. Here, membership of the nation is based on ethnicity, which means that it is not open to everyone.

Extreme right parties are often criticized for being *racist* and *xenophobic*. However, racism and xenophobia are often used loosely and interchangeably. Therefore, some conceptual clarity is needed. *Racism* has been defined by Mudde as '[t]he belief in natural (hereditary) and permanent differences between groups of people with the centrality of a hierarchy of races' (Mudde, 2000: 187). This is a fairly strict definition. However, Mudde (1995: 211) has also highlighted the distinction between 'new' racism, on the one hand, and 'classical' racism on the other. Classical racism represents the ambition to preserve racial purity and the belief that ethnic groups can be ordered into a hierarchy. New racism focuses on cultural differences instead of genetically inherited characteristics. New racists argue that cultures should be kept separate, but do not believe in an ethnic hierarchy. Hence, new racism is sometimes referred to as 'culturism' (see also Fennema, 1997: 478–9).

If the definitions of racism are applied strictly, open racism is unusual in the modern extreme right. Classical racism is very hard to find, while new racism is somewhat less uncommon. In practice the wording of party programmes and manifestos is often ambiguous. An example is the 1997 election programme of the Norwegian Progress Party, which includes the following paragraph:

> There is reason to fear that continued immigration of asylum seekers, only approximating the extent that has taken place in recent years, will lead to serious antagonisms between ethnic groups in Norway. It is not immoral to believe that reactions against this immigration should be taken into consideration, as a precaution against conflicts. Nor is it immoral to believe that precautions should be taken against too rapid changes in the unified character of our population. It is incorrect to call such views racism, as they are not based on notions of some races being more valuable than others. (Norwegian Progress Party, election programme 1997–2001, section 'Norge og Verden'. Translation by author. See also Hagelund, forthcoming.)

The key here is the words 'the unified character of our population' (*det helhetspreg som vår befolkning har*). If this is taken as meaning cultural characteristics, the statement could be regarded as a case of new racism, or culturism. If, on the other hand, it is taken as referring to genetical characteristics it could even be regarded as a case of classical racism, although the latter interpretation is negated by the subsequent denial of the existence of a racial hierarchy. What this example shows is that, in practice, it is very problematic to apply definitions of racism to actual texts or statements. Clear-cut examples, such as the statement by Jean-Marie Le Pen, leader of the French Front National, that 'some races are more equal than others' are rare (Hainsworth, 2000b: 25).

Xenophobia is a Greek word which means 'fear of strangers' (Mudde, 1995: 212). These strangers may, but need not, be ethnic groups. Xenophobia could be targeted at any group of people regarded as 'strange' or deviant. Thus, xenophobia can be fear of people from a foreign country, but also fears of groups such as sexual minorities or religions.

While racism and xenophobia often appear together, they are not synonymous. A racist does not, by definition, have to be xenophobic, and vice versa. It is, at least in theory, possible that the racist is against inter-racial marriages and believes that certain ethnic groups are more advanced than others, without having any fear of the groups considered as less advanced. Conversely, a person expressing xenophobic sentiment does not have to believe in a racial hierarchy, or even in the separation of cultures. Racism is ideological, while xenophobia is psychological. The racist claims that there are scientifically proven general differences between different groups of people, and that these differences should lead to political consequences such as repatriation or segregation. Xenophobia is more of an attitude, according to which the alien group is blamed for different societal ills (Betz, 1994: 172–3).

If racism is difficult to find in the modern extreme right, there is plenty of evidence of xenophobia against ethnic or religious groups. The Belgian Vlaams Blok is one of many examples, with its reference to immigrants as 'guest terrorists' and portrayal of Muslims as fifth columnists of an expansionist and cruel religion (Mudde, 2000: 103). An even more blatant example is a statement by a member of the Danish Progress Party: 'What is the difference between a Muslim and a rat? The rat does not receive social benefits' (*Berlingske Tidende*, 20 October 2001; http://www.berlingske.dk).

Exactly what *anti-democracy* means depends on what we mean by democracy. Mudde (1995: 214) argues that there are two main definitions of democracy – procedural and substantive. According to the former, democracy is a legal framework, with universal suffrage and free choice between candidates and/or parties. Anti-democracy in this sense could mean the advocacy of a dictatorship or a reduction in the right to vote. According to the substantive definition of democracy, all citizens are equal, and human rights and liberties are central. Seen this way anti-democracy would mean restrictions in, for example, freedom of expression and equality before the law.

It is rare to find anti-democracy openly expressed by modern extreme right parties.

This is certainly true if the procedural definition is applied. There are, however, parties such as the Front National in France, whose policy of national preference, by which citizens of French origin have priority to social benefits, housing, etc., could be regarded as anti-democratic in the substantive sense (Hainsworth, 2000b: 24–5). This is because they wish to base citizen rights on ethnic rather than citizenship criteria, meaning that not all citizens are treated as equal. Nevertheless, fully-fledged anti-democracy is rare in today's extreme right. To some extent this can be explained by tactical considerations, but also by legal restrictions. An often discussed example of a legal framework designed to curb anti-democracy is Germany, where parties on the extreme left as well as extreme right have been banned. Less drastic measures have also been taken, for example the decision in 1992 by the *Verfassungsschutz* to collect information on the Republikaner party (More, 1994).

While open anti-democracy is hard to find, the relationship between extreme right parties and democracy is not completely unproblematic. Anti-establishment sentiment is a key part of their rhetoric, and the democratic system is often described as corrupt and ineffective. The extreme right often ridicules the political system and the other political parties (Mudde, 1996b). Whether this amounts to actual anti-democracy is a different matter. There is not much to suggest that the modern extreme right parties want to abolish democracy in favour of a Nazi-style dictatorship. Such ideas may still exist in neo-Nazi sects, but not in parties with serious electoral ambitions (see, however, Schedler, 1996: 302–4, who argues that anti-political establishment parties can be regarded as 'semi-loyal' to democracy).

However, the extreme right often displays authoritarian tendencies. There is much emphasis on law and order, and criticism against the perceived permissiveness in modern society. The concern for law and order, often connected with demands for a stronger police force, fits well into Mudde's fifth and final core feature in the extreme right ideology, the advocacy of a *strong state*. Still, the commitment to a strong state is not unequivocal. There is, for example, a remarkable absence of militarism in the propaganda of the contemporary extreme right. A related problem is the view on the role of the state in the economy. The modern extreme right is often attributed with a market liberal and pro-capitalist approach (Taggart, 1995: 38). According to Kitschelt (1997: 5, 19–21), this is a key part in the winning formula of pro-capitalism and authoritarianism that extreme right parties need to adopt in order to be successful. A limited welfare state together with a strong law enforcement apparatus is certainly not an impossible combination. However, as Mudde has shown, this is hardly a core part of the modern extreme right ideology. In his study of five extreme right parties, he finds that the welfare state is not at all rejected, as long as the benefits are confined to the nation's 'own people' (Mudde, 2000: 174–5, 189). This policy, called *welfare chauvinism*, has grown in importance in the West European extreme right since Kitschelt's book was written.

Whether the growing significance of welfare chauvinism represents an ideological change or just a tactical shift is difficult to assess. It does not necessarily mean that the pro-capitalist position has been abandoned. Welfare chauvinism is not necessarily the same thing as redistribution of income and wealth, and the apparent turn towards more openness to the welfare state does not appear to be accompanied by a general reassessment of economic principles.

To sum up, none of the five core features discussed in this section is completely unproblematic. As has been argued, modern extreme right parties can hardly be called racist or anti-democratic. This is supported by Mudde's study of five extreme right parties (the German Republicans and DVU, the Dutch Centre Democrats and CP'86 and the Belgian Vlaams Blok). He found that they have a common ideological core, which consists of nationalism, xenophobia, welfare chauvinism and law and order (Mudde, 2000: 177). Thus there is some, but not total, overlap between the five literature-based core features and the components of the common ideological core found in the parties analysed by Mudde. The overlap consists of nationalism, xenophobia and law and order (the latter being a key characteristic of the strong state). Anti-democracy and racism are among the literature-based core features, but are not found in the common ideological core of the five studied parties. One component of the common ideological core, welfare chauvinism, is not included among the literature-based core features, unless it can be regarded as connected to the advocacy of a strong state.

Thus, there are some remaining ambiguities regarding the contents of the ideology of modern extreme right parties. However, Mudde's work is an important contribution. The picture is beginning to clear. True, the ideological characteristics attributed to extreme right parties are not unique to them. Nationalism and xenophobia, the most clear-cut ideological characteristics, appear in other parties (even the French Communist Party; see Kitschelt, 1997: 98). However, what makes the extreme right distinctive is that nationalism and xenophobia are core components of the party ideology, in other words, components that are found in the vast majority of extreme right parties, and that form a significant part of their general political outlook. Therefore, Mudde concludes that extreme right parties have an ideological core which is distinct from possible borderline ideologies such as left-wing extremism and neo-conservatism (Mudde, 2000: 178–9).

IS 'EXTREME RIGHT' AN APPROPRIATE LABEL?

One of the controversies about the extreme right is whether it is really an appropriate label for the parties dealt with here. There are several alternatives, such as 'neo-fascist/ Nazi', '(new) radical right', 'far right', 'populist right' or 'new populist', often with derivations. This array of designations raises several questions. One is the link between today's extreme right parties and traditional fascism. According to one school of thought, the post-war extreme right is a continuation of the inter-war fascist and Nazi movements (Mudde, 1995: 204–5; Kitschelt, 1997: 1). It is indeed true that some of today's extreme right parties have direct or indirect links with inter-war fascism. The most obvious example is the Italian Alleanza Nazionale, which was formed under the name Movimento Sociale Italiano (MSI) in 1946, as a successor of Mussolini's fascist party. The MSI never tried to hide its fascist links, but in 1995, when it changed its name to Alleanza Nazionale, it declared that the era of fascism was over. Traditional fascism lives on in the small MSI-Fiamma Tricolore, which defected from Alleanza Nazionale in protest against the reorientation. Less direct, but traceable, links can be found in, for example, the German National Democrats (NPD) and the British National Party (Ignazi, 1992: 9–10).

However, the vast majority of today's extreme right parties have no historical or ideological links to 'old' fascism. Indeed, links to inter-war fascism are by no means a reliable indicator of how radical a party is today. After the reorientation in 1995, the Alleanza Nazionale has been comparatively moderate in its rhetoric and policies, careful to maintain its respectability. At the same time, some parties that cannot be traced back to inter-war fascist organizations are very radical in their hostility to ethnic minorities. An example is the Front National in France, with its advocacy of a national preference policy, mentioned above.

The lack of historical links is one reason why 'neo-fascist' or 'neo-Nazi' are not particularly well-chosen labels. Another reason is ideological. Fascism and Nazism still exist in several militant racist groups throughout Europe and the USA. However, a comparison between the ideology of modern extreme right parties on the one hand and traditional fascism and Nazism on the other suggests important differences. The main features of fascist ideology are: strong nationalism, an organic perspective of state and nation, corporatism, racism, anti-democracy, authoritarianism and a leadership cult. Nazism shares these features but is usually attributed a more aggressive form of racism. The main difference between fascism and Nazism is often regarded to be the latter's fierce anti-semitism (for more elaborate discussions on fascism and Nazism see, for example, Sternhell, 1979; Neocleous, 1997; and Renton, 1999).

Fascism and Nazism are not completely distinct from the modern extreme right ideology. Most importantly, nationalism is a core feature in the new as well as old extreme right variants. Still, the differences outweigh the similarities. Modern extreme right parties may be strongly nationalist but their form of nationalism is not expansionist or militaristic. They do not view the nation as an organism and do not advocate the state being re-organized according to corporatist principles. They may be led by charismatic personalities but there is no leadership cult comparable to the one associated with the likes of Hitler and Mussolini. Elements of racism can be found in some modern extreme right parties but it is difficult to find examples of classical racism, with its emphasis on a biologically defined racial hierarchy. As for anti-semitism, there are examples of modern extreme right parties dabbling with anti-Jewish statements, but clear-cut cases of anti-semitic rhetoric or policies are rare (Hainsworth, 2000a: 10). Another important difference is the perspective on democracy. Modern extreme right parties, with their mockery of democratic institutions and 'anti-establishment' rhetoric, can hardly claim to be loyal defenders of democracy. However, they have shown no signs of wanting to overthrow the democratic system in favour of a dictatorship, something which was one of the key characteristics of inter-war fascist and Nazi movements. Thus, while there are some ideological similarities and, in some cases, historical links, between

the modern extreme right and classical fascism and Nazism, the differences outweigh the similarities. Admittedly, some modern extreme right parties are more radical than others. There are, indeed, groups and movements that continue the fascist and Nazi traditions. Still, there is not much evidence of classical fascism and Nazism surviving in modern political parties. Therefore, it is not justified to label today's extreme right parties 'neo-fascist' or 'neo-Nazi'.

Another possibility is to use or include the word *'populist'*. Hans-Georg Betz (1998: 4) argues that a definition of populism must consist of three core elements. First, the *structure of argumentation*. Populists claim that there are simple solutions to societal problems. They believe in 'common sense' as superior to technocracy and expertise. Populists also argue that common sense can be found in the 'common man', but that he has not been given the chance to use it. The second core element is the *political style and strategy* of populism. Populists claim to speak for ordinary people, whose opinions, sentiments and demands have not been articulated. They also have a set of clearly defined enemies. It is often easier to determine what, and whom, populists oppose, than what they are in favour of. When they are in favour of something, it is often referred to in vague terms. The vagueness is illustrated by the concept of the *heartland* (Taggart, 2000: 95–8). The 'heartland' is not a word used by populists themselves, but a term that captures a mythical ideal existence for which populists yearn. It can, for example, be the one's country 'as it once was', before it – allegedly – was destroyed by politicians, immigrants or other alien forces.

The third core element of populism is, according to Betz, *ideological*. The populist ideology consists of a producer ethic based on individual effort. Populists believe in a fundamental harmony of interests, which is the basis of their belief in democracy and egalitarianism. However, populists believe that the existing political and economic system serves only the few at the expense of the many.

Then, why not call the parties in question 'populist'? Certainly, any of the modern extreme right parties share several of the characteristics of populism outlined above. The problem is that, as should already be apparent, populism is something more than an ideology. Indeed, the ideological element of populism identified by Betz is not universally accepted. There is much to suggest that the most important aspects of populism are not ideological but a form of political style and appeal (Canovan, 1999: 3). The populist appeal can appear in many ideological shapes: left, right, centre, ecological or something else. Thus, it is difficult to argue that the different forms of populism contain common ideological characteristics.

This is a problem when we are looking for a suitable label for the parties dealt with in this chapter. The purpose of such a search is to be able to find them a place among other groups of political parties or 'party families' (von Beyme, 1985: 29–31). In other words, we wish to be able to classify the parties in question in the same way as other parties are classified as socialist, conservative, liberal, etc. There are several possible criteria for the classification of parties (Mudde, 2000: 2–5; Gallagher et al., 2001: 202–3), but it can be argued that party ideology is the most appropriate (Mudde, 2000: 5). Thus, if we accept party ideology as the criterion for classification, 'populist' is not a particularly useful term.

Of course, the designation 'extreme right' also has its problems. First, the word 'extreme' can be questioned. It is generally assumed that the parties we are dealing with here are extreme compared to other parties, although this assumption has not been backed by comparative empirical evidence. But political extremism can also have another meaning. According to the 'extremism-theoretical' school, extremists on the left as well right reject democracy (Mudde, 1996a: 242–3; Mudde, 2000: 177; see also Fennema,

1997: 481–6). The parties we are talking about here cannot be classed as extremist in this sense, since they, as already mentioned, do not want to overthrow democracy.

Secondly, are the parties in question really to the right? While ideological features such as nationalism and xenophobia can be argued to be rightist rather than leftist, that is not the whole story. Extreme right parties are by no means necessarily to the right in economic terms. In some cases they are, or have been, strongly pro-capitalist. However, as has been argued above, this is not a core feature of the extreme right ideology. Thus, 'extreme right' is hardly an ideal choice of words. The problem is that none of the possible alternatives is better. As we have seen, labels including 'fascist', 'Nazi' or 'populist' have significant problems. Other possibilities, such as '(new) radical right' and 'far right' offer little extra information or precision. Mudde's (2000: 180) conclusion is that we may just as well stick to the term 'extreme right', as there is no better alternative. For some reason, there seems to be a reasonably general understanding of what 'extreme right' entails, and overall agreement about which parties should be included under this heading (for a list of such parties, see Mudde, 2000: 185–6).

CONCLUSION

In this chapter it has been argued that there is a family of political parties that can be labelled 'extreme right'. Just like any other party family, its defining characteristics are ideological. The extreme right ideology consists of a number of features that, one by one, are not necessarily unique in comparison to parties belonging to other families. Taken together, however, they form a core that makes the extreme right a distinctive group. This is an important assertion. The extreme right is not merely a more extreme form of conservatism. Nor is it just another form of extremism which can be classified together with, for example, radical leftists or ecologists. It is a group of parties that occupy their own unique position in the ideological space.

That it is a worthwhile exercise to study this group of parties is an understatement. The extreme right is no longer a fringe phenomenon. Although there are variations across Europe, the overall situation is that the extreme right party family is growing in electoral strength and political significance. This could well turn out to be one of the most significant recent ongoing changes in Western Europe. Parties whose ideological core includes nationalism and xenophobia look like having obtained an established position in several party systems. Other parties are beginning to have to treat the extreme right as a competitor with serious vote-winning potential. It is not particularly far-fetched to assume that this could have long-term implications for the general political climate. At the same time, it is important to note that this political challenge does not come only from political parties. There are other groups and movements on the extreme right which provide at least as serious a challenge. Racist and neo-Nazi/fascist groups have an elaborate agenda to cause havoc and distress, with the ultimate aim of destabilizing democracy. They sometimes revert to terrorist methods, and members of racist organizations have been convicted of crimes, including murder (Bjørgo, 1995; for more recent information refer to the website of the European Monitoring Centre on Racism and Xenophobia, EUMC; http://eumc.eu.int/).

It may not be justified to equate the extreme right party family with Nazi, fascist and militant racist groups. As has been argued above, the tag 'fascist' or 'Nazi' is not appropriate for today's extreme right parties; at least not as a collective party family name. Neo-Nazi and fascist groups, on the other hand, are often labelled as such out of their own choice. Extreme right parties have agreed to play according to the political and democratic rules, even if they sometimes do so grudgingly. The non-partisan groups have as their main purpose to break the rules. On the other hand, there are some similarities. There are those who would argue that the non-partisan groups on the extreme right are part of the same political force as the extreme right parties. Certainly, they share important political values and characteristics, such as their lack of respect for democracy and their hostility to multiculturalism. There are also some cases where connections between extreme right parties and openly neo-fascist/Nazi groups have been shown to exist, for example in the German NPD (Backer, 2000: 113).

Regardless of how these differences and similarities are assessed, parties as well as other groups on the extreme right provide a challenge which deserves continued attention, by students and scholars as well as by the general public. In order to understand contemporary politics it is becoming increasingly necessary to understand the extreme right.

Summary

- The term 'extreme right' is problematic since its ideological components are not necessarily extreme nor unambiguously to the right.
- The extreme right ideology contains five core features: nationalism, racism, xenophobia, anti-democracy and a strong state.

- Nationalism is a key element in the extreme right ideology. Distinction can be made between ethnic and state (civic) nationalism, where the former is more extreme.
- Racism and xenophobia often appear together but they are not synonymous. Racism is ideological, while xenophobia is more of an attitude.
- Modern extreme right parties are hardly respectful of democracy but are not anti-democratic in the sense that they want to overthrow democracy in favour of another form of government.
- Modern extreme right parties place heavy emphasis on law and order. However, they are not unequivocally in favour of a strong state.
- Modern extreme right parties are often attributed with strong market liberalism. However, this is not a defining characteristic. Many extreme right parties are welfare chauvinist, which means that they advocate a welfare state, as long as the benefits are confined to the nation's 'own people'.
- The modern extreme right parties are ideologically distinct from classical fascism and Nazism.
- Populism is not primarily an ideological concept, and is therefore not an appropriate label when classifying parties according to ideology.
- Therefore, it is still defensible to use the label 'extreme right', if only because there are no better alternatives.

TUTORIAL QUESTIONS

1. **What are the similarities and differences between the modern extreme right ideology, on the one hand, and fascism and Nazism, on the other?**

2. **How can the use of the label 'extreme right' be justified?**

3. **According to Mudde, the extreme right ideology contains five core features: nationalism, racism, xenophobia, anti-democracy and a strong state. Do you agree that these are the most central ingredients? Should one or more of them be omitted? Should any other element be included?**

FURTHER READING

For further study on the modern extreme right ideology it is impossible to avoid Cas Mudde's work. The best overview can be found in *The Ideology of the Extreme Right* (Manchester: Manchester University Press, 2000). Highly recommended also is his article 'Right-wing

Extremism Analyzed: a Comparative Analysis of Three Alleged Right-wing Extremist Parties (NPD, NDP, CP'86)', in *European Journal of Political Research*, **2**: 203–24.

Paul Taggart (2000) *Populism* (Buckingham and Philadelphia, PA: Open University Press) provides a theoretical discussion on populism.

Herbert Kitschelt with A.J. Mc Cann (1997) *The Radical Right in Western Europe* (Ann Arbor, MI: Michigan University Press, first paperback edition), is theoretically ambitious and offers a broad comparative analysis on the conditions for extreme right success.

Another comparative piece is Hans-Georg Betz (1994) *Radical Right-wing Populism in Western Europe* (Basingstoke: Macmillan). It is very readable, but possibly getting somewhat dated.

Among many anthologies with country-specific chapters on extreme right parties, Paul Hainsworth (ed.) (2000) *The Politics of the Extreme Right: from the Margins to the Mainstream* (London: Pinter) and Hans-Georg Betz and Stefan Immerfall (eds) (1998) *The New Politics of the Right: Neo-populist Parties and Movements in Established Democracies* (Basingstoke: Macmillan) are recommended.

REFERENCES

Backer, S. (2000) 'Right-wing Extremism in Unified Germany', in Paul Hainsworth (ed.), *The Politics of the Extreme Right: from the Margins to the Mainstream*. London: Pinter, pp. 87–120.

Betz, H.-G. (1994) *Radical Right-wing Populism in Western Europe*. Basingstoke and London: Macmillan.

Betz, H.-G. (1998) 'Introduction', in H.-G. Betz and S. Immerfall (eds), *The New Politics of the Right: Neo-populist Parties and Movements in Established Democracies*. Basingstoke and London: Macmillan, pp. 1–10.

von Beyme, K. (1985) *Political Parties in Western Democracies*. Aldershot: Gower.

Bjørgo, T. (ed.) (1995) 'Terror from the extreme Right'. Special issue of the journal *Terrorism and Political Violence*, **7**(1).

Canovan, M. (1999) 'Trust the People! Populism and the Two Faces of Democracy', *Political Studies*, **47**, 2–16.

Eatwell, R. (2000) 'The Rebirth of the Extreme Right in Western Europe?', *Parliamentary Affairs*, **53**: 407–25.

Fennema, M. (1997) 'Some Conceptual Issues and Problems in the Comparison of Anti-Immigrant Parties in Western Europe', *Party Politics*, **3**: 473–92.

Gallagher, M., Laver, M. and Mair, P. (2001) *Representative Government in Western Europe: Institutions, Parties and Governments*. New York: McGraw-Hill.

Hagelund, A. (forthcoming) 'A Matter of Decency? The Progress Party in Norwegian Immigration Politics', *Journal of Ethnic and Migration Studies*, **29**.

Hainsworth, P. (2000a) 'Introduction: the Extreme Right', in Paul Hainsworth (ed.), *The Politics of the Extreme Right: from the Margins to the Mainstream*. London: Pinter, pp. 1–17.

Hainsworth, P. (2000b) 'The Front National: from Ascendancy to Fragmentation on the French Extreme Right', in Paul Hainsworth (ed.), *The Politics of the Extreme Right: from the Margins to the Mainstream*. London: Pinter, pp. 18–32.

Ignazi, P. (1992) 'The Silent Counter-Revolution: Hypotheses on the Emergence of Extreme

Right-wing Parties in Europe', *European Journal of Political Research*, **22**: 3–34.

Kitschelt, H. with A.J. McCann (1997) *The Radical Right in Western Europe*. Ann Arbor, MI: Michigan University Press (first paperback edition).

More, G. (1994) 'Undercover Surveillance of the Republikaner Party: Protecting a Militant Democracy or Discrediting a Political Rival?', *German Politics*, **3**: 284–92.

Mudde, C. (1995) 'Right-wing Extremism Analyzed: a Comparative Analysis of the Ideologies of Three Alleged Right-wing Extremist Parties (NPD, NDP, CP'86)', *European Journal of Political Research*, **27**: 203–24.

Mudde, C. (1996a) 'The War of the Words: Defining the Extreme Right Party Family', *West European Politics*, **19**: 225–48.

Mudde, C. (1996b) 'The Paradox of the Anti-party Party: Insights from the Extreme Right', *Party Politics*, **2**: 265–76.

Mudde, C. (2000) *The Ideology of the Extreme Right*. Manchester: Manchester University Press.

Neocleous, M. (1997) *Fascism*. Buckingham and Philadelphia, PA: Open University Press.

Norwegian Progress Party, election programme 1997–2001, in *Vi vil..! Norske partiprogrammer 1884–2001, versjon 1.1* (CD-Rom with Norwegian party programmes and manifestos). Bergen: Norsk Samfunnsvitenskapelig Datatjeneste (NSD).

Renton, D. (1999) *Fascism. Theory and Practice*. London and Sterling, VA: Pluto Press.

Sartori, G. (1976) *Parties and Party Systems: a Framework for Analysis*. Cambridge: Cambridge University Press.

Schedler, A. (1996) 'Anti-Political Establishment Parties', *Party Politics*, **2**: 291–312.

Sternhell, Z. (1979) 'Fascist Ideology', in Walter Laqueur (ed.), *Fascism: a Reader's Guide*. Harmondsworth: Penguin/Pelican, pp. 325–406.

Taggart, P.A. (1995) 'New populist parties in Western Europe', *West European Politics*, **18**: 34–51.

Taggart, P.A. (2000) *Populism*. Buckingham and Philadelphia, PA: Open University Press.

See also chapters

29 Feminism

Kimberly Hutchings

Feminism is a political ideology with a variety of distinct strands (Whelehan, 1995). However, all feminist viewpoints are based in some way on the argument that women are of equal significance to men when it comes to formulating political goals and values. This does not necessarily mean that all feminists think that men and women have the same goals and values or that men and women should always be treated as if they are the same. It is important to note that feminist democratic theory has been focused largely on criticizing and offering alternatives to liberal democracy. This is because encounters between feminist movements and democratic ideas and institutions have been most common in the context of liberal democratic regimes.

Liberal feminism shares the basic assumptions of liberalism but argues that there has been a deep inconsistency in the application of liberal individual rights (including political rights) to women (Whelehan, 1995: 25–43). For liberal feminists the reason why there has been this inconsistency is to do with bias and prejudice against women which has its roots in pre-modern, *patriarchal* forms of thinking and social order. The patriarchal view that women are inferior to men is, it is claimed, demonstrably irrational. For liberal feminism, when it comes to the public realms of law, politics and employment, there is no significant difference between women and men. The message of liberal feminism is probably best formulated as that of 'equal rights for women'. A famous early articulation of this argument was made by Mary Wollstonecraft in her book *A Vindication of the Rights of Women* (1792/1975). Movements such as the suffragette movement in the early years of the twentieth century in the UK and elsewhere, campaigning for women's right to vote, were firmly based on the idea that men and women were equal. The growth of the feminist movement in western countries in the 1960s was also largely of a liberal feminist kind, calling for equality of treatment for women within the liberal democratic and welfare state. Outcomes such as equal pay and anti-sex discrimination legislation are examples of the goals of this kind of feminism. It looks forward to a world in which genuine equal opportunities apply for women in the public sphere (Friedan, 1965; Richards, 1982).

Radical feminism argues that liberal feminism overlooks the fact that modern liberal democracies are still inherently patriarchal (Whelehan, 1995: 67–87). In other words, the ways in which women are disadvantaged or excluded in contemporary democracies are not just a historical leftover, but are part of the structure of liberal society and its reliance on a division between the private realm of family and personal relations and the public realm of legal, social, economic and political relations. According to this view, the achievement of equal rights does not in itself deal with the basic roots of the subordination of women. It is argued that these roots are located not in the public realm of law, politics and employment but in the organization and ideology of the private realm of family, sex, sexuality, reproduction and domestic work. In addition, according to radical feminists, the prevailing male-biased ideology enforces the notion that women are naturally different from, and inferior to, men. As long as women give birth and take primary responsibility for the care of children and family they are excluded from the masculine world of the public sphere, even if they may have equal rights on paper to participate. The feminist politics inspired by radical feminism draws attention to the importance of differences between men and women and argues for the need to address the power relations inherent in the split between public (masculine) and private (feminine) spheres and roles. This leads to a focus in practice on dealing with issues such as domestic violence or rape. In addition, radical feminists have been concerned to challenge sexist ideologies which label women as inferior beings, one example of this is the radical feminist campaign against the denigration of women as 'sex objects' in pornography (Mackinnon, 1987; Dworkin, 1988).

WHAT'S WRONG WITH LIBERAL DEMOCRACY FROM A FEMINIST PERSPECTIVE?

Feminist critics of liberal democracy, whether liberal or radical, begin with the claim that liberal democracy excludes women and fails adequately to represent them and respond to their needs and interests. This critique is grounded on empirical evidence from existing liberal democracies. Feminist critics point to the fact that, with a few exceptions (mainly located in the social democratic Nordic countries), the proportion of women in politics in liberal democracies is far lower than the proportion of women in the population as a whole. Many liberal democracies did not even give women the vote until relatively late

in their evolution. Feminist critics also point to the fact that women's interests have often been neglected in the formation and implementation of legislation within liberal democracies, and that it is a struggle to get and to keep issues of particular importance to women high on the political agenda. One example of this would be the specific problems women face in combining family life with paid employment, which feminists argue are neglected in employment and social security legislation which takes a male head of household as the norm. It should be apparent that the feminist critique of liberal democracy has two aspects to it: on the one hand, it is to do with procedural issues and the relative absence of women among political activists and decision-makers; on the other hand, it is to do with substantive objections to the outcomes of policy-making and legislation in male-dominated liberal democracies.

For liberal feminists the lack of women in politics can be explained only on the grounds of the continuing existence of unfair barriers or prejudices against them, since it is axiomatic for liberal feminists that there is nothing inherent in women which would make them less able to be active citizens and politicians than men. The assumption of liberal feminists is that the struggle to include more women in politics is a stage on the way to a position in which a genuine level playing field will have been established and the sex of the politician will become irrelevant. Similarly, for liberal feminists there is no necessary connection between liberal democracy and the neglect of women's interests. To the extent that liberal democracies fail in this respect, there must still be illiberal institutional and ideological leftovers from earlier times which are distorting the ways in which liberal democracy should work.

Radical feminists draw attention to the ways in which the norms inherent in liberal conceptions of democracy and citizenship, although they are presented as gender-neutral, are actually *masculinist*. In other words, they reflect assumptions which fit with male lives and with values which are traditionally associated with men. This criticism of liberal democracy goes deeper than the argument that democratic participation fits more easily with most men's life-style than with most women's, though this can be seen as one effect of liberal democracy's masculinism. At a more fundamental level, it is argued that the concept of the citizen in liberal democracies is of an 'unencumbered self', an independent and rational being who voluntarily 'contracts in' to political society. He may have dependants (wife, child, servants) but is never himself envisaged either as dependent or as pregnant. This way of thinking about citizenship is one which puts the status of those who are dependent, including women, into doubt. The most famous formulation of this feminist critique of liberal conceptions of citizenship can be found in Carole Pateman's critical reading of the idea of the 'social contract' in the work of thinkers such as Locke, who is one of the founding fathers of liberal political thought (Pateman, 1988). According to Pateman, if you read the canonic texts of liberalism carefully, you find that the social contract upon which political society is founded is actually a contract between men. Women are included in the liberal polity with an ambiguous status in which they are judged not fully capable of consent in their relations with men. The slogan of the French Revolution in 1789 was 'Liberty, Equality, Fraternity'. Pateman argues that the meaning of 'fraternity' should be taken literally – sisters are not included (Pateman, 1988; see also Wollstonecraft, 1792/1975).

In conjunction with this view of the nature of citizens is a view about the values appropriate to citizenship and to political participation. According to radical feminist criticisms of liberal democracy, these values give priority to abstract and universal principles and goals such as human rights and national self-determination and denigrate values associated with the private sphere of dependence and the specific responsibilities involved in relationships of love and nurture. For radical feminists, the shortcomings of liberal democracy both procedurally and substantively are rooted in liberal democracy itself, and not an unfortunate distortion of it.

WHAT SHOULD BE DONE?

It is clear from the outline of liberal and radical feminisms given above that they have quite distinct philosophical starting points and political programmes. However, in spite of these differences, if we look at the history of liberal and radical feminist critiques of liberal democracy, we see that there is a tendency for the two strands to come together. In practice, liberal reform transmutes into a more radical political programme as the difficulties of including women within the liberal polity on the same terms as men become apparent. At the same time, as Anne Phillips has argued, the revolutionary programme of radical feminism, which begins with the rejection of liberal democracy, transmutes over time into the more reformist agenda of a politics of presence (Phillips, 1993, 1995).

Faced with the fact of the low levels of participation of women in politics, the first step for a liberal feminist would be to make sure there were no legal blocks to women's participation. Women must have equal rights to vote, to stand for election, to belong to political parties, trade unions and so on. If these rights are in place, then there must be other kinds of barrier or prejudice in operation which are denying women equal opportunities. The liberal feminist therefore looks at other rights, such as rights to work and to equal pay, which may also form blocks to women's capacity to participate in the public sphere. If these rights are in place, then there must be other kinds of barrier at work, perhaps at the level of ideology, in which women are being discriminated against in practice (for instance in candidate selection processes) because it is assumed that women are less capable than men, or that a politician 'needs a wife'. Alternatively, it may be that the 'double burden' of family as well as employment responsibilities is preventing women from acting on their rights. Yet again, the explanation could be that women are not putting themselves forward because they lack confidence in their own abilities as politicians or, for instance, because they could not combine their family responsibilities with the hours of work institutionalized in the Westminster parliament.

Once the liberal feminist asks the question of why it is that women do not participate in democratic politics to the same extent as men it is difficult for her not to find her analysis pushed beyond the level of formal equality of right for individuals to a set of substantive issues about women's (as a group) structural position within liberal polities and the ideological assumptions that are associated with that position. Although the liberal feminist begins from the conviction of women's essential sameness to men as rational agents, she finds herself perpetually confronted with women's difference and the perception of that difference in explaining why it is that women are not present in democratic politics in equal numbers to men.

Liberal feminists are committed to the idea of equal opportunities as the key to a genuinely inclusive politics. However, if equal opportunities involve more than equality of formal rights to inclusion in politics, then liberal feminists find themselves engaged in arguing for strategies for inclusion targeted at the informal but deeply embedded ways in which women are excluded. In some cases this poses no problems for a continuing fundamental commitment to liberal ideals. For instance, monitoring to make sure equal opportunities practices are followed in selection and election processes, or promoting the ideal of political participation for women through organizations like the 300 Group (which aims for equal numbers of women and men in the Westminster parliament) would both be acceptable on liberal grounds. However, things become more difficult for liberal feminists when policies of positive discrimination in selection and election processes are suggested (such as all-women

shortlists for selection of candidates or formal quotas). Things become more difficult still, from the point of view of the liberal acceptance of the split between public and private spheres, when the argument is made (on liberal grounds) that what is needed is a complete reform of the division of labour within the family (Okin, 1989). If one adopts either of these recommendations, one is attributing deep significance to the ways in which women are different from men. In the former case, one is giving special treatment to women to compensate them for the lack of a genuinely 'level playing field', which is something which cuts against the liberal emphasis on the need to treat individuals without discrimination on grounds of sex. In the latter case, one is going against a crucial aspect of liberal ideology which has been to limit interference of government into the private sphere. In other words, these ways of addressing women's exclusion from the political sphere justify non-liberal means as a way of arriving at the liberal end of all individuals being able to be treated equally (the same).

It is at this point that radical feminists criticize liberal feminists for not following through the implications of their own analysis and for remaining attached to a view of equality as sameness. For radical feminists, women's difference not only explains the reasons for their political exclusion, but also provides a resource for re-thinking democracy along non-liberal lines. The grounding insight of second-wave feminism, that the 'personal is political', directed feminist attention to relations of power in operation within reproduction, family and work and away from formal political institutions. In the earlier days of second-wave feminism, radical feminism was characterized by a distrust of the idea of representation and by a commitment to direct, participatory models of democracy in terms of the ways in which feminist groups themselves were organized and made decisions. The most common feature of suggestions for change emerging from radical feminist re-thinking of democracy involve some kind of *reversal* of the priority given to the principles, goals and practices of the public sphere of politics over those characteristic of the private sphere. This feminist politics of reversal can take various forms. Some well-known examples challenge the framework of liberal democratic thought altogether and are associated with a radical politics of resistance and subversion or with the rejection of liberal democracy as an inherently masculinist enterprise (Mackinnon, 1987; Pateman, 1988). However, as Phillips points out, this more radical rejection of liberal democracy has been succeeded by a rather different approach, one which focuses on re-thinking notions of citizenship along alternative lines (Phillips, 1993). There are two broad directions in which this re-thinking has proceeded within feminism: first, in relation to an ethic of care; secondly, in a feminist return to a civic republican tradition in thinking about citizenship and participation.

Feminist attempts to re-think the meaning of citizenship and political participation from the perspective of the values inherent in caring (traditionally private/dependence) as opposed to contractual (traditionally public/independence) relations remain part of the tradition of a feminist politics of reversal. Examples of such work include Tronto's, which draws attention to the 'privileged irresponsibility' of those beings who approximate most closely to the traditional liberal view of the independent citizen and argues for the need to recognize the actual inequalities and dependencies which are masked by liberal assumptions about independent selves (Tronto, 1993). The idea of 'privileged irresponsibility' refers to the position of citizens who are cared for by others in terms of their material and emotional needs and are therefore free to operate independently within the public sphere. The old-fashioned view that every politician 'needs a wife' is a reflection of the reality in which people with power (often men) depend on people without power (often women). But the state does not recognize this dependence or reward the carers who are making activity in political life possible. Tronto's argument requires both that the reality of inequality between citizens (often between male and female citizens) is addressed rather than airbrushed out of the picture, and also points to the crucial role played by practices associated with the private sphere in underpinning democratic politics. Tronto argues that care needs to be valued as an essential practice and should be given explicit recognition in policy-making within liberal democratic states.

Tronto's arguments have recently been taken further by Mackay (Mackay, 2001), who picks up on the idea that caring practice involves values and virtues which sustain democratic politics. In Mackay's case this leads her to examine the ways in which women in politics both bring different values to bear on politics and policy-making and also practise democratic politics in a distinctive way. Specifically, Mackay is interested in the ways in which some of the experience and know-how associated with caring work in the private sphere are manifested in the day-to-day practice of women politicians (Mackay, 2001: 172). Mackay concludes that there is evidence that the ways in which women practise democratic politics are different from those of men, and that women do draw on the resources of their private sphere experience in their public role as political activists. For Mackay, therefore, the presence of women in politics itself becomes a route to improving and enriching the nature of democracy within existing liberal democratic states.

The development of an ideal of citizenship and participation oriented by the values and virtues of care in feminist theory has been accompanied by a rather different alternative feminist re-thinking of citizenship and participation within the liberal democratic state. This development returns feminism to the civic republican tradition of thinking about politics, which has also been recently revived in communitarian thinking (Young, 1990, 2001; Mouffe, 1992; Phillips, 1995). The feminist critique of liberal democracy, in both liberal and radical forms, was originally focused on the ways in which women were excluded from politics and the ways in which liberal democracies failed to recognize and respond to women's specific interests and needs at the level of substantive outcomes of the political process. In the case of both liberal and radical feminism, the problem with liberal democracy was not the exclusion of women from participation in politics in itself, but that that lack of participation either reflected or perpetuated a situation in which women's interests and needs were overlooked and actively discriminated against. The recent turn of feminist theory to the civic republican tradition resurrects the ancient idea that participation in politics is a good in and of itself, not simply in terms of its consequences. Whereas liberal conceptions of citizenship are grounded in the idea of rights and protections enjoyed by the citizen as an individual, republican conceptions of citizenship are grounded in the idea of the intrinsic value of acting in the public realm to articulate and further common ends which transcend any individual interest. Rather than political goals being given in advance and rooted in either individual or collective (women's) identity, common goals emerge within the activity of political deliberation and action.

The civic republican turn in feminist thinking is in part a reaction to the old radical feminist politics of reversal. One of the most important developments, both theoretically and practically, within the feminist movement since the beginning of second-wave feminism has been the argument over whether the idea of 'women' as a collective category makes any sense. Both liberal and radical feminism rest on claiming the political significance of shared identities. In the case of liberal feminism, it is the identification of women as human and in all relevant respects the same as men which is crucial. In the case of radical feminism, it is the inherent difference of women from men (whether biologically or socially grounded) which is the lynchpin of the analysis of women's oppression. Within the women's movement since the 1970s, the idea that women can be

grouped together as being essentially the same has come under increasing criticism. In particular, lesbian feminists and black feminists have argued that the category of women works as an exclusive norm in radical feminism much as the category of human does in liberalism. In other words, 'women' actually refers to heterosexual white women and their defining experiences and has nothing to say about women who do not fit this norm (hooks, 1982; Whelehan, 1995: 88–105, 106–12). Over time, feminists have responded to this critique of the category 'women' by acknowledging a plurality of identities and interests among women and feminists and by incorporating that acknowledgement in responses to questions such as those involving appropriate forms of democracy for feminists.

It is somewhat ironic that feminists have returned to civic republican ideals of citizenship since these have traditionally been even more exclusive of women than liberal ones. In the ancient world, women were deemed unfit for citizenship and participation in the *demos* because of their confinement to the private sphere and, in particular, because of the fact they could not bear arms and fight for the protection of the political realm. In fact, the feminist take-up of this more participatory view of citizenship has tended also to be modified by an attachment to liberal ideals of individual rights in which all adults are deemed to have equal rights of participation (to speak and be heard) in the public sphere. Here feminists have come to engage in debates about the ideal of 'deliberative democracy' which have been most famously forwarded by Habermas (Habermas, 1992; Phillips, 1995; Young, 2001). Some feminist thinkers, such as Benhabib, have incorporated elements of the ideal of care along with civic republicanism and deliberative democracy in order to formulate an adequate democratic ideal (Benhabib, 1992, 1996). This kind of synthesis exemplifies the extent to which the programmes of liberal and radical feminism in relation to liberal democracy have become modified over time and now tend to converge on questions of presence and procedure as opposed to more substantial assertions about the nature of women's needs and interests (Phillips, 1995).

CONCLUSION

The contribution of feminism to understanding democracy is clearly one that overlaps with that of other critical ideological traditions, from Marxism to communitarianism. However, there are certain specific insights that feminism provides which can be argued to be of particular value. Above all, feminism provides a reminder that equality and rights at the level of formal, legal relations are not in themselves enough to ensure a kind of democracy which is inclusive of all citizens. This can be ensured only if democracy is sensitive to systematic ways in which individuals are excluded or inhibited from democratic participation by structures such as the division between the private and the public spheres. The second lesson of feminist inter-

rogations of liberal democracy, therefore, is the importance of enabling equal participation for all citizens, even if this may involve treating some citizens differently. The radical feminist critique of liberal feminism insists that equality cannot be equated with sameness or equal treatment with same treatment if the rhetoric of equal opportunities is to become at all meaningful. This mounts a serious challenge to standard liberal accounts of the preconditions for democracy. The third lesson to be drawn from feminist work on democracy, one inherent in work drawing on the ethic of care, is that the politics of reversal can enrich both the practice and outcomes of political processes and institutions. The final lesson, however, which emerges from political arguments within the feminist movement, is that it is a mistake to assume that democratic politics is simply about the fair reflection of pre-given interests deriving from fixed identities. Instead, democratic politics needs to be understood as involving the testing and re-working of pre-existing interests in a process of political deliberation which is open to all.

Summary

- Liberalism is associated with the view that there is no necessary connection between the ideological position taken by a representative and his or her own identity. Nevertheless, in attempting to tackle the ways in which women are excluded within contemporary politics, liberal feminists find themselves logically drawn to non-liberal modes of addressing evident inequities in order to boost the numbers of women in politics as a stage on the way to the situation in which the sex of the politician can become irrelevant.
- For radical feminists, liberal democracy is not only structured to make participation difficult for women, but it remains inhospitable to the values and virtues associated with women and femininity. For radical feminists, the presence of women in politics makes a direct difference to politics both substantively and procedurally.
- For feminist civic republican or deliberative democrats, the point of extending women's presence in politics is part of a larger project in which space is

created for plurality within the public sphere and therefore for deliberation about common action from a variety of perspectives, including different feminist perspectives.

TUTORIAL QUESTIONS

1. **Is positive discrimination (for example, all women shortlists in political parties) inherently anti-democratic?**

2. **Do women have common political interests because they are women?**

3. **Does genuine democracy require state intervention in personal and family life?**

FURTHER READING

Mary Wollstonecraft (1792/1975) *A Vindication of the Rights of Woman* (Harmondsworth: Penguin Books), originally published in 1792, can be seen as the founding argument for women's inclusion in liberal democratic politics.

Carole Pateman is one of the most influential contributors to feminist arguments about liberalism and democracy. Her *The Sexual Contract* (Cambridge: Polity Press, 1988) is a classic reference point for contemporary feminist debate.

Anne Phillips's work has been crucial to developing feminist ideas about democracy within the UK. See her *Engendering Democracy* (Cambridge: Polity Press, 1991) as well as other works cited below.

Judith Squires (1999) *Gender in Political Theory* (Cambridge: Polity Press) provides an excellent and detailed account of contemporary debate in feminist political theory.

Ruth Lister (1997) *Citizenship: Feminist Perspectives* (Basingstoke and London: Macmillan) explores feminist debates about citizenship in both theory and practice, drawing on literatures and examples from different parts of the world.

REFERENCES

Benhabib, Seyla (1992) *Situating the Self: Gender, Postmodernism and Community in Contemporary Ethics*. Cambridge: Polity Press.

Benhabib, Seyla (1996) 'Toward a Deliberative Model of Democratic Legitimacy', in S. Benhabib (ed.), *Democracy and Difference: Contesting the Boundaries of the Political*. Princeton, NJ: Princeton University Press.

Dworkin, Andrea (1988) *Letters from a War Zone: Writings 1976–1987*. London: Secker and Warburg.

Friedan, Betty (1965) *The Feminine Mystique*. Harmondsworth: Penguin.

Habermas, Jürgen (1992) *Between Facts and Norms*. Cambridge, Mass.: MIT Press.

hooks, bell (1982) *Ain't I a Woman: Black Women and Feminism*. London: Pluto Press.

Mackay, Fiona (2001) *Love and Politics: Women Politicians and the Ethics of Care*. London and New York: Continuum.

Mackinnon, Catharine (1987) *Feminism Unmodified: Discourses on Life and Law*. Cambridge, MA: Harvard University Press.

Mouffe, Chantal (1992) *The Return of the Political*. London: Verso.

Okin, Susan Moller (1989) *Gender, Justice and the Family*. New York: Basic Books.

Pateman, Carole (1988) *The Sexual Contract*. Cambridge: Polity Press.

Phillips, Anne (1993) 'Must Feminists Give Up on Liberal Democracy?', in D. Held (ed.), *Prospects for Democracy*. Cambridge: Polity Press, pp. 93–111.

Phillips, Anne (1995) *The Politics of Presence*. Oxford: Clarendon Press.

Richards, J. Radcliffe (1982) *The Sceptical Feminist: a Philosophical Inquiry*. Harmondsworth: Penguin.

Tronto, Joan (1993) *Moral Boundaries: the Political Argument for an Ethic of Care*. New York: Routledge.

Whelehan, Imelda (1995) *Modern Feminist Thought*. Edinburgh: Edinburgh University Press.

Wollstonecraft, Mary (1792/1975) *A Vindication of the Rights of Women*. Harmondsworth: Penguin.

Young, Iris Marion (1990) *Justice and the Politics of Difference*. Princeton, NJ: Princeton University Press.

Young, Iris Marion (2001) *Inclusion and Democracy*. Oxford: Oxford University Press.

See also chapters

30 Environmentalism

John Barry

Environmentalism or 'green politics', as is it sometimes called, is a very new political movement and ideology, perhaps the most recent of all political ideologies. Having its roots as a 'new social movement' in the 1960s (like the feminist movement), environmentalism has emerged as a permanent feature of modern politics. Adding a new colour 'green' to the political spectrum, Green political parties and movements propose radical policies across a range of environmental and non-environmental areas, use exciting and innovative forms of political action (direct action against road-building in Britain, or Greenpeace dinghies stopping whaling ships, consumer boycotting of large corporations), and all in all offer a very different and refreshingly unique style of politics and new political concerns to the existing political system in liberal democracies.

Despite its central concern with environmental issues, environmentalism as a new social movement and a political ideology has, since its origins, also been organized around the relationship between democracy (in theory and practice) and the environmentalist political agenda (in terms of both political means/strategy and ends). This chapter will outline and explore the relationship between environmentalism and democracy.

Environmentalism is rather unusual in that it encompasses both radical democratic and anti-democratic proposals, policies and schools of thought. The anti-democratic position holds that the root cause of the environ-mental crisis is to be found in the democratic organization of society in general and in particular the unregulated multiplication of wants and desires which the modern (liberal) democratic system is based upon and maintains. On this view, greater state authority, order and regulation are absolutely needed to deal with the various environmental problems facing modern societies. On the other hand, there are those who hold that the solution to environmental problems requires more not less democracy and suggest the democratization of the state, the cultivation of a robust and active sense of 'environmental' citizenship, more open, transparent modes of public policy-making and the extension of democratic norms to the economic sphere.

'SURVIVALISM' AND 'ECO-AUTHORITARIANISM'

The popular perception of environmentalism is of well-meaning, passionate and committed people organized into groups to struggle for a variety of 'good things'. Some of these 'good things' include environmental protection, animal rights, minimizing waste, more ecologically sustainable production and decreasing consumption. But one of the main political aims associated with environmentalism is democracy, and the extension of democracy, openness and transparency in political, economic and social life. Thus, it may strike many people as odd that there is an 'anti-democratic' environmentalist position, or environmental wing.

The anti-democratic position on environmental politics was first articulated in the early 1970s against the backdrop of a popular conception of an 'ecological crisis', the ending of the post-war era of economic growth, full employment and abundance with severe resource scarcity, especially oil as a result of the oil crisis in 1972. In keeping with the popular mood of impending ecological crisis and catastrophe numerous environmentalist publications were produced. Two significant ones were the famous and influential *Limits to Growth* report (Meadows et al., 1972) in the USA, and *Blueprint for Survival* (Goldsmith et al., 1972) in the UK. Both explained the causes and dynamics of the ecological crisis as being related to the inherently unsustainable character of contemporary western society, that is, western advanced industrial societies were undermining the ecological conditions of their own survival. They also proposed that radical and immediate solutions were required if these societies were to survive.

Closely associated with this view has been the survivalist or eco-authoritarian position. Authors such as William Ophuls (1977) and Garret Hardin (1977) argued that democracy was the problem and basic cause of the ecological crisis, not the solution, and democracy was counterproductive when faced with ecological threats to survival. William Ophuls argued that with the advent of the ecological crisis, interpreted as a return to ecological scarcity (following 'the limits to growth' thesis), 'the golden age of individualism, liberty and democracy is all but over. In many important respects we shall be obliged to return to something resembling the premodern closed polity' (Ophuls, 1977: 145). He interpreted this in terms of a (benign) technocratic dictatorship. Ophuls sees a strong link between the necessary technological solutions to environmental problems and undemocratic politics. Given the complexity

and expert knowledge (scientific and technological) required to solve the ecological crisis, democracy as 'rule by the many' is inappropriate to the task of saving society from ecological catastrophe. He calls for a 'priesthood of responsible technologists' (Ophuls, 1977: 159) and is explicit about the authoritarian and anti-democratic status of a more ecological society (sometimes called a 'steady-state society'). For him:

> the steady-state society will not only be more authoritarian and less democratic than the industrial societies of today . . . but it will also in all likelihood be much more oligarchic as well, with only those possessing the ecological and other competencies necessary to make prudent decisions allowed full participation in the political process. (Ophuls, 1977: 163)

According to the eco-authoritarian view, post-war liberal democracies fostered consumptionist life-styles, and were based on a materialist view of the 'good life' towards which the majority of people aspired. There is a multiplication of consumption desires for more and more goods and services, all of which demand increasing levels of ecological resources, materials, land, energy, which results in more and more pressure and damage to the environment (locally, nationally and between nations). Democratic elections within these societies were simply 'beauty contests' about which party (whether of the 'left' or 'right' was immaterial) will give, or promise to give, people higher levels of material affluence (as reflected in higher Gross National Product, employment and personal disposal income). Liberal democracies are systematically and structurally 'locked into' an 'environmentally destructive cycle' meaning they are unable and unwilling to impose limits on consumption and dominant 'materialist' life-styles, and therefore the consequent human destructive impact on the environment.

If, however, as the ecological critique suggested, the era of abundance was coming to an end, as a result of growing ecological scarcities in resources and the ability of the eco-system to tolerate the stress human activities were placing on it (especially pollution limits, population growth, land use, habitat destruction, soil erosion, etc.), then scarcity, not abundance, characterized the condition society faced. And a return to scarcity meant the erosion of the conditions which sustained western notions of democracy, liberty and freedom. Given that democracy encouraged environmental destruction by stimulating popular demands for more and more consumption, energy, jobs, income, etc., to the continued survival of society, the cost for saving society from ecological catastrophe was the abandoning of democracy. Identifying, coping and/or solving environmental problems are technical matters of expertise, best left to those with the requisite knowledge. Democracy is at best superfluous and at worst a hindrance in times of crisis, when decisions (tough and often unpopular decisions) have to be made for the sake of social survival.

RESPONSES TO ECO-AUTHORITARIANISM

There are a number of responses from within the environmental movement to the extremely pessimistic diagnosis and solution proposed by the eco-authoritarian view.

Questioning the link between 'democracy' and 'scarcity'

Why should a less materially affluent society necessarily lead to the rejection of democracy? There is nothing intrinsic to democracy as a procedure and system for making political decisions that makes it dependent upon economic affluence and wealth. Viewed as a system of government and decision-making procedure, democracy is not about promising or delivering material wealth, nor does it require economic affluence as a necessary condition for its existence.

Democracy, according to many environmentalists, does require some level of economic *security* and socio-economic equality, but not rising levels of absolute social wealth. For many Greens the issue is the distribution of social affluence not its absolute level (a position they share with left-wing ideologies and movements such as socialism-Marxism, feminism and anarchism).

Distinguishing liberal democracy from democracy per se

The main object of the eco-authoritarian argument is the modern liberal democratic state as it exists in the 'western' world. The rejection of democracy and the proposal of anti-democratic, centralized, authoritarian solutions confuses democracy and liberal democracy. However, liberal democracy does not exhaust the types of democracy available to society, as there are many non-liberal forms of alternative democratic government. This leaves open the possibility that different understandings of democracy are compatible with (indeed may be required for) solving environmental problems.

The limits of expertise and non-democratic decision-making in the face of complex ecological problems

There are good reasons seriously to doubt that a small elite (though perhaps benign) of experts could come up with the 'right' or most appropriate course of action for society to take in the face of the complexity, inter-relatedness and uncertainty that characterizes most ecological problems. Rather than the closed, self-contained decision-making by an elite, the environmentalist perspective is that democratic decision-making, which encourages open-endedness, the exchange of ideas and views, is better and superior as a decision-making process under conditions of uncertainty. Technocratic/expert solutions may not just be normatively undesirable (because they are undemocratic) but also ineffective (because they assume complete knowledge of the complexity and contingency that characterize ecological problems, something which is impossible to have in principle). While the solving of environmental problems will definitely require the input and knowledge of experts, this knowledge is a necessary, not a sufficient, condition for political decision-making about environmental problems. Experts should be 'on tap, but not on top', as it were.

Environmental problems are not just 'technical' problems

Environmental problems have many dimensions and significance for society, only one of which is their 'technical' character as problems to be 'solved'. Many environmental problems from global climate change, habitat destruction, animal welfare, water or soil scarcity, are also moral/ethical questions raising issues about social and global justice, the 'good life' and our obligations to future generations among others. Given the inherently normative character of environmental problems, decisions concerning environmental problems need to be made through decision-making procedures and institutions which involve everyone and not just a few, that is, a democratic decision-making procedure.

Having shown the contradictions and limits of the eco-authoritarian, anti-democratic position, the next section discusses the necessary connection between democracy and environmentalism.

ENVIRONMENTALISM AND THE EXTENSION OF DEMOCRACY I: POLITICAL PRACTICE

Why can it be argued that, in opposition to the eco-authoritarian view, the solution, or at least a major part of the solution, to the ecological crisis is *more*, not *less*, democracy?

Democracy and the environmental movement

As a result of activities such as lobbying for greater public access to information, particularly scientific data, strengthening 'freedom of information' and 'right to know' legislation, to arguing and helping to create more open forms of public policy-making, the environmental movement – and Green political parties – have been at the forefront of efforts to 'democratize' state institutions and help create a more democratic and accountable form of political decision-making on environmental matters (Paehlke, 1988). The environmental commitment to democratic norms is also expressed in the movement's use of the tactics of 'civil disobedience', and the explicit link made by the environmental movement between such modes of political strategy (for example in the UK anti-roads movement) and democratic claims. Such extra-parliamentary forms of political protest are explicitly justified and expressed in terms of their being legitimate forms of democratic action and expressions of democratic citizenship (Doherty, 1996).

Green parties have long been associated with promoting policies and political proposals for the extension of democracy and democratic accountability to more and more areas of social life, from opening up economic practices, scientific and technological developments to democratic scrutiny, the increased democratic regulation of corporations and public bodies, agencies and institutions to the promotion of local democracy and decentralization of political power and decision-making. They are also widely regarded as the most democratic type of political party in terms of their internal organization and decision-making processes, in comparison to non-Green parties. From consensual modes of decision-making, the rotation of elected representatives, the election of central party spokespeople and officers, to transparent and open policy-making process, Green parties are the most internally democratic political parties, despite the logic of electoral competition that has led to Green parties adopting more 'profession' party structures.

Democracy and sustainable development

Equally, one of the central aims of environmentalism, 'sustainable development', has at its heart a concern with extending democracy and enhancing democratic institutions and citizenship participation in decision-making. A very good example of the link between democratization and environmentalism is 'Local Agenda 21'. This policy was proposed and adopted at the 1992 Rio 'Earth Summit' organized by the United Nations with the official title of 'United Nations Conference on Environment and Development'. The Rio conference established that the goal of sustainable development required local authorities to consult widely and involve a range of 'stakeholders' within their local communities to develop their own environmental plans for achieving sustainable development. Thus the LA21 process is about linking sustainable development explicitly to democracy and democratization. According to the United Nations Association, '[a]s Local Agenda 21s turn into local sustainability plans, they reveal that sustainable development is not just about environmental protection and the meeting of social needs. *It's also about the revival of democracy itself'* (in Jacobs, 1996: 113; emphasis added).

ENVIRONMENTALISM AND THE EXTENSION OF DEMOCRACY II: POLITICAL THEORY

Along with arguments for the characterization of environmentalism in practice as committed not just to the defence of democracy, but its radical extension and deepening, there are a variety of theoretical arguments one can make for 'Green democracy'.

Democracy against the market

Theories of Green democracy explicitly make the democratic regulation of the economic sphere and the market a necessary condition for the achievement of sustainability and other Green goals, such as greater socio-economic equality and the redistribution of social wealth to achieve social justice. A typical statement of this extension of democracy from a Green perspective is Jacobs's statement that, '[m]arkets must . . . operate within the constraints imposed by public decisions made for the common good. The market should be servant to society, not master' (Jacobs, 1996: 111). Here Greens, together with socialists, call for the external democratic regulation and possible planning of production, energy use, transport, etc. by the state (including the local and supranational state), with the aim of achieving sustainable development (see Kenny and Meadowcroft, 1999) and other goals such as equality and social justice.

Secondly, on the question of the democratic regulation of the market, Green arguments for democracy overlap with arguments from 'Green political economy' about the necessary extension of democratic norms and practices within the economic sphere itself, in terms of greater opportunities for workers, consumers and citizens to have a 'voice' in matters of production, consumption and distribution, rather than these being left to the tender mercies of the unregulated free market (Barry, 1999).

Thirdly, arguments for such democratic extension of control, accountability and popular (including state) power to the 'private' sphere of the economy are also based on Green democratic arguments in favour of promoting environmental (and other) interests individuals have as 'citizens' (aimed at the common good) over 'consumer' interests (which are private and necessarily narrow) and over corporate producer interests. Sustainable development and the transition of society away from its current unsustainable development path is more likely to occur if environmental protection is articulated within a democratic, political process rather than a market, economic one.

Democracy against bureaucracy and centralization

Environmentalism does express scepticism (if not sometimes outright hostility) to the centralized nation-state in general, and more specifically the state's ability adequately to deal with environmental problems and achieve or promote other environmentalist ends. In particular, environmentalism is concerned about the bureaucratic and centralized character of the modern nation-state, which makes it ill-suited to deal with the complex, changing, dynamic and non-routinized processes of environmental change.

There are four interrelated points that ground this scepticism.

1. Democracy is not co-extensive with the institutions of the nation-state: From the environmental political perspective, democracy and democratic practices, such as citizenship and democratic decision-making, must go beyond the nation-state, to encompass transnational, international and global dimensions.

2. Environmentalism is concerned with fostering a 'democratic society' and not just a democratic 'political system': The Green democratic vision is one which goes beyond what is conventionally understood to be the democratic political sphere (local and central government, the state and its agencies, political parties, periodic elections, etc.). While environmentalism wishes to democratize the state (through such reforms as decentralization and local empowerment), it also wishes to see this process extended to 'civil society'. As Jacobs puts it:

It is therefore at the local level that a fully democratic society is constructed. The role played in this by voluntary and community groups is crucial, empowering people whose voices are otherwise unheard, enabling participation in the democratic process. Strengthening the role and capacity of local community groups is therefore a essential part of democratic reform. (Jacobs, 1996: 115)

3. Decentralization: Decentralization of political power and authority has been a consistent Green political principle from its origins. Political decisions should be made at the lowest possible level for democratic and ecological reasons. The democratic reasons have to do with transparency and accountability of political decisions that are held to increase in line with the proximity of those who make them to the affected community. The ecological reasons have to do with the concern that local rather than distant decision-making is often the most effective, matching the political decision-making level to the ecological problems at hand. It follows that for some environmental problems the most appropriate level is the national or even the global levels (think of climate change).

4. Citizen empowerment: Those who are affected by a decision have a right to a say in the decision-making process, which is to say that environmental decisions should not be made by (unelected) bureaucrats and civil servants alone, but should include opportunities for public participation. This has implications for existing state administrative processes from the planning system, public inquiries and legislative decision-making, including proposals for more citizens' initiatives, referendums, and other opportunities for active citizen political participation and agenda-setting such as one finds in cantons in Switzerland and certain states in America. Furthermore, the 'greening' of democratic citizenship requires the extension of the scope of citizenship beyond the 'normal' political arena to include, for example, citizens 'doing their bit' (recycling waste, repairing goods instead of buying new ones, using public transport as opposed to the car, etc.) to help achieve a less unsustainable development path for society.

Democracy against technocracy

Another reason for preferring democratic, political as opposed to non-democratic, non-political technical decision-making processes is the indeterminacy of environmental issues. Because of the complexity and interrelatedness of human–ecological interaction, we cannot make decisions once and for all to 'finally solve' or 'deal with' the various environmental problems we face, in some definitive sense. Ecological conditions can change, and change very quickly, and this leads to a strong prima facie case for democratic, public and 'open' as opposed to 'closed' decision-making systems in order to deal with and respond to changed ecological conditions. In other words, democracy is more flexible than technocratic decision-making to deal with the complexity and quickly changing character of social–ecological interactions.

GREEN POLITICS AND THE EXTENSION OF DEMOCRACY TO NEW 'MORAL CONSTITUENCIES'

Given that a key dimension of the environmentalist position is that all those affected by a decision should have some opportunity either to take part in it, influence it or challenge it, environmental politics poses some very novel (not to say difficult) challenges for representative democracy in practice and democratic theory as a whole. There are at least three interrelated new interests or 'moral constituencies' which Greens suggest for inclusion in the democratic process, as a result of being affected by the environmental decisions made by the current, territorially-bound democratic nation-state. These are future generations, affected non-citizens beyond the state, and the non-human world, which lead to various proposals regarding the extension of democracy across time, space and species.

Future generations

Given that the decisions we make today will have long-lasting implications for the lives, hopes and quality of life of those who will come after us, in terms of the environmental conditions and resources we leave them, Greens argue that the interests of future generations be represented in current decision-making, the results of which will have environmental consequences for them. The spirit of the change to our current limited representation of interests can be seen in a Native American Indian saying commonly used in Green political debate: 'We don't inherit the earth from our parents, we borrow it from our children.' Of course whether we can or ought to include future generations in democratic decision and exactly how the representation of their interests can be affected are extremely difficult issues, but this debate has been a central one in Green democratic theory.

Affected non-citizens

Another constituency of affected interests that Green politics proposes for inclusion in democratic decision-making arises from the fact that environmental issues and problems do not respect borders, thus leading to a situation where the effects of policies or consumer or producer decisions in one country or part of the world can have ecological (and social and economic) consequences for people living in another.

Equally, ecological conditions create webs of causality between distant places, so that my individual decision to buy a mahogany toilet seat, or Nike trainers, establishes a causal connection with the place, institutions and ecological conditions where production or extraction took place – the factory or company, rainforest, indigenous people, etc., of which I may not even be aware. Here the gap between consumption and production permits individual (and collective) consumption patterns and decisions to be considered exempt from moral or ethical consideration, such that the only relevant criteria are whether we like and can afford the particular commodity in question. Against this ignorance and complacent attitude Greens point out that there is a link between production (somewhere else) and consumption (here and now), an ethically significant causal relationship for which moral responsibility should be acknowledged for those consumption decisions. A more poignant example is the fact that the devastation caused by global climate change in many parts of the developing world is as a result of energy policies by the developed world. The rich, Northern countries consume most of the world's fossil fuel (coal, oil and gas mainly) that results in carbon dioxide emissions which are the main cause of climate change. These countries enjoy the benefits of the energy produced, yet the ecological costs are largely borne by countries in the non-developed world, which, unlike the developed world, are ill-equipped to cope with climate change. The logic of the Green democratic position is that there should be representation or inclusion of the voices of these affected non-citizens outside the borders of the state in democratic decision-making. That is, given global ecological conditions, the relevant *demos* or 'people' is no longer the territorially delimited one found within the borders of the nation-state. The Green democratic challenge to existing theories and practices of democracy on this issue is how to include the voices and concerns of individuals, communities and states outside the democratic nation-state, such that the *demos* (at least for environmentally related decisions) includes the interests (and perhaps the representatives) of non-citizens.

The non-human world

Perhaps the most radical proposal Green democratic theory advances is the extension of the *demos* to include the non-human world. Since the interests of the non-human world (individual animals, animal communities, habitats, landforms, rivers, seas, forests, etc.) are affected (usually negatively) by democratic decisions made by humans, these interests of the non-human world ought and should be represented somehow in the decision-making process. Since the non-human world (like future generations) is actually not able to participate directly in democratic decision-making, it is necessary to find ways whereby their interests are represented. Some humans or some democratic institution (like the constitution or specific laws or decision-making rules) are charged with this task of representing the interests of non-humans in the democratic process (Dobson, 1996). In other words, while democracy is *by the people* and *of the people*, does it follow that it also has to be confined to being *for the people*? (Eckersley, 1996). The Green democratic call for 'enfranchising the earth' (Goodin, 1996) is of course an extremely radical position with which many people are very uncomfortable. But then, if we look back over the course of democratic history, we would find many people being uncomfortable with proposals to extend democracy to include the working class, the uneducated, women, non-whites, and others. Seen in this context the Green call for the expansion of democracy beyond humanity can be seen as simply the rounding out of the democratic project, its full flowering as the best way to protect the vulnerable by giving them 'voice' and presence in political decision-making.

CONCLUSION

Green democratic theory and practice is perhaps the most comprehensive and radical of all forms of democratic theory, and one that is set to grow in importance as this century progresses. It has at its disposal a range of concerns, principles and values which ideally equip it to deal with the democratic challenges and opportunities which will arise in the debates and struggles around the social, environmental, economic, ethical and political dimensions of globalization.

Summary

- Environmentalism/Green politics is the most recent and, in many respects, the most radical, exciting and innovative political movement and theoretical perspective on democracy.
- While there were early responses to the ecological crisis in the 1970s which proposed authoritarian, non-democratic forms of decision-making, these can be shown to be both flawed and not truly environmentalist positions.
- In political practice environmental politics and the environmental movement is extremely democratic in its modes of internal organization and modes of engagement with the political system.
- There is a whole variety of theoretical arguments used by Greens to suggest that the solution to environmental problems and issues requires more not less democracy, relating to questions about the regulation of the market, the non-technical character of environmental issues and a suspicion of the bureaucratic and centralized state.
- Green politics proposes the extension of democracy across time, space and the species barrier in looking at radical ways in which to include the voices and interests of future generations, affected non-citizens outside the borders of the state and affected non-humans.

TUTORIAL QUESTIONS

1. **Does environmentalism in practice (within social movements and Green political parties) live up to environmentalism's radical democratic theoretical claims?**

2. **What sort of institutional arrangements might be required in order to realize the democratic resolution of environmental problems?**

3. **'Environmentalism is about achieving certain substantive outcomes or ends (the sustainable society, environmental protection, a post-materialist economy, etc.), but democracy is about procedures. What guarantee is there that democratic procedures will realize environmental ends?**

FURTHER READING

For an introduction to Green political and moral thought, see J. Barry (1999) *Environment and Social Theory* (London: Routledge); A. Dobson (2000) *Green Political Thought* (London: Routledge, third edition); N. Carter (2001) *The Politics of the Environment: Ideas, Activism, Policy* (Cambridge: Cambridge University Press); and R. Eckersley (1992) *Environmentalism and Political Theory* (London: University College London Press).

Detailed accounts of 'Green democratic theory' can be found in J. Barry (2001) 'Democracy', in J. Barry and E.G. Frankland (eds), *International Encyclopedia of Environmental Politics* (London: Routledge); A. de Shalit (2000) *The Environment: Between Theory and Practice* (Oxford: Oxford University Press); J. Radcliffe (2000) *Green Politics: Dictatorship or Democracy?* (Basingstoke: Macmillan).

There are three excellent edited volumes devoted to examining the relationship between environmentalism and democracy: B. Doherty and M. de Geus (eds) (1996) *Democracy and Green Political Thought* (London: Routledge); W. Lafferty and J. Meadowcroft (eds) (1996) *Democracy and the Environment* (Avebury: Edward Elgar); and F. Matthews (ed.) (1996) *Ecology and Democracy* (London: Frank Cass).

More recent work on the relationship between Green politics and liberal democracy can be found in M. Wissenburg (1998) *Green Liberalism: the Free and the Green Society* (London: University College London Press); J. Barry and M. Wissenburg (eds) (2001) *Sustaining Liberal Democracy* (Basingstoke and London: Palgrave).

REFERENCES

Barry, J. (1999) *Rethinking Green Politics: Nature, Virtue and Progress*. London: Sage.

Dobson, A. (1996) 'The Environment and Representative Democracy', in W. Lafferty and J. Meadowcroft (eds), *Democracy and the Environment*. Avebury: Edward Elgar.

Doherty, B. (1996) 'Green Parties, Nonviolence and Political Obligation', in B. Doherty and M. de Geus (eds), *Democracy and Green Political Thought*. London: Routledge.

Eckersley, R. (1996) 'Greening Liberal Democracy: the Rights Discourse Revisited', in B. Doherty and M. de Geus (eds), *Democracy and Green Political Thought*. London: Routledge.

Goldsmith, E. et al. (1972) *A Blueprint for Survival*. London: Tom Stacy.

Goodin, R. (1996) 'Enfranchising the Earth and its Alternatives', *Political Studies*, **44**: 835–49.

Hardin, G. (1977) *The Limits to Altruism*. Indianapolis, IN: Indiana University Press.

Jacobs, M. (1996) *The Politics of the Real World*. London: Earthscan.

Kenny, M. and Meadowcroft, J. (eds) (1999) *Planning Sustainability*. London: Routledge.

Meadows, D. et al. (1972) *Limits to Growth: a Report for the Club of Rome's Project on the Predicament of Mankind*. New York: Universe.

Ophuls, W. (1977) *Ecology and the Politics of Scarcity*. San Francisco, CA: W.H. Freeman.

Paehlke, R. (1988) 'Democracy, Bureaucracy, Environmentalism', *Environmental Ethics*, **10**: 4.

See also chapters

31 Democracy and the Islamist Paradox

Abdelwahab El-Affendi

It has become a truism to remark, especially following the 1990s worldwide 'democratization rush', that the Muslim world (that vast expanse of land extending from Indonesia to Morocco, with 50-odd countries, over one billion inhabitants and a bewildering variety of peoples) is somewhat resistant to democratization (Goldberg et al., 1993; Salamé, 1994). Numerous explanations were ventured to account for this apparent resistance, ranging from cultural explanations (Kedourie, 1994; Lewis, 1996) to appeal to socio-economic factors (persistence of patriarchal or clientele relations, the prevalence of the rentier state, the lag in economic or social development, the weakness of civil society, etc.) (Sharabi, 1988; Salamé, 1994; Garnham and Tessler, 1995; Norton, 1995, 1996).

Closely related to this issue is the proliferation and ascendancy of political and social groups that make an explicit appeal to Islam. These groups (known as 'fundamentalist', 'Islamist', 'extremist' or 'radical' depending on the perspective adopted) currently represent the most powerful opposition to (mostly autocratic) incumbent regimes in many countries. In some countries (Sudan, Iran, Afghanistan, Algeria), they have either come to power or have come very close to getting there. Some of these movements joined power-sharing arrangements in a number of countries (Jordan, Kuwait, Yemen, Malaysia, Indonesia, Pakistan). The strength of these groups has been cited by those opposing democratization as a justification for the *status quo*. Democratization, it has been argued, could only benefit these 'anti-democratic' groups (Miller, 1993). An apparently insoluble paradox thus presents itself: true democrats should resist democracy in Muslim countries.

CONTENDING WITH ISLAMISM

The paradox has been emphasized by a recent judgment (31 July 2001) by the European Court of Human Rights in Strasbourg, in which the Court dismissed a petition by the Refah party, the main Islamist party in Turkey, against a January 1998 ban by the Turkish Constitutional Court. The Court decided, by four votes to three, that there had been no violation of Article 11 (freedom of assembly and association) of the European Convention on Human Rights, and that the Turkish government was right to dissolve the party. Disregarding Refah's protestation that it had consistently respected Turkey's secular constitution, the Court ruled that the Turkish state was entitled to take pre-emptive action to block a political programme that might jeopardize civil peace and the country's democratic regime.

This ruling gives an authoritative normative stamp to practices already embarked upon by incumbent regimes and endorsed by major international powers. The so-called 'Islamism debate' (Kramer, 1997) has been raging in western policy circles for some time now. Policy-makers have been anguishing over whether to support democratization in Muslim countries, but by and large they have opted for *realpolitik* options: democracy is to be supported where possible, and only prudently (Kramer, 1997). However, this did not resolve the normative or intellectual issues involved.

The target of this ruling is also interesting. Refah party is a moderate Islamist party, so much so that it is indistinguishable from its secular rivals. According to one observer, Turkish Islamism, 'far from being a danger to democracy, can sanction it and consolidate the parliamentary regime, as parties owing allegiance to Catholicism have done in Germany' (Bayart, 1994: 292). At the time of initiating the proceedings against Refah in Turkey, the party was in power and its leader Necmettin Erbakan was the elected prime minister. The party was the largest in parliament, with over 22 per cent of the vote and 155 seats (out of 550). This made the process even more problematic from a democratic perspective.

But if Refah is not a typical Islamic party, its predicament is typical of most Islamist groups. During the same period, the Egyptian Muslim Brotherhood (*al-Ikhwan al-Muslimun, Ikhwan* for short) made significant electoral gains, in spite of remaining officially outlawed. *Ikhwan* continues to dominate the professional organizations and has also become the largest opposition bloc in parliament following the October 2000 elections. The situation in Egypt mirrors that in many other Arab countries, including Algeria, where the *Ikhwan* branch sided with the military but was upstaged by a novice Islamist group, the Islamic Salvation Front (FIS), which won the bulk of parliamentary seats in the 1991 elections before the military stepped back in and halted the process. Since then over 100,000 people have been killed in violence precipitated by the coup. In Syria, membership of the Brotherhood carries the death penalty. Tunisia prides itself in having 'eradicated' its own moderate Islamic group, the Ennahda party, and shows 'zero tolerance' for its activities. Iraq and Libya employ equally harsh policies. However, a number of Muslim countries permit Islamist groups to function legally, or even share power. In addition to the countries mentioned above where Islamist parties are allowed to share power, Islamists operate more or less freely in Bangladesh, Indonesia, Lebanon, Pakistan and Malaysia. A number of Arab countries also permit Islamists to operate, but under severe restrictions.

ISLAMISM AS A PHENOMENON

In current discourse, Islamism refers to a cluster of movements which emerged in the twentieth century and which insist that religious values should play a decisive role in public life. These include a wide range of diverse groups, from the quasi-secular Refah and Ennahda, to the very militant Islamic Jihad (Egypt), Hamas (Palestine) and Armed Islamic Group (Algeria). The Islamist phenomenon can be traced back to nineteenth-century reformist trends, in particular the school of Sayyid Jamal El-Din al-Afghani (1839–97), an enigmatic figure believed to be of Iranian origin. His experiences at a time when the perceived unity of the Muslim world was still a (rapidly disappearing) reality (he was thrown out of Egypt and Iran, harassed by the British in India and lived in exile in Europe for some years before ending up in Istanbul where he died a virtual prisoner of the sultan) led him to conclude that the phenomenon we now know as modernity posed a serious and existential threat to the Muslim community. Colonialism and western ascendancy represented the outward manifestations (and most serious aspect) of this challenge, even if the loss of vitality by Muslim societies and the decline of their spiritual and intellectual vitality remained the underlying cause of the problem (Keddie, 1968). Afghani proposed a twin strategy of a quest for Islamic intellectual and religious revival and of resistance to colonialism.

These themes of religious reformism and struggle for self-determination were to dominate Islamist discourse, while Afghani's ideas, and those of his most prominent disciple, the Egyptian Muhammad Abduh (1847–1905), were influential in shaping the intellectual climate in which the first major Islamist group, the Muslim Brotherhood, emerged in the 1920s. By that time, most of the Muslim world had fallen under western colonialism, while the Caliphate, the focal institution that symbolized Muslim unity since the death of the Prophet in 632 CE, was abolished in Turkey in 1924. This was a traumatic development for many Muslims, even though the Caliphate had by then become a purely symbolic institution.

The Muslim Brotherhood was founded in Egypt in 1928 by a charismatic young schoolteacher, Hassan al-Banna (1906–49) and had a turbulent history in Egypt and elsewhere. It was banned in 1948 and its leader assassinated in February 1949 (by government instigation, it has been alleged). Restored to legality following the military coup of July 1952, it soon fell out with Nasser and was finally banned in 1955. However, the movement continued to expand and establish branches or offshoots in most Arab countries and beyond.

Another major Islamist group, the Jamaat-i Islami, was founded independently in India in 1941 by a journalist, Sayyid Abu'l Ala al-Maududi (1903–79). The Jamaat-i Islami had a less troubled history and continues to operate legally in Pakistan, which became its main base, as well as in India and Bangladesh. Theoretically, the Jamaat is more hard-line than *Ikhwan*. Maududi condemns existing societies as un-Islamic and incapable of reforming from within. Only the establishment of a parallel Islamic society which would retrace the steps of the early Muslim community of self-purification, withdrawal and finally reassertion of power and influence could achieve the necessary task of re-Islamization (Maududi, 1947; Adam, 1983: 105–10).

Jamaat did not become a mass movement as *Ikhwan* did, but its founder had significant ideological influence. Maududi's ideas were adopted by sections of *Ikhwan*, under the influence of the prominent Egyptian Islamist thinker, Sayyid Qutb (1903–66), seen by many analysts as the prime influence in the resurgence of Islamist radicalism and violence from the 1970s (Kepel, 1985). However, this (widely accepted) proposition is put into question by the fact that Maududi's uncompromising ideological rhetoric induced conservatism or political inaction, rather than violence, in its original setting. The direct causes of radicalism and violence may thus have to be sought in the political context, rather than in ideology. The interaction of these movements with their milieux remains an evolving and dynamic 'learning process' (Kramer, 1997: 141–2). They have conducted themselves differently in areas where stable democracy prevailed (for example, South Asia) than in the brutal realm of Arab politics. Even in the Arab world, various Islamic groups displayed different attitudes. The branches of the Muslim Brotherhood in Jordan, Kuwait, Saudi Arabia and most Gulf states supported the royal families and were careful to operate within the confines permitted by the system. This contrasts with the experiences in Syria, Libya, Iraq, Tunisia and Egypt, where conflict erupted. Even in one country, such as in Algeria or Egypt, different Islamist groups reacted differently to regime brutality.

In addition to these pioneering movements, a number of other movements have emerged either independently or through indirect influence by these, in Indonesia, Malaysia, Algeria, Morocco and, more recently, the Central Asian republics.

GENERAL CHARACTERISTICS

It is clear from these preliminary remarks that Islamist movements exhibit a remarkable diversity of approaches and opinions, even though they claim to appeal to the same source of legitimacy: Islamic religious values and traditions. Many attempts have been made to develop a typology of these movements, but none appears satisfactory (Arjomand, 1995: 182–6; Entelis, 1997: 43–67). The most important distinction is that between radical (or extremist) groups and moderate ones. The former, a minority, adopt uncompromising attitudes, do not engage in regular politics and usually advocate violence. They do not recognize the legitimacy of existing states, whether democratic or despotic, and pose as the ultimate arbiters of who and what is Islamic. They also question the legitimacy of the more moderate groups, which they condemn as not genuinely Islamic. Examples of these are the Islamic Jihad and the Islamic Group in Egypt, the Armed Islamic Group in Algeria and, of course, Usama Bin-Laden's *Qa'idat al-Jihad*. The more moderate groups (such as Muslim Brotherhood, Refah party and the Tunisian Ennahda) accept the legitimacy of existing states, especially if they are democratic, and agree to work peacefully to achieve their goals. Some, such as Refah, the Indian branch of Jamaat, or even Hizbollah in Lebanon, have made express commitment to the secular system in which they operate.

Islamist movements represent, to a great extent, a modern phenomenon, even though some authors regard them as the continuation of certain strands of 'scriptural fundamentalism' (Arjomand, 1995: 179–86) or other modes of traditional reformism (Esposito and Voll, 1996: 21–32). Some commentators rightly point out that it does not make sense to speak of fundamentalism outside the context of modernity, while others even regard them as modernizing or westernizing agents (Gellner, 1995: 284–7; Kramer, 1997: 51–64). This puts them in sharp contrast to tradition-alist revival movements that sometimes co-existed with them spatially and temporally. Refah party's quasi-secular approach, for example, is the antithesis of the Afghan Taliban's lonely quest to turn the clock back by basing itself almost exclusively on pre-modern traditions and attitudes. (Taliban, recently bombed out of power by the United States, does not qualify as an Islamist movement according to the criteria adopted in this chapter. The movement led by Ayatollah Khomeini in Iran is a marginal case, although I am inclined to classify it with Taliban and the Saudi monarchy as an attempt to reassert pre-modern realities.) In many countries, ulama-led or sufi-led traditionalist movements often presented themselves as rivals to Islamist groups and allied themselves with regimes or secular parties against them.

The typical leader of an Islamist movement is a layman, usually a professional, educated in the west or in a modern western-style university. He is (no 'she' yet) usually very conscious of the overall modern context, and his ideas are not self-contained within the tradition, but represent the product of dialogue with modern ideologies and normative concerns. Membership of Islamist groups is generally described as lower middle class plus an assortment of marginalized groups. However, Islamists come increasingly from the educated strata of society, mostly urban, young, from the science faculties, and less from the human and social science disciplines.

Islamists distinguish themselves from rival political movements pursuing the same goals of self-government and national reconstruction in that they insist on national revival being pursued within the specific parameters of Islamic orthodoxy. This objective has often been expressed in the terms of demands for implementation of Islamic law (sharia) and for a stronger state role in enforcing Islamic values. Another, little noted, characteristic of these movements is that they are cult-like. Adherence to an Islamic group is not just signing up to a political party, but is also a commitment to a personal life-style, involvement in certain social networks and generally transforming the way a person organizes his or her life.

Analysts have usually tried to comprehend the rise of Islamist groups by applying the secularization thesis in reverse, linking the phenomenon to various social and cultural factors. Gellner (1994, 1995) argues that Islam is secularization-resistant because it has its own in-built 'Protestantism' which adapted perfectly to modernity. A number of explanations are offered for this apparent 'refutation of the secularization thesis' (a claim not conceded by some who contend that Islam has succumbed to practical secularization from the beginning (Lapidus, 1975)). These explanations include: the excess of oil money after the early 1970s oil shock, increased misery and pauperization of the masses, rapid urbanization and dislocation of the traditional order, the impact of the June 1967 Arab defeat in the war with Israel, loss of legitimacy by regimes and the discrediting of the dominant secular nationalist and socialist ideologies, crisis of identity, among others (Esposito, 1983: 10–14; Pipes, 1983; Entelis, 1997: 93–122). The restrictions on political activity and on the growth of civil society by despotic regimes is also said to have left Islamist groups at an advantage, since they could rely on the religious infrastructure (religious indoctrination, mosques as meeting places, religiously related income sources) in a manner not available to their secular rivals. The attempt by regimes to manipulate these groups in the contest with secular opponents has also been noted (Salamé, 1994: 78, 210–14).

As in the case of such complex phenomena, no single factor can fully account for the rise and endurance of Islamism. Some explanations are problematized by the implicit acceptance of classical modernization theory and its assumptions on the inevitability of secularization (Binder, 1988: 76–84). What is indisputable is that Islamist movements appear not only to be growing in strength, but also to have achieved 'hegemony in public discourse' (Sivan, 1998). At the same time, there is a perception that these groups are facing inevitable failure, in spite of this hegemony, especially given the inherent self-contradiction in their programmes and the unfeasibility of the 'partial modernization' project they advocate (Tibi, 1988: 1–8, 127–41; Roy, 1994: 60–74).

From the perspective of democracy, the more moderate movements exhibit both a consciousness of modern democratic norms and a desire to accommodate them, even if they hedge this with many reservations. Most Islamist thinkers accept the notion of basic human rights, even though they may disagree on which rights to support (El-Affendi, 2000). It is also interesting to note that the structures of these movements are largely democratic. The leader is elected by members, as are the various executive and consultative councils, another innovation. This goes to prove that whatever alternative these movements envisage to democracy, they did not find it suitable to organize their own affairs.

Even where they have come to government, as in Iran and Sudan, the Islamically inclined leaders have accepted in principle the trappings of democracy: elected officials and assemblies, division of powers, popular sovereignty, universal suffrage and accountability to the people. In Iran, of course, the principle of *wilayat al-faqih* allows the Guide to overrule all elected bodies in the name of the law. But the Guide is himself indirectly elected.

THE ISLAMISTS IN POWER

Iran represents a special case, both because Shiism is dominant there and also because it has a militant Islamic government in power. The branch of Shiism dominant in Iran holds that no actual legitimate leader exists since the disappearance of the sect's twelfth Imam in the ninth century CE. A charismatic Iranian religious scholar, Ayatollah Ruhullah Khomeini (1902–89), developed in the early 1970s a doctrine that transformed Shii quietism during the 'wait for the return of the imam' into militant activism. The doctrine of *wilayat al-faqih* (the authority of the learned man (or class)) stipulated that, in the absence of the imam, men of learning and piety should stand in for him and assume the reigns of government (Martin, 2000: 100–28). Khomeini was able to implement this vision after the revolution which toppled the shah in February 1979 and made Iran one of the first modern Muslim states to reverse the process of secularization to which almost all Muslim nations had succumbed (except for Saudi Arabia, which had never adopted overt secularism). The Iranian constitution is a hybrid document, establishing a republic with a parliament and president, separation of powers and ultimate submission to popular will, but vesting supreme authority in a supreme leader who has to be a *faqih* (Martin, 2000: 147–73).

The doctrine was opposed by both secular groups and Islamic groups, including the (Islamist) Iran Freedom Movement, led by Mehdi Bazargan, the first prime minister of revolutionary Iran, as a well as conservative *ulama*. The current reformist trend led by President Mohamed Khatemi, who was elected to the presidency by a landslide for a second term in 2001, does not openly oppose the doctrine, although its professed democratic ideals are in open conflict with it.

Other countries experienced Islamization bids, as in Afghanistan, where the Taliban ((religious) students), who advocate an ultra-traditionalist interpretation of Islamic doctrine, came to power in 1996 as a reaction to endemic infighting between the warlords who rose against the Soviet invasion in 1979. Only in Sudan, however, did a modern Islamist movement come to power. Led by Dr Hassan Turabi (1932–), a legal scholar educated in London and Paris, the movement has emerged as an *Ikhwan* offshoot in the 1950s and gradually increased its influence (El-Affendi, 1991). It made its bid for power in June 1989, shortly after being ejected from a coalition government because it was seen as

an obstacle to ending the civil war which had raged since 1983.

Islamist rule in Iran, Sudan, Saudi Arabia and Afghanistan has been associated with persistent civil conflicts and widespread complaints about human rights abuses. There have been persistent complaints that minorities, women and dissidents were targeted for maltreatment and denial of rights. Some abuses are specific to these regimes (restrictions on women's rights, application of corporal punishments, etc.). However, the bulk of alleged abuses are more familiar: harassment and silencing of opponents, torture, persecution of minorities and the abridgment of freedoms of expression and assembly. The abuses have been at their worst in Taliban-ruled Afghanistan. Both Iran and Sudan have experienced some liberalization in the last few years, but the regimes remain repressive and conflict-ridden. In addition, Islamist regimes remain riven with internal infighting which only goes to confirm that there is no agreed 'Islamist' approach to governance any more than there is a 'secular' one.

Islamist rule has also revealed the problematic nature of appeal to Islamic principles in general and sharia law in particular. The four current Islamist regimes (Saudi Arabia, Iran, Sudan and Afghanistan, which still professes adherence to Islamic law, even after Taliban) have adopted different versions and interpretations of Islamic law in spite of a general agreement that the sources of law should be the traditional interpretations of basic texts (the Quran, the Prophet's example or *sunnah*).

Another significant feature noted by some observers pertains to the paradoxically 'secularizing' impact of Islamist movements, even where they have attained exclusive power (Kramer, 1997: 69–83). In Iran, the ultimate appeal to *raison d'état* was made official by the passing of a constitutional amendment in 1989 that created a council (the Expediency Discernment Council of the System) empowered to overrule the exigencies of Islamic law if the interest of state so dictated (Articles 111 and 112 of the Constitution). Elsewhere

Islamist rulers have shown a tendency to disregard Islamic injunctions when it suited them. Of equal significance is the fact that Islamists in power (and outside it for that matter) have shown a tendency to engage in squabbles and disputes which puts into question one of their most basic tenets: that Islamic values offer a firm guide about how to conduct public affairs. In the recent split among Sudanese Islamists, which saw the Islamist leader Turabi put in jail by the faction now in government under President Omar al-Bashir, both factions invoked Islam, but this common reference failed to resolve their disputes.

These developments tend to confirm the worst fears of those who argue that Islamist rule would be a disaster. Needless to say, the 11 September 2001 terrorist atrocities in the United States, of which Islamist extremists were accused, have increased suspicions of all Islamists even further. It has also led to a rolling back of civil rights even in established democracies. This only goes to demonstrate that the 'Islamist question' is going to continue to have an impact on the world scene and affect perceptions of democracy well beyond Muslim countries.

CONCLUSION

The Islamist paradox presents a serious challenge not only to stability in Muslim nations, but to many assumptions of political theory. This paradoxical role (being popular and representative as well as exhibiting anti-democratic tendencies) is symptomatic of the structural instability of modern Muslim societies, which do not seem to have been able to develop a decisively secular order nor to be able to revert to a fully Islamic order. As one observer put it, the central question presented here is this: why has the reference to religion become politically useful and effective in Islamic societies? 'Such a question bears less on theology or political thinking (not to mention religious sociology), than on

the analysis of the discourse and its effects' (Salamé, 1994: 8).

The question is thus not about Islamist movements (religious revivalist movements exist almost everywhere) but about the structure of Muslim societies and the overall socio-cultural context which makes the discourse of Islamist movements so effective. Making democratization in Muslim countries conditional on the eradication of Islamism is thus problematic not only because it appears unrealizable, but also because it misses the point. Some of the strongest Islamist movements have emerged in the most secularized Muslim countries, such as Turkey (eight decades of militant secularism), Algeria (four decades of socialism preceded by a century and a half of culturally aggressive French colonialism), Iran, Lebanon, Palestine and Tunisia.

On the other hand, the countries that did not pursue such aggressive anti-Islamist policies appear to have enjoyed more stability. Among the few Muslim countries that have escaped this crisis, the most remarkable is Malaysia, the only Muslim majority country to have maintained a stable and thriving democracy throughout its independent history Although Malaysia's democracy leaves a lot to be desired, the country is a rarity of multicultural co-existence and economic success. Malaysia is also one of the few Muslim countries to have a legal Islamic party, which is now the main opposition in addition to being the ruling party in a number of states in the federation. It is also to be noted that while Islamist parties operate legally in many countries, none of the takeovers by Islamic regimes (Sudan, Iran, Afghanistan) has occurred democratically. One must conclude that it is no coincidence that Islamist parties appear to thrive most where they are banned, while democracies fare better where these parties can operate legally.

Advancing democracy in Muslim countries and safeguarding it worldwide would thus appear to call for a 'democratic' solution to the Islamist question. The most viable strategy would be to create a broad alliance of democratic forces, which is to include moderate Islamists, with the aim of striking an inclusive 'democratic bargain' (Salamé, 1994: 200–22; Esposito and Voll, 1996: 6–10; Entelis, 1997: 66–71). This is already happening in Algeria, Tunisia and Egypt, among other countries. However, the most interesting playing out of this probable coalition has been Indonesia. It was a supreme irony for this staunchly secular country that, when the Suharto regime was toppled in 1998, moderate Islamist leaders were at the heart of the coalition that took over, a coalition which proved solid enough to withstand the constitutionally problematic toppling of President Abdul Rahman Wahid, himself a prominent religious leader, in 2001. Both common sense suggests and experience thus confirms that a democratic approach of inclusion is the best approach from the perspective of securing stability in Muslim societies, pretty much like everywhere else. The Muslim world, it would appear, is not the 'exceptional' case it has been trumpeted to be.

Summary

- There is a widespread perception that Muslim societies are somewhat resistant to democratization, a characteristic that has been explained by cultural, political, global or socio-economic factors.
- The Muslim world has also been experiencing a religious revival characterized by the proliferation of Islamist groups which seek to enhance the role of religion in public life and advocate a stricter adherence to religious norms both in private and public life.
- Islamist groups represent a modern phenomenon, both as a reaction to modernity and as its consequence. They have emerged in the twentieth century in countries that were British colonies at the time, and among groups that have benefited from a modern education.
- While these groups were very small at first and doubly marginalized *vis-à-vis* traditional society and the modern sector, they have witnessed a rapid growth in following and influence, in particular since the 1970s.
- These movements have succeeded so far in gaining power in only one country: Sudan. However, powerful Islamization trends have swept other countries, in particular Iran and Afghanistan.
- The rising influence of these groups and the fear it provoked has induced a resistance to democratization by incumbent elites, with full support from the west.
- This has created a dilemma which appears difficult to resolve, but without such a resolution the prospects for democracy in the Muslim world will remain very dim indeed.

TUTORIAL QUESTIONS

1. **Present two different arguments which aim to justify why Muslim societies have failed to democratize. Can you offer a refutation of these arguments?**

2. **Some analysts (for example, Miller, 1993; Kramer, 1997) argue that it is pointless to try to distinguish between moderate and extremist Islamist groups. Can you present one argument for, and one against, this proposition? What is your own viewpoint?**

3. **'Islamist movements are an obstacle to democratization in Muslim countries because they do not believe in democracy and are intolerant of others.' Discuss.**

FURTHER READING

Dale F. Eickleman and James Piscatori (1996) *Muslim Politics* (Princeton, NJ: Princeton University Press) is a good introductory work, which is also informed and sophisticated.

Abdelwahab El-Affendi (1993) 'The Eclipse of Reason: the Media in the Muslim World', *Journal of International Affairs*, **46**: 163–93, examines the way media control plays a central role in sustaining a non-democratic order in the Middle East.

Charles Kurzman (1988) *Liberal Islam: a Source-Book* (New York: Oxford University Press) is a good anthology of works by Islamist thinkers who advocate pluralism.

Ann Elizabeth Mayer (1991) *Islam and Human Rights: Tradition and Politics* (Boulder, CO: Westview Press) follows the debate on human rights in Islamist discourse.

Elizabeth Özdaga and Sune Persson (eds) (1997) *Democracy, Civil Society and the Muslim World* (Istanbul: The Swedish Research Institute) present one of the best discussions on pluralism and civil society as it relates to Muslim societies.

REFERENCES

Adam, Charles J. (1983) 'Maududi and the Islamic State', in John Esposito (ed.), *Voices of Resurgent Islam*. Oxford: Oxford University Press, pp. 99–123.

Arjomand, Said Amir (1995) 'Unity and Diversity in Islamic Fundamentalism', in Martin E. Marty and R. Scott Appleby (eds), *Fundamentalisms Comprehended*. Chicago, IL: Chicago University Press, pp. 179–98.

Bayart, Jean-François (1994) 'Republican Trajectories in Iran and Turkey: a Tocquevillian Reading', in Ghassan Salamé (ed.), *Democracy without Democrats? The Renewal of Politics in the Muslim World*. London: I.B. Tauris, pp. 282–99.

Binder, Leonard (1988) *Islamic Liberalism: a Critique of Development Ideologies*. Chicago, IL: University of Chicago Press.

El-Affendi, Abdelwahab (1991) *Turabi's Revolution: Islam and Power in Sudan*. London: Grey Seal Books.

El-Affendi, Abdelwahab (2000) 'Reviving Controversy: Islamic Revivalism and Modern Human Rights', Encounter, **6**: 117–50.

Entelis, John P. (ed.) (1997) *Islam, Democracy, and the State in North Africa*. Bloomington, IN: Indiana University Press.

Esposito, John (ed.) (1983) *Voices of Resurgent Islam*. Oxford: Oxford University Press.

Esposito, John and Voll, John (1996) *Islam and Democracy*. Oxford: Oxford University Press.

Gellner, Ernest (1994) *Conditions of Liberty: Civil Society and Its Rivals*. London: Hamish Hamilton.

Gellner, Ernest (1995) 'Fundamentalism as a Comprehensive System: Soviet Marxism and Islamic Fundamentalism,' in Martin E. Marty and R. Scott Appleby (eds), *Fundamentalisms Comprehended*. Chicago, IL: Chicago University Press, pp. 259–76.

Goldberg, Ellis et al. (eds) (1993) *Rules and Rights in the Middle East: Democracy, Law and Society*. Seattle, WA: University of Washington Press.

Garnham, David and Tessler, Mark (eds) (1995) *Democracy, War and Peace in the Middle East*. Bloomington, IN: Indiana University Press.

Keddie, Nikki (1968) *An Islamic Response to Imperialism*. Berkeley, CA: University of California Press.

Kedourie, Elie (1994) *Democracy and Arab Political Culture*. London: Frank Cass.

Kepel, Gilles (1985) *The Prophet and the Pharaoh: Muslim Extremism in Egypt*. London: Al-Saqi Books.

Kramer, Martin (ed.) (1997) *The Islamism Debate*. Tel Aviv: The Moshe Dayan Centre.

Lapidus, I.M. (1975) 'The separation of state and religion in the development of early Islamic society', *International Journal of Middle Eastern Studies*, **6**: 363–85.

Lewis, Bernard (1996) 'Islam and Liberal Democracy: a Historical Overview,' *Journal of Democracy*, **7**: 52–63.

Martin, Vanessa (2000) *Creating an Islamic State: Khomeni and the making of a new Iran*. London: I.B. Tauris.

Maududi, Abu'l Ala (1947) *The Process of Islamic Revolution*. Lahore.

Maududi, Abu'l Ala (1969) *Islamic Law and Constitution*. Lahore: Islamic Publications.

Miller, J. (1993) 'The Challenge of Radical Islam', *Foreign Affairs*, Spring: 43–56.

Norton, Richard Augustus (1995 and 1996) *Civil Society in the Middle East, Vols I and II*. Leiden: E.J. Brill.

Pipes, Daniel (1983) *In the Path of God*. New York: Basic Books.

Roy, Oliver (1994) *The Failure of Political Islam*. Cambridge, MA: Harvard University Press.

Salamé, Ghassan (ed.) (1994) *Democracy without Democrats? The Renewal of Politics in the Muslim World*. London: I.B. Tauris.

Sharabi, Hisham (1988) *Neopatriarchy: a Theory of Distorted Change in Arab Society*. New York: Oxford University Press.

Sivan, Emmanuel (1998) 'Why Radical Muslims Aren't Taking Over Governments', *MEIA Journal*, **2** (online).

Tibi, Bassam (1988) *The Crisis of Modern Islam*. Salt Lake City, UT: University of Utah Press.

See also chapters

32 Cosmopolitanism

Nicholas Rengger

This chapter examines the emergence and character of one of the more diffuse but influential movements to have come to prominence in the last few years: cosmopolitanism. While it has ancient roots, it has developed a distinct modern character and in the current context, although I shall say something about its origin and history, it is naturally with modern versions of cosmopolitanism that I shall principally be concerned here. It is also rather more diffuse than some other movements and ideas discussed in this book (there are no 'cosmopolitan parties', though there are certainly parties that have cosmopolitan ideas) and I shall try to illustrate both the reasons and the consequences of this diffuseness in this chapter. However, my primary goal will be to offer an overview of modern cosmopolitanism as a whole and to gesture at least towards what I take to be its strengths and weaknesses.

HISTORY

The term 'cosmopolitan' is taken from the Greek compound term *Kosmou-polites*, literally 'citizen of the *Kosmos* (or, as we might say, universe)'. The origin of the use stems from the so-called 'Hellenistic' period of ancient Greek thought (roughly the third century BCE to the first century BCE). A number of the Hellenistic schools contributed to its evolution, most obviously the so-called 'cynics' (famously the cynic Diogenes), the Epi-

cureans (that is the followers of Epicurus), and, most especially, the Stoic school founded by the philosopher Zeno of Citium (from the word *Stoa*, a painted colonnade, where Zeno lectured). However, it was the popularity of Stoic philosophy at Rome that really established 'cosmopolitanism' as an important movement in ancient life and thought. Writers (and political actors) as important as Marcus Tullius Cicero, Seneca and the Emperor Marcus Aurelius were convinced Stoics and both their writings and their example have been influential from their own time to ours.

In general terms, ancient cosmopolitanism was predicated on a view of the universe as a rational ordered whole. The central human faculty that allowed us to reason, think and speak (known to the Greeks as the *logos*) is embedded in the universe. Humanity and nature are thus one. If humans recognize this they will act congruently with the rational in nature – as the Stoics tended to say they will 'follow nature'. Roman Stoics especially were also fond of an image that emphasized human community as a set of concentric circles. We live in at least two communities, Seneca tells us, the local community into which we were born and the wider community 'which is truly great and truly common. In which we look neither to this corner or to that but measure the boundaries of our nation by the sun'.

These assumptions were, of course, easier to combine when the political unit that occupied centre-stage was a unified empire that occupied much of the known world. Although the Romans were, of course, aware that other societies and cultures existed (and not just nearby but much further away as well), it was much easier to see the empire as the fundamental political unit, in the words of the commentator Lactantius: 'the city that sustained all things'. Roman Stoics, and thus Roman 'cosmopolitans', therefore tended to elide the difference between what would later become termed 'moral' and 'institutional' (or 'political') cosmopolitanism, a distinction we shall look at in detail later on.

Ancient cosmopolitanism did not truly survive into the medieval period. Although elements of Stoicism were influential on early Christianity, the collapse of the Empire and the emergence of the barbarian kingdoms doomed political cosmopolitanism, and moral cosmopolitanism became merely a feature (and a decreasingly significant one) of Christian doctrine. The closest medieval Europe came to developing a 'cosmopolitan' version of Christian theology was with the emergence of the Natural Law tradition; however, many other tributaries fed this development as well.

Only in the fifteenth and sixteenth centuries did cosmopolitan ideas begin to surface again. This was part of the recovery of classical thought undertaken by the Renaissance. However, not really until the eighteenth century did writers begin once more self-consciously to use the term, as they did especially during the so-called European Enlightenment. Cosmopolitan ideas were widespread in the Enlightenment and philosophers such as Montesquieu, David Hume and Adam Smith did a good deal to develop a distinctly 'modern' cosmopolitanism, though all were powerfully influenced by ancient (especially Roman) models. Perhaps the most important such writer, however, is the German philosopher Immanuel Kant (1724–1804) (Reiss, 1970). Kant's 'cosmopolitanism' is articulated in the philosophical system he developed from his fifties onwards, usually called the 'critical phil-

osophy' and composed principally of the three great 'Critiques': the *Critique of Pure Reason* (1781/87) the *Critique of Practical Reason* (1788) and the *Critique of Judgement* (1790). Most of Kant's explicitly political writings, however, postdate these three. His 'cosmopolitanism' was chiefly expressed in a series of essays written in the 1780s and 1790s. The most important essays in this context are: 'What is Enlightenment?' (1784); 'The Idea of a Universal History' (1784); 'On Theory and Practice' (1793); and, especially, 'On Perpetual Peace' (1795), to which should be added one late book, the *Metaphysics of Morals* (1797).

Enlightenment – and especially Kantian – cosmopolitanism emphasized that the community relevant for full moral judgement was the human community as such. In this sense it echoed ancient cosmopolitanism. However, the manner in which this claim was made and pursued was very different. While it is obviously true that there are many human cultures and many human practices, Kant's assumption was that at least in principle they could be brought under the rule of reason and that human societies would move, no doubt hesitantly and clumsily, towards progress. This was not any longer, however, a unity of humanity with nature, but rather the realization of a specifically human opportunity. That, after all, was what Enlightenment was about. As he put it in his essay on what is Enlightenment: 'Enlightenment is the emergence of man from his *self-incurred* immaturity' (emphasis added), where immaturity is 'the inability to use one's reason without the guidance of another' (Reiss, 1970).

However, while Kant was clearly a moral cosmopolitan, there is more of a question as to whether he was also a political cosmopolitan. He is explicit in not advocating a world state (on the ground that it would, in all probability, be despotic), but at the same time seems to advocate (especially in the *Metaphysics of Morals*) a system of cosmopolitan law in which traditional state sovereignty would gradually disappear. As we will see, this dilemma is one that has remained salient for cosmopolitans to this day.

Throughout the nineteenth century cosmopolitanism as a self-conscious set of ideas was largely limited to small groups of intellectuals, who saw themselves as heirs to the Enlightenment, although its moral force can be observed from time to time in political events. It was an important element, for example, in the setting up of the International Committee of the Red Cross in 1864 and, indeed, the general move to codify the laws of war which resulted in the Hague conventions of 1899 and 1907. It also became entwined with the liberal optimism that obtained in many circles as the nineteenth century progressed and that is generally supposed to have been buried by the outbreak of war in 1914. Yet it emerged again after 1945, in the context of the ideas underlying the Nuremberg and Tokyo trials, in many of the early statements of the fledgling United Nations (for example, the Genocide convention (1947) and the UN Charter on Human Rights (1948)). Today its most obvious political constituency is the growing global human rights regime, and movements dedicated to it (such as Amnesty International), and it is increasingly present in environmental movements and movements dedicated to establishing just and fair procedures for global governance as well.

If this is a (very) schematic account of the roots and emergence of modern cosmopolitanism, the question still remains: how exactly should we understand it and what are its main claims? To answer this question, however, we need to recognize that in contemporary thought there are two general senses of the notion of cosmopolitanism that are influential, though one is very much more common and influential than the other. I shall call this first cosmopolitanism *universalist cosmopolitanism*, since its central focus is the universality of moral judgement and what follows from this politically (though there is, as we shall see, some debate about this). Its (currently less influential) cousin, by contrast, I shall term *particularist cosmopolitanism*, since

the focus here is less on the universality of moral judgement but rather the indeterminacy of all existing political and moral claims. The 'cosmopolitanism' thus advocated develops in a very different way. Let me offer a brief discussion of each in turn.

UNIVERSALIST COSMOPOLITANISM

Let us look first, then, at 'universalist cosmopolitanism'. As Charles Beitz, one of its most important academic advocates has defined it, this view comprises two essential elements: 'it is inclusive and non-perspectival'. These imply that it seeks to see the whole that encompasses all local points of view and it seeks to see each part in relation to the whole. Beitz then goes on to argue that (as we have already seen) this can be divided into two main types. The first (and he suggests more basic) of these he calls 'moral cosmopolitanism' and argues that its crux is the idea that each person is equally a subject of moral concern and that in the justification of choices one must take the prospects of everyone affected equally into account. The second view is what Beitz (2001) calls 'institutional cosmopolitanism' (and which some other authors, for example Kim Hutchings (1999), have more recently termed 'political' cosmopolitanism). This view holds that the moral claims associated with moral cosmopolitanism imply that existing institutional/political arrangements governing world politics, at various different levels, are unjust or inappropriate and that therefore they should be reformed and redesigned to be both effective and more justifiable ethically. At its most extreme, versions of institutional cosmopolitanism advocate some form of world government, but more usual deployments of this idea would emphasize various kinds of federal, or confederal structures, together with what is increasingly being called 'cosmopolitan law'. In all versions, however, the existing structures of the states system would be significantly diminished.

In contemporary moral and political philosophy, cosmopolitanism of various different kinds has become extremely influential. At the risk of simplifying an exceedingly complex tale, I shall suggest here that there are four increasingly influential versions of universalist cosmopolitanism. Of course, they overlap to a greater or a lesser degree, and there are some prominent cosmopolitans who do not (quite) fit into any of these categories. I shall say something about each in what follows, before discussing some wider aspects of universalist cosmopolitanism.

Consequentialist cosmopolitanism

The first is usually called consequentialist cosmopolitanism. The most common version of this is one variety or another of utilitarianism, which emphasizes that the bedrock of moral choice should be the maximization of beneficial outcomes ('utility') to action and minimization of harmful outcomes. Its concern is primarily with the consequences of actions. It fits Beitz's definition (it is both inclusive and non-perspectival) and is open to both moral and institutional interpretations. Leading moral and political thinkers associated with this view would include the moral philosopher, bio-ethicist and animal rights campaigner Peter Singer, the political theorist Robert Goodin and a number of leading economists and public policy scholars of various stripes. The essence of consequentialist cosmopolitanism is that it emphasizes the moral significance of consequences, but argues that the relevant consequences are strongly inclusive in Beitz's sense. Thus, as Singer has most famously argued, on utilitarian and consequentialist grounds, the vast disparities of wealth that exist between the rich few and the poor many in contemporary world politics is simply immoral and unjust and it is incumbent upon all of us to seek to remedy it by various different means.

Deontological cosmopolitanism

The second version – and perhaps at the moment, certainly among scholars, the most influential one – is generally referred to as 'deontological'. Deontologists (the term implies an emphasis on intentions and obligations) tend to argue for the rights and (especially) obligations we have under the moral law. While, of course, outcomes are important (especially in the public realm) moral judgement rests as much on intentions and on structures of rights and duties as it does solely on outcomes. The most common philosophical root for deontologists would be some form of Kantianism. Leading philosophical advocates of a broadly deontological cosmopolitanism would include Beitz himself, Henry Shue, Thomas Pogge and Onora O'Neill. However, while there is broad agreement between deontological cosmopolitans, one area where they differ is the emphasis they wish to place on rights. Some – like Shue and Beitz – place a very heavy emphasis on rights as the key tool for establishing cosmopolitan norms both ethically and politically. Others – O'Neill is perhaps the most influential example – are more suspicious at least of how the rights culture has become embedded and see notions of duty or obligation as more fruitful. All would agree, however, that (for example) justice requires substantial global redistribution of resources.

Critical theory

Both consequentialist and deontological cosmopolitanism are becoming especially influential in the Anglophone philosophical community. However, over the last few years, the German tradition of 'critical theory', and especially its most distinguished contemporary representative Jürgen Habermas, has developed a different way of framing the cosmopolitan challenge. Habermas has developed a version of universalist cosmopolitanism which does imply a strict link between moral and political cosmopolitanism, and which even (perhaps) places the priority on political (and legal) cosmopolitanism. In addition to Habermas, leading political thinkers associated with this approach would include James Bohman, Nancy Fraser, David Held, Axel Honneth and Andrew Linklater. This way of articulating cosmopolitanism is perhaps best seen as a species of philosophical history that takes the hallmark of human moral progress to be the gradual increase in who is included in the sphere of moral concern. Linklater has argued such developments inevitably bring institutional and political change in their wake and that we are now living in an age when citizenship and political loyalties are 'post-Westphalian', that is to say not limited to the state or the states system. Of course, this does not imply any *inevitable* evolution or any specific institutional form, but it does suggest that a 'just world order' will require very considerable institutional redesign.

Perhaps the most directly influential political cosmopolitans in recent years have been those, most especially perhaps David Held (1995), who have argued for the concept of 'cosmopolitan democracy'. This takes the previous argument in a very particular direction. It suggests that existing social forms will continue to become more and more dysfunctional unless the social system best adapted to corralling and managing conflicts and disruptions – democracy – can be effectively globalized. Clearly this would amount to a very substantial redesign of the existing international system and would put in place at least aspects of real 'global governance' if not global government.

Cosmopolitan capabilities

A fourth version of universalist cosmopolitanism has also emerged over the last few years. It has emerged from the (originally distinct and then joint) work of the 1998 Nobel laureate in Economics, Amartya Sen, and the influential classicist, philosopher, literary critic and public intellectual, Martha Nussbaum. Known chiefly as the 'capabilities approach', it seeks to overcome some of the perceived difficulties of other versions of universalist cosmopolitanism (of which more in a moment). At least in Nussbaum's version – and it is Nussbaum's version that is becoming increasingly influential – it owes a good deal to ancient cosmopolitanism as well as to the Enlightenment.

Its basic argument suggests that we pay greater attention to what it means to be *capable* of what Nussbaum calls 'fully human functioning'. We can, she thinks, develop a sense of the range of possibilities that proper human functioning requires *as capabilities*. Moral and political choices should, she argues, reflect this notion. In other words, political institutions should be assumed to be working well when people who live under them have the capability of fulfilling any one of a wide range of possible life choices. Note that for Nussbaum having the capability to do something does not imply that there is any requirement to do it, or any necessary superiority in doing it. Thus, to use an example she has herself used, the practice in many societies of female genital mutilation should be abandoned because its practice disables those on whom it is inflicted from the capability fully to enjoy sexual relationships. The *capability* to take part in such relationships is part of good human functioning, but this says nothing about whether one should take part in such relationships. For Nussbaum, it is perfectly possible that a woman might choose to live a celibate life and this would be a perfectly legitimate choice; the point, of course, is that female genital mutilation *denies* her this choice, deprives her of the capability to exercise choice and that is why it is wrong (Nussbaum, 1994).

The implications of this view are clearly in tune with universalist cosmopolitanism. The development of 'good human functioning' is Nussbaum's version of the Stoic injunction to 'follow nature' and she argues that our moral and political lives should revolve around this claim. It follows, therefore, that (for example) state boundaries have an entirely derivative significance (though not necessarily no significance) and it would also follow that there might (though not necessarily would) be substantial institutional reform required in order to fulfil the tasks of moral obligation and political legitimacy.

Universalist cosmopolitanism, moral or political

In addition to the above, of course, there have been important contributions to universalist cosmopolitanism that do not quite fit into any of the above categories. Brian Barry, for example, certainly a leading cosmopolitan theorist, probably has most in common with deontological cosmopolitanism but his work has elements of consequentialism in it as well (Barry, 1991). Again, Jonathan Glover, who has worked with Sen and Nussbaum in the WIDER (World Institute for Development Economics Research) projects that helped to develop the capabilities approach, has recently articulated a strongly cosmopolitan view of moral and political life but one rooted in a psychological and naturalistic approach (Glover, 1999). A final point would be to emphasize that much contemporary religious thinking and practice is cosmopolitan in effect, if not always explicitly so, in that it can serve to undercut narrower and more partisan particularist perspectives.

The division between moral and political cosmopolitans remains a major source of the diffuseness mentioned at the outset, however. There is no clear division of these approaches into moral and political cosmopolitans. Singer has implied, for example, that the institutional structures of the contemporary world are largely irrelevant for whether or not cosmopolitan moral choices can be made. We can – and he thinks should – choose to give a 'tithe' of a small percentage of our income to lessen global (or even local) hunger, notwithstanding whether the world is politically organized along state lines or more as a global federation. Some other utilitarians, however – for example Robert Goodin – have implied that at least some institutional reframing is probably necessary. Equally, while most leading deontological

cosmopolitans are broadly inclined to at least some institutional reform, only Pogge appears to be a fully-fledged 'political' cosmopolitan, an ambiguity shared (so far at least) by the likes of Nussbaum and Sen. Of the above approaches the only one that seems committed to at least certain forms of institutional cosmopolitanism is critical theory, part of whose argument is predicated on the dislocating effects of globalization (and most obviously present in the recent work of Habermas, Linklater and Held) and whose sense of the importance of 'cosmopolitanism' is primarily political *rather than* ethical.

PARTICULARIST COSMOPOLITANISM

The above versions unquestionably represent the most influential versions of cosmopolitanism in current academic discussion. However, there is, I think, a rather different version that is also increasingly significant. I have called this 'particularist cosmopolitanism, which sounds like a contradiction but serves to highlight certain key differences between these two approaches. Particularist cosmopolitans are suspicious of universalism. For them the route to identifiably cosmopolitan *political* understandings is by denying the universalisms inherent (they think) in existing justifications of moral and political practices. Universalism, as they would have it, denies difference. To be sensitive to difference, to recognize the fluidity and hybridity of identity is to recognize our 'commonness' without requiring us to think that there are 'universal' norms of any kind.

This sort of cosmopolitanism has become increasingly influential among political and moral theorists drawn to so-called 'continental' thought (as opposed to the 'Anglo-American' orientation of most universalist cosmopolitans). There is more sympathy among critical theorists for this kind of cosmopolitanism than among other universalist cosmopolitans, perhaps for this reason. Good examples would be William Connolly, Fred Dallmayr, Bruce Robbins, Bonnie Honig and

Rob Walker. They tend to be critical of moral universalism but also suggest that most extant examples of political cosmopolitanism merely reify untenable dichotomies (self/ other, inside/outside, secular/religious). For them, political cosmopolitanism is better associated with local sites of resistance to unjust practices, specific and concrete social movements rather than 'top down' attempts at institutional or political redesign. 'Democracy', they often suggest, is best seen as a state of mind or a way of being political, rather than as requiring particular universalistic structures (though they do not deny that democratic politics does require some structures and that these structures are better than others).

However, in one sense both kinds of cosmopolitanism are united. Both take the state-centred states system to be at best a partial, and more usually an entirely inappropriate, mode of political association for the 'late modern', 'globalizing' age in which we live. Even moral cosmopolitans, who may not be specifically critical of the institutions of the states system as such, usually end up criticizing the practice of states and especially so-called 'realist' or conservative modes of statecraft which emphasize military force, state interest and *realpolitik* as the guide to state behaviour. At issue between moral and political cosmopolitans of all types is whether state practice can *in principle* be changed, or whether the state form itself must be transcended in order plausibly to start constructing a properly just world.

WHAT'S THE MATTER WITH COSMOPOLITANISM?

Perhaps the greatest strength of cosmopolitanism in general in the current context is its insistence that moral (and perhaps, though more ambiguously, political) claims cannot be bounded by the cultures, nations, norms or ethnicities with which the earth is littered. Although universalist and particularist cos-

mopolitans would differ profoundly about the manner in which such boundaries should be understood and mediated, both would deny they should have limiting force. Thus, in an era of 'globalization' – a rather amorphous term which seems to emphasize the decay of traditional boundaries and the replacement of borders with 'flows' – a political idea which claims that it can create value that is centred on the human person, and not on the 'national/cultural/ethnic, etc., has an especial appeal. At the same time, cosmopolitanism seems to speak to those – and in the west at least they are many – whose conception of politics emphasizes issues that are impossible to corral under traditional headings (such as gender or sexuality or even rights, understood in certain ways). And it speaks to a world where decisions are increasingly transnational, where multilateralism is increasingly the norm and where international institutions and agreements have proliferated astonishingly over the last 30 years.

Many would argue, however, that cosmopolitanism seems to fly in the face of the reality of rooted differences for which people are prepared to die and to kill. The oldest argument against cosmopolitanism is that of self-confessed 'realists': that to hope for universal moral truth (and even more for a politics unmediated by force and fraud) is the worst of all delusions and more likely to encourage, rather than prevent, the very behaviour it seeks to avoid. Yet cosmopolitans have rarely been so naïve as to think that theirs is an easy or simple path. Marcus Aurelius, who spent the last 18 years of his life on campaign against the enemies of Rome, can hardly be said to have been ignorant of the willingness of some to deny the 'cosmopolitan truths' of others. Moreover, the point of asserting cosmopolitan ideas in the modern world, for many, is precisely to overcome the existing divisions that create so much conflict and hostility. It is hardly an argument against cosmopolitanism as such that there are some people who cannot bring themselves to be cosmopolitans.

But perhaps there is a more deep-seated problem with cosmopolitanism; one that is not so easily set aside. In its modern versions at least, cosmopolitanism is the latest and perhaps most coherent version of a desire that has very deep roots in most cultures, but especially in the modern west. This is the desire to believe that the life of a society displays progress and, at least in principle, any society can learn, and will have learnt, from its past mistakes. The cosmopolitan assumption (whether universalist or particularist) must be that 'we' (whoever the 'we' refers to) can make moral and political progress. Cosmopolitanism, in other words, is one of the most powerful vehicles remaining that can carry the belief in progress that has proved so central to the secular cultures of the west. It has to some extent, perhaps, inherited the mantle of the more ambitious schemes of liberalism and socialism that characterized twentieth-century political thought, and seems to dress them up very neatly for the globalizing politics of the twenty-first century. Yet, however well caparisoned, it is still a theory of progress. Do we think that we have made moral progress in the twentieth century? Can we in the twenty-first? To answer yes to either suggests, surely, a triumph of hope but hardly a hope that is at all well founded empirically. We will have to see.

Summary

- Cosmopolitanism has two main sources: ancient thought (especially Stoicism) and the European Enlightenment.
- Contemporary cosmopolitanism has two principal versions: universalist (very much the dominant one) and particularist.
- Universalist cosmopolitanism has four main versions (consequentialist, deontological, critical theory, capabilities), though also some that are not easily identitified with any of the above.
- Cosmopolitanism is best seen as the latest way of conceptualizing the possibility of moral and political progress. Is this plausible?

TUTORIAL QUESTIONS

1. **Which form of universalist cosmopolitanism appeals to you and why?**

2. **Is particularist cosmopolitanism really cosmopolitanism at all?**

3. **If the essence of cosmopolitanism is the belief in moral progress, how plausible is it today?**

FURTHER READING

Martha Nussbaum (1994) *The Therapy of Desire* (Princeton, NJ: Princeton University Press) provides a good account of the background to ancient cosmopolitan thought.

For excerpts of Kant's relevant essays, see *Kant's Political Writings* (ed. H. Reiss) (Cambridge: Camridge University Press, 1970).

Good discussions of universalist cosmopolitanism can be found in the following texts:

Charles Beitz (2001) *Political Theory and International Relations* (Princeton, NJ: Princeton University Press, second edition (1979)).

Thomas Pogge (2002) *World Poverty and Human Rights* (Cambridge: Polity Press).

Onora O'Neill (2000) *Bounds of Justice* (Cambridge: Cambridge University Press).

Andrew Linklater (1997) *The Transformation of Political Community* (Cambridge: Polity Press).

David Held (1995) *Democracy and the Global Order* (Cambridge: Polity Press).

David Crocker (1995) 'The Capabilities Approach', in Jonathan Glover and Martha Nussbaum (eds), *Women, Culture and Development* (Oxford: Clarendon Press).

A good collection of essays that illustrates particularist cosmopolitanism is Peng Cheah and Bruce Robbins (eds) (1999) *Cosmopolitics* (Minneapolis, MN: University of Minnesota Press).

REFERENCES

Barry, Brian (1991) *Liberty, Power and Justice*. Oxford: Clarendon Press.

Beitz, Charles (2001) *Political Theory and International Relations*. Princeton, NJ: Princeton University Press.

Glover, Jonathan (1999) *Humanity: a History of the Twentieth Century*. London: Jonathan Cape.

Held, David (1995) *Democracy and the Global Order*. Cambridge: Polity Press.

Hutchings, Kimberly (1999) *International Political Theory*. London: Sage.

Nussbaum, Martha (1994) *The Therapy of Desire*. Princeton, NJ: Princeton University Press.

Reiss, H. (ed.) (1970) *Kant's Political Writings*. Cambridge: Cambridge University Press.

See also chapters

Index